Shadow Mothers

The publisher gratefully acknowledges the generous support of the General Endowment Fund of the University of California Press Foundation.

Shadow Mothers

*Nannies, Au Pairs, and the Micropolitics
of Mothering*

Cameron Lynne Macdonald

UNIVERSITY OF CALIFORNIA PRESS
Berkeley   Los Angeles   London

University of California Press, one of the most distinguished university presses in the United States, enriches lives around the world by advancing scholarship in the humanities, social sciences, and natural sciences. Its activities are supported by the UC Press Foundation and by philanthropic contributions from individuals and institutions. For more information, visit www.ucpress.edu.

University of California Press
Berkeley and Los Angeles, California

University of California Press, Ltd.
London, England

Library of Congress Cataloging-in-Publication Data

Macdonald, Cameron Lynne.
    Shadow mothers : nannies, au pairs, and the micropolitics of mothering / Cameron Lynne Macdonald.
        p. cm.
    Includes bibliographical references and index.
    ISBN 978-0-520-22232-8 (cloth : alk. paper)—ISBN 978-0-520-26697-1 (pbk. : alk. paper)
    1. Child care.   2. Au pairs.   3. Nannies.   4. Child care services.
5. Motherhood.   I. Title.
    HQ778.5.M33   2011
    306.874'3—dc22   2010030922

Manufactured in the United States of America

19   18   17   16   15   14   13   12   11   10
10   9   8   7   6   5   4   3   2   1

This book is printed on Cascades Enviro 100, a 100% post consumer waste, recycled, de-inked fiber. FSC recycled certified and processed chlorine free. It is acid free, Ecologo certified, and manufactured by BioGas energy.

Dedicated with gratitude to the memory of Louise Jones

CONTENTS

PREFACE

Those of us who make observing social life our profession often draw from our own lives in forming our research interests. The concept of delegated care is rooted in experiences that have helped define my life story. I recount three here, each from a different period of my life, and each formative in its own way.

. . .

I first met Louise Jones when I was about five years old. We probably bumped into her at my grandmother's apartment on a day when she was there doing the housecleaning, but in my memory, we were going to visit royalty. I knew Louise had to be special because, around her, my father got fussy about my behavior in ways that he usually did not. Maybe I should curtsy? She seemed very tall to me, and I remember noticing her wide, flat cheekbones and smooth skin the color of prunes. As I grew older, stories of Louise permeated my childhood: how, when she called my father in for lunch, her voice would drop down as low as gravel and rise to the skies with a swooping, "Doug-LAS!" How she was soothing and relaxed during those times when my grandmother was anxiety-producing, how she was always humming spirituals, and how she and my father used to sit at the small kitchen table and listen to Kate Smith on the radio.

My father credits Louise for his healthy development. My grandmother was widowed when he was three. A nervous woman and ambivalent about having children, my grandmother had found it difficult to cope with single motherhood. Recently, when I asked my father about Louise, he reminisced about how comforting she had been:

So OK, my being sick with Louise was always associated with comfort, easiness, calmness, quietness. With my mother it was enemas, anxiety, and a present. Very mixed, very complicated. I always felt like Louise understood me, accepted whatever I was feeling. My mom was always wanting me to do better in school. Always, always, always. Even if I got mostly A's, which I sometimes did. She'd say, "You need to bring your other grades up." But Mom always wanted me, *needed* me to be the best. Louise didn't need me to be anything. Just home on time and not get hurt or hit by a car or something. So she was very accepting.

My father continued to send Louise cards on Mother's Day and flowers on her birthday for as long as I can remember.

Of course, there was another side to Louise's story. She had moved north during the Great Migration, to live with her sister. She had never had access to much education, so she worked as a domestic her entire life. At age forty, she married George Jones, a New York City sanitation worker, who gave her a settled working-class life. But they never had any children. Her children were the white children, like my father, whom she raised, and who, long after she had moved on to a new position, continued to adore her from a distance.

After George died and she could no longer care for herself, Louise went to live with nieces and nephews. When she died, word spread through the small network of white children (now grown) who had loved her. Of course, they all phoned Louise's family to ask about her death and about funeral arrangements. And of course, her family found these intrusive "strangers" somewhat off-putting. Although my father understood why no one had told him that Louise was declining or contacted him about the funeral, he felt sad, guilty, and a little bit betrayed.

· · ·

The summer I turned sixteen, I worked as a full-time, live-in nanny for a family with three children: Prentice, five; Tommy, three; and Lily, eighteen months. I spent two months with the family at their lake house in Maine. My job was to care for the kids while their mother, Monica, studied for the Bar Exam and their dad, Lloyd, was, well, being Dad. The boys were fun, and I got to teach them how to swim and hike, but they spent a fair amount of time with their father. Lily's care was my primary job.

The house had no electricity, gas, or phone, and I was still young enough that playing "Little House in the Big Woods" still seemed like great fun. I was a seasoned babysitter of several years, but I had never before taken full care of a baby from waking to sleeping. Lily spent most of her days perched on my hip as I did other chores around the house; but she also played in the sandy shallows of the lake as I delighted in every new sound she made, and she toddled around after her beloved older brothers. Though I didn't like Lloyd much, I worshipped Monica, loved the boys, and adored Lily. She was the first baby I had ever bonded with and everything about her enchanted me.

Monica and I got along well, too, cooking meals on the old Franklin wood stove and playing with the kids during her study breaks. Since I was in my "I want to be a lawyer/writer/actress" phase, I glommed onto her as a potential role model. Monica seemed to like me, too. Before our summer time together was half over, she and I had agreed that I would have a standing, every-Friday babysitting gig with the family. I was thrilled that I would get to see little Lily grow up.

The day we left for home, everything changed. When the boat arrived to take us from the lake house, Lily stumbled and fell. Monica swept her up to comfort her, but she was inconsolable. Ultimately, Monica had to hand Lily to me so I could calm her. After that event, we made the three-day drive home from Maine in steely silence, Lloyd and Monica in the front seat and me in the back with the children. When we had to divvy up rooms at motel overnights, Lily and I bunked together, since there was no question of separating us at that point. I wasn't sure what I had done wrong, but at the end of that long drive back, the family dropped me off at home. They paid me my summer's wages, and I never heard from them again.

I was devastated. I felt guilty and ashamed. I was certain that I had crossed some invisible line that I should have seen. My mother drew on her own experience in childcare and kindergarten-teaching to explain that, while sad, this was all very normal. She described the many times that parents, particularly mothers, were upset when their children called her "Mrs. McMommy" instead of "Mrs. Macdonald." She tried to convince me that Lily's attachment to me and Monica's reaction were both normal, and that they were both signs that I was doing my job well. If Lily hadn't bonded with me, then I would have failed as a caregiver. I tried to take this in, but to my sixteen-year-old self, my mother's reasoning seemed a bit of a stretch. It seemed to me that if I really had done my job well, I would still have my every-Friday babysitting gig. Couldn't we just move on?

. . .

I am a big believer in symmetry. When I was collecting the data for my dissertation, I was aware of how my experience helped me understand the way the nannies I interviewed felt. I imagined that by the time I revised this manuscript for publication, I would have my own children, and that I would come to understand first-hand a bit of how the mothers I interviewed felt. I never dreamed that I would earn enough to hire a nanny, but I imagined that my children would grow attached to a family daycare provider (a caregiver who provides care for multiple children in her own home), or a center worker, and that I would have to make sense of that. I would have to learn to trust those I loved to another's care.

Instead, I learned about this kind of trust from a different teacher. Mid-way through my last year of graduate school, my husband was diagnosed with non-Hodgkin's lymphoma. At first we were told that his prognosis was good, that although he would need six months of disabling chemotherapy, he had an 80 percent chance of full remission. We looked at it as a blip on the road to the life we had planned. I continued to write my dissertation, cared for him during his recovery from each round of chemo, and in between times, we continued to try to start the family we had long hoped for, only this time with the help of a clinic and the sperm he had banked before the chemotherapy rendered him sterile.

Eighteen months into his cancer journey, the disease was back—this time requiring a bone marrow transplant. We had moved to a new town and I had my first tenure-track job. The hoped-for pregnancy had not materialized. He was too sick to work. When we went through the pre-transplant screening for the procedure that could save his life, the social worker explained to me that I needed to find a way to ensure that someone would be with him at all times. I would either need to quit my job, hire someone else, or find friends and family to help. I kept gesturing to my health insurance benefit packet, helpfully opened to the page marked "home care benefit," hoping that she would realize her error. I couldn't quit my job: who would keep the roof over our heads and pay for health insurance? Obviously, our insurance would provide home health care.

It did not. The fine print explained that we were eligible for home health care only if the patient required lifting, and even then, the coverage was only for two hours a day. Instead, I would have to rely on friends, strangers really—we had only lived in the new town for nine months—to help look after him, monitor his medications, make sure his IV didn't kink, call 911 when he spiked a fever. The social worker handed me a book entitled "Share the Care," which was designed to help people like me set up a care network. So I did what I had to do: every time someone said to me, "I'm so sorry to hear about your husband. If there's anything I can do. . ." I would respond, "We're having an organizational meeting next week." Ultimately, thirty people joined that care network. I didn't know any of them very well, and I was terrified by how fragile my husband had become after only the first of the many rounds of high-dose chemotherapy the transplant would require.

At the end of one organizational meeting, I started sobbing. A volunteer, who happened also to be a retired nurse, came up to me and asked what was wrong. "I know you guys want to help," I wailed, "but NO ONE can take care of him the way I can!" It seemed impossible. How would I ever be able to trust these people with the person I loved most in the world? She patted my hand gently and said in a very calm tone, "Of course not. No one loves him the way you do. But maybe there are things we have to offer him that you lack." My jaw dropped. Undone by my own argument.

ACKNOWLEDGMENTS

My husband's long illness, his death, and my bereavement all have left their mark, shaping both me and this book. I have been the recipient of countless acts of support, encouragement, and kindness. I have many people to thank.

First, I must thank the women who gave me their time and their stories during the two waves of data collection in the late 1990s. Their willingness to speak openly about topics that often made them uncomfortable was an act of bravery that I deeply respect. It is often the minutiae of our daily lives that leave us most exposed. I hope I have succeeded in conveying these generous women's stories with the respect they deserve.

Second, I am deeply grateful to the professors who inspired me to become a sociologist and to pursue this project: Arlie Hochschild, Carmen Sirianni, Karen Hansen, Anita Garey, and Rosanna Hertz. My dissertation writing group, Faith Ferguson, Henry Rubin, and Jean Elson, and the Boston Area Feminist Sociology Reading Group also merit special mention for keeping me afloat and engaged during the first write-up of the data.

After the second round of data collection, and after my husband's death, a new group of colleagues and mentors were instrumental as I reconceived the project and wrote the book you see today. My invaluable, wonderful writing group—Caroline Knapp, Cristina Rathbone, Kathleen Coll, Kimberly McLain DaCosta, and Laura Miller—read draft after draft. My colleagues at the University of Wisconsin–Madison provided critical and insightful feedback, especially Myra Ferree, Pam Oliver, and Gay Seidman. I am also indebted to Sharon Hays, Mary Tuominen, Pamela Stone, and Arlene Kaplan Daniels, each of whom commented on at least one draft of the entire manuscript.

The Sociology Department at the University of Connecticut, the Committee on Degrees in Social Studies at Harvard, and the Bunting Institute at Radcliffe each gave me temporary homes where I could work and write in between bouts of cancer care. During these phases of intermittent contact with the project, student research assistants helped me keep my hand in the work: Sandra Olarte and Sylvia Gutierrez recruited and interviewed the Spanish-speaking nannies in the study; in the wake of the Louise Woodward trial, Miishe Addy recontacted and conducted phone interviews with the twenty Boston-area nanny placement agencies I had originally interviewed; Ilana Sichel assisted with coding and updating my reading list; and Jessica Brown and Jenna Nitkowski wrestled my massive bibliography into a citation software program. Katherine Mooney, editrix extraordinaire, transformed the text from bloated to streamlined. Sara Phyfer served as a relentless proofreader.

And (almost) last, though not least, thanks to my parents: Doug Macdonald, my father, for caring for me the way Louise cared for him, and my mother, Sherry Macdonald, for reading drafts, helping with transcription, and offering her insights as a daycare worker, kindergarten teacher, and "Mrs. McMommy" to hundreds of kidlets over her thirty years in early childhood education. Most of all, thanks to Rob, Julie, Jitterbug, and Fenway for giving me a new life.

Introduction

Childcare on Trial

"One Less Baby, One More Volvo"

—PICKET SIGN, 1997 TRIAL OF BRITISH AU PAIR LOUISE WOODWARD

Seventy percent of all mothers in the United States work outside the home.[1] Most rely on some form of paid childcare. Despite these realities, the American public remains ambivalent toward mothers who leave their children in the care of others. Reactions to one subset, women who could ostensibly afford to stay at home but do not, are especially intense. When Court TV provided gavel-to-gavel coverage of the trial of eighteen-year-old Louise Woodward, a British au pair, for the 1997 death of baby Matthew Eappen,[2] viewers nationwide were mesmerized. Everyone, it seemed, had an opinion; public sentiment was divided as to whether Woodward was innocent or guilty. There was remarkable unity, however, in the public's vilification of Matthew's mother. Picketers marched daily outside the Middlesex County Courthouse in Cambridge, Massachusetts, often holding placards picturing baby Matthew's face. A sign carrying the slogan given in the epigraph to this chapter captured the hostility I heard expressed over the airwaves and in conversations on subways and buses concerning who was *really* to blame for baby Matthew's untimely death.[3]

Deborah Eappen and her husband, Sunil, had employed Louise to look after their two children while he worked full-time as an anesthesiologist and she worked part-time as an ophthalmologist. Putatively *not* a suspect in the murder case, Dr. Deborah Eappen was put on trial in the court of public opinion and found guilty. Regardless of who was directly to blame for Matthew's death, it was the baby's mother who was deemed ultimately responsible. She was seen as derelict in her maternal duties because she had hired an au pair so that she could work three days a week outside the home.[4] Deborah Eappen noted in an interview, "People write to us that we are greedy, that we did it, that we made poor decisions, that

I am at fault. I am shocked at the way people have been to me and that I have to defend myself."[5] The vehemence of these attacks was directed not just at Matthew's mother, but at all "Volvo-class" working mothers: women who presumably were married to high-earning husbands and also presumably could afford to stay home.

The year before the Woodward case became front-page news, I was in the Boston area conducting interviews with mothers and nannies for this book. A Caribbean nanny recounted an experience that spoke to the caregiver's side of the public vehemence expressed at Volvo-class working mothers. Celine, a forty-two-year-old nanny from Trinidad, was running errands with her two-year-old charge, Gregory. As she chatted with a friend, the cashier at the local drugstore, Celine remembered that she was nearly out of baby wipes. She asked her friend to watch Gregory (who was seated in his stroller) while she ran to the aisle to get the wipes. When she returned to the checkout stand, she was accosted by a white woman who identified herself as an "at-home mom." The woman began to yell at Celine for leaving the toddler unattended. The more Celine protested ("I would never leave my Gregory with a stranger!"), the more heated the other woman's language became. Finally, she said, "I don't blame you—I blame your employer." Celine's friend tried to intercede, but to no avail. The argument escalated, and, Celine told me, the other woman "called me a nigger. Well, that was it. I got really mad, and then the manager told us to leave." Both women exited, but they continued arguing outside the store. Eventually, the police came, separated them, and sent them home. For Celine, the drugstore encounter was proof of the "really racist" attitude of people in the community where she worked. No doubt it was, but the vehemence with which she was accosted suggests an additional trigger. Caregivers who are visibly different from the children in their care learn to expect to be censored by strangers—although this usually takes the form of hostile stares and whispered comments rather than dramatic confrontations.[6] Unlike their peers who can "pass" as their charges' mothers, these nannies signal to the public that some mothers have chosen to shirk what many consider to be their most important adult responsibilities.

Although neither the Woodward case nor Celine's experience at the drugstore are commonplace events, both reflect a continuing ambivalence the American public feels about what constitutes "good enough" mothering, especially among a certain class of mothers. A nationwide poll reported in 2003 that 72 percent of respondents agreed that children *already* spend too much time in daycare or with babysitters; in a poll conducted in 2005, 77 percent agreed with the statement that although "it may be necessary for the mother to be working because the family needs money, it would be better if she could stay home and take care of the house and children."[7] This judgment is clearly linked to social class; working mothers like Dr. Eappen, women who seem financially able to stay home, are the most stigmatized for working. At the other end of the class spectrum, poor women who rely on public assistance while they stay at home to raise their children are judged as negative role models for those children.[8] Although the belief in at-home mothering is strong, so is the belief in child improvement. Some children, it seems, are better off with their mothers whereas others would benefit from professional care, and these children are categorized by race and class.

Never before have the daily lives of so many American mothers been so at odds with prevailing beliefs about children's needs. This historical period is particularly significant in that it is *white middle-class women* whose approach to parenting is viewed as deviant. At the time of my interviews, in the late 1990s, 63 percent of college-educated mothers of infants worked outside the home.[9] Parents are also working longer hours away from home; among families with dual earners, the average number of hours per week the two parents worked away from home peaked at 115 in 1999 and has not declined significantly since then.[10] Despite these realities facing working families, our ideas about how best to raise children remain firmly built on the ideal of the ever-present, continually attentive, at-home mother. Advice books, parenting magazines, and general cultural sentiment have converged to "raise the bar" of expectations for mothering young children so high that even full-time at-home mothers would be hard-pressed to meet them.[11] For mothers who work outside the home the task is literally impossible: meeting these expectations *requires* the presence of a full-time mother as the primary caregiver. Some resolve this dilemma by redefining mothering so they can delegate certain aspects to a carefully chosen stand-in. In-home caregivers help maintain or even extend this redefinition of "mother-work" as they negotiate with their employers who does what aspects of childrearing and what the resulting division of labor *means* to each party.[12]

Celine's story, reactions to Woodward's trial, and the subsequent polling data are evidence of the deeply held and conflicting opinions surrounding motherhood, work, race, and social class. At the time of Woodward's first trial, I had just completed interviewing the fiftieth woman in a research sample that ultimately expanded to eighty women: thirty mother-employers and fifty in-home childcare providers. I was surprised by the media portrayals of women like those who were participating in my study. Although I found tension, sadness, and occasionally difficult working conditions in these women's relationships, their problems did not result from the fact that the mothers worked, nor did they arise from the kinds of childcare workers they employed. Instead, these problems, ironically, stemmed mainly from the same set of beliefs about mothering that generated the public outcry at the Woodward trial. Both sets of respondents, mother-employers and their childcare providers, believed in the value of at-home mothering. Contests over the definition of the "good mother" and whether the mother-employer or the mother-worker was ultimately the better caregiver lay at the root of most mother-nanny conflicts.[13]

This book analyzes the micropolitics of interactions inside these linked lives. By micropolitics, I mean the ways that "power is relayed in everyday practices": the "small wars" that go on in everyday life as individuals and groups jockey for position.[14] This is a particularly apt approach to understanding the division of labor in the contested terrain of mother-work. As the journalist Caitlin Flanagan points out, "The precise intersection of many women's most passionate impulses—their profound, almost physical love for their children and their ardent wish to make something of themselves beyond their own doorstep—is the exact spot where nannies show up for work each day."[15] Inside these relationships, we see how both mother-employers and mother-workers view what it means to be a "good mother" and what it means to commodify portions of this role.

The conflicts I observed between nannies and employers over seemingly minor activities such as naptimes, play dates, and "time-outs" reflect not only their competing views on mothering but also the constraints placed on both sets of women by larger structural forces—for example, the nature of "all-or-nothing" careers (for the mother-employers) and the assumption that domestic workers are "part of the family" (for the mother-workers). They also reflect deep-seated differences in class-based beliefs about parenting. Although these larger cultural and institutional forces are evident in many areas of public and private life, they crystallize in the employer-nanny relationship.

During the interviews I conducted with mothers and caregivers, I searched for answers to some simple but provocative questions. What kinds of caregivers do mother-employers seek? What are the implications of the race, class, age, legal status, and education of the childcare worker in how each of the two parties defines the work? How do professional-class working mothers interpret their own status as mothers in light of the fact that someone else does the bulk of the day-to-day care? From the perspective of the mother-worker, what does it mean to be paid to love someone else's children? Do childcare workers enter the relationship with agendas that contradict or compete with those of their employers? What are the costs and consequences of the kind of emotional labor in-home childcare providers perform?[16] How is the paid caregiver's role within the family and within the children's lives defined by both parties? How do both parties define and maintain the boundary between mother and "not-mother"? In answering these questions, this book sheds light not only on contemporary understandings of motherhood among middle-class women, but also on the changing boundaries between family and community, home and work, and love and money.

CRITICAL FRAMEWORKS

Mothers employed outside the home, commodified childcare and housework, work-family tensions: none of these are new phenomena. Sociologists, policy analysts, and feminist theorists have been writing about the challenges facing dual-earner families, the politics of contemporary motherhood, and the working and labor market conditions of domestic workers for many years. This book benefits from this research but also significantly extends and frequently challenges the insights this research provides, placing childcare at the center of the analysis of contemporary family life. In what follows, I outline the broad contours of the research most relevant to understanding the micropolitics of mothering in the context of commodified childcare.

Doing the "First Shift"

This book directs attention to the division of childrearing labor during the "first shift" in family life. Existing research reflects continuing ambivalence concerning the role of childcare workers in the lives of working families. Work/family researchers have long focused on increased male participation in the "second shift" (i.e., the housework and parenting that takes place at the end of the workday) as a panacea for the dilemmas facing dual-earner families.[17] Many studies indicate that a more equitable division of labor in the second shift would solve problems facing working mothers, including lack of sleep, inadequate leisure time, marital stress, and unequal access to career advancement.[18] In practice, though, for dual-earner families, increased paternal participation is only a partial solution. In recent years, men's involvement in childrearing has risen, but husbands still lag behind their wives by eighteen hours per week.[19] Aside from those parents who provide childcare themselves by working complementary shifts, most working families must rely on someone outside the family to provide childcare during at least some part of the working day.[20] The exclusive focus on fathers' housework and childcare ignores the critical role of "friendly intruders" in the lives of children.[21]

How working parents negotiate the division of childrearing labor during the hours they are at work remains poorly understood. Much of the literature on dual-earner families treats children as if they exist in a state of suspended animation while their parents are away. By focusing primarily on how fathers can assist at home, most of the existing research reinforces the notion of the nuclear family as an isolated unit that limps along on its own limited resources. In contrast, I argue that a realistic view of family life in dual-earner households must include the role played by caring adults from outside the immediate family.

Mothering Ideologies

This book also brings the role of paid childcare workers into debates about the meanings of mothering. Feminist scholars have documented the cultural lag between beliefs concerning good mothering and actual mothering practices.[22] These authors argue that middle-class American mothering ideals, and the beliefs about children's needs that accompany them, are cultural and historical remnants that are no longer realistic. Feminist researchers call for a redefined and expanded notion of "the good mother" that moves beyond "the sacrificial mother" to include working as a way of supporting the family economically and of modeling for children the value of work and independence.[23] Although most agree that any new model of good mothering must include a flexible workplace and coparenting partners, few feminist scholars address how paid childcare workers fit into this redefined notion of mothering.[24]

Specifically, and most obviously since the nineteenth-century switch from father-centered childrearing to mother-centered childrearing, U.S. discourses on mothering have insisted that the mother "take entire care" of her children. Middle-class mothers were exhorted to dispense with servants; those in the classes below were urged to give up working outside the home.[25] This ideology of "intensive mothering" was (and continues to be) class-based in other ways as well. Traditionally, the policies and professional advice aimed at mothers have been differentiated by social class, and women from different classes typically interpret these mothering messages in different ways.

In particular, concerns about how the middle and upper classes will reproduce themselves, and mothers' role in that status attainment, express the tensions between the career aspirations of middle-class women and the assumption that these strivings are in direct conflict with their children's needs. This is a dilemma of long standing. For example, more than a hundred years ago, when women were finally being admitted into the halls of higher education, this change was framed as a way to make them better *mothers,* not as a route to joining their male peers in the professional labor force. The broad concerns about the fate of white, middle-class motherhood were voiced by S. Weir Mitchell in the somber warning he delivered to Radcliffe students at the beginning of the twentieth century: "I believe that if the higher education or the college life in any way, body or mind, unfits women to be good wives and mothers, there had better be none of it. If these so affect them that they crave merely what they call a career as finer, nobler, more to their taste than the life of home, then better close every college door in the land."[26]

Nonetheless, the number of college-educated women continued to rise, and they married in ever greater numbers and continued to produce smaller families.[27] Indeed, throughout the twentieth century, the number of working women showed a steady increase, but it was not until the last few decades of the century that Dr. Mitchell's nightmare became a reality: the majority of college-educated women with young children were in the workforce. They are now there to stay.

But these mothers, and the millions of others now in the workforce, have not decreased their hours of childcare. In fact, contemporary mothers spend more time interacting with their children than their own mothers spent with them.[28] They have offset their higher hours of paid work and greater amount of time with their children by spending fewer hours cooking and cleaning, lowering standards in the latter and outsourcing much of the former. They have also cut back on sleep, leisure, and time with their partners in the hope of meeting increasingly strident, and increasingly mother-centered, cultural expectations regarding childrearing. These intersecting tensions form the broad context for the social pressures that face middle-class mothers today. Ours is a distinctive historical moment.

The childcare-employer relationships I describe in the chapters that follow are not inevitable; they are not the natural outgrowth of women's innate characteristics. They result from a confluence of historically specific cultural and ideological forces. As the psychologist Shari Thurer notes, "If an intense, one-on-one, exclusive mother relationship were, in fact, essential, we would have to conclude that except for a brief period in the fifties, most cultures, past and present, in its absence, produced damaged people."[29] Given that they did not, the outsized worry aimed at children of mothers who work outside the home must result from a unique intersection of cultural and institutional changes. As the sociologist Anne Swidler has pointed out, during times of social and cultural upheaval, common sense often hardens into dogma.[30] Cultural expectations regarding childrearing have become more strident precisely *because* of the profound shifts in mothers' labor force participation. As working outside of the home shifted from the provenance of poor or unmarried women to the norm, even for mothers with young children and for those who could putatively "afford to stay home," cultural criticisms of working mothers have become increasingly shrill.

This book challenges the assumptions of intensive mothering by asking why we assume childcare must be framed as a last resort for families who require a second (or first) income, rather than as the welcome addition of more loving adults into a child's life.

Commodified Care: Childcare, Housework, and Global Capitalism

This book also refocuses the typical understanding of paid domestic workers. A large body of research approaches domestic work, and to a lesser extent childcare, from the perspective of the care provider.[31] With the formation of "global cities" comes both a wealthy class of knowledge-workers, who need and can afford domestic help, and a labor pool of predominantly immigrant women to fill those needs at low wages.[32] These studies of domestics and other care-workers tend to describe a broad swath of workers who usually have been selected for study based on their race/ethnicity and national origin rather than on their job description.[33]

There are some major drawbacks to that approach. Studying a single category that simultaneously includes day cleaners, nanny-housekeepers, mother's helpers, and maids with wide-ranging responsibilities overlooks the fact that there is a significant difference between delegated, commodified *mothering*, and delegated, commodified *housework*. Moreover, this distinction has crucial implications for how employers hire and manage childcare workers versus domestic workers. Critical differences in the demographic composition of the market in domestic labor emerge when the job is childcare-only rather than childcare-secondary.

Finally, within the single category of childcare, the age of the children is an influential factor. Intensive mothering ideologies are strongest in advice directed at mothers of preschool-age children. Servant-mistress tensions combine with mothering ideologies in the preschool childcare labor market in ways that shed light on broader tensions concerning childrearing for a wage.[34] Arguably, the conflict between mothering ideologies and the need for paid childcare workers is the trip wire on the feminist road to gender equality. As Flanagan points out regarding the feminist professional caught between egalitarian ideals and her need for affordable childcare, "She had wanted a revolution; what she got was a Venezuelan."[35]

The Public-Private Divide

This book's close examination of commodified mother-work challenges assumptions concerning the self-sufficiency of the nuclear family and the permeability of the public-private divide. Some scholars, and many parents, believe that work performed out of love and work performed for a wage are fundamentally incompatible. Many observers express a "concern that encroaching commodification threatens to irrevocably evacuate from motherhood all that is best and most powerful about it."[36] The philosopher Jean Bethke Elshtain speaks for most conservative critics of paid childcare when she writes, "It used to be that some things, whole areas of life, were not up for grabs as part of the world of buying and selling." Today, in contrast, "nothing is holy, sacred, or off-limits in a world in which everything is for sale."[37] In fact, some scholars argue that labor with a caring component pays less than similarly skilled jobs because employers believe that keeping wages low limits the labor pool to those with truly altruistic motives.[38]

Even feminist theorists like Barbara Katz Rothman voice concern over what is lost when the work of the family is outsourced: "Mrs. Smith's Frozen Pie Company is not an intimate experience, either for the consumer or for the provider of the service. Wiping a child's behind or nose, settling an after-school squabble between siblings, putting on a new Band-Aid, unsticking the zipper on the toddler's snowsuit—*these* are intimate services."[39] As more women have entered the labor force, services formerly performed by mothers and wives have been taken over by service and manufacturing industries: laundry, the production of food and clothing, cooking, and cleaning. In general, we view these products and services as labor-saving conveniences, and consider the frozen pie from Mrs. Smith's a fair substitute for mom's homemade recipe. Other services traditionally in the mother's sphere have been appropriated by professionals: education; care of the sick, the disabled, and the elderly. These professional services are generally viewed as superior to the informal care provided by wives and mothers. Of course, the distribution of these services—who can afford to outsource, who stays out of the labor force to provide them, and who provides them while in the labor force—varies according to social class. Whether delegated or family-provided, ensuring the quality of services otherwise known as "reproductive labor" remains women's responsibility.

In much of the scholarly literature, and in the minds of the general public, child-care is the last remaining area of women's "sphere" in which mothers are viewed as irreplaceable. According to the sociologist Viviana Zelizer, that view is misguided. She argues that exchanges of affection and intimacy have long coincided with monetary exchange, and that "people devote significant effort to negotiating meanings of social relations and marking their boundaries. They do so especially when those relations involve both intimacy and economic transactions." In her view, maintaining these boundaries requires "relational work" that involves "distinguishing those relationships from [ones] with which they might become confused," and constantly renegotiating and repairing relationships when confusion does arise.[40] This book builds on Zelizer's insights by examining the intimate and economic negotiations between mother-employers and childcare providers, the relational work they entail, and the consequences of failing to navigate them successfully.

. . .

The majority of mothers in the United States are not full-time, stay-at-home parents. But because the American public remains haunted by the ghost of June Cleaver, ever-present for husband and children with pearls firmly in place, social policies more often reflect this sentimental vision rather than the realities of dual-earner families and the enormous pressures on mothers who work outside the home. The United States lags behind all other industrialized nations in supports for working parents and other adult workers who must care for dependents. It is in this moment of misalignment between cherished ideologies and daily realities that we enter the lives of the mothers and nannies in this study.

STUDY DESIGN

This study examines the delegation of mother-work, not the division and delegation of other aspects of motherhood, such as conceiving, gestating, and bearing children, the creation of family ties, or the economic support of children.[41] I define mother-work specifically as those daily tasks involved in the care and protection of small children. For example, in interviews with mother-employers and with the caregivers they hired and supervised, I asked about various mothering practices, including feeding, diapering, bathing, disciplining, and playing with children. I also asked about the relational tasks involved in mother-work: the soothing, stimulating, and forging intimate connections that are part of the everyday practices of raising infants and toddlers.[42] Although separate from motherhood as a social role or identity, mother-work represents a significant component of what it means to be a mother. Therefore, the practice of delegating mother-work to a paid caregiver could be expected to challenge fundamental understandings of motherhood.

My findings are based on data collected in the mid to late 1990s, during interviews with thirty mother-employers and fifty caregivers. The mother-employers were employed at least thirty hours per week outside the home and had at least one child younger than school age during the period in which they employed in-home care. The majority held high-status positions as doctors, lawyers, engineers, managers, teachers and professors, artists, and writers. The interviewees included single and married mothers, mothers with one to five children, mothers with children at various stages of development, and mothers from different ethnic and socioeconomic backgrounds. Of the thirty mother-employers interviewed, eight were women of color.[43]

The childcare providers represent the range of in-home caregivers: I interviewed ten European au pairs,[44] fifteen U.S.-born nannies, and twenty-five immigrant caregivers from all parts of the globe. Fourteen caregivers had children of their own and viewed their mothering experience as their job training; twelve had some formal training in early childhood education. Three of the immigrant workers had been professionals, either medical or educational, in their home countries.[45] Of the fifty caregivers, fifteen worked on a live-in basis and thirty-five lived out. The live-in caregivers earned salaries ranging from $100 to $300 per week, plus room and board, and the live-out caregivers earned from $80 to $500 per week. The caregivers worked from thirty to seventy hours per week.

Thirty-two of the interviewees were part of mother-caregiver dyads. Therefore, almost half of the interviews represent two perspectives from the same household, providing a unique opportunity to analyze divergent interpretations of each mother-caregiver relationship. The women who were not part of mother-caregiver dyads offered equally valuable perspectives in that they were less likely to perceive their employment relationships as successful. Finally, I supplemented the perspectives of the employers and employees with information gleaned in interviews with twenty nanny and au pair placement agency owners and managers. These informants sketched the broad outlines of nanny and au pair contracts for me and explained how placement agencies participate in negotiations between employers and caregivers. Ultimately, I conducted in-depth, tape-recorded interviews with a total of one hundred individuals.

I chose to study childcare in the employer's home, as opposed to daycare provided in an institutional setting (center daycare) or in the caregiver's home (family daycare), for several reasons. First, it is a one-to-one relationship between employer and employee. Because I was interested in how women negotiated commodified childcare, I sought a childcare arrangement that resembled the Weberian "ideal type" of mother-provider negotiation. An ideal type is a heuristic model that allows the researcher to construct a model that accentuates the critical characteristics of the phenomenon under study while deemphasizing other aspects. Although not statistically typical, the mother-nanny relationship emphasizes the kinds of direct negotiation concerning the division of mother-work that I sought to understand.[46] In the more common forms of childcare, the caregiver-parent interaction is shaped by center or owner policies, by the needs of multiple children and their parents, and often by the needs of multiple employees. Conversely, in her own home, a mother has (or is believed to have) the power to choose and direct care so that it meets her needs and those of her children. Thus, *how* she selects and manages in-home care reflects what does and does not matter to her as a mother—and what does and does not matter reflects her mothering ideology.

Second, professional-class working mothers who employ in-home childcare workers generally have the financial resources to choose among competing types of care. I wanted to explore how women who are able to select *any kind* of care arrangement go about creating a personally satisfying division of mothering labor. Professional-class mothers are also of interest because they are especially aware of and influenced by the dominant cultural expectations surrounding childrearing.[47] In delegating the labor of mothering, their decisions are likely to be shaped by the middle-class childrearing paradigm and its expectations regarding children's psychological, emotional, and cognitive development.[48]

Third, I was keen to understand how women who had broken so many traditional barriers to equality in the workplace dealt with traditional mothering ideologies at home. To be clear, I had no intention of trying to position professional-class women as "the norm," a practice that has justifiably been criticized by work/family sociologists.[49] Rather, I sought to understand what professional-class women who had succeeded in all other areas of their lives could reveal about childrearing and delegating childcare. Seventeen of the thirty mothers I interviewed could be considered true trailblazers at work: they were either the first or the only women to have reached their positions in their particular firms or lines of work. Most were overtly feminist in their orientation toward work and marriage. I imagined that they would be the group, if any, who would bear witness to the emergence of "postgender" parenting strategies.[50] As it turned out, they were not, but this was also an effect, ironically, of their career success and resulting social class.

Finally, my research choices were influenced by broader structural conditions and events. As I was carrying out the study, public concern over children being deprived of adequate parenting, over gender equity at home and at work, and over immigration and the potential exploitation of low-wage immigrant workers rose. Anger over the widening gap in earnings and social class grew as well. When I first began the research, the Zoe Baird and Kimba Wood scandals were breaking news.[51] By the time I completed the first wave of interviews, reactions to the Louise Woodward case, as well as numerous nanny references in popular culture, had made it clear that Americans' ambivalence about childcare was crystallizing around professional women and their nannies.[52] Although not the statistical norm, the childcare arrangements of professional-class working mothers had come to represent a politically and emotionally charged cultural symbol.[53] It seemed to me that a satisfactory understanding of the mothering and employment strategies attributed to this now-iconic form of childcare required going inside it—exploring what mattered to the two sets of women involved—rather than taking popular-culture portrayals at face value.

Because most nannies are paid under the table, available statistics on their numbers and their racial and ethnic distribution in the labor force are unreliable. Thus, in designing the sample, I did not aim for random generalizability; instead, I used a strategy of "maximum variation sampling."[54] Within the boundaries of the population I wanted to study, I sought as many different types of arrangements as possible. I had assumed, based on other research, that the majority of nannies would be undocumented immigrants, but I quickly discovered otherwise. Boston-area childcare workers cluster in three main groups: immigrants, au pairs, and American-born women. I recruited care providers from each of these groups and then sought to interview their employers.[55]

These interviews elicited rich and detailed accounts of explicit rules and implicit expectations, stories of the "nanny from hell" as well as accounts of the "angel who holds us together." I asked the nannies and au pairs what brought them to childcare work, what they looked for in a prospective employer's family, and how they felt about the conditions of their work. They responded with often poignant, sometimes humorous narratives of what it feels like to be the cornerstone of family life and yet often be denied adult-level autonomy and authority.

Mother-employers generally expressed satisfaction with their current childcare providers and with the quality of their children's care. Not all of the fifty caregivers were satisfied with their employers, but they all expressed a deep commitment to the children in their care. I was able to directly observe their affection for and pride in their charges, since many of the interviews took place with the children present. Likewise, the mothers strove to be conscientious employers.

My respondents' attitudes and actions may reflect self-selection; nannies who were abusing their children or employers who were abusing their nannies most likely would not have agreed to be interviewed. The situations I observed did not, for the most part, include evidence of nanny abuse or of the stereotypically heartless employers and childcare providers that often are portrayed in the media and in some research. Both sets of women in the study tried hard to make their relationships work. The problems they experienced were, therefore, more subtle, more intractable, and in many ways more heartbreaking.

OVERVIEW

The book's remaining chapters are grouped into four thematic sections: cultural and structural constraints that shape the mother-nanny relationship; resolving the ideal mother/ideal worker conflict; nannies' perspectives on their employers' management strategies; and alternative models of the mother-nanny relationship and avenues for change. Each is described below.

Cultural and Structural Constraints

The mother-nanny relationship is not shaped by free-floating, unconstrained actors. The first section (chapters 2 and 3) outlines the cultural and structural constraints that shape the needs and expectations mothers and nannies bring to their employment relationship.

Chapter 2 discusses the contradictory forces shaping the mother-employers' lives. Although trailblazers in male-dominated fields, they find themselves in the awkward position of having to continually prove their devotion to work.[56] They find they must constantly pass "the test of manhood" to confirm their career-orientation, a test that becomes more difficult once they have children. They simultaneously, and perhaps paradoxically, embrace the tenets of intensive mothering. Reading volumes of advice literature, they evaluate their own mothering practices as falling short of the "ideal mother" norm, and they seek in-home childcare as a way to approximate mother-care while they are at work. They experience what I call "blanket accountability," the sense that they are responsible for everything that happens in their children's daily lives, regardless of who provides the actual care. They are consequently torn between hiring an at-home mother to support them as they pursue their demanding careers, and the desire to *be* that at-home mother for their children. It is this conflict that feeds the mother-employers' deep ambivalence and guides their strategies for managing their childcare workers.

Chapter 3 introduces three types of nannies common in the Boston area and describes their different routes to nanny work, as well as the problems they face in an occupation that is legally and socially defined as being "part of the family" rather than as doing skilled work. The caregivers I interviewed work with very young children in childcare-only positions. They consider themselves more skilled than other domestic workers; they also take pride in the quality of care they offer, especially as compared to care offered at daycare centers. Nonetheless, their identities as professional mother-workers trap the nannies in conflicts over whether their work should be governed by market norms or by more flexible, but potentially exploitative, family norms. They also embrace mothering as a work ethic, a cultural norm that binds them ever tighter to the children in their care and, paradoxically, leads them to negotiate against their own economic interests.

Resolving the Ideal Mother / Ideal Worker Conflict

The second section (chapters 4–6) analyzes how mother-employers attempt to resolve their "ideal mother / ideal worker" conflicts by hiring, managing, and monitoring nannies. The most common coping strategies involve managing the nanny as if she were an extension of the mother herself: a shadow mother. Managing the nanny to produce shadow motherhood begins with screening and selecting a caregiver. Chapter 4 outlines the logics working mothers use to find and hire the employee who will provide the right "fit" for their child and for their child's developmental stage.

Chapter 5 presents management and monitoring strategies put in place after the caregiver has been hired. The mother-employers use nanny management strategies that range from micromanagement to benign inattention that assumes the existence of an intuitive connection between employer and nanny. Each of these seemingly polar-extreme approaches treats the caregiver as an extension of the mother, rather than as an individual with her own distinctive relationship to the children. In both management strategies, the goal is to orchestrate the daily lives of the nanny and children to mirror the employer's image of the care she imagines she would provide if she were an at-home mother herself.

Chapter 6 focuses on a different kind of management strategy: managing both the image of the mother-nanny division of labor and what that division of labor means. The employers I interviewed believe strongly in the ideal of "being in the mother-appropriate places at the mother-appropriate times."[57] This leads them to devise a complex supervisory subtext that delineates what aspects of childcare the nanny is to engage in and what aspects are "mother only." Care in hiring and daily management can transform an in-home care provider into a trustworthy channel for her employer's childrearing practice. The makeover to shadow mother is not fully realized, however, until the nanny not only acts as a mother-extension but also fades into invisibility when she is not needed, and carries out her responsibilities in ways that provide no threat to her employer's image as the child's primary attachment.

Nannies' Perspectives

The third section (chapters 7 and 8) presents nannies' perspectives and their responses to employer management strategies. Most of the nannies and their employers interpret what it means to be a "good mother" differently, and most have strong opinions regarding who is best at fulfilling that ideal. Since the everyday actions and expectations of the two sets of women are rooted in their (separate) understandings of ideal motherhood, their competing ideologies become the battleground on which employer-employee tensions emerge. Chapter 7 describes the working conditions, including employer attitudes and family atmosphere, that nannies report wanting most. I term this much-desired scenario the "third-parent" ideal. All the nannies long for their employers' recognition of the important contribution they make to family life. Few receive this recognition. Chapter 8 examines the ways in which nannies accommodate and/or resist employer-imposed definitions of their role and limitations on the bond they forge with the children in their care. Ironically, a key form of resistance involves attempting to "outmother the mother." In this sense, the notion of the ideal mother holds both sets of women in thrall. They each comply in their own, albeit very different, kinds of subjugation to the same unrealistic, culturally defined ideals.

Alternatives and Avenues for Change

The final section (chapters 9 and 10) examines alternative employer–childcare provider relationships and explores avenues for change. The initial fifty-eight interviews I conducted for this study indicated that most of the working mother–nanny relationships were distorted by a "recognition deficit"—neither party could recognize or validate her own contribution to the childrearing endeavor without simultaneously negating that of the other. Some of the relationships, though, showed glimmers of mutuality, respect, and cooperative childrearing. These exceptions suggested that mother-employers who were not straining to meet ideal-mother and ideal-worker standards might approach managing childcare differently and be less likely to rely on shadow-mother strategies. I interviewed an additional twenty-two women, recruiting mothers who worked part-time or flextime, and those who had been raised by mothers employed outside the home, with the idea that these women might offer counterhegemonic approaches to managing childcare.[58]

Among this group, partnership strategies prevail. These mother-employers treat childcare workers as individuals whose relationships with the children are distinct from the mother-child bond rather than extensions of it. Similarly, in this group husbands and wives share childrearing responsibilities more equally. Partnerships also are the only employer-employee relationships that explicitly challenge the ideology of intensive mothering by acknowledging the contributions paid caregivers make to childrearing and family life. Chapter 9 describes these relationships and shows that paid childcare can be incorporated into family life in ways that benefit all the participants.

In chapter 10, I apply the insights found in this study to other forms of childcare. Across the childcare spectrum, caregivers seek to be valued with both fair pay and recognition for their caring and altruism: a tension that is central to the frustrations of the nannies I interviewed. Furthermore, intensive mothering is inherently class-based. Not only are mothers' specific concerns shaped by social class, but also the conflicts between nannies and mothers arise primarily from the class-based nature of mothering ideologies. Class transmission is work, and it is women's work. Negotiating this gendered work between women of different classes is a central problem facing those I interviewed. In my concluding remarks, I argue that concerns for the dignity of care should transcend anxieties over the maintenance of status.

2

Mother-Employers

Blanket Accountability at Home and at Work

PRELUDE: JESSICA AND ANABEL*

I first met Jessica at the consulting firm where she worked as the sole female partner. A tall and athletic-looking thirty-eight-year-old, she seemed the epitome of success: her blonde hair was perfectly coiffed, her beige suit was beautifully tailored, and her accessories bespoke affluence rather than conscious attention to accessorizing. She welcomed me into her oak and pastel office with the gracious-ness of a seasoned hostess and the firm handshake of a corporate veteran.

Jessica was the highest earner among the thirty mothers I interviewed, making more than three hundred thousand dollars per year. She had been happily married to Steve, a self-employed business owner, for two years. She described Steve as an active coparent for their eleven-month-old son, Sammy. She considered herself "lucky" to have found the perfect au pair in Anabel, an eighteen-year-old from Scotland. As we talked, however, what seemed like a dream life began to sound a bit like a nightmare, and Jessica's composure gradually gave way to tears.

Although her firm prided itself on being "family-friendly," Jessica's pregnancy had caused her work status to plummet. Many of her normal responsibilities had been taken away from her as a result of her pregnancy, and her colleagues' once

---

*The "preludes" in this book are vignettes that present the stories of particular mother-employers, caregivers, or employer-caregiver dyads. Each prelude illustrates a theme salient to the chapter it accompanies.

Each time a new mother or nanny is introduced, I provide a description of her age, ethnicity, and occupation. Subsequent references will use the name only. Please refer to the appendix for full lists of mothers and nannies in this study.

respectful treatment had shifted to subtle and not so subtle belittlement. For example, on a conference call with the president of a prospective client company, when the client asked, "So how are you, Jessica?" the senior partner in her firm cut in, reporting, "Well actually, she's not doing very well right now. You should see her! She's really quite under the weather. She's *pregnant*." To this, the client responded, "Whoa, you better watch it. You got to be careful with things like that." This exchange was followed by the jovial laughter of male bonding. On another occasion, in a meeting, a colleague referred to what Jessica might be doing in the future, "when she's not busy making babies."

Initially, Jessica had hoped to supplement the nine-week unpaid maternity leave she had taken with additional time off in the future. But, she explained, "I don't think you can take off a couple of years from a career—a high-level career—and come back at the same level. That is, for women. Now, if I were a man and I was, you know, going on a golf tour for two years or whatever, I'd go right back at the same level. But I think once you've taken off a couple of years to raise children, that you're somehow diminished in the professional world." She added that in her workplace, there was a curious double standard about parenting: "One of the guys who works for me has two kids who are here in the office as we speak. . . . But if I brought my child in, I think there'd be an awful lot of crossed eyes, you know, looking at me funny and saying 'She can't work. Her child is here. What's the problem? Where's the childcare?'" Presumably a mother could not have her child at the workplace and concentrate on other things. At least not a *good* mother.

In male-pattern careers like Jessica's, employees are expected to be able to make work their first priority, either because they have no family responsibilities or because they have someone else at home to take care of them. As a woman, she was expected to work harder to prove that her commitment would not be hampered by her pregnancy, by the birth of her first child, or by having an infant at home. Her male coworkers did not face similar hurdles. Fatherhood is widely understood as not adversely affecting workplace commitment; in some cases, male workers earn bonus points for being trailblazing, involved fathers and sensitive "new men."[1]

Much as at the office, on the surface Jessica's situation at home appeared ideal. Steve ran his own business and had the flexibility to drop in at home during the day. He had become an actively involved parent. According to Jessica, Anabel was the dream au pair. She was energetic, compliant, and completely in love with Sammy. But Jessica described feeling a "deep, deep hurt that even to this day, Sammy wants Anabel, or he wants Steve, and I'm third. And I worry. I feel like, 'Is our relationship ever gonna recover from that? Is he ever gonna be more mommy-oriented? I hope so.'" From her perspective, she was failing on two fronts. She was no longer the unencumbered worker that her male-pattern career demanded, and she felt she was not present enough in her son's life to establish herself as his "primary attachment," as the advice books she read told her she should. Like most of the mother-employers in this study, Jessica was burdened by a sense of what I call "blanket accountability" both at home and at work: no matter where she was, she was held accountable for what went on at her workplace and in her son's life.

Also, like most of the mother-employers I interviewed, Jessica relied on childrearing advice books as a lifeline. She reported that Steve felt she was "*far* too much of a book mom," but Jessica saw the books as a way to ensure that she would not make the mistake of raising her child the way she had been raised, and she had no female role models. "My friends are all at home with their kids," she explained. "And my professional friends either don't have children or have much older children." Relying on the guidance of childrearing experts created serious problems for Jessica, however. Most of the books she read admonished her to focus her entire attention on Sammy's development. At work, she was under increasing pressure to demonstrate even greater commitment, and yet fulfilling her responsibilities as a mother required that she spend more, not less, time with her son.

This conflict gave rise to a mix of contradictory expectations and feelings that colored her relationship with Anabel: "I wanted her to love him and adore him during the day when *she* was with him. And at night or anytime that I was home, I wanted her to not be loving and adoring toward him. I wanted her to just take a step back and be very hands-off with him. Which is sort of impossible to ask a person to shut off all the time." Anabel managed to accomplish the "impossible" most of the time. Jessica acknowledged that her au pair was "very understanding" of the conflict Jessica faced and "really [tried] to help me with that." As I will discuss in the coming chapters, Jessica was similar to the other mother-employers I interviewed in that her management of her caregiver was structured by her need to be the primary parent and the concomitant desire that her childcare provider be a "shadow mother."

When I interviewed Anabel, we met in the family room of Jessica's spacious home. Anabel was solidly built, with cornflower blue eyes, a face splashed with freckles, and an unruly mass of red curls. She spoke with a thick brogue, and during the interview she spent as much time talking to Sammy as to me. He used her as a human jungle gym while we talked. When I asked how she felt about Sammy, she replied, "Achh, I love him to death. It's going to be so hard to leave. He's *such* a good little boy, he really is." Like most of the nannies and au pairs I interviewed, Anabel clearly was as in love with the child as his mother was. But like her peers, Anabel was aware that protecting Jessica's role as Sammy's primary attachment was a critical aspect of her job. She mentioned that the baby, who was just beginning to talk, "sometimes" said "dadadada" and "very occasionally," "mama." With a somewhat rueful laugh, she added, "We all clap and cheer when he says 'mama.'" Anabel also recognized that she was responsible for shoring up her employer's sense of importance in the family. When Jessica lamented that

Sammy was almost a year old and she felt she had not spent any time with him, Anabel objected and firmly asserted, "Oh Jessica, you've spent loads of time with him and he loves you very much."

Despite her au pair's reassurances, blanket accountability weighed heavily on Jessica. To cope with her fear of failing Sammy or in any way jeopardizing his well-being and successful development because she was away at work, she created an array of rules. Anabel could not drive the car with the baby or walk with him anywhere but to the local park. She could not have the television on during the day, and her phone time was limited to ten minutes. The phone time limit was eventually revised: "I talked to one of my friends who's an at-home mother, and she said, 'Hey, I'm home with kids all day; [the phone] is your connection to the world. You *need* to get on the phone.'" Jessica's freshly raised consciousness had its limits, however. She gave Anabel permission to talk on the phone for "half an hour at a time when [Sammy's] asleep," but when he was awake, the ten-minute rule held. Although Jessica admitted that the restrictions she imposed on her au pair's mobility and use of the car and the phone would have been difficult for her to follow if she had been the one staying at home, she kept the rules in place. They were essential to her sense of being in control of her son's care, even when she could not provide that care herself.

Anabel voiced few complaints; she adapted. Her love for Sammy led her to feel responsible for finding a suitable replacement for herself when her au pair contract year ended. She assumed that if she handpicked the next care provider, all would be well. What Anabel did not know was that when her contract ended, Jessica planned that she, not another au pair, would replace Anabel. Because she earned 85 percent of her family's income and covered all of its medical benefits, Jessica was worried about how leaving her job would affect the family's economic stability, but at the time of our interview, reducing her fear of maternal inadequacy was a more pressing need.

. . .

The mother-employers I interviewed represented the generation who benefited from the advances of second-wave feminism. They all worked in male-dominated occupations—they were physicians, dentists, corporate and nonprofit executives, professors,[2] attorneys, engineers, military officers, and scientists. Most were the first or only women to reach their standing in their workplaces. Others worked in the arts as writers and filmmakers, and others filled midlevel jobs in teaching and management. Like their professional and managerial female peers, they were somewhat late labor force entrants. They had started their careers after accumulating an average of twenty-one years of education, including, for most, postgraduate training.

Because they also started their families later, however, their career and parenting aspirations were on a collision course.[3] Most were having their first child just as they were reaching the period of peak productivity and career consolidation. Like Jessica, they found themselves caught in the crosscurrents created by the competing ideals of the "unencumbered worker" and the "good mother."[4] The harder they tried to be ideal mothers, the less time they had to focus on work; the more they tried to be fully present for work demands, the less time they had for their children. As we will see, the feminist beliefs that had opened doors for them at school and at work did not help them when they tried to balance career and family. They challenged neither the assumptions about the ideal "unencumbered" worker nor those about the ideal "at-home" mother. Instead, most accepted their job demands and they embraced intensive mothering more strongly than less affluent women might, and with a class-based emphasis on child perfectibility.

This chapter examines these dilemmas, exploring the standards and expectations that define the ideal mother and the ideal worker, and how these shaped the thoughts, feelings, and actions of the mother-employers who participated in my study. These working mothers took very seriously the notion that they were personally responsible for how their children "turned out." They adopted a notion of blanket accountability, which asserts that no matter how loving and competent the nanny or au pair they employed was, their own absence from the home might be depriving their children of something irreplaceable, the absence of which might even deeply flaw their children's development. Worse, if such damage did occur, it was not likely to be apparent until after the child had grown and it was too late to change. The notion that time spent away from a young child is "unrecoverable" haunted these women. "I'm constantly paranoid," was how one mother-employer put it, explaining that she "reassessed" her employment decision "every week," trying to decide whether by remaining at a job she "loved," she might be failing to fully satisfy her sixteen-month-old daughter's needs.

Blanket accountability went beyond concern for physical safety and emotional well-being to worries about successful class transmission. What Sharon Hays has termed "the ideology of intensive mothering"[5] has accelerated in recent decades, increasingly focusing on successfully achieving developmental benchmarks. The new competitive mothering ideology is aimed squarely at middle-class mothers and admonishes them to prepare their infants and toddlers to compete for the coveted slots in the preschool that will ultimately destine them for Harvard. Most theorists of class transmission describe the process as effortless, if not inevitable.[6] These theories also assume that the reproduction of social class is women's work, and that it always privileges the upper classes. Nonetheless, the middle- and professional-class mothers I interviewed described class transmission as their job, a difficult job they had to delegate to a surrogate.

For the mother-employers I interviewed, this strong sense of blanket account-ability, coupled with the fact that someone else was doing the bulk of the day-to-day childcare, presented a nearly impossible challenge. They felt compelled to find a way to remain in their jobs; be knowledgeable about what was best for their children and ensure that the children were receiving this kind of nurture and developmentally appropriate stimulation every day; and, though gone from home, nevertheless retain supremacy in their children's psychic lives. If, as experts suggest, the bond between mother and child is "indivisible," how can these working mothers share the care of their children with others and still be ideal mothers? If their careers require an "all-or-nothing" level of commitment, how can these mothers meet their workplace demands and excel in the high-level jobs they hold? Is Jessica right when she says, "I don't think you can take off a couple of years from a career—a high-level career—and come back at the same level"? How do mothers who hold high-powered jobs respond to the array of duties, responsibilities, expec-tations, opportunities, and constraints that shape their home and work lives? How do these responses affect the type of care they try to provide for their children?

To answer these questions, this chapter begins by examining some of the most important sources of the mother-employers' beliefs concerning their responsibili-ties as mothers: a contemporary childrearing ideology (as presented and inter-preted in advice books, popular media, and academic research) that calls for an omnipresent mother who invests most or all of her energies in her children's care, a class-based ideology of "competitive mothering,"[7] expectations rooted in fragmented memories of their own mothers' childrearing practices, and standards based on what the study participants imagined, and what the media maintained, at-home mothers did with their children.

The second part of the chapter turns to the workplace, focusing first on how the expectations and standards associated with the prevailing model of the "unen-cumbered worker" compete with mothering ideals, and then considering some of the factors that keep affluent mothers in the workforce. Last, the chapter explores how the anxieties produced by work demands and feeling inadequate as mothers lead most of the mothers I interviewed to act as "maternal gatekeepers," or at least to be ambivalent about including fathers in an already fragmented childrearing endeavor.[8]

THE NEW MOTHERHOOD IDEAL

In the mid-1990s, Sharon Hays coined the term *intensive mothering* to describe the "child-centered, expert-guided, emotionally absorbing, labor intensive, and financially expensive" approach that dominates childrearing in the United States.[9] In the decade and a half since then, demands on mothers have only expanded, fed by changes in experts' opinions regarding the importance of mother-child attachment, by new research pointing to the period from birth to age three as a critical time for brain development, and by the notion of child perfectibility as an attainable goal, particularly for educated, affluent mothers.

The Primacy of the Mother-Infant Bond

In the mid-1990s the first waves of data from the National Institute of Child Health and Human Development's (NICHD) Study of Early Child Care and Youth Development began to appear in the media. This study, and particularly the media "spin" it received, played an important role in ushering in a new era of scientifically guided childrearing. The NICHD research started from the assumption that the mother is the person with whom the child establishes its "primary" bond; thus, good mothering begins with forming that primary attachment and continues with efforts aimed at sustaining it. Experts in child development started with the assumption that a successful mother is the primary and often the only caregiver for her children during the critical years from birth to age three. She bonds with her child and transmits, through all of the attachment activities of infancy, toddlerhood, and early childhood, a sense of security and well-being. Though designed as a study of the effects of various early childcare settings on child development, the NICHD study analysis focused not only on the effects of various types of nonmaternal care but also on the effect of maternal absence. The assumption that maternal absence is inherently damaging is evidenced by the study's heavy reliance on Mary Ainsworth's "strange situation test."[10]

Study reports produced mixed findings on the effects of nonmaternal care, finding for the most part that the quality of childcare was more significant to healthy development than the fact of maternal presence or absence.[11] Media coverage of the study, however, was not so sanguine. Shortly after publication of the first findings, which showed that neither the type of setting nor the duration of care made a difference in children's levels of attachment to their mothers, the *New York Times Magazine* published an article on Romania's orphans and their "attachment disorders," linking these to the plight of children of U.S. working mothers.[12] Media coverage of the NICHD study also emphasized a more minor finding, that some at-risk children placed in daycare were, by age six, "smart and nasty."[13] Despite evidence to the contrary provided by follow-up research on the same children, the takeaway message from the media's coverage of the multiyear study was that children in extrafamilial childcare were at risk for problems later in life.

The Birth-to-Three Fetish

During the same period, the convergence of high-profile conferences, such as the White House–sponsored Starting Points event, and the wide dissemination of new research findings through publications like *Rethinking the Brain—New Insights into Early Development* intensified the "myth of the first three years."[14] Extrapolation from the premise that the brain creates its primary neural pathways during the birth-to-three period led some experts to conclude that a child's long-term cognitive functioning depends almost entirely on the kinds of stimulation received during this period. As the Harvard child psychiatrist Felton Earls proclaimed, "A kind of irreversibility sets in. There is this shaping process that goes on early, and then at the end of this process, be that age 2, 3 or 4, you have essentially designed a brain that probably is not going to change very much more."[15]

Statements like this sparked a flurry of cognitive-stimulation marketing activity, including the "Baby Genius" and "Baby Mozart" series, and the attendant fear that if a parent did not ensure that her child was exposed to these stimuli, the youngster would fall behind academically before reaching preschool. A nationwide survey of parents with children younger than three—conducted after the "critical period" findings were made public—found that 92 percent believed that their children's educational successes would be influenced by their birth-to-three cognitive experiences, and that 85 percent feared that if they did not provide proper stimulation, their babies' brains would not develop properly.[16]

Neurologists attempted to clarify that the new findings did *not* imply irreversibility. They explained that children's brains do not need special shaping; their brains are resilient and prone to growth and development well past the first three years of life. Thus, "no unusual interventions [are] required, and only the grossest neglect [seems] to impede the process in normal babies."[17] This reassuring corrective to the birth-to-three myth, however, appears to have been much less widely disseminated and much more tentatively embraced by the general public.

The Perfectible Child Hypothesis

Parents' reluctance to risk not taking an active role in "designing" their children's brains is understandable. Even as neurologists were trying to replace myth with fact, childrearing experts, synthesizing the basic tenets of intensive mothering and the implications of the latest research on neural development, stimulation, and attachment, had identified an exciting new possibility: raising perfect children. The perfectible child hypothesis is summed up in the words of the psychiatry professor Richard Chase. In *Newsweek*'s 1997 "Your Child: From Birth to Three" special issue (which sold one million copies), he asserted, "We can make most children smarter and more interesting than we make them now."[18] Statements like those made by Drs. Earls and Chase placed enormous pressure on parents, especially mothers.

"Can" quickly became "ought" among the middle- and upper-middle-class participants in this study. They were, like Jessica, "book moms" who tended to "approach mothering like a doctoral dissertation."[19] They studied advice manuals to learn about behavior patterns, illnesses, and developmental milestones.[20] They tried to align their own expectations and behavior with the experts' pronouncements regarding parental involvement, bonding, and the importance of cognitive stimulation. But when they evaluated their own performance against the standards of contemporary childrearing, most concluded that the mothering they were providing was not up to par.[21]

During interviews, the study participants' anxiety about their children's development—and their role in overseeing it—was palpable. Much of the power of the cultural ideal of the good mother as omnipresent and personally responsible for all aspects of childrearing lies in the fact that, by definition, it cannot be tested. Not one of the mother-employers I interviewed was sure how much time, attachment, involvement, attention, or stimulation would be enough to produce a perfect child or what the long-term repercussions of falling short might be.[22] Not surprisingly, first-time mothers were the most anxious, and those with flexible schedules or those who worked part-time were the least. All the mother-employers, though, worried that by deviating from the at-home norm, they risked being seen as bad mothers and therefore as having failed at one of the primary responsibilities of adult womanhood. The cultural ideal of the good mother is so strong that even women who lack the time or flexibility to approximate the at-home mother strive to produce the image of the at-home mother. They do so because they are accountable not only to others, but also to themselves and to the ideal of motherhood they embrace.

For the professional-class women I interviewed, this sense of what I call blanket accountability was almost impossible to overcome or even temper. Most of the mother-employers lacked the access their nannies had to peers in the same situation; they had no opportunity for the "reality checks" provided by regular exposure to playground-based "folk wisdom" in which their nannies, for example, were immersed. Just as important, neither the study participants nor most other mothers in the United States have a counterideology to draw on. No popular belief system challenges the notion that regardless of who cares for children, their own mothers are ultimately responsible for the children's physical, emotional, and psychological well-being and for all aspects of the quality of the care the children receive. To this already daunting list of responsibilities, professional-class mothers add another: the duty to see to it that their children are equipped to maintain or improve their social class standing.

COMPETITIVE MOTHERING

U.S. society's long-standing emphasis on individualism has given rise to a "rhetoric of competitive mothering."[23] Each family, and indeed each mother, is expected to marshal and transmit the economic, social, and cultural resources needed to reproduce or enhance children's class status. Childrearing strategies that result in one's children having a competitive edge are particularly important to middle- and upper-middle-class parents, since this helps preserve their advantageous class standing.[24] The mother-employers were well aware that today, mobility is as likely to be downward as upward, so they felt it was essential that their children gain the skills and attributes that would ensure their success. They believed that the good mother not only loves her children but also transmits what Pierre Bourdieu has termed *habitus*,[25] which is transformed into cultural capital as children age.[26]

For Bourdieu, the concept of habitus indicates both what is natural and what individuals find comfortable or expected. The transmission of habitus in childhood translates into power because, as Lareau points out, "Cultural training in the home is awarded unequal value in dominant institutions because of the close compatibility between the standards of child rearing in privileged homes and the (arbitrary) standards proposed by these institutions."[27] In comparing middle-class, working-class, and poor families, Lareau found that both black and white middle-class parents tended to deliberately foster their children's perceived gifts, to schedule multiple enrichment activities, and to model for them interactions based on a sense of entitlement. As children age, this approach gives these children greater advantage relative to their peers.

As we will see, various concerns about delegated mothering intertwine in mothers' accounts. They worry about their children's safety, the quality of nurturance they receive, their psychological bonds to parents and others, and, perhaps most vexing, about how to transmit cultural capital and habitus through caregivers who may not naturally carry the same social and cultural assumptions. Unlike their own mothers, who could presumably transmit middle-class habitus through their very presence, through exposure to their tastes and judgments, likes and dislikes, the mothers in this study had to "contract" this transmission. The difficulty of transmitting upper-middle-class habitus through a working-class maternal figure becomes an increasingly pressing problem as mothers consider hiring, training, and supervising their nannies.

Measuring Up to At-Home Mothers, Real and Imagined

Habitus informs what individuals consider normal and natural in childhood and family life, and in that sense also shapes standards of mothering. The mother-employers framed their understanding of what constituted a "normal" childhood based largely on how they had been mothered. And, since the standards against which they measured their own attempts at childrearing incorporated what they recalled of their mothers' practices, as well as what they learned by reading advice books and media accounts of the latest research, they had yet more reasons for judging their own mothering as falling short of the mark. Most were constantly calculating how much time they had (or had not) spent with their children over the previous day (or week, or month) and trying to find ways to compensate for areas in which they saw themselves as not measuring up to the ideal.[28] Suzanne, who at thirty was the vice-president of a successful dot-com startup as well as a first-time mother, explained, "The model that I grew up with is obviously not the model that I'm doing right now, so it's very, uh, difficult for me to assess what the impact is of what I'm doing—the long-term impact of what I'm doing. And that—you know—stresses me out. [*laughs*] I'm not sure [I'm home enough]. . . . I mean, I don't—I spend, uh, maybe—it has been pretty bad, like, you know, an hour and a half, maybe two hours a day with her." Interviewees who had been raised by stay-at-home mothers, and these were in the majority, tended to feel more ambivalent about working than those who had not.[29]

Mary Anne, a white thirty-four-year-old research scientist with a two-year-old daughter, described her mom as the "perfect nurturing mother." She recalled that her mother "did everything with us," was "with us all the time," and was "involved in every part of our lives." Now that she was raising a child, Mary Anne found that "a lot" of her own practices were modeled on her mother's—even though she, unlike her mother, worked outside the home. Thirty-three-year-old Teresa, a Latina mathematics professor, said that when her mother "freaked" over her plan to put her first child in day care at fourteen months, Teresa found herself feeling the same way her mother did: "I remember feeling like, 'How can I really be his mother if I'm not the one who he comes to? Truly, the person who is with him is the mother.'" Eventually, a colleague with two healthy, happy children helped Teresa see her mother's attitude as "just [her mother's] personal bias rather than fact."

Even those who had been raised by working mothers often felt inadequate in comparison. Alicia, a Latina writer who, at twenty-nine, was younger than most of the mothers who participated in the study, said she had been raised "by the typical supermom of the seventies." Because Alicia "always [felt] divided between them [the children] and the rest of my life," she considered herself inferior to her mother, who had combined a challenging academic career with raising a family. Alicia could have viewed her mother as a positive role model for her own mothering practice; instead, she saw her as possessed of extraordinary personal characteristics that Alicia herself lacked. Interestingly, whether the comparative case mother worked or stayed home, the women I interviewed emphasized their *personal* characteristics rather than their *institutional* (home or work) supports.

Regardless of whether or not they had been raised by an at-home mother, all the mother-employers shared the same great dilemma, namely, how to transmit their cultural capital and habitus through an intermediary. Their own mothers executed their responsibilities through their very presence in the home, where they were able to "naturally" expose the children to their tastes and judgments, likes and dislikes. My interviewees, by contrast, had to "contract" the transmission of habitus. In most cases, their childcare providers' backgrounds were very different from their own. Thus, few nannies or au pairs shared their employers' social and cultural assumptions. As we will see in the chapters to come, the difficulty of transmitting upper-middle-class habitus and cultural capital through a working-class maternal figure is a pressing problem for the mother-employers.

Mythical Moms

In addition to trying to live up to their recollections of their own mothers' practices, the mother-employers tried to meet standards they presumed their nonemployed counterparts were achieving. Most were deeply affected by the media's frequent, and frequently negative, comparisons between working and at-home mothers.[30] Mary, a white thirty-seven-year-old part-time physician, mentioned a recent *Boston Globe* article "about new respect for at-home moms" and recalled comments she had heard from a friend who is part of a group of full-time mothers. Then she mused, "So sometimes when I see these other people and I talk to them, I feel like maybe they're more 'serious' about mothering, you know what I mean? They know a lot about mothering issues and that stuff, and I wonder if maybe I'm not serious enough about it." The at-home mother ideal was particularly powerful since most of the working moms knew very few other mothers in situations like their own. Their work lives were dominated by men with at-home wives, by other working women who had either grown children or no children, and by the saintly at-home mother depicted in the media, whose childrearing knowledge and capacity for self-sacrifice both seemed infinite.

The belief that at-home mothers perceived them as "free riders" propelled many of the mother-employers to devise ways to emulate the image they held of the at-home mother. For instance, as a member of a local community where "there are a lot of nonworking mothers" who "are doing all these wonderful support things [in their children's schools]," forty-three-year-old Carol, a white college teacher with three children, said she "felt very guilty about not being part of the PTO." Although she spent two hours per week as a volunteer aide in the classroom, Carol felt her efforts paled in comparison to those of the at-home mothers: "There is a group of women that put in *incredible* amount of hours doing stuff. I haven't made any part of it. I feel guilty for that. Not guilty [*pause*] but, yes, *guilty.*"

Mothers in a Man's World

Working and parenting are not inherently contradictory activities. In other Western industrialized nations, government and workplace policies, reinforced by cultural norms, combine to make working and parenting viable and, in some cases, gender equitable.[31] The United States, however, offers no comparable support, so working families must find private solutions to what are essentially public problems—and it is women who most frequently take on the task of "solving" the work-family dilemma.[32] For low-income mothers, that often means working multiple jobs, leaving children in understaffed daycare, working for low pay and no benefits, and being "practical" about the limits of the mothering they can provide their children.[33] For the professional-class women I interviewed, the work-family dilemma took a different form and exacted a different, but still burdensome, toll. While the norms of blanket accountability prompted them to emulate "ideal" at-home mothers, their careers demanded that they emulate the professional ideal of the "unencumbered worker."

THE UNENCUMBERED WORKER

As the law professor Joan Williams and others have pointed out, the work world, especially the world of professional and managerial work, is based on the model of an unencumbered male worker.[34] This model, which has changed surprisingly little over the past few generations, despite dramatic increases in the number of women in the workforce, assumes the normal worker is free of family responsibilities because he is single or because he has a wife at home to both care for his family and bolster his career.[35] Thus, salaried jobs tend to be "all-or-nothing" positions, in which the incumbents typically put in long hours and must be prepared to accommodate last-minute changes in plans and schedules.[36]

Studies of women in high-status occupations indicate that these workplaces tend to demand "virtually single-minded commitment" and tend to force women to choose between being a worker and being a mother.[37] This happens in part because the unencumbered worker model assumes a worker whose career trajectory proceeds without interruption. Women who work in male-dominated careers thus find themselves pitted against a career clock that presumes they will be able to devote themselves to career-building during their prime childbearing years. Meanwhile, the ideological standards and cultural expectations associated with motherhood pressure women to devote themselves to their families. Those, like the mother-employers in my study, who try both to have children and to compete with male peers (and with female peers who have few or no family responsibilities) find themselves in an often untenable bind between hyperfeminine caregiving expectations at home and hypermasculine productivity demands at work.

Passing the "Test of Manhood"

Given the pervasiveness of the unencumbered worker model in male-dominated occupations, simply becoming pregnant can place women in professional-level jobs in these fields on the defensive at work. Many of the mother-employers recounted experiences like Jessica's—all the credibility and respect they had accrued in their career "banks" seemed to have magically vanished when their pregnancies became apparent.[38] And, again like Jessica, many also found that being pregnant raised doubts about their work ethic and prompted a scaling back of their workplace responsibilities.[39]

Rosanna Hertz argues that for professional/managerial-class women, "having a child and caring for them becomes a 'test of manhood.'"[40] The new mother must demonstrate her determination to stick to the male career model or risk being explicitly or implicitly placed on the "mommy track."[41] The majority of the mother-employers I interviewed faced this test with their first pregnancies. Maternity leaves, despite being part of most of the women's employment packages, often occasioned manhood tests. Joyce, a black thirty-seven-year-old physician, told me that after she had cleared her leave with the clinical director of the hospital where she worked, she still had to pass a test of manhood administered by one of her male colleagues: "He asked me, 'Well, are you gonna be paid for your maternity leave? Or should I go to the clinic and tell them that they should provide extra coverage out here, which they can pay for because you're not here?' And I said, 'No. When you had your knee surgery, were you paid?' 'Yes.' 'You were out for a month and you got paid.' So, yeah. But I mean, he was fine with it." Joyce successfully defended her right to a maternity leave because she couched it in "male" terms her colleague could understand: having a baby is like having knee surgery. As Anne Crittenden has remarked, "When and if [working women] do give birth, they are expected to treat the event like an appendectomy, take a brief time-out for recuperation, then resume the truly important business of business."[42]

Leigh, a white thirty-eight-year-old British primary-care physician in private practice, was back to the "truly important business of business" almost immediately after the birth of her child. She recalled that "when [the baby] was born, I was on the phone that afternoon with patients, and I went back to work within a week. I had less time than people take for a regular vacation." Joyce had a longer leave, but the gradual "ramp-up to full time" that she had negotiated with her director did not materialize. When she came back to work, "I was back full-time. You know, I didn't ease into it. I was just back." Others in high-level positions mentioned that, although they had taken maternity leaves, they had come back to work before their allotted leave time was up. Some, like Jane, a white thirty-four-year-old corporate vice-president, were explicit that they had done so in response to job demands: "[My leave was] very short—full time, about three weeks. And I had a C-section. My choice was basically—I had a very small staff. I reported directly to the chairman. The business was having tremendous difficulties, and it was either I resigned or I went back to work, so there wasn't a lot of option there."

The nature of the top-tier positions that women like Jane and most of the other mother-employers held demands that their incumbents *not* use the many benefits associated with these jobs.[43] Furthermore, women who take parental leave experience financial penalties over the life of their careers. Sylvia Hewlett found an 11 percent salary gap between those who took less than one year out of the workforce and those who took none; there was a 37 percent salary gap between those who spent three or more years out of the workforce and those who had taken no time off.[44] As a group, my interviewees averaged eight weeks of maternity leave, half of it paid. The mother with the least maternity leave took two weeks unpaid, and the mother with the most leave received eleven months of unpaid leave. The women in more flexible jobs, such as artists and writers, tended to have the most maternity leave, followed by women in academic professions. At the other end of the spectrum were the doctors, lawyers, and corporate executives, who rarely had more than the federally mandated twelve weeks, and often received much less.[45]

The mother-employers I interviewed did not challenge the male-pattern career norm: rather, they viewed it as just one more hurdle among many in their professional lives. Pat, a white forty-two-year-old career military officer, said of her rapid return to work after the birth of her second child, "because I nursed and because of my body build, I was able to go right back to my [military] uniform. So, I mean no one even knew I had the baby." In the test of manhood for mothers with male-pattern careers, this represents the ultimate success.

Pat had a compelling reason to hide her pregnancy. Being visibly pregnant can curtail a woman's career advancement opportunities. Pat had hoped to protect a very recent promotion to a much-desired post: "No one of my rank worked at that high a level. I was the first one. . . . And so I was [pause] concerned—[chuckles]— that I was going to lose my job and be sent somewhere less exciting, you know, less stimulating. And so I hid the fact I was pregnant until I was six months along. I just kept buying larger and larger clothes." To her surprise, despite her efforts, Pat's superior officers knew she was pregnant. She heard through the grapevine that a search for her replacement had been initiated: "They had all assumed that I would turn in my resignation and leave because the work was just too hard for me, because I was having a baby, because all their wives had said it was so hard, and 'She can't work when she has that little one at home.'" As a pioneer in an all-male bastion of power, Pat believed she had a responsibility to be a trailblazer, challenging some of the entrenched expectations of the workplace on behalf of other women:

> I had a professional need to come back to work to prove to them that—not necessarily that I had to, I mean I had the *luxury*, I guess, if I had wanted to stay home, because my husband worked and I had the education to do many other things—there are a lot of people in the military who don't have those choices, where they are the sole person. And I just thought, if I can just make it through this tour so that the next person that's hired after me doesn't have to go through the arduous thing that I had to go through, then we have won a major victory; however small it is in the grand scheme of things, we've made a change.

Pat was successful in proving that pregnancy need not be a hindrance in a high-level position, and she continued to prove it when her second child was born. When women like Pat and the other mother-employers in the study succeed in passing the test of manhood, however, they ultimately reinforce a norm that is harmful to them, individually and as a group. For women in "all-or-nothing jobs," the long-term career cost of scaling back is extraordinarily high.[46] Noting that "women in high-powered traditionally masculine careers are less likely to have children and more likely to fall off the fast-track," Joan Williams emphasizes that that outcome "doesn't represent their free unfettered choice. It represents the structure of traditionally masculine careers."[47] The experiences of the few study participants who chose to scale back their hours confirm this.

"You Just Have to Sort of Rationalize"

Elaine, a white thirty-four-year-old corporate vice-president, dropped to a three-day workweek after the birth of her second child. "I made a decision that I was not going to miss another child's infancy," she explained. She tailored her job so that she could meet her responsibilities by working at the office three ten- to thirteen-hour days each week. She told me this scheduling change resulted in professional losses "like advancement, titles, money, opportunities." Then she quickly added, "They're really not important to me." She did acknowledge, though, that she resented the fact that she had lost the possibility of retaining her identity (and benefits) as a full-time worker not because she was working fewer hours or producing lower-quality work but because she had reduced her office "face time."

Some of the mothers I interviewed also pointed out the imbalance between the continued high quality of the work they produced and the heavy penalties associated with scaling back. For example, Linda, a white thirty-nine-year-old attorney, cut back to a thirty-five-hour workweek—considered part time at her firm—as her family grew. She was well aware of what this decision had cost her: "It's taken away in the sense that I would have been a partner by now, and it's slowed down the partnership track and I probably don't have—I know I don't have as much experience as colleagues of mine who graduated with me, who have been to court several times and have much more power. But . . . I've sort of changed my priorities. . . . I think, 'Well, I have three kids at home and I get to see them a lot more.' So, you just have to sort of rationalize." Even after having been mommy tracked, these part-timers continued to require full-time in-home childcare because they still worked long hours, and they still needed the flexibility to be able to respond at short notice to changing job demands. Thus, what women like Linda must "rationalize" is that they incur a significant career loss—fewer chances for promotion and growth, lower income, and less status—but gain only modestly with respect to fulfilling the cultural expectations associated with being a good mother.

The seven mothers I interviewed who classified themselves as working part-time at some point in their careers averaged thirty-six hours for a "part-time" week (as opposed to the average fifty-one hours per week among the twenty-three who classified themselves solely as working full-time).[48] The part-timers typically worked away from home ten to thirteen hours per day, three to four days per week. They also brought work home and spent significant hours working in the "home office." Regardless of whether a professional/managerial-class worker is full-time or part-time, or whether she is unencumbered or has a family, she is expected to put her work commitments first.[49]

WHY WORK? THE EVER-RECEDING HORIZON OF CAREER SECURITY

Although it seems self-evident that every adult has the right to seek gainful employment, working mothers with young children are held accountable to mothering norms that emphasize putting family first. Several commonly held assumptions make mothers in professional/managerial positions additionally vulnerable to public censure. They are assumed to have high-earning spouses, and thus their own jobs are "luxuries"; they are assumed to *owe* their children the benefit of direct exposure to their class background, educational level, and professional standing; their justifications for being in the workforce, whether these be personal meaning, stimulation, or social interaction, are assumed to be insufficient; and women, not men, are assumed to be the ones who must choose between income and childrearing. In short, for the women I interviewed, class transmission is women's work. Ironically, class transmission also became a reason to stay in demanding jobs.

All of the mothers I interviewed agreed that they would like to work less, or said that a part-time schedule would be their ideal. Still, all argued that they *needed* to work.[50] The most frequently cited reason was the ever-receding horizon of career security. Because they had struggled to achieve legitimacy in male-dominated occupations, these women were acutely aware of the fragility of their career trajectories. Most felt they could not risk scaling back; they could not afford to be shunted onto the mommy track. My respondents consistently referred to themselves as having "been lucky" in their career choices or of having been "at the right place at the right time." As a result, they felt a sense of urgency—a need to capitalize on the opportunities they had gained—combined with an acute awareness that they faced a very narrow window of opportunity. Many of those who seriously considered taking time off felt they needed to put "just a few more years" in the career bank first, and then they would be sufficiently established to safely cut back. Given the ever-changing demands of their careers, it is unlikely that any of the mother-employers I interviewed would achieve the plateau of career safety at which they could channel more energy toward home. The need to keep abreast of the latest developments in their fields was important. They were measured against the standard of the male career trajectory, an uninterrupted upward climb. Taking time off from a demanding profession could place them hopelessly behind their peers. This concern was most apparent among the professionals (doctors, lawyers, engineers), but it was also a worry for managers and executives.[51]

Some mother-employers, in addition to citing economic need, mentioned the importance of the stimulation and sense of self they gained from having a work life. Carol was the most vocal about the "right" to work, not out of economic need but because work was of inherent value to the self. Interestingly, she also had the least economic justification for working, since her salary represented only 15 percent of her family's household income. This was a sore point. As she pointed out, "We pay as much for our childcare or more than what I make at [work]." To Carol, "The bottom-line argument is often that many families require the income. Well, to me it's far more complex than that—we deserve to define ourselves in other ways, and I don't think our kids are getting hurt for it. If I were working forty, fifty hours a week, [my husband] were working forty, fifty hours a week—yeah. It's not right to have kids in that situation, at least for me. But this allows me to work, [and] maintain a family and a home."

Joyce cited the important sense of structure and accomplishment she gained from working outside the home: "When I was home on maternity leave, it was good, but it was also—I never knew where the time went. I didn't have the same kind of goal accomplishments at the end of a day or at the end of a certain period that I had when I was working. And though I knew that I was taking care of him, it wasn't quite the same in the short term. And I need some of those things also. To make me feel good about what I'm doing." Most of the mothers in this study had to and had come to value the structure and sense of reward and recognition that is built into the professional careers. Like Joyce, many felt it was important to look back on some concrete accomplishment at the end of the day. They also valued the adult interactions of the workplace, and the sense of self-worth that came from taking part in the outside world, away from home and family.

Although few needed to work for subsistence, the mother-employers I interviewed cited economic need as their primary reason for working.[52] Despite their large incomes, they perceived this need as quite real, in part because of the broader climate of economic scarcity and instability. The loss of one income due to downsizing or divorce can lead to a precipitous drop in a family's standard of living. Two incomes provide a safety net to offset the steady dismantling of the social services these baby-boom-generation mothers and fathers had come to take for granted.[53] As Katherine Newman has pointed out, the economic setbacks of the 1970s and early 1980s and the rising cost of home ownership led many women to feel they faced a choice between starting a family at a young age or delaying in order to earn enough money to attain or maintain a middle-class standard of living.[54] Large numbers, including the professional-class mothers I interviewed, made the latter choice, and the economic downturn of the first decade of the twenty-first century no doubt validated that decision.

More important, study participants reasoned that their substantial salaries, combined with their ongoing financial vigilance, would protect their children's future careers and class standing. Some viewed their salaries as the difference between home ownership and renting. For others, like Bonnie, a white thirty-six-year-old engineer with three young children, continuing to work made the difference between one school district and another: "I mean, we could make it on my husband's salary, but . . . without my salary, we could probably afford to live [only] in [neighboring town], where the college attendance rate is about 60 percent. And I'm just not willing to take that chance." Although working outside the home was often a strain, she felt she needed to work because the "chance" that her children would fall into the noncollegiate 40 percent was not one she was willing to take.

Jessica also emphasized working to plan for Sammy's future educational needs. She focused on the long term and foresaw needing to cover the costs not only of his college education but also of graduate school: "I absolutely feel like I want the option of being able to send him to private school . . . if his needs are that that's where they can provide the best education for him, based on the type of student he is, I want to be able to do that. And in this day and age to say, 'Well, my child is gonna go to college and that's it.' Well, I don't know. Maybe he will need the assistance of graduate school." Other mothers concurred. Based on their own career experiences, it seemed likely that to support a middle-class lifestyle, their children would need to attend graduate or professional schools after college. Like Jessica, they wanted to be able to afford the cost of this additional education for their children.

They also felt that in order to reach graduate school, they needed to get into the right college, and in order to do this, they needed an array of expensive enrichment activities that they would have purchased for their children whether or not they worked outside of the home. They spoke of how their children would need an elite preschool and a competitive private school or a public school in an affluent district. All of these perceived needs pressured the mothers I interviewed to stay on the high-earning career fast track. Ironically, in the context of competitive mothering, being a good mother frequently meant working to fund these enrichment activities at the same time that working outside of the home often felt like being inadequate as a mother.

Finally, although only a few mothers mentioned it, the prospect of divorce and its economic consequences loomed in the background of their career decision making. Given that nearly half of all marriages currently end in divorce, a mother who allowed her career to stall because she chose to stay home with her children might be risking her children's economic future. If her marriage were to fail, she might find that she was unable to reenter the labor market at her former level. Conversely, as Jessica pointed out, the decision to stay in the labor force for her son's benefit could hurt her in the long run if she were to divorce. If her ex-husband were to remarry, Jessica feared she could lose custody: "So I feel like I have all that responsibility, yet on the other hand, if we got divorced, I could lose my child." This is a minor trend in custody cases. Fathers who remarry are beginning to sue for custody and are winning in cases where the mothers are working.[55] Their status as mothers defines these women as insufficiently committed workers; their status as workers defines them as insufficiently committed mothers.

Surprisingly, despite the sometimes overwhelming difficulties the highly educated and career-oriented women I interviewed faced as they tried to juggle their work and home responsibilities, almost none of them considered increased government or corporate support for working and mothering to be a right. Rather than challenging the ideology of intensive mothering, they embraced it. Rather than seeking change in the male-pattern career, they sought success within its boundaries. Thus, the structural and ideological constraints that create the ideal mother/ideal worker dilemma remained intact and unquestioned in their own lives as well as in society at large. Also surprisingly, the gendered division of labor at home went unchallenged. As discussed in the next section, the women chose to "outsource" much of the household labor, and they reserved for themselves—and their nannies—most of both the work and the pleasure of childrearing.

INTENSIVE MOTHERING AND
MATERNAL GATEKEEPING

Most sociological studies of how working wives and mothers attempt to find gender equity in dividing household labor with their spouses argue that a more equitable division of labor in the "second shift" would solve many problems facing working mothers, including lack of sleep, inadequate leisure time, marital stress, and unequal access to career advancement.[56] Yet it is in the division of labor during the *first* shift that the definition of what it means to be a good mother is most contested. Perhaps because they had delegated so much of the first shift to their nannies, the majority of the mother-employers I interviewed did not seek to increase their husbands' participation in the second shift, and especially not in the area of childcare; nor did they seek additional assistance in managing the nanny's labor during the first shift. Both childcare and nanny-management were too bound up in intensive mothering to delegate to husbands and fathers.[57]

Nevertheless, one-half of the mother-employers described their husbands as equal sharers.[58] The explanation for this seeming anomaly probably lies in what constitutes the second shift in these families. Almost every household had extra help, in addition to childcare, for cooking, cleaning, and errands. Neither parent normally did the "dirty work" of the second shift. The slice of the housework and childcare pie mothers and fathers divided between them was very slim and thus required little negotiation.

So, when the working mothers I interviewed spoke of husbands who shared, they were referring to sharing the "quality time" of childcare, such as weekend family outings or evening bedtime rituals. As Joan, a white thirty-eight-year-old corporate executive with an eleven-month-old daughter, explained, having paid help meant that when she and her husband were at home, their focus could be entirely on their daughter: "The time that we have together is limited, but I really do think it's good. And a lot [of] that is kind of enabled by somebody like Melanie [their nanny], you know, who can kind of do a lot of things for us during the week. I mean, she does errands for us, she does stuff for us. And we have somebody [else] who cleans the house for us. I was laughing with Bill, you know, the *infrastructure* we have built just to allow us to work—it's, like, disgusting! [*laughs*]"

Still, even sharing "quality time" could be stressful. Some working mothers felt threatened when a child preferred daddy to them. Others, like Suzanne, whose husbands had more flexibility at work, sometimes envied their husbands: "Well, my husband's been in sort of a unique situation in that he was in graduate school when Lindsay was born, and so for a year and a half, kind of had that at-homeness. And he's just transitioned into working and he, uh, keeps on joking that he'd like to stay home. I told him that's not an option [*laughs*]." Thus, in some cases, an important part of husbands' second-shift work entailed helping their wives have time for "quality time" with the children. Since Suzanne's work schedule was more demanding than her husband's, she gratefully acknowledged that he often did the cooking in the evenings, which allowed her what she called "face time" with her baby. Interestingly, she used a term most frequently associated with time at the office to describe how she scheduled time with her child at home.

Perhaps because most of the mother-employers—and most of the nannies—believed in some version of intensive mothering, they saw themselves as "sharing the same role,"[59] and viewed the children's fathers either as outside the mother-child-nanny equation or as a threat to its delicate balance. This perspective is particularly striking given that a number of the fathers in the sixty families I studied either worked fewer hours than their wives or were described as equal sharers of second-shift household tasks.

The most significant spousal tensions over the second shift arose around selective sharing. Some men were actively involved in their children's lives, but on their own terms. They might participate in activities such as organized sports or weekend outings but leave the more mundane daily childrearing tasks to their wives. Yet, in most of the families in which the mother was responsible for morning and evening childcare, this was explicitly her choice. Many, already feeling displaced by their nannies' central role in the children's lives, were unwilling to share even the less emotionally rewarding areas of care with their spouses. The more they shared, the more they risked experiencing what Jessica described as the "deep, deep hurt" of coming not first, but second or third, in their child's affections.

Selective sharing was most problematic with regard to hiring and supervising the nanny. When a new childcare worker was needed, the father usually took part only after the mother had screened dozens of applicants. The father would attend a meeting with the top candidate to add his stamp of approval. Mary Anne, who was thinking of replacing her nanny, told me that her husband thought the whole hiring process should be up to her. On the one hand, she felt he should be involved as well: "If I were to hire someone else, I would certainly want him to meet them, as well, because I think it's—our child, so we can both do it." On the other hand, her husband's feeling that the final decision should be hers "because I'm the one that would deal with them, and I'm here in the morning when they arrive," was "fine" and "work[ed] out well." Most of the mother-employers were like Mary Anne. They wanted their husbands to be involved in finding and selecting the person who would care for their child, but they also wanted the final hiring decision to be theirs alone.

Similarly, husbands and wives frequently divided supervisory labor unequally. One parent would do the morning "handoff" to the nanny, and the other the evening. The quality of the handoff varied between mothers and fathers, however. Mothers more often did the interactive work of information exchange, giving morning instructions or taking the evening debriefing, while fathers merely relieved the nanny at the end of her shift. This imbalance was further complicated by the fact that most mothers wanted to be the supervisor and childcare expert, making fathers' efforts in this area superfluous. Joan, for instance, who described the division of childrearing labor as "absolutely fifty/fifty" between her and Bill, her husband, said that she, not Bill, was "*definitely*" Melanie's supervisor, and that this hierarchy was evident to them all: "I think Bill would agree. Um, you know, I think that Melanie sees me as kind of the boss just because we spent so much time together at the beginning, and I really was much more the person giving her direction. Um, and maybe it's something about being the mom, I don't know." Among the fifty nannies I interviewed, only one said that she would call the father first if a question arose concerning the children. In this family, the mother was almost unreachable at work, and the father was a pediatrician. In all other cases, mothers considered themselves the nanny's primary supervisor and the nannies concurred.[60]

Reserving the role of supervisor to themselves helped working mothers maintain a distinction between the nanny's childcare responsibilities and other household chores. Most felt strongly that childcare should come first. Fathers were less likely to be concerned with keeping control over the nanny's job description. Describing her husband Michael's efforts to train their nanny, Suzanne made it clear why mother-employers might find sharing supervisory responsibilities with their spouses difficult: "I think that she [Violet] considers me, like, the ultimate authority, and in fact, I think that, often, that is the case. You know, my husband will . . . tell her, like, that, you know, it's OK to do this or OK to do that, and it's not really OK with me." Believing in blanket accountability, the mother-employers I interviewed felt entirely responsible for what went on at home during the first shift. It is therefore not surprising that their childcare standards would be higher than their husbands'.

Still, fathers had their uses in the nanny-mother relationship. They often acted as a go-between. Disagreements and hurt feelings occurred in even the most harmonious mother-nanny relationships; fathers frequently were called on to restore peace. Jessica described as "very helpful" the interpretive work Steve did when she was feeling frustrated by her lack of face time with Sammy: "He did talk to her [Anabel] at one point and explain[ed] to her that I really needed time alone with Sammy. And that I needed to build my own relationship with him, and that I was having some difficulties with that." This was a familiar scenario in the families I studied. When tensions mounted past the point where a mother and nanny felt comfortable discussing the problem, the father would go back and forth between them, explaining and smoothing over. Fathers took on this role not because the women could not communicate—in fact, this happened frequently in families in which the mother and the nanny were quite close—but because the stakes were too high or the issue too emotionally charged for the women to negotiate successfully on their own.

An even more frequent role for fathers was to serve as the family's designated "bad guy."[61] Many mothers confessed to sending their husbands to speak to the nanny about difficult or unpleasant issues like negotiating pay or denying a request, even when the potentially upsetting decision had originated with the mother. Debbie, a white thirty-four-year-old corporate lawyer with two young children, was frank: "If there's anything extra that I want to ask of her, I usually have him ask. [*laughs*]" Doing so was a form of insurance. If a mother made the nanny angry, she feared that the caregiver might direct this anger at the child. Interestingly, the mother-employers never expressed a similar worry regarding a nanny's reaction to the father. Anger at the father was expected; anger at the mother was too dangerous to risk.

Nannies and mothers also colluded in defining fathers as ignorant of childcare and household tasks. Conspiring this way reinforced the bond between nanny and employer and bolstered the women's sense of the value of the role they shared. Furthermore, this kind of collusion increased their awareness that they did indeed share a special role, one from which the father stood apart. Jointly defining the father as the "bad guy" could reduce tensions during difficult negotiations around family work. For example, when Jane and her nanny Sarah, a white twenty-four-year-old from Iowa, were renegotiating Sarah's contract, Jane's husband, Peter, balked at paying Sarah the same salary for fewer hours. Jane and Sarah's shared perception that Peter simply failed to *understand* Sarah's importance to the family the way Jane did defused the situation. Sarah explained: "I think Peter doesn't really know how much I do. . . . And Jane, she's like, 'Well, if you leave, I'm just going to be doing all the cooking and the laundry again, and I don't have time to do all that—that's why we have you here.' . . . And Peter just kind of went along with her—he kind of just does, so it worked out well."

The role fathers played also points to an important distinction between supervising childcare workers and supervising domestic workers. Judith Rollins argues that both the domestic worker and her (female) employer are subordinate to the male head of the household, that this subordination shapes the women's relationship, and that because the work to be divided is "women's work" it is devalued.[62] In Rollins's scenario, both women are the man's servants. This is only partly true in homes where nannies are employed. Fathers appear to be able to serve as "go-betweens" and "bad guys" in the mother-nanny relationship precisely because the work of childcare is not their primary concern. It is in some senses defined as beneath them; yet it is simultaneously defined as *beyond* them. Nannies and mothers frequently referred to fathers as inept at various aspects of caring for young children. Suzanne said of Michael, "He doesn't like to ask [their nanny, Violet, to do tasks], that's the thing. He'll have Violet, like, sitting in a chair while he's running around." Another mother remarked of her husband, "He's *afraid* to give the baby her bath." Of a different father, a nanny complained, "He's even more clueless than *she* [the mother] is."

Mothers' and nannies' perceptions of fathers highlight a critical difference between childcare and housework. Childcare assigns a degree of power to the primary parent and is emotionally gratifying in a way that housework is not. Therefore, the mother-employers were loath to give up control of childrearing, even as they wished their husbands would do more. And those who perceived their husbands as "equal sharers" really perceived them as doing as much of the second shift as they wanted them to do. No more, no less.

CONCLUSION

The mother-employers I studied relied heavily on expert advice and worked hard to live up to all the standards and expectations associated with contemporary approaches to childrearing among the middle and upper-middle classes. They accepted as valid the central tenets of the ideology of intensive mothering, including the notion that the grown child is the "finished product" of the mother's labor. They were haunted by the underlying message of the notion of the perfectible child: if they *could* build a better child, they *should*. Moreover, although it is impossible for a mother to work outside the home and not share some mothering tasks with someone else, the mother-employers I interviewed understood the responsibilities of motherhood as being fundamentally theirs alone. In shouldering the burden of blanket accountability, they accepted full responsibility for every aspect of their children's development, despite not being present to perform all the necessary mother-work themselves.

In almost all cases, the mother-employers were in high-paying positions. Still, they voiced multiple fears about economic insecurity. They aimed to achieve a stable toehold for their children on the ladder of upward mobility. Even those whose careers provided a second income argued that it was their earnings that made possible the house in the good school district, the private school, the tutors, the special lessons and activities—advantages they hoped would secure their children's place in the managerial/professional class. Their income also provided a cushion against layoff, divorce, or illness, and most of them were conscious of this.

These mother-employers' career decisions brought them affluence and success, but also placed them in multiple actual and potential binds. They tried to simultaneously address the demands of blanket accountability and buy their way out of conflicts over the second shift by outsourcing housework and by closely monitoring who performed what childrearing tasks. Yet, even when they managed to find vocabularies to counter cultural pressures as women, as workers, as wives, and as mothers, and even when they were able to accommodate competing structural demands, they found that succeeding in one area of their lives risked failing in another. If they found the "perfect nanny," who "adored" their child, they jeopardized the bond between the baby and themselves, an attachment crucially important to fulfilling their maternal duty to promote and protect their children's future development. If they were fortunate enough to keep their marriages intact, they still faced the double-bind of either risking "stalled-out" careers or missing what they considered to be important phases in their children's development.

Compared to the majority of mothers who work, these women's dilemmas are not severe.[63] The fact that they are privileged makes their work/family problems and their economic worries relative, but it does not make them any less real. They struggled to meet cultural standards, expectations, and personal beliefs about motherhood, even as these burdened them with full responsibility for their children's well-being. They were determined to hold on to jobs they loved and needed, even as these positions exacted enormous and unrealistic demands, given their dual roles as workers and mothers. Caught in a vise between the cultural pressure of the ideology of intensive mothering and the structural rigidity of male-pattern careers, and with no public policy shifts on the horizon, they turned to a private solution to a public problem. They hired a wife.

Nannies on the Market

PRELUDE: MARGARITA, LURA, AND ASTRID

My Spanish-speaking research assistant and I met Margarita at a local park where she was watching the three-year-old in her care. Now forty-nine years old, Margarita, who is Ecuadorean, had come to the United States about twenty years earlier to assist her daughter, who was pregnant with her first child. Margarita stayed, her husband joined her, and she worked in factories for several years.

In 1984, she took her first childcare job. Over the years, she became downwardly mobile. She moved from $250 a week for live-in childcare, to $150 a week live-out, to her current job, which paid her only $100 per week for live-out work. But she took pride in her decision to accommodate the family's economic situation and in "raising" her employers' children. Here, Margarita used the word *educar*, which means to give a proper upbringing, to teach respect and manners, to form a child into someone who will grow up to be a respectable adult. For her, fulfilling this mission was more important than the money she earned. As she explained of her third employer's child, "I taught him to be calm, to greet people, to not misbehave, and it seems the boy learned to be very respectful and so his parents said, 'Thank you, Margarita, because you are guiding him.' . . . In school he will learn, but [thanks to you], he will not be *maleducado*."[1] Like many immigrant mothers who are far from their own children and grandchildren, Margarita used her employers' children as emotional substitutes. On her first job, she recalled coming "to love that child as if he were my own grandson. . . . And if you look at that photo [*shows us*], you can see that even now that child loves me."

Although she had longed to return to Ecuador, every time she planned to do so, it seemed that something would get in the way. Now both her husband

and her parents were deceased, her children were living in the United States and Europe, and there was no longer a place for her in Ecuador. Like most of the immigrant women we interviewed who came from South and Central American and Caribbean countries, retaining a place within their families back home was essential to happiness and even survival. Many women who, like Margarita, had planned to return home to retire discovered that there was no longer a role for them in their communities of origin. Those who were widowed, had no adult children to live with, or, even worse, were divorced found life in their home countries socially isolating and economically uncertain. Many of the immigrants we interviewed had left their home countries originally because of failed or abusive marriages. Their stories reveal a combined economic pull and social, economic, and cultural push that kept them in the United States longer than they had intended. The children in their care provided them with an important source of comfort and meaning.

. . .

I met Lura when she responded to an advertisement for the study I had placed in a local paper. She had worked as a nanny for ten years after leaving Iowa at age twenty. A friend invited her to Boston for vacation. Lura's first reaction was, "I can't afford [to visit]. I'm going to college. I can barely afford that. . . . Then my mother saw an ad in the [local] newspaper. Someone wanted a nanny." Lura planned to work for a short while, experience city life, and save for college: "I was going to study business and computer science and get a job that made lots and lots of money . . . but then I fell in love with it here [in Boston]. Fell in love with the kids. So I said, 'I'm not going back.' I started taking classes once in a while, but I couldn't really afford that either. So I'm just stuck with this." Like many of her American-born peers, she found that what had started as a lark turned into a way of life. Before long, she had found a boyfriend and, because her live-in employers did not like the idea of a man coming to the house, had traded her live-in job for a live-out one that paid $350 a week, with full benefits.

Lura married her boyfriend and her new career as a nanny proceeded well until their son was born. She worked until two weeks before his birth, and although her employer wanted her to come back after maternity leave, she declined. The family had twin toddlers. Lura felt that "with the twins walking, it wouldn't work. Either they would be slighted or he [Lura's baby] would be slighted. I couldn't do it." At the time of our interview, she was unemployed and, despite excellent references, was having a hard time finding the right job—one where she could bring her son to work. She explained, "Ideally I would like to find somebody that had [a child] the same age as him that would let me bring him along and take care of them together. . . . [T]hey could kind of grow up together and be friends." This scenario presented problems, however, because "most people say, 'Well, we want one-on-one with our kids, so we don't want your kids here.'"

Ultimately, Lura wanted to work from her own home and operate her own family childcare center. But she and her husband shared a small two-bedroom apartment that would not qualify as a licensed family daycare. She knew she would have to wait "until we can afford to buy a house. Then I could have a family daycare. But that will be about five years from now." With the shift in her priorities that put her son's needs first, Lura's employment opportunities diminished. She considered leaving childcare work altogether, but, she shrugged, "To get what I would call a normal job, [employers] would say, 'Well, what have you been doing for the past eleven years?' Well, I've been taking care of kids."

. . .

I was introduced to nineteen-year-old Astrid, a Swedish au pair, by her employer, Bonnie. Astrid came to my apartment and I interviewed her over coffee. She explained that she had become an au pair because she hoped more experience working with children would improve her employment prospects as a preschool teacher when she returned to Sweden. She looked down on au pairs who "just think that they come here to have fun and they don't know how much work it is." She worked ten hours a day, four days a week, plus weekend evenings, caring for three children: Josh, age four, Emma, two, and baby Madison, four months. She described Bonnie as an understanding employer, because she stayed home with her children one day a week and "knows what it's like." As for Bonnie's husband, Astrid said, "I don't think he could handle the kids for even one week all by himself."

Astrid admitted somewhat sheepishly to having a favorite (Emma) among the three children and to finding Josh sometimes difficult to handle. He talked back and hit her, but "he knows what time-out is, so that's good." Josh missed his previous au pair and wanted to write to her. "Sometimes he mixes us up," Astrid explained, "Like, 'Do you remember the time we did that?' But I wasn't here then." She thought the one-year turnover was probably hard on him. Josh had begun asking her when she was going to go home, whether they would have a new au pair, and what her name would be.

The only other difficulty Astrid mentioned was isolation. She lived in a basement room in Bonnie's three-bedroom suburban home. She was allowed to have friends over, and she and the kids played frequently with nannies and au pairs in the neighborhood. But during the day, she had no access to a car. Both parents drove to work, leaving her with the three children and without many options for outings. She said that during the summer, "We have picnics, we play outside all day, it's fun." But in the cold winter months, "the kids go stir-crazy." I asked her if she had discussed the problem with Bonnie, but, like most au pairs, Astrid was reticent with her "host parents," rationalizing that her working conditions were "only for a year." The few frustrations she had went unmentioned.

. . .

Professional childcare is one of America's least socially and economically valued occupations, and those who provide this service are among the most dependent and vulnerable of workers. All forms of childcare are poorly paid.[2] Most childcare workers, including the nannies and au pairs in this study, family daycare providers, and daycare center workers, have fewer economic opportunities than the parents of the children they care for.[3] Among in-home care providers, occupational inequities go far beyond the problem of low wages. Working *inside* of the family, these workers are defined as *outside* of labor law. Thus, they have little recourse in disputes with employers, whether these disagreements concern hours, working conditions, or pay.

Socially, the norms that define their work may further undermine their position. Nannies and au pairs often use childcare work as a means of fulfilling their own version of intensive mothering. Moreover, they frequently are considered, and often prefer to consider themselves, "one of the family," the equivalent of an older daughter or a beloved aunt. In practice, this means that they must conduct their work negotiations from the complicated perspective of fictive kin, balancing their strong loyalties to the children in their care against their own needs and desires for regular hours, a clear job description, and decent pay. The mother-employers with whom they negotiate, in turn, must weigh their children's well-being against their own needs and desire for a competent, flexible worker whose wage demands will not strain household finances. Finally, since childcare providers and their employers rarely come from the same class and cultural backgrounds, they each bring a different set of perspectives and values to the task of childrearing. Here, too, nannies and au pairs must develop ways to accommodate their employers' wishes without violating their own beliefs and principles. This chapter examines these tensions and the many factors that drive them.

WHO WORKS AS A NANNY AND WHY?

Many studies of childcare and domestic work suggest that almost all nannies are immigrants, and that most of the domestic and childcare workers in a given region are from the same group (e.g., Latinas in Los Angeles or women from the Caribbean in New York).[4] These studies draw on Shellee Colen's concept of "stratified reproduction."[5] "Physical and social reproductive tasks are accomplished differentially according to inequalities that are based on hierarchies of class, race, ethnicity, gender, place in a global economy, and migration status and that are structured by social, economic, and political forces."[6]

This concept needs to be defined more broadly, however, to encompass the range of in-home childcare workers I found when recruiting interviewees: I sought caregivers based on their job description rather than immigration status or ethnic origin, and found white American-born nannies like Lura, European au pairs like Astrid, as well as immigrant women, both documented and undocumented, like Margarita, all filling nanny roles for young children. The more diverse pattern I found in the Boston area raises important questions about these perceptions, and about the critical distinction between in-home childcare and other forms of domestic work. More complex factors shaped employers' childcare hiring preferences. As chapter 4 shows, rather than hiring from the most populous or inexpensive immigrant group, the mother-employers I interviewed strategically matched their perceptions of their childcare needs to their perceptions of the qualities and traits of specific ethnic groups. Elaine spoke for most of the mother-employers I interviewed when she described how she perceived New York and Los Angeles employers: "There are areas in the country where, you know, 'that [ethnic group] is where the "help" comes from.' And I guess I never viewed any of these childcare providers as 'the help.' This is not 'the girl' who lives downstairs, because this isn't a housekeeper. This is a crucial part of our family." Elaine's remarks address regional hiring preferences but, more important, they speak to the distinctions most employers I interviewed made between caring labor and menial labor, between childcare and housework.[7]

Racial/ethnic hierarchies were expressed differently when the job was defined as childcare-only as opposed to housework, or to some combination of these two sets of responsibilities. This implies that interpretations of the dimensions of race and ethnicity in employer-employee relationships found in earlier inquiries into the racial/ethnic dynamics of domestic work need to be more nuanced and more sensitive to the ways individuals define the work. I found three distinct groups of in-home childcare providers. As I show in this chapter, each faced distinct challenges getting and leaving jobs, as well as different experiences and conditions at work.

The women most frequently represented in media portrayals of nannies are immigrants, often undocumented, who come to the United States from developing countries. The second are young American women, primarily Caucasians from rust-belt and farm-belt communities in the Midwest, who migrate to urban areas for work. The third are au pairs, women between the ages of eighteen and twenty-five, who come to the United States from Europe, South America, and Asia on short-stay, "cultural exchange" visas. Members of all three groups are represented in the population of childcare workers in the greater Boston area, and in this study. Each group's characteristics and how these characteristics shape their career patterns and working conditions are described below. Perhaps surprisingly, race and ethnicity were not the deciding factor in working conditions or pay among these women: legal status was, whether for the foreign-exchange au pair or the undocumented immigrant.

Immigrants

My research assistants and I interviewed twenty-five immigrant women who worked as nannies.[8] They ranged in age from twenty-one to sixty-six, and their legal statuses varied.[9] They had a wide range of educational and professional backgrounds. Some had worked as professionals in their home countries; others had no formal education or previous training. Their reasons for coming to the United States also varied. Some, like Rosa, a thirty-two-year-old immigrant from Honduras who had been forced to leave her two school-age daughters behind, were fleeing the stigma of divorce or the danger of an abusive relationship; others, like Pilar, a twenty-one-year-old from El Salvador, were political refugees, seeking jobs in order to support family members they had to leave behind. Others, like Esther, a sixty-four-year-old from China, brought at least some of their children with them, hoping to provide them with better educational and economic opportunities in the United States.

All but one of the immigrants worked on a live-out basis, in homes located in areas close to Boston, accessible by public transportation.[10] Most were on the job very long hours, an average of fifty-six per week. Although not all were willing to disclose their earnings, those who did reported weekly salaries ranging from $80 to $450. Among the immigrant women I interviewed, those with working papers, a good command of English, and experience with childcare earned as much or more than their American-born Caucasian counterparts.[11] Those who worked illegally or who had language difficulties earned much less, and often faced more difficult working conditions as well. Lonehl, a thirty-five-year-old naturalized citizen originally from Barbados, noted that employers seemed to reason that women without legal status "really need the job," and that this led them to treat these nannies "worse than if you're legal." According to Anne, a thirty-four-year-old Jamaican nanny, "If you can't speak English—you're dead. You're just dead meat . . . you're totally a slave."

Most of the immigrant interviewees were sending part of the money they earned to someone else—parents, children, or other relatives at home. Some were working to support and/or care for relatives in the United States. To this financial burden, many added the stress of daily guilt and worry resulting from having to leave their children behind when they came to the United States.[12] The majority would have preferred a different kind of work. As Esther, who had abandoned a medical career in China, said wryly, "Actually, I wasn't seeking to be a babysitter for the rest of my life." Many others concurred; they did not see themselves as being nannies indefinitely. They spoke of going home once they had earned enough money, or of changing careers once they had working papers or sufficient language skills. They had no sense of how or when these future scenarios might take shape, however.

Undocumented immigrant nannies had especially narrow options. Pilar, for example, knew that she was earning too little in her first job ($150 per week for fifty hours of live-out work), but, as she said, "I needed a job so badly—I have to help my parents." Like most of the undocumented workers we interviewed, Pilar had relied on personal networks ("my brother-in-law") to secure employment. Finding employment this way can have social as well as financial consequences. If an undocumented nanny's employer refuses to let her take the children on outings outside the home, or denies her time off to build broader personal networks, she may become isolated and completely dependent on her employer. Immigrant women we interviewed mentioned others who were not allowed to go to the more popular playgrounds and parks lest they connect with other nannies who could help them (see chapter 8). Many of the undocumented interviewees were over-worked and underpaid. Many also had limited English skills. This compounded their legal vulnerability and kept them tied not only to a low-wage occupation, but also to a specific employer and exploitative working conditions.

Changes in U.S. immigration laws in the latter half of the twentieth century curtailed the practice of domestic-labor employers sponsoring their employees for citizenship.[13] Although never as popular in the United States as in Canada, employer sponsorship is now nearly impossible. Employer sanctions instituted in the 1986 Immigration Reform and Control Act have had a chilling effect on the number of employers willing to sponsor undocumented immigrants, since the application process means admitting that one is breaking the law. The immigration act of 1990 drastically reduced the number of low-wage workers who could become naturalized on work visas. In the low-skill "other" category, which includes nannies among other so-called unskilled workers, the usual quota is a mere five thousand per year. In 1996, Congress passed the Illegal Immigration Reform and Immigrant Responsibility Act (IIRAIRA), which added the final nail in the employer sponsorship coffin. Immigrants who wish to change their visa status (from student or tourist to work visa, for example) must return to their home country to effect this change. The IIRAIRA also stipulates, however, that any immigrant who has overstayed her visa and leaves the country must stay away for three or ten years, depending on the length of her overstay. Even under the best circumstances, an employer-sponsored nanny is likely to wait seven to eight years to receive a green card.[14]

The new laws prompt more and more immigrant caregivers to work for extended family members, who are the only people who can legally act as sponsors. Although the previous legal provisions gave employers significant power over their domestic workers and led to unfair and exploitative practices, the new laws create hardships as well.[15] Women whose undocumented status and lack of networks limit their work opportunities to jobs with relatives or countrymen are especially vulnerable and have been taken advantage of by these individuals, who demand that they work around the clock at extremely low wages.[16] Ynez, a forty-six-year-old undocumented immigrant with five children to support at home in Honduras, worked for a relative in the Boston area, initially earning $80 per week (live-in). As her relatives' finances grew tighter, Ynez's salary dwindled to $30 per week. Her work schedule, 7:00 a.m. to 5:00 p.m. six days a week, did not change. Ynez knew her salary was too low, but "they were my family also," she explained, "and we were helping each other." She was searching for a new job against the wishes of her extended family, but so far her search for a new job had been unsuccessful, she said.[17]

Groups such as the National Organization for Women and the American Immigration Lawyers Association have urged that protective measures be instituted, including designating "home care workers" as a special category for immigration purposes.[18] Unfortunately, issuing immigrant women "special visas" would effectively imprison them in the domestic labor pool. Although as legal workers they might have more flexibility in choosing among employers, their right to remain in the United States would last only so long as they worked in private households. This is simply a continuation of U.S. policies that would keep immigrant "women of color as a superexploitable, low-wage labor force."[19]

European Au Pairs

At the time of my initial interviews, as many as thirty-two thousand au pairs were coming to the United States annually, channeled through eight U.S.-licensed au pair foreign-exchange agencies.[20] Agencies charge families an annual fee ($3,500–$4,000 during the study period) for administrative costs, air transportation, training, minimal health insurance, and support from a local counselor. Au pairs must post a deposit ($500), refundable upon completion of their year of service. They receive a weekly stipend ($100–$125), plus room and board and a tuition reimbursement ($500).[21] Agency regulations stipulate that au pairs are to perform childcare-related tasks only and to work no more than forty-five hours per week. Their visas restrict their stay to twelve months, with an optional additional month for travel.[22]

The ten au pairs I interviewed ranged in age from eighteen to twenty-six, with an average age of twenty-two. Some had come to the United States for fun, to see a new country, or to take a break after completing high school or college. Others hoped the job would improve their marketability at home. For example, Berenice, a twenty-five-year-old European au pair, held a law degree, but she needed fluency in English to gain work as an attorney in her native Spain. Elsa was a certified physical education teacher, but she needed more experience working with children in order to succeed in Sweden's competitive childcare job market.

Au pairs are issued visas that identify them as "visitors" participating in a "cultural exchange" program. Their working conditions and pay rates are overseen not by the Department of Labor, but rather, since 1999, by the Bureau of Educational and Cultural Affairs within the State Department, and before that by the United States Information Agency (USIA).[23] When public controversy erupted in December 1991 over the case of Olivia Riner, a Swiss au pair who was charged with arson and murder, the au pair program came under closer scrutiny.[24] In 1994, after proposing various improvements in the program, the USIA was deluged with more than three thousand letters from U.S. families who opposed the changes—especially the plans for shortening working hours from forty-five to forty and for restricting the care of children younger than age two to women older than age twenty-one.[25] Although the cracks in the au pair system may create unstable childcare situations in which homesick teens work long hours in isolation with infants and toddlers, parents who benefit from this relatively low-cost childcare option advocated against changes to the policy. In the end, work hours remained the same and no age limit was imposed, but training in child safety was added and the weekly stipend was slightly increased.

Since 1998, the sending countries for au pairs have shifted, with Western Europe now surpassed by Eastern Europe, South America, and Asia.[26] Three factors in particular have slowed the flow from Western Europe. First, the Louise Woodward murder trial in 1998 caused an uproar abroad and led some Western European women to shun jobs in the United States. The grizzly murder of the Swedish au pair Karina Holmer in Boston in 1996 similarly shifted Scandinavian perceptions of the desirability of working in the United States. Finally, the establishment of the European Union in 1993 broadened prospective au pairs' options. Their working hours are more strictly regulated in Europe than in the United States and, as EU citizens, these young women can promptly seek other employment should their au pair placement become unpleasant.

Although representatives from the State Department would not confirm or deny the dramatic shift in sending countries from Western Europe to Eastern Europe, South America, and Asia, my interviews with au pair agency owners confirmed this shift; and they, at least, attributed it to the murder cases and to economic opportunities for European women resulting from the establishment of the European Union. Similarly, the mother-employers I interviewed after 1998 noted the shift. For example, Teresa, who had grown up in the United Kingdom, said that she had hoped to find a British au pair but almost none were available in the aftermath of the Woodward case: "And so I thought, 'Perfect. I'll get someone in England and I'll have my brother who is from England, I'll hail him to go over and meet with this woman and find out what they're like . . . [but] there were only Eastern Europeans. As I said, I don't know anything about Eastern European culture." Finally, although recent articles tout the fact that there were 22,000 au pairs in the United States in 2007 (an 86 percent increase from 1998), this figure is 10,000 au pairs *fewer* than the total number here at the time I started my research. Clearly, both the number and the origin of au pairs working in the United States have changed.

U.S. regulations for au pair working conditions also play a role. In theory, au pairs in the United States have at least one and one-half days off per week and their duties are limited to childcare, doing the children's laundry, and cooking for the children. In practice, working parents often find it difficult to adhere to these restrictions. Many of the au pairs spoke of working fifty or sixty hours per week and of being asked to cook for the family, clean the house, do the household laundry, and run family errands. Some asserted that they did not mind doing this extra work, but others wanted their employers to abide by the contract provisions.[27] When problems arise, au pairs have the option of bringing a grievance against the family. The local agency coordinator will intervene and attempt to mediate or to place the au pair with another family. But if these efforts fail, the au pair is sent home and she forfeits her security deposit. In addition, she does not receive certification as an experienced childcare worker.

These certificates, which are awarded to all au pairs who complete one year of service, are important vouchers for those who plan to continue in a childcare career. Au pairs' desire for certification undermines the State Department's protective regulations. Cases of maltreatment of au pairs by host families are rarely reported. And even when mistreatment is brought to the attention of agency staff, offending host families often continue their relationship with the agency for years, committing the same kind of abuses with each new au pair placed in their homes. Twenty-one-year-old Liv, an au pair from Sweden, described just such a scenario. She succeeded in having her first host family banned from the agency's program only after she had carefully documented the family's excessive demands and inappropriate behavior toward her and had transferred to a new family. She was the *sixth* au pair who reported such experiences with this host family.

Liv's assertiveness was not typical. Because they were young, far from home, and financially and emotionally invested in their au pair experience, most of the au pairs I interviewed preferred not to seek help with work-related problems. Instead, most tried to make it through their year-long commitment relying on their own resources. For example, Kristina's employer directed her to stay in the house for eight to ten hours a day with the two small children in her care. She had no outside contact or access to transportation. She had not discussed these conditions with her local coordinator. "I was kind of afraid I would get into trouble and the things would get worse if I asked [the agency] to talk to them," she explained. Kristina chose to remain where she was because receiving her certificate of completion was a top priority. She had a college degree in early childhood education and planned to work in childcare when she returned home to Sweden.

. Furthermore, like many au pairs, Kristina viewed her employers as surrogate parents, which increased her fear of confronting them. This framing is one the State Department encourages, with its references to au pairs' employers as "host parents" and its tendency to emphasize the educational and cultural goals of the program over its labor market components. The difference in expectations between au pairs, who come to the United States seeking a cultural-exchange experience in a "host family," and those of employers, who seek a low-cost childcare worker rather than a "guest daughter," often result in their defining their mutual obligations differently. This, in turn, increases the opportunity for problems and the likelihood that these difficulties will go unresolved.

Most of the au pairs I interviewed, like most of the American-born nannies, viewed their childcare work as temporary, a transitional stage before starting college, for example, or before beginning careers in childcare in their home countries. Those who planned to work in center-based daycare anticipated combining this career choice with motherhood, explaining that they would bring their own children to work with them.[28] An important consequence of understanding their work as transitional was that these au pairs often did not consider their wages low. In fact, some did not consider the pay they received as *wages* in the true sense. One young woman I interviewed, justifying her $400 monthly salary, remarked, "Well, I get room and board. And besides, it's just spending money." Her views may have stemmed from minimal prior exposure to the labor market or from the fact that because her visa was limited to one year, she considered her $2.22 hourly wage a temporary circumstance. Many foreign au pairs return to the United States illegally and continue to work at similarly low wages, however; there are no legal impediments to repeatedly renewing a contract at the same pay rate. Viewing the work as temporary and their salaries as only "spending money" can lock these women into poor working conditions and long hours at low wages.

American-Born Nannies

Most of the fifteen American-born nannies I interviewed were young high school graduates who had few employment options.[29] They viewed working as a nanny as a way to save money for further education, to see another part of the country, or to "buy time" before marrying or settling into a real job. Upon completing high school these women found their options limited. The decline of manufacturing in rust-belt states made finding a job with a living wage or a husband who earned one virtually impossible. Most had secured their first jobs through agencies. Many nanny agencies specialize in recruiting young women from the Midwest and Far West, in part because families looking for nannies often explicitly prefer mid-western "farm girls," associating them with strong "family values." As one agency owner confided, her clients wanted a "nice fresh-faced kid," someone from "young, white America." All of the midwestern nannies I interviewed had been placed in their first jobs by agencies.

Experienced nannies disdained these intermediaries. They secured their positions themselves, relying on newspaper ads or word of mouth. "If you go to an agency," Lonehl explained, "you're really thinking this agency is helping you and they're really not. They're just out to make money. So I mean, it's a win-lose situation." Since placement companies risk losing commissions if nannies fail to fulfill their contracts, they have a strong business interest in protecting the placement, as opposed to enforcing the contract. They have little to offer women like Lonehl, who had both experience and good local references. Nannies without these advantages, by contrast, needed the placement agencies initially.

Some of the American-born nannies reported struggling to gain their families' and friends' acceptance and approval of their work choices. For example, Colleen, a white twenty-five-year-old who came to Boston from Ohio after receiving a degree in early childhood education, described her father as reacting negatively to her decision "right off the bat." He wanted her to get "a good, sound job with a company." Similarly, April, a white twenty-four-year-old graduate of a Boston-area college, took a nanny job as an "interim step." Her mother was disappointed and disapproving. "She was paranoid that I'm going to be a nanny for the rest of my existence," April reported. Still, the American-born nannies, like the documented immigrants in the study, generally were the best treated and best paid of the in-home childcare providers. Half received some type of health insurance, and half had taxes withheld by their employers. They worked an average of forty-nine hours per week, and they tended to make more (an average income of $1,000 per month live-in and $1,600 per month live-out) than au pairs or undocumented immigrants. Although most described their jobs as involving childcare only, many also did housework and cooking. Those who did housework, however, generally did this work on their days off and were paid extra for it.

The American-born women had been in nanny jobs for an average of five years. The majority had gradually transitioned from viewing nanny work as an interim step to being "professional mothers." The hoped-for postsecondary education had not materialized. They had found partners and now either already had children of their own or were planning to start families. Their typical career trajectory involved first working as a nanny, then bringing their own children with them to their nanny jobs, and then hoping to open their own in-home centers. Helene, a white twenty-nine-year-old midwesterner who came to Boston after high school because her sister was working as a nanny and knew people who could offer her a job, was typical. What had begun as a lark and as a way of keeping her sister company gradually grew into a career. She met her future husband, shifted to a live-out job so that she could spend more time with him, and at the time of our interview was trying to become pregnant. Like many of her peers, Helene wanted to be a stay-at-home mother, caring only for her own children. Since this was not financially possible, she hoped to find a situation where she could care for her child and others, preferably in her own home.

As a group, the American-born nannies made it clear that becoming full-time, stay-at-home mothers was their ultimate, but generally financially unattainable, goal. There is a sad irony to their family daycare dream. Nannies who cared for children in their own homes would almost certainly have to take a cut in pay, and they knew this.[30] They wanted pay commensurate with what they perceived as their level of skill, but their strong orientation toward "at-home" mothering inclined them to put a higher value on working conditions that would enable them to combine being a mother with earning a living. Most of the caregivers in the study expressed a similar commitment to the value and importance of being a stay-at-home mother. As the next section explains, nannies' perspectives and actions, like those of their employers, were shaped in important ways by their interpretation of the principles of intensive mothering.

MOTHERING IDEOLOGIES AMONG CHILDCARE WORKERS: INTENSIVE MOTHERING AS A WORK ETHIC

The goal of using childcare work as a bridge to at-home motherhood offers insight into how the caregivers I interviewed perceived the responsibilities of mothering.[31] In a job with low to moderate pay, very little security, and no benefits, nannies and au pairs garner much of their self-esteem through viewing themselves as skilled and caring mother figures. Thus, mothering ideologies, despite their built-in class and cultural biases, shape their work ethic.

Lupe, a twenty-nine-year-old immigrant from Mexico and the mother of a young baby, explained how nanny work offered her a way out of the work/family dilemma: "I was not going to work if I could not bring her. She is still too young to be left in the charge of someone else or something like that. So let's say that this is a benefit of being a babysitter."

Other nannies viewed their work as a way of making up for the fact that they could not be present for their own children. Rosa told me, "It was very important for me to be with children. I felt the need. I felt as if being with them was like being with my own daughters, and I knew that my own daughters were in Honduras with someone who was not their mother, and I said to myself that in the same way that I took care of this child, someone is going to take care of my daughters." She could not change the economic realities that forced her to leave her daughters behind, but by "doing [her] very best" for the child in her care, Rosa, like other, similarly positioned immigrant women, believed she was somehow insuring equally good care for her own children.[32]

Nannies and au pairs were strong believers in their own version of intensive mothering. They put little stock in "book knowledge" (a point discussed in chapter 7), but they did agree with the child development experts that children younger than three should have focused attention from a dedicated caregiver. They also believed in the value of at-home mothering, even if it involved a substitute mother. Many felt that institutional daycare settings in the United States failed to provide high-quality care. Most would not even consider center-based work. Lura told me, "You have to have an early childhood education degree, and they pay less than being a nanny." April described the places where she interviewed as "horrible": "I thought, 'Maybe I could work in a daycare center for a while.' I called places and they were accredited and I'd go for an interview and you think, 'I should stay here and work. Save these poor kids!' You know? And there's so many places, I can't believe that they're accredited, and they're horrible."

Other nannies defined their job responsibilities on the basis of their own mothering practice. They saw themselves as "molding" the children in their care, and "being the mother while the parents are away." They took on intensive mothering as a work ethic because being a good mother was the ideal they most valued. As chapter 8 explains, this understanding of their role as ideal mothers often led nannies and au pairs to put the needs of the children first, even if this meant refusing to perform requested housekeeping tasks when those would take them away from providing good childcare, or even when their view of the children's needs put them on a collision course with their employers' childrearing views.

CLASS, CULTURE, AND CHILDREARING BELIEFS

Whether the nannies and au pairs I interviewed came to childcare work through economic need and limited options or through a love of children and the choice of childcare as a career, once inside childcare work, they all undertook their jobs based on childrearing beliefs and practices they drew from their own backgrounds as well as from their hands-on experiences with their employers' children. The cultural repertoires that guide childrearing practices in working-class and poor families differ from those that guide the middle and upper-middle classes. Because very few childcare workers share their employers' class and cultural background, disagreements and misunderstandings regarding "the best way" to raise children are common.

Middle- and upper-middle-class parents engage in "concerted cultivation." They enroll their children in multiple activities designed to develop a range of talents; and they pursue a disciplinary style that involves reasoning and negotiation rather than direct commands. Working-class parents are more likely to adopt the "accomplishment of natural growth." These parents emphasize unstructured play over organized activities, "hanging out" with kin rather than arranging play dates with peers, and reliance on parental care rather than care by specialists.[33] These class distinctions in childrearing strategies directly reflect the conflicting views between most of the mother-employers and nannies I interviewed. Although both sets of women believed in following the *form* of intensive mothering (child-centered, labor-intensive, and expert-guided), the *content* of their mothering ideologies varied by class and culture. The mother-employers created and followed a version of concerted cultivation for infants and toddlers; the nannies believed in applying the values associated with the accomplishment of natural growth.

Most nannies disagreed with the practice of scheduling an array of activities for children, especially infants and toddlers. Chantal, a forty-two-year-old nanny from St. Lucia with ten years of childcare experience, was especially frustrated with her employers' expectation that she provide the infant in her care with some activity outside of the house every day. "And they always ask, 'Did he go out today?' Like if I don't bring him out, it's going to be a problem. . . . Sometimes it's really cold. We could just stay in and play. But I will find somewhere to go with him, the library or something, because they just don't like him to be in the house. 'Take him out. It doesn't matter what, take him out!'" Helene liked her employers and generally was happy with her working conditions. Nevertheless, she rejected the idea of bringing her own hoped-for baby to work with her because she judged the environment too hectic for healthy development: "I would cut out a lot of the activities. I think it's way too much. . . . They are wonderful parents. I mean they do pretty well considering how much they work. But I just think they need to have a little more time with their kids—*quality* time. Not time running them around to their activities. . . . 'We gotta go to baseball. We gotta go to hockey. We gotta go here and there.'" The idea of unscheduled play may have been anathema to most employers, but most nannies believed that "hanging out" and unstructured play were best for preschool-age children.

Class and cultural background also shaped expectations regarding how involved caregivers should be in children's play. Lupe, recalling her childhood in Mexico, explained that "in many Latin American countries . . . they leave children to play by themselves for hours and hours." Like most immigrant nannies, she argued that this greater freedom and independence helped children to develop social skills and self-reliance. Chantal told me, "Back home [in St. Lucia] it is different. We are not all over the children like here. We let them play with each other. Learn a little independence." Unlike many of her peers, Lupe saw some advantages in her employer's approach to childrearing: "She would always be thinking about what can be done with the children to have them use their time fully. . . . Here I have seen that it is good that children . . . have activities that would better help them develop."

Valerie, a white working-class nanny from Rhode Island with two years of experience, was baffled by her employers' expectation that she engage in structured play "all the time" with the two older children in her care, ages five and eight. The children told her that they did not want her to be involved in all of their play, and Valerie decided to respect their wishes: "They like me to do arts and crafts with them and play soccer with them, and sometimes we get on the floor and play Legos. But when they're playing Star Wars, or Power Rangers, or something like that, they don't want me playing, because I don't know their little story line." In Valerie's mind, there was a difference between supervising the children and making sure they were safe, and "always having to be up to your butts playing with them."

Employers' practices regarding their children's behavior was another area in which class-based distinctions arose. Unlike middle- and upper-middle-class parents, who prefer to reason with children, working-class parents expect children to follow directions without questioning them.[34] Corinne, a twenty-eight-year-old nanny from Kenya with five years of experience, was appalled by her employer's efforts to reason with her toddler about her daily departure for work. In Corinne's view, reasoning with a toddler was just "asking for trouble"; she felt that parents' work lives were something that children simply needed to accept as a fact of life.

Others, although respectful of their employers' wishes with regard to discipline, were skeptical of the effectiveness of the frequent use of "time-outs." Recalling their own upbringing, nannies often wished that their employers would be more strict with their children. Chantal, for instance, felt that misbehavior on the part of the older children in her care should have more consequences—"not abusing or anything, but my mom was more stern, so that you are going to know that she's serious about it." Sarah, a twenty-four-year-old from Iowa who took care of boys ages eight and two, often found their behavior a cause for concern. Sarah's employer, in contrast, generally was happy with her sons' actions. One of Sarah's nanny friends told me that both she and Sarah came from the Midwest, where "we have different values." In Boston, "The kids are pampered. . . . Out here, the kid does something wrong and the parents say, 'No, don't do that,' and the kid just does it over again." Most nannies concluded that the reasoning approach associated with concerted cultivation resulted in whiny, spoiled children who were disrespectful of their parents. These contrasting, class-based childrearing beliefs set the stage for many tense, yet usually unspoken, conflicts between employer and employee.

FAMILY NORMS AND MARKET FORMS

Relations between nannies and their employers were further complicated by the legal and social status accorded the household worker in fact and in law. Although, as Elaine stated, her nanny was not "the girl" or the housecleaner, nanny work is still regulated according to the legal definition of domestic work. Furthermore, most employers and some nannies believed that they are more "one of the family" than a true employee, compounding the structural labor market disadvantages that make nannies and au pairs vulnerable to overwork and underpayment. Precisely because they work inside the private sphere of recreation and repose, domestic workers historically have been excluded from the right to organize and from the provisions of worker-protection laws. More important, however, nannies and au pairs themselves are ambivalent about what role they should play in the family and what norms should govern their work relationships.

Domestic Work and Labor Law

Among the childcare workers who participated in my study, none had any knowledge of what legal rights or protections might apply to them in the two areas that concerned them most: on-the-job accidents (most had no health insurance)[35] and sexual harassment and abuse. In fact, their recourses were few. Nannies come under the category of "domestic workers" with respect to labor law. This categorization explicitly excludes them from the provisions of key federal labor laws, such as the National Labor Relations Act (NLRA) and the Occupational Safety and Health Act, and most federal antidiscrimination laws. Likewise, state laws offer few protections. For example, many states mandate that a business must have four or more employees to be considered under sexual harassment statutes;[36] and all but a few states explicitly exclude domestic workers from worker's compensation laws or make the few laws that do include them almost unenforceable. The lack of protections leads legal scholars such as Katherine Silbaugh to argue that "these [federal and state] exemptions paint a picture of a *kind* of work that does not look like work, even when it is done for pay."[37] Laws characterizing domestic labor as outside the realm of workers' rights and protections, Silbaugh explains, result from a two-step logic: that the work of the home as performed by the wife has no monetary, but only affective (emotional) value; and that as extensions of the housewife's labor, domestic workers' rights are the same as those that accrue to the housewife and mother, namely, only those associated with affection and self-sacrifice.

In the area of wages, domestic workers fare slightly better, since the Fair Labor Standards Act specifies that they are entitled to the minimum wage, and that live-out domestics are entitled to time-and-a-half for overtime. Almost none of the women I interviewed were aware of these provisions, however, and none had ever received overtime pay, even though forty of the fifty childcare workers I interviewed worked more than forty hours per week.[38] Similarly, many nannies did not know that it was their right as employees to have taxes and social security contributions withheld from their paychecks; others did know but preferred being paid under the table, because their wages were already so low.

Perhaps the most important way in which the law fails nannies and other domestic workers is by denying them the right to collective bargaining. This provision of the NLRA leaves them isolated when they are negotiating with their more powerful employers; it makes them dependent on unscrupulous nanny placement agencies for work; and it contributes to their ignorance of the few rights they do have.[39] The nannies I interviewed were acutely aware that they were on their own during negotiations with employers who had greater resources, and often greater knowledge, than they had. April summed up the situation this way: "There's no advocate for you and you've got to entirely be like a little island within yourself, and if you're going to fight about things and make sure you get rights, you're going to have to do it all [by] yourself." Eventually, many nannies became savvy negotiators. But even well-paid nannies wished there were a forum that would represent their collective interests. No one, however, had any idea who would represent them or how to organize on their own.[40]

During one of the "bitch sessions" that occurred periodically among the nannies at a local playground, I asked, "What do you think needs to be changed?" Lonehl responded: "I think that down in city hall they should set up something for either the au pairs that come here, or for the immigrants who come over here with no papers, for them to talk to someone. I mean, they have all these talk shows with bad nanny situations, but they never put on the good nanny situations. You know? And they never have nannies on a show talking about the people they work for, so 'Tell Oprah!' Let's do that. You know what I'm saying?" Unfortunately, although there have been great strides in unionizing daycare center workers, family daycare providers, and housecleaners, none of these campaigns include nannies, who are still left to negotiate on their own.[41] These negotiations are complicated by the nanny's special "place" in the family.[42]

Market-Based versus Family-Based Exchange

The notion that nannies are "part of the family" and therefore not entitled to workers' rights is not limited to labor law. It also permeates commonsense understandings of the caregiver-family relationship. The nannies I interviewed thus frequently found themselves awkwardly poised on the line between employee and fictive kin, working for money and working for love. This dilemma is much less evident in institutional daycare, where policies and administrative hierarchies are already in place when parents and children enter the childcare setting. In that context, market-based norms, with their explicit rules and obligations, are more the rule.[43]

Because nannies work in the homes of the families they serve, the norms applied to their work frequently are what I refer to as *family* exchange norms, in which it is not unusual to expect flexibility, accommodation, and even sacrifice for the good of the group.[44] This shift from market exchange to family exchange profoundly transforms how family members and employees understand the nature of childcare work. For example, as "part of the family," nannies are often expected to do work that is not in their contracts and to be flexible with respect to "on-duty" and "off-duty" time.[45]

The blurry line between worker and family member is complicated by the fact that some nannies, particularly young live-in nannies and au pairs, often *want* to be considered "part of the family."[46] Sarah echoed the sentiments of many others when she said of her first employer, "I didn't want to be just an employee to [the family]." Her member-of-the-family status had drawbacks, though. Her room was right next to the baby's room, so she frequently was the first one to get up with him when he cried; and once he was old enough to get out of his crib and open doors, she found she had no privacy.[47] Moreover, as Sarah discovered, it was difficult for nannies to try to impose market-based norms when they were in a job with strong family norms: "They're always slipping in extra stuff that's not really in your contract, and how far do you go? Do you stick totally by your contract, or do you say, 'Well, it's fine to do a few extra things because I live here too?' " Sarah concluded that working long hours was a reasonable exchange for the rewards she received from being an integral part of her first employer's family.

Some mother-employers recognized that being considered part of the family could translate into an endless workday for their childcare providers. Leigh, for example, noted, "That is the hard line to say, 'Are they still working? Or, are they doing this for fun?' " This lack of clarity between family-based and market-based norms was especially problematic when mothers wanted their nannies to disappear at the end of the workday, as an employee would, while nannies wanted to stay and have dinner with the family, or vice versa.

Most of the older, immigrant nannies refused to live in. Lonehl, who was one of the older, more experienced nannies I interviewed, remarked, "I think the biggest abuses come in when you live in. Um, you're supposed to have a set time to get off. The people, they take advantage of that. Like if the child wakes up [at] twelve at night, they expect you to get up, and you're off [duty]." Although Lonehl did not live in, she "covered" for her employer, Elizabeth, by spending the night with daughter Chloe when Elizabeth had to travel for work. For this, she was paid extra. The majority of the live-out nannies I interviewed wanted to work set hours for set pay and to base their relationships with their employers on market norms. They wanted their workday to end at a set time, and they wanted their employers to realize that they had lives, and often families, of their own.

Employers' failure to recognize these needs frustrated their caregivers.[48] Chantal found she was always thirty minutes late for her GED class: "They said at the beginning that they would *ask* me [about overtime]. . . . But they don't do it. They just, like, tell me, and that's it. And I'm supposed to just fit them in and change [my plans]." Other nannies emphasized the importance of being given fair notice of an impending layoff. As one explained, "As soon as the child is old enough for daycare, they [employers] don't care. They don't care if you are homeless. They don't care if you need the money or not. Lots of times, they don't give you enough notice to find another job." Or, as a Puerto Rican care-worker who bounced from eldercare to childcare jobs told me, "They either die on you or they go to preschool."

Meanwhile, many mother-employers said they chose live-in care precisely because it offered them flexibility. They wanted someone whose hours could be adjusted to the demands of a working mother and whose primary devotion was to her employer's family. Debbie described her decision to hire an au pair this way: "I'd pick Miranda [her daughter] up at six, and if I was a minute late—you know the family daycare lady was nice, but she had places to go and things to do." With an au pair, Debbie paid less for childcare than she did when her daughter was enrolled in family daycare, and she could schedule her au pair's workweek to match her own needs. She elaborated on how the quality of her life had improved significantly when she hired Annika: "I'm home by six, and my children are eating and the laundry is done. The beds have been made and the preparation of my dinner is under way, and all that stuff that I usually had to do has been taken care of." When Annika was not as flexible as Debbie would have liked, she attributed this to a flaw in Annika's personality ("She is the kind of person who likes to have things really structured.") rather than to the fact that her nanny, like her previous family daycare provider, might have "places to go and things to do."

The mother-employers also wanted workers who would make their employers' families their priority, over and above their commitment to parents, siblings, or friends, for instance. This was why Leigh, for one, preferred European au pairs over American nannies: "[I was] set on European[s] because I wanted them to be part of the family. I felt that with American[s] . . . they would, even if they lived in, they probably would tend to go home [on days off], and I needed the person here in the house and have our family as their priority and not their family as their priority."

And Mary Anne, like the employers Lura described, was reluctant to hire a nanny who wanted to bring her own child to the job: "I wanted someone whose primary purpose here was to take care of Jennifer. . . . I felt that if they brought their own child . . . [they would] be watching him as he was crawling into every-thing, and maybe neglect Jennifer."

These are examples of how stratified reproduction works. The mother-employers defined their own children's needs in opposition to the needs of their caregivers' families. And because they saw their own children as needing the full, undivided attention of a caregiver whose presence was solely for their benefit, many preferred young women who were far from home and who had no chil-dren of their own, or immigrant women whose children were living elsewhere.

Underlying employers' belief that their children required undivided attention is the assumption that their children were more valuable than the caregivers' children. Violet, Suzanne's Caribbean nanny, worked to support the children she had been forced to leave behind. Suzanne acknowledged that it took great "strength" to leave one's children in order to provide for them. At the same time, her conviction that "it's not something that *I* could do" alluded to a fundamental difference between her approach to mothering and Violet's, with the clear implication that Suzanne's commitment was the deeper of the two.

In addition to devaluing the nanny's family, stratified reproduction helps reveal the all-encompassing nature of the nanny job. Although many commercial employers might wish they could use family obligations to justify discriminatory practices, it would be illegal for them to do so. But nannies, as a subset of the domestic workers category, are not protected by antidiscrimination laws. Because the informal norms regulating their work often are family norms, it is not surprising that some employers feel comfortable controlling their nanny's life outside of their home as well as her work inside of it.

Which Norms Should Guide Wage Rates?

Mother-employers and childcare providers also struggled over whether to apply market or family norms when negotiating wages. Sarah recounted gratefully how she and her first employers did "things that an employer and employee don't really do for each other": "If I needed my paycheck at the beginning of the week instead of the end, or if I needed extra money because I was going someplace, they'd pay me a couple of weeks early. They helped me out when there was something wrong with my car, or if I needed to go to a dentist or something." Christine's employers gave her an MCAT class for Christmas the year she was considering medical school; Melanie's employer bought her a subway pass every month; and Anne's employer always included her and her children in outings for the employer's children. This blurring of family and market norms, and the exchange of kindnesses it entailed, emerged, in part, from the nature of childcare work itself. Many mothers mentioned their hope that whatever good feeling they were able to "cultivate" between themselves and their nannies, whether through gifts or other thoughtful gestures, would translate into the nanny expressing warmth toward the children. Similarly, nannies understood that love and kindness for the children were part of their work, and they appreciated it when the affection they expressed was returned in kind by their employers.

Judith Rollins noted the "maternalism" employers displayed toward their domestics and explained this as one way employers asserted their superiority.[49] Many of the mother-employers in my study also were maternalistic, but this attitude was more often motivated by a sense of their own dependency (see chapter 5) and vulnerability to the whims of their childcare providers. Gift-giving and other family-based exchanges were a kind of insurance policy against maltreatment of their children. Despite this difference in the source of their maternalism, though, the outcome often was the same as in Rollins's study: nannies felt obligated to define their own needs in terms of the needs of the family, and to repay kindness with kindness. As a result, they often felt unsure about their rights as workers.

In some cases, the women I interviewed did *not* feel confused about their rights but felt unable to assert them. Julie, a twenty-year-old nanny from Montana, described her frustration over her employer's "I-know-what-is-best-for-you-dear" approach to the amount of her weekly paychecks: "She kept saying that I was making $200 a week, and my checks were only $175. And she would say, 'Well, the twenty-five dollars is in an escrow account for you and when you're done with the job at the end of the two years, then you'll get the check.' And she kept calling it my *bonus*. But it was money that I had already earned that she was keeping out of my paycheck . . . [and] making it sound like she was doing something really nice for me." In effect, the twenty-five dollars a week changed Julie's job from a fee-for-service position to a form of indentured servitude. The "bonus" added up as the weeks went by, and forfeiting it was not an option she was willing to contemplate.

Julie's story is also an example of how placement agencies collude in enforcing family norms if doing so is in employers' best interests. Even though this odd arrangement was not in her contract, Julie had no recourse in this dispute because once her contract was signed, the agency that had arranged her placement had a financial incentive for ensuring that she fulfilled her commitment. If she did not, they would be forced to refund the fee they had charged her employer. With the contract signed, the remainder of Julie's interactions with the family were conducted under family-based norms in which she was treated like an adolescent member of the household, with none of the rights accorded an employee.

It was in the area of setting wage rates that differences between mother-employers' and nannies' invocations of family-based and market-based norms were most apparent. Mother-employers tended to use market logic, asking friends and agency owners for information on the "going rate." For example, Mary Anne explained that she had calculated Esther's pay (which, at seven dollars per hour, was at least one dollar below market rate for the study period) based on what she had learned was acceptable from interviewing other candidates and on what she felt she could afford. Most likely, her calculation also included a presumption that a lower wage would be acceptable to Esther, who, as an older immigrant, was likely to have limited options. Alicia said that in setting Leticia's salary, she had used "no real scientific method": "Someone said six dollars an hour and I did six dollars an hour." For Leticia, an undocumented immigrant, a low-wage job probably seemed preferable to no job. Mothers applied market logic to the wages of nonimmigrants, as well. April described her experiences with this mentality. "You know, they [parents] want you to be educated, but they want to pay you [*makes a raspberry*] for what you're doing." After a determined search for a better situation, April concluded, "You feel like saying to them [employers], 'What do you think you're going to get when you offer that much money? What right do you have to offer such a poor pay and no benefits?'" In addition to using market logic, most mothers I interviewed based their caregivers' salaries on a rationale derived from the ideology of intensive mothering. Mothers felt they had to justify their own right to work outside the home. Therefore, the nanny's work must not only fit *around* the mother's working day but also fit *inside* her paycheck.[50] Mothers who earned less than 50 percent of their household income, regardless of how high that household income was, paid the lowest wages and usually hired au pairs or undocumented immigrants. At the other end of the spectrum, mothers who earned more than 50 percent of their household incomes, regardless of the total, paid among the highest wages, whether for live-in or live-out help. Notably, most employers did not calculate the nanny's wage as a *household* expense, but as the mother's own expense, incurred by her choice to work outside of the home.[51]

For their part, when it came to determining the economic value of their work, most of the nannies I interviewed backed away from market norms and invoked an emotionally laden, family-based norm, in effect asking, "How much is your child worth to you?" Lura told me, "When I first got [to Boston], people would pay more to kennel their dog than to have somebody take care of their kids." Marisol, a thirty-seven-year-old immigrant from Nicaragua, compared the relatively large amounts of money her employer spent on clothes for her son with the relatively small amounts she paid Marisol for ensuring the boy's daily safety and well-being. She wondered out loud about the morality of her employer's choices. Regardless of how their pay rate was determined, though, most nannies felt that their work was undervalued.[52] Some became embittered at the sight of the families they worked for prospering while they struggled to get by. A nanny from the Caribbean articulated this sentiment perfectly: "They should wash our feet and drink the water for how they get ahead at our expense, and we fall behind."

CONCLUSION

Like the mother-employers I interviewed, nannies entered the employment relationship constrained by specific cultural values and institutional barriers. Where their employers valued a professional-class version of intensive mothering that emphasized concerted cultivation, nannies held to a more traditional set of beliefs about good parenting that mirrored both their own upbringing and their defense of at-home mothering as a valued role. Viewing intensive mothering as a work ethic had its costs, however. Most important, it put them in a bind between valuing their relationships to the children as "like family" and wanting to view their contracts with the employer-mothers in a more businesslike manner. These tensions blossomed as mother and nanny attempted to negotiate the day-to-day care of a particular set of children.

Legal constraints on nanny work also come into play. Although attachment to the children in their care is the major reason the nannies I interviewed cited for not leaving bad jobs, the fact that they had no recourse to collective bargaining or to setting up their own cooperative placement agencies to replace private agencies that more often protected their own profits than the employees they placed, and the fact that they had almost no legal standing in employment law all contributed to their inability to make bad jobs better. This, too, would have its consequences in how mother and nanny negotiate their joint caregiving project.

4

"They're Too Poor and They All Smoke"

Ethnic Logics and Childcare Hiring Decisions

PRELUDE: JOYCE AND STACY

I met Joyce in her hospital office. Her straightened hair was cut in a bob and her dark chocolate complexion contrasted sharply with the lab coat she wore. As I interviewed her in her cluttered office in the downtown hospital where she practiced pediatric oncology, construction workers were busy repairing the HVAC system in the ceiling directly above us. I jumped at the sound of each loud clang, but Joyce's calm professional demeanor never faltered. She continued steadily describing how she came to hire Stacy, her nanny.

Well before the birth of Ellis, Joyce's now eleven-month-old son, she began an exhaustive search for the right caregiver. Joyce is Afro-Caribbean and her husband is an immigrant from Africa. Their nanny's race, she explained, was an important consideration: "Um, I would have liked to have someone black. Um, just because of the—some identification issues—and because we were in a neighborhood that is almost all white, so just to have a little bit more of that diversity issue." Joyce used several agencies in her search for a black nanny, and she and her husband also contacted friends and family in New York City, hoping to find a Caribbean caregiver: "I'm originally from New York, so [I] asked people there . . . like the woman who I grew up with. Her mother is from Barbados and she said, 'Well, maybe I can help you find someone.' And she had found a couple of people who were in Barbados who were thinking about coming up here, and who I called and talked to."

Once she began screening candidates, it became clear that finding "the right person" might prove difficult: "Some people, over the phone, [there] were language issues. . . . And I feel that especially in the ages where my son is gonna be learning how to talk, he needs to hear English. And I also have to be able to communicate with the person who is working for me. Or some people who had very heavy accents, so it was hard to understand them." Because "the person was spending, or would be spending, a lot more time with Ellis than I would be during his waking hours," Joyce eliminated women with "very thick" accents. "That prevented me from even interviewing people in person, just from phone conversations," she recalled. Her preference for a black nanny was further undermined by the fact that many Caribbean nannies are not licensed drivers. This was a concern, given that Joyce and her husband lived in the suburbs but anticipated having their child "involved" in multiple activities: "The other thing is that we wanted to have someone who wouldn't necessarily be solely restricted to the house. I know a lot of women from the Caribbean do work as nannies, but are not as interactive with the rest of the community in terms of getting children outside and into groups and other things that we wanted him to be involved in. And so, in the end, it [race] didn't matter, as long as it was the right person."

When Joyce gave in and started looking for nannies from the United States, she quickly discovered a second racial problem—that of *her* race:

> In the ad we made it very clear that we were a black family, because we live in [suburb] and there are not many black people who live in [suburb]. There may be some issues with people working for black people. Which, um, I hadn't really thought about before, but I have another friend who is a black physician who had a baby in March. She was looking for childcare, and she said sometimes, you know, when she opened her door for the person who was coming for the interview, they would look very shocked. And so in order to avoid that, I was up front and said, "Black professional couple seeks nanny."

This wording did not solve all of her problems, though. "You know," she told me, "I got one person who said, 'Oh, I work with colored people all the time.'" "*That* person was out," she added, laughing.

When Joyce was beginning to despair of finding any nanny at all, much less a black nanny, a young woman working in the local area as a nanny responded to the ad, explaining that she was phoning on behalf of a friend. The friend was Stacy, a twenty-one-year-old blonde from Nebraska who had worked for a family in the area the year before and wanted to return. Joyce and her husband, Hasani, agreed to interview Stacy by phone. The interview went well, and Joyce was particularly pleased to learn that Stacy still had nanny friends in a nearby suburb, so Ellis would have playmates through Stacy's nanny network. After the interview, they met with Stacy's friend so that she could check out the nanny apartment in the basement. In the end, Joyce and Hasani hired Stacy, sight unseen.

When I first met Stacy, she was sitting on the floor in Joyce and Hasani's modern-looking living room, holding baby Ellis. She frequently interrupted our conversation with coos directed to him and cries of "I just think he's so cute!" directed to me. She considered Joyce and Hasani excellent employers. They gave her freedom to plan Ellis's day and to make play dates with other nannies in the area. They also went out of their way to make her feel included. They invited her to Ellis's medical checkups, on vacations, and even on a trip to visit Joyce's family for the baby's christening: "I went to . . . her family's for Ellis's christening. They live on Long Island. So, I got to meet her mom and her dad and the whole family. So it was like, it was kind of funny. I just felt this. . . . I was, like, the only white person there. So I stuck out like a sore thumb. But I had fun. I mean, they went all out for this christening." Stacy hoped to stay for "at least a few years—as long as they'll have me . . . and [as long as] they don't have any more kids! [*laughs*]" Then she modified her position, saying that she probably would stay if Joyce and Hasani had one more child. "But," she added, "I don't know what their plans are."

Stacy loved Ellis. Her only difficulty at the moment was that "he will not nap. I mean, he'll fall asleep in your arms, but the second you put him down, he wakes up." Fortunately, he seemed satisfied with Stacy's solution—a "U-shaped pillow-type [thing]" she placed Ellis in when she laid him down in his crib. "He thinks someone is still holding him," Stacy explained, "and he sleeps for an hour or so. But otherwise, I have to hold him, and then I don't get anything done." In this respect, she sounded just like the other nannies and mothers I interviewed: the continual task of adapting to a child's developmental changes can be frustrating at some points and pleasurable at others.

When Stacy accepted the job, she knew her employers were black. She remembered the exchange she had with them during the telephone interview: "[Hasani] said, 'What exactly did your friend tell you about this job?' And I said, 'What do you mean?' And he said, 'Well, what'd she tell you?' I knew what he was getting at after this point. They wanted to know if I knew they were black. And Joyce's like, 'Hasani, just say it.' And I said, 'Um, you want to know if I know you're black.' And he said, 'Yeah.' And I said, 'Yeah. And I'm white.' And it was just kind of . . . 'cause, you know, it didn't matter to me. It doesn't." When she took Ellis out in public, though, Stacy found that to other people, race does matter. Her nanny group accepts her and loves Ellis unquestioningly, but strangers frequently express their disapproval of the combination of a white woman and a black baby. In her previous position, Stacy often "passed" as the mother of her employer's children. "People would always stop me and say how much they looked like me and things. But I don't think they look like me at all. But when I go out with Ellis, I get so many stares. . . . And it's 'cause—I don't know if they're just, like, 'black baby with white woman,' or what." The reactions from whites tended to be somewhat patronizing; she noted that those from blacks were more likely to be openly hostile, adding, "Black women stare at me more. Sometimes blacks are real . . . like they don't want white people raising their children. So I find that I get stared at."

Stacy understood some of the politics behind black women's discomfort at the prospect that she might have adopted Ellis. She was not hoping to "pass" as Ellis's mother. What she wanted was to be able to love and care for him as she would any child in her care. At the end of the interview, she sighed and said, "I mean it doesn't really bother me, but some days it does."

. . .

This chapter explores the hiring practices of the working mothers I interviewed. Why did they choose a nanny over a childcare center or a family childcare home? What factors shape the labor market from which they choose their caregivers? What "logics" guide their choice of a particular type of childcare provider? Specifically, to what extent do working mothers take their caregiver's race and ethnicity into account? As discussed in chapter 3, the employers I interviewed did not simply hire the least expensive workers to fill their childcare needs, a finding that contradicts those in many other studies of nannies and domestics.[1] Nor, in choosing from a particular ethnic group, did they seek either to establish a status hierarchy or to maintain ethnic similarity. Rather, they applied ethnic stereotypes strategically and selectively according to their perceptions of their children's needs and the availability of workers from particular ethnic groups. As this chapter also shows, using ethnic logics leads employers to objectify and commodify their childcare providers.

In their efforts to recruit the right nanny, the mothers who participated in this study said they relied on agencies, word of mouth, and advertisements in local papers. In the beginning phases of advertising, screening, and winnowing the pool, they also relied on their own vague ideas concerning the "type" of person they wanted to hire. Most mother-employers denied seeking a particular type; instead, they mentioned looking for "someone reliable," "someone nurturing," or "someone who could socialize with the baby." When our discussions went further, however, it became clear that these were not ethnically neutral traits. Most employers had a specific set of ethnic "markers" in mind when they were recruiting caregivers— that is, they associated particular languages, demeanor, values, and so on with particular groups of people. They then equated these characteristics with a set of childrearing abilities. This chapter explores the symbolic nature of race, ethnicity, and nationality as these characteristics apply to nanny hiring decisions. Having reduced the nanny to one element in their overall childrearing system, employers typically proceed to "bundle" childcare services around the nanny, or through a series of multiple nannies, to create what they imagine to be an ideal maternal substitute. The fact that mother-employers feel compelled to hire, fire, and, as we will see in the chapters that follow, manage and supervise their childcare workers to emulate this ideal expresses how they use management of the childcare worker to ease the pressure to simultaneously be the perfect (at-home) mother and the ideal (male) worker.

ETHNIC LOGICS

Like many middle- and upper-middle-class mothers, the employers I interviewed understood mothering as involving not only nurture but also the transmission of cultural and social capital.[2] They were keenly aware of their responsibility, *as mothers,* to make certain that their children were socialized properly, beginning in infancy. Babies need to make secure emotional attachments; toddlers need exposure to their peers so that they can begin making the right friends; preschool and school-age children need opportunities to learn to interact correctly with other adults and children. All youngsters also need age-appropriate cognitive stimulation, and all need to learn to "consume" culture in class-appropriate ways— whether through hearing Mozart in the womb or through visiting museums as toddlers. To ensure that these needs would be met, the mother-employers I interviewed took great care in selecting their child's mother-surrogate.

Employers used race, ethnicity, and immigration status strategically to select qualities they wanted to impart to their children. They were as likely to seek "otherness" in their nannies as they were to seek similarity. When racial/ethnic characteristics enter childcare hiring decisions, it is generally not to establish a hierarchy, since in this market an employer-employee hierarchy already exists. Rather, the employer has attached a specific *meaning* to the caregiver's ethnic background, a meaning that imbues the candidate with certain desired characteristics, so the employer wants to hire what she interprets as that *kind of person.* I call this process of linking childcare-specific needs to perceived ethnic traits "ethnic logics."

Two factors, in particular, shape the use of ethnic logics in childcare hiring decisions. The first is the "service triangle" (employer-service-customer);[3] employers who take the attitudes and emotional needs of the customer into account may ascribe certain service capacities to certain "types" of people. In the case of hiring a nanny, the mother-employer assesses her child's (i.e., the customer's) needs and matches them with the kind of person she believes is most likely to meet those needs. Thus, the perception of her child's developmental stage, personality type, and level of socialization all go into a calculus that determines, first, whom the mother is likely to hire, and later, how she is likely to manage the nanny. (Chapter 5 explores the management component.) The "commodification of emotion" also comes into play in hiring a childcare worker. This term refers to the ways that the worker's personal characteristics, including her presentation of self, *are* the product.[4] Because of these two factors—the service triangle and the commodification of emotion—discrimination takes a different form when applied to caregivers. The worker as a person with certain ethnic or ethnically stereotyped characteristics is relevant to the employer's assessment of customer needs, and expectations are to be met on the job.

Childcare providers bring emotional aspects of the self, sometimes a deep personal connection, to their work. How do mother-employers find these aspects and screen for the qualities they seek? The answer is complicated. According to Robin Leidner, managers often routinize or "script" interactions between workers and customers so that the service experience is both uniform and high-quality.[5] If the interactive work is too complex to script, employers rely on hiring the right "type" of individuals and on training and motivating them to perform as if the work *were* scripted or directly supervised. Childcare is particularly difficult to script. Caregivers must be able to respond to children's needs autonomously and immediately.

Furthermore, to the extent that child-caregiver interactions are understood as directly influencing early childhood development, the stakes are high in the search for the correct "type" of worker. This implies that ethnic stereotypes may be especially salient in childcare hiring decisions, because hiring criteria are individual and subjective, and because decisions are made based on a dearth of "individuating information."[6] That is, most childcare seekers know very little about the real qualifications of childcare providers because there is little consensus about what constitutes the appropriate "skill set." In addition, parents seeking childcare rely heavily on informal networks, word of mouth, and "gut instinct" in making their decisions, all conditions likely to lead to the use of stereotyping as a "cognitive shortcut."[7]

In making their hiring decisions, mother-employers strategically translate ethnic stereotypes into tangible caregiving skills, such as language, education, or nurturance, and then further equate those skills with less tangible characteristics, such as the ability to transmit culture or class. This translation process is as salient for white parents as it is for parents of color. The desirability of particular ethnic characteristics varies a great deal from employer to employer, however, and often changes even for a single employer, as the child being cared for progresses from one developmental stage to the next. This means that hiring decisions frequently have very little to do with caregivers' objective qualifications. For the most part, ethnic logics are formed by a somewhat *illogical* equation of employers' core assumptions about ethnicity and a second set of perceptions regarding their children's needs.

Ethnic logics differ from standard notions of stereotyping or discrimination in that they do not operate as a blanket set of beliefs about a particular ethnic group, but rather change over time, across regions, and from one context to another. In this way, they resemble Ann Swidler's theory of culture as a "toolkit" from which individuals can draw the symbolic means to a given end.[8] A cultural logic is a resource. It enables individuals and collectivities to create "strategies of action" for solving the problems at hand—in this case, how to match employee (the caregiver), service (her specific child-related skill or skills), and customer (the child). Swidler emphasizes that "strategies of action make sense only within a social world."[9] In this case, the "social world" in question is the combination of the culture of competitive mothering and the need to delegate aspects of mothering to paid subordinates. These strategies are not necessarily the result of rational or even conscious choices; although people conform to everyday norms and standards of behavior, they may not be aware that they are doing so; and although their actions are interest oriented, they are, at the same time, embedded in a social and cultural world that shapes both their choices and the resources they draw on to realize those choices.

Elements of the problem at hand shift frequently; thus, strategies of action may not appear logical or consistent, and they may include "irregularities and even incoherences."[10] This is because practical logic is driven by necessity, not by symbolic coherence.[11] Instead, "habits, traditions, customs, beliefs—the cultural and social legacy of the past—filter and shape individual and collective responses to the present and future. They *mediate* the effects of external structures to produce action."[12] This means, according to Swidler, that "institutions both shape culture and structure the situations in which particular cultural elements will be brought to bear."[13] We can observe how employers deploy strategies of action as they filter their hiring decisions through children's social networks and through childrearing norms articulated in advice books.

EXTERNAL INFLUENCES: EMPLOYMENT SUBCULTURES AND CHILD DEVELOPMENT ADVICE

In selecting their childcare providers, the mothers I interviewed relied heavily on word of mouth. As a result, they adopted their local areas' preferences for (and aversions to) nannies from specific ethnic groups.

Neighborhood-Specific Subcultures

Preferences were not consistent across hiring networks: an ethnicity deemed ideal in one neighborhood typically was viewed as off-limits in another. For example, Carol, a college instructor from a suburb north of Boston, told me that she had wanted to hire an Irish immigrant, but her friends had advised her not to "because they don't have driver's licenses because they're too poor [to own cars], and they all smoke." Meanwhile, in the Beacon Hill area of Boston, virtually all of the nannies were Irish immigrants. Thirty-eight-year-old Joan, a white corporate executive from that area, explained, "We were talking to friends who said, you know, you just have to place your ad in the South Boston newspaper, because that's where all the Irish nannies are." Interestingly, neither employer spoke about what caregiving *skills* Irish nannies might or might not have. Rather, this group simply was preferred in one region and avoided in another. Thus, ethnic logics not only are tailored to employers' somewhat fuzzy conceptions of the job and the ideal candidate but also are neighborhood-specific, reflecting employer networks, nanny networks, and, most important, *baby* networks (playgroups).

Employers were especially concerned to hire a nanny who could socialize their children into local playgroups. At-home mothers are notorious for excluding childcare workers from their networks, and most mother-employers knew this. Elaine noted that in her suburban neighborhood, where most of the mothers did not work outside the home, some children were ostracized because their mothers worked: "There are certainly lots of playgroups in which a nanny is certainly not welcome, because the playgroups are to some degree for the kids, but they are largely for the mothers. So there is a piece that he misses out on because I'm not at home." In most areas, nannies form their own playgroups. Since the nanny is the point of contact for play dates, organized activities, and contact with other children, it is essential that she fit in with these local groups. If she does not, the children in her care are likely to become socially isolated.[14]

As Joyce noted in recounting her search for a nanny, she hired Stacy in lieu of a woman of color in part because Stacy could socialize with the nannies in Joyce's largely white suburb, where the majority of nannies were white midwesterners who worked on a live-in basis. This calculus worked in the opposite direction for mothers hiring in urban areas. Mary, a white physician, was typical of this group. She described hiring Ronda, her thirty-four-year-old African American live-out nanny, this way: "Ronda was very enthusiastic and it works out really well for her. It's on the T [Boston's metropolitan area rapid transit system], and she doesn't have a car. She has all these friends in the area who are working here, so it was actually a nice match in that way." Like most employers who lived in Cambridge, Boston, and Brookline, Mary used the local nanny network to find a woman who would fit in with the local playground culture. Following the local hiring culture, she chose a woman of color who worked on a live-out basis.

Local subcultures also reflect differences between suburban and urban living. In the Boston area suburbs, parents could save money by capitalizing on the extra space in their houses, hiring nannies and au pairs who lived in.[15] In addition, suburban life required that the nanny have her own car, or at least a driver's license, which eliminated most immigrant caregivers. The parks I observed in the affluent suburbs were filled with live-in au pairs and white American nannies from all over the country. By contrast, city dwellers in affluent neighborhoods tended not to have space for a live-in nanny, but they had sufficient income to pay a higher live-out rate. And, with easily accessible public transportation, driving was not an issue. The parks and playgrounds in these areas were dominated by Latina, Caribbean, and Irish immigrant caregivers.

The use of ethnicity to hire "into" local nanny networks speaks to neighborhood variations in hiring patterns, and to how these patterns are reproduced.[16] One ethnic group may initially have become popular in a particular area for pragmatic reasons, but over time successive waves of employers will continue to hire women from that group so that their children will not be socially ostracized from local nanny-centered playgroups and networks.

Advice Literature and "Bundling" Services

Ethnic logics are further complicated by employers' perceptions of the changing needs of their "customers," the children, as they develop, and how these needs are framed by childrearing advice books. Advice literature, which the mothers I interviewed read assiduously, shaped the decisions they made as employers in two ways. First, most interpreted expert advice on early childhood development in a racialized way and hired accordingly. The scientific literature stresses the importance of the development of a secure attachment with an infant and notes, "Security is associated with prompt responsiveness to distress . . . moderate, appropriate stimulation, and interactional synchrony, as well as warmth, involvement, and responsiveness."[17] When asked what they looked for in a nanny, the mothers I interviewed emphasized these qualities and looked for them as they evaluated potential and current nannies. A warm and responsive caregiver was suitable for infants but, according to the literature, toddlers needed more.

Mothers also used expert advice to help them "bundle" childcare services. Typically, mothers would hire caregivers whom they viewed as endowed with a baseline set of expert-approved qualities and then supplement these with other services, including additional enrichment activities for the children (lessons, playgroups, or preschool) to offset any deficiencies the nannies might have in providing cognitive stimulation or teaching the children how to socialize with peers as the children moved into their toddler years. In some cases, bundling meant adding services that the nanny herself was not contracted to perform (cooking, cleaning, gardening, or pet care). In general, however, the goal was to match a particular skill set to a given stage of child development, replacing the caregiver or supplementing her services as the child entered a new stage.

In interviewing prospective nannies, employers conducted their own versions of the "strange situation test." They assessed interactions between children and nannies. Did she cuddle the baby? How did the baby respond to her? Did she get down on the floor to play? Was the child sad to see her go? The importance mothers assigned to these signals of attachment is clear in the explanation thirty-six-year-old Naomi, a physician, gave for hiring Yvonne, a forty-two-year-old woman from Jamaica: "And I think I knew pretty soon after she came that she was the right person for us, because she seemed so comfortable with the baby. She just picked her right up, bounced her, and the kid was asleep." These assessments of individual facility with children were quickly generalized: Naomi attributed

Yvonne's facility with infants to "Jamaican voodoo," and concluded that Caribbean women must be good with infants. Similarly, Suzanne hired Violet, who was also older and from the Caribbean, not because of the cognitive stimulation or socialization she could provide Suzanne's baby daughter, Lindsay, but because she viewed Violet as "religious" and therefore trustworthy, and "nurturing" and therefore good for an infant.[18]

As children began to grow, mothers perceived their needs as changing. Now they needed to go out into the world, to be "perfected" (see chapter 2 for a discussion of the culture of perfectibility) by participating in organized activities such as gymnastics and in enrichment programs such as arts and crafts for toddlers. Especially in the suburbs, the nanny would need to drive in order to meet these evolving needs. In fact, as children grew, the nanny's ability to drive took on such importance that it could eclipse her many other competencies. This was the case with Yvonne. Naomi explained that as her son Nathan entered toddlerhood, she "knew he would be starting a program this summer, and we'd want them to start going places." Yvonne could not drive, so, as happens to many immigrant nannies, her charge aged out of her capabilities.

The majority of mother-employers I interviewed followed expert advice to the letter in pairing their nannies' services with their children's presumed developmental needs. They moved directly from bundling infancy with someone they thought could provide nurture to bundling toddlerhood with an "active" nanny. The new nanny would need language skills to meet the toddler's developing speech acquisition needs. Her work would be supplemented by classes that could provide cognitive and social stimulation. This commitment to offering a steady flow of age-appropriate enrichment prompted many mothers to replace or supplement informal playgroups and individual classes with preschool, thus coordinating enrollment to match (or even anticipate) their children's movement to a new developmental stage.

Most began enrolling their children as soon as they were eligible, generally at age two years, nine months. Alicia, a twenty-nine-year-old Latina writer, offered this explanation for enrolling Magdalena, her just-eligible toddler, in a Montessori school: "[Now] I feel like I'm not responsible for her entire development. I guess that's it. It's not like she's actually taking a break from developing during those hours; she's actually getting something out of those hours. So that helps me a lot." The family's nanny, Leticia, and Leticia's daughter were adept at teaching Alicia's two daughters perfect Venezuelan Spanish and were highly nurturing caregivers. Nevertheless, Alicia was concerned because Leticia fell short in "parenting theory" and "curriculum," both of which she felt her toddler needed.

Other mothers shared Alicia's concern that their caregivers' skills might not meet their preschool or soon-to-become-preschool-age children's needs. As

Suzanne remarked, "I don't know what the right answer is . . . like when Lindsay starts, like, going 'Why, why, why?' I don't know how Violet is going to respond. If she's going to give answers that I [*pause*] like? If she will be able to provide the sort of breadth and depth of experiences [for Lindsay]? Will she take Lindsay to, like, the children's museum?" Similarly, Joyce looked ahead to a time when Stacy might not be able to provide Ellis with all the necessary "developmental things": "His needs will change over time and that will call for reevaluation of what his childcare is, and we've begun to think about that in terms of when he gets to be two and needs more exposure to other kids to learn things like sharing and how to play, and more developmental things. . . . [W]e want him to be able to fit in." As these quotations suggest, the transition to preschool for a child could signal an impending transition to unemployment for a nanny. As the child grew older, providing appropriate cultural capital loomed larger.

For some mothers, shifting from the older, often immigrant woman they had hired during their child's nurture-needing infant years to a younger woman, either an au pair or a midwestern migrant who would supply their stimulation-needing toddlers with developmentally appropriate cognitive and social input, was emotionally wrenching (see chapter 5 for a description of one mother's struggle over the decision to replace her child's nanny). Many parents, though, took a pragmatic view, based on their interpretation of the advice literature. Their growing children needed new services, and therefore they needed a new caregiver. Employers' new definitions of what services were needed could mean a change in the preferred sex of the childcare provider, as well as in age and ethnicity. One family that I followed for several years switched to a male au pair when their children, both boys, reached school age and needed to be socialized into the world of organized sports and boys clubs.[19]

Nanny Turnover as a Childrearing Tool: Protecting the Mother's Place

For some employers, it was not so much a desire for new services as for new faces; by frequently replacing caregivers, these working mothers hoped to make themselves the rock-steady center of their children's lives. As Amy, a white thirty-four-year-old manager, said of her au pair arrangement, "I think a year is a good amount of time. I'm also selfish; it also means that the baby still connects with you because this person is only here for twelve months. And that person turns over. So, the baby knows who I am and that I'm always there. And that's important. I think I would feel a little less secure in my work and balancing routine if this person could potentially be there for five years of her life."

A similar ambivalence regarding the place of the nanny was evident in mothers' efforts to simultaneously maximize and minimize the importance of their children's bonds with paid caregivers, particularly in discussions of the effects of nanny turnover. The need to feel good about her childcare arrangement may lead a mother-employer to maximize the nanny-child bond, to emphasize that her provider is "great" and that her children "love" the nanny. This same need, though, may lead her to minimize the effects of nanny turnover on her children's emotional well-being. For example, Jane, a thirty-four-year-old white executive, described her children's reactions to the departures of various nannies as not a problem for her sons, ages eight and two and a half. She said that because her older son had been in daycare, "he deals with transitions incredibly well, so, for him, if a person is living here [or has left], it isn't that big an issue." She saw her younger son, Matthew, as being similarly emotionally robust. She said that he and his first nanny, Cindy, who was with him from birth to eighteen months, "adored each other," but, according to Jane, their separation had little impact on Matthew's "overall well-being." "Well, he's young enough so that, you know, he talks about her all the time. I mean he understands and says that Cindy went home to be with her mommy and daddy. I think he missed her, but it doesn't seem to have had any huge impact on his overall well-being. . . . I guess my sense has always been if *family life* is stable enough, that the transitions of *childcare people*, as long as they're not constant changes, aren't going to have any terrible effects" (my emphasis).

Jane's distinction between "family life" and "childcare people" is revealing. Although Cindy had spent more time with Matthew than anyone else in the family during the first year and a half of his life, Jane did not view her as an integral part of her son's family, psychologically or symbolically. Moreover, she seemed untroubled by the inherent contradiction in both emphasizing the benefits of her child's bond with his nanny and downplaying how much its loss might affect him.

Not surprisingly, mothers and nannies often disagreed in their appraisals of the effects of nanny turnover. Sarah, the white twenty-four-year-old nanny working for Jane at the time of our interview, interpreted the impact of Cindy's departure much differently: "I think Matthew is having a hard time because he's been through so many nannies. I mean, he still talks about his other nannies. I was good friends with Cindy, his first nanny, and I have a picture of her upstairs. And he'll go and see it and ask when she's coming back. And the same for his second nanny. He wants to know why they're gone. . . . [H]e doesn't really understand why they left him. And he also asks me when I'm leaving." Sarah voiced a common concern about the effects of a succession of caregivers on children's ability to trust. She said that she was having difficulty getting through to Brian, her eight-year-old charge: "Brian isn't willing to get close to anybody because he knows that eventually they're going to leave."

In contrast, other employers, who had learned the hard way about the effects of too much turnover, were less sanguine about their children's ability to weather the comings and goings of numerous caregivers. Carol explained that her children refused to cooperate with Berenice, their fifth au pair. She said that her three boys were becoming "jaded," and thus unable or unwilling to form an emotional attachment with someone they knew would be leaving in a year. She described the children's response to their new au pair as being "like somebody on their sixth or seventh divorce and remarriage. . . . [Y]ou know it's temporary now." As a result, Carol felt it was now time to find a childcare worker who could be part of the family's life for a period of years, allowing her children to once again feel safe bonding with their caregiver.

Although the logic of achieving the best fit for a given age often dictated a high level of nanny turnover, turnover also served another function. In the context of intensive mothering, maintaining a relationship with the same caregiver over a period of time, whether that period was more or less than a year, involved keeping a balance between the value of providing children with a long-term bond and the necessity of ensuring the mother's own role as the "most constant person." Frequent turnover made certain that parents, and particularly mothers, would remain their children's sole constant in an ever-changing childcare world.

All of these strategies point to the ways that hiring decisions are informed by expert advice, including the mandate that the mother remain the central and primary caregiver. They show, as well, how mother-employers' perceptions of caregivers reify certain services the caregiver might provide, and thus obscure any view of the caregiver as a whole person with a unique relationship to the child. The mothers in this study generally did not try to hire individuals who would adapt to their children's changing needs; they simply changed the purveyors as the kind of services they required for their children changed.

Hiring and firing decisions thus served several purposes. They enabled mothers to create an optimal match between their perceptions of the caregiver's skills and their children's developmental needs; they enabled mothers to perceive themselves as in control of their children's upbringing precisely because they were creating this optimal match; and they relegated caregivers to fixed, temporary roles in children's lives. This approach to childcare raises an obvious question. Parents, like all other human beings, have both strengths and weaknesses; they are better suited for one childrearing task, or one age group, than for another. Yet parents are expected to learn, and children are expected to adapt to their parents' varying levels of competence. Why cannot the same be said of paid caregivers? By choosing to define their childcare provider as a bundle of childrearing services and not as an evolving individual who might develop and change with the job, many mothers in this study implicitly embraced a long-standing (though rarely acknowledged) class-based assumption: that the cultural capital and social skills of middle-class mothers are irreplaceable and can be approximated only by a carefully orchestrated array of services.[20]

USING ETHNIC LOGICS TO ENSURE TRANSMISSION
OF SKILLS, VALUES, AND CULTURE

Mother-employers used stereotypes strategically, as "tools" to help them solve the problem of ensuring that certain qualities and experiences would be transmitted to their children even when they, the mothers, were not present. Their ethnic logics translated race and ethnicity into personality, and translated personality into the types of emotional labor and interactive displays they considered most important.

Nurturance

One mother hired a caregiver from the Caribbean because, in her estimation, women from the islands were "very religious" and "very good with children and stuff like that." A second noted that her caregiver grew up in Jamaica, where she had "always worked as a domestic with either children or elderly people— watching over them. And she did more than just babysit. She really took *care* of people." For these employers, Caribbean origin signified a particular orientation toward nurturing. This kind of stereotyping was not limited to women of color, but extended to European au pairs and to American-born women from various states. Amy concluded, after a trip to London, that a Scandinavian au pair would be superior to a British au pair: "Having seen London and seen what the teenagers and the young women there were looking like, it struck me much more like it was too city and sophisticated. . . . I sort of had an image of it being more quiet, a little bit more laid back, in terms of the Scandinavian countries—and [I admit] that comes totally from ignorance. I've never been to a Scandinavian country." Ironically, despite Amy's desire for a milk-fed country girl, her au pair came from Stockholm. Other mothers shared this view of British au pairs as frighteningly worldly and of Scandinavian au pairs as from rural backgrounds that made them wholesome and nurturing. Another mother-employer's annotation to her application for an au pair captures this perspective nicely: she requested the "European version of the all-American girl," and added that she preferred someone from a Scandinavian country.

For many white parents, whiteness served as a proxy for a constellation of traits related to nurturance—wholesomeness, safety, and shared culture. For others, whiteness was a proxy for middle-class values. But there was whiteness and there was *whiteness.* The owner of a nanny placement agency explained to me that nannies from the Midwest were very popular, especially among employers who sought a live-in caregiver, not simply because the relative lack of economic opportunities in their home states made these young women affordable. Most of her clients, the agency owner said, were looking for "a nice, fresh-faced kid." They wanted "someone from young, white America" to come live with them and were "not open to" candidates of color. Other white employers, however, turned to the "blackness as nurturance" trope. Significantly, these two types of employers expressed no other race-specific attitudes other than assumptions about their children's needs and the childrearing-specific traits of certain ethnic groups.

Employers commonly assumed that similarity in one area, such as race or national origin, would translate into similarity in another, such as childrearing values or other cultural norms. Lynet Uttal notes that "because racial ethnic group membership serves as a marker, it is used to assess whether or not there is a cultural fit, and whether or not values will be shared, styles will be shared, and practices are culturally similar,"[21] but she emphasizes that ethnic similarity is more important for parents of color than for white parents. I found, however, that ethnicity was significant for both groups of parents, although in slightly different ways. One white mother expected that the British au pair she hired would share her family's values, since she and her husband were English. She reasoned that since "we were brought up in the same culture," a British au pair would "intuitively" grasp her approach to childrearing, thus removing any need for training. Other white parents instead valued immigrant women or women of color, but for the same reasons—they equated ethnicity with culture, and culture with particular childrearing characteristics. This group of mother-employers typically viewed certain ethnic groups as exotic and their members as endowed with special caregiving qualities (Naomi's attribution of skills in "Jamaican voodoo" to her nanny Yvonne is one example).

The African American parents I interviewed also sought ethnic similarity in hiring, although, like Joyce, they were not always successful. Caroline, a thirty-five-year-old African American history professor who hired an African American nanny, explained why she made that choice: "I thought that if there was sort of racial parity among us, then there's a common ground, there's a sense of solidarity in the project of caring for these children. And that maybe it would take away some of the edge of inequality inherent in the relationship of employer/employee, to the extent that, well, they might feel more comfortable working for a black couple as opposed to a white one. And assuming that they do feel more comfortable, and they *can* feel more comfortable because, after all, we *are* all black." Racial and ethnic similarity did add a level of comfort (on both sides) in many families that hired women of the same race. This similarity did not, however, close the gap in social class and culture. Caroline told me that her nanny's evangelical Christianity disturbed her, as did the fact that her nanny frequently took the children to McDonald's, when she preferred that they eat low-fat meals.[22] Caroline found that class trumped race: "In cultural terms, we don't have a lot in common. . . . It's mostly because of class, it turns out. So, politically we're not similar; our education and backgrounds are hugely different. So it's sort of like the inequalities of class are much more apparent. So the racial as proxy for cultural commonality equation doesn't work. Because we don't even like the same black music, you know?" Her firsthand discovery that racial similarity did not translate into cultural comfort prompted Caroline to try a different hiring strategy. When she looked for her next caregiver, she chose a Brazilian mixed-race au pair from a middle-class background.

Teaching Skills and Transmitting Culture

In more than two-thirds of the childcare relationships I studied, one or both parents shared a racial and/or language heritage with the caregiver, and in more than one-third of the cases, at least one parent and the childcare provider were of the same ethnic group or national origin.[23] Employers did not always seek ethnic similarity per se, however. Instead, they translated similar ethnic background into tangible skills, such as language, and into intangible skills, such as the ability to transmit specific cultural capital.

The ability to speak and teach proper English or Spanish were the tangible skills most commonly sought. Good English was a must for most parents, even those who, like Joyce, came from immigrant families. Sometimes this preference was a cause for racial guilt or anxiety. Joan talked about attending a diversity program at work and then feeling "a little guilt" about her choice of nanny. She recalled that during her search for a caregiver, "when I got someone whose English I had difficulty understanding, I was not inclined to pursue that phone call back because I was concerned about the kids not, not developing their English properly, or not being able to understand." Many employers I interviewed expressed similar sentiments, but like Joan (and Joyce), their children's language development took priority over their concern for nondiscriminatory hiring practices.

Good Spanish was just as important as good English. When asked, most employers of immigrant nannies explained that they hired these childcare providers for their language skills. All of the Latina nannies I interviewed were employed by families with at least one Spanish-speaking parent, and these families were very particular about the *type* of Spanish they wanted taught to their children. Puerto Ricans and Dominicans make up the majority of the Latino population—and a significant proportion of the documented immigrant workers—in the greater Boston area,[24] but employers' language preferences made members of these groups the least likely candidates for the higher-paying, childcare-only jobs. "My Spanish is not the sort of Spanish that they would want their children learning," one Puerto Rican would-be nanny noted. The Latina childcare workers who qualified for this study were from Mexico, Guatemala, Ecuador, Honduras, Venezuela, and Chile. All had been hired *because of* their ethnicity and national origin, not in spite of it or because an immigrant nanny might be cheaper; and all had been hired to teach specific skills or to transmit a specific cultural background (or both) to their charges. Rosa described the emphasis her employers placed on her language skills this way: "The children spoke Spanish [with me] because the parents wanted the children to learn Spanish well, and they said, 'Well, Rosa, here they learn Spanish with you because Puerto Rican Spanish is not good,' they would tell me. 'The Mexican Spanish, they sing,' they would tell me."[25]

Other mothers viewed their children's acquisition of a second language purely as skill enhancement. For example, Alicia, whose family is from Argentina, was confident that she could instill "cultural pride" in her children. "Linguistics" was another matter. This, she said, was "the thing I'm most worried about," and the primary reason why she had hired a "Venezuelan Spanish" nanny. The nanny understood her role clearly, explaining to me that "those children—tomorrow they will go to the university and those who have more than one language, who are bilingual, make more money." For most families, however, the tangible asset of language was no more important than the intangible asset of cultural transmission. Rosa told me that her employers wanted her not only to teach the children to speak Spanish but also to make sure that "the children should not forget their roots." The fact that Rosa was Honduran and her employers Cuban did not seem to trouble them.

Most of the Latin American employers and nannies I interviewed were similarly unfazed by the incongruity of hiring a childcare provider to transmit "cultural values" when the caregiver, although Spanish-speaking, was of a different national origin and cultural background. This was also the case when employers wanted to convey African American culture to their children, but conveyed it through immigrant women who happened to be black. Nannies were occasionally critical of this use of ethnic logics, but more often agreed. Nilda, a twenty-six-year-old Afro-Caribbean nanny from Montserrat, spoke admiringly of how her employer hired her because "[the baby] is adopted, and she's white and she wanted an African American person to more or less be there for him, to teach him. . . . I know it's pretty important for a child to identify their own cultures or their own race, but she's doing that by hiring me and having him participate in things that are culturally geared towards him. There's nothing she's not doing." Nannies were often acutely aware of class and cultural differences between themselves and their employers, but they also knew the importance of strategically emphasizing certain similarities.

For their part, Latino parents seemed comfortable with the idea that a shared language was indicative of broader similarities. For example, Paula, a white thirty-nine-year-old psychologist, and her Cuban husband hired only au pairs from Spain. She described their decision to replace use of a daycare center with a live-in au pair after their third child was born as based on their desire to "get a Spanish-speaking person in the household . . . and we can do the cultural piece, and have flexible childcare, more hours, and, ultimately, [pay] less money per hour." Paula pointed out several other advantages associated with a Spanish au pair: "The Spanish culture really loves kids," Spaniards tend to have an "effusive affect," and their culture is known to be "affectively alive." Although some might argue that Spain and Cuba have little in common beyond language, for Paula, the ethnic marker of Spanish national origin translated into the tangible benefit of Spanish language skills, as well as the intangibles of "doing the cultural piece" and emotional warmth and zest.

At first glance, it might appear that these employers were simply using "statistical discrimination," generalizing from an individual to an entire class.[26] I would argue, however, that they were strategically deploying a range of stereotypes that allowed them to feel confident about the quality of services provided by an individual. That they were engaging in similarity-attraction, inferring the existence of similarity in attitudes based on ethnic similarities, is also a possibility.[27] But the parents I interviewed sought similarity in some childrearing situations and difference in others. These stereotypes were not consistent, nor did they reflect whether the employers viewed the group as a whole negatively or positively. Rather, the mother-employers I interviewed strategically selected from among available stereotypes to connect the type of person with the type of service they sought.

Ethnic logics create a complex employment calculus that takes into account a wide range of factors: the child's developmental stage and needs, the local childcare culture, beliefs about ethnic and cultural similarity and difference, and the nature of the childcare services being purchased. This calculus creates an idiosyncratic use of stereotypes as tools. It also commodifies ethnic characteristics, with the result that certain types of workers become defined as more or as less desirable, and also that employers routinely generalize about caregivers' qualities on the basis of one ethnic or racial attribute. They extrapolate from a set of preconceived notions about race or ethnicity to a sense that they can trust the caregiver or that the caregiver might transmit some valued set of characteristics to their child(ren). For childcare workers, this tendency on the part of employers makes it advantageous to market themselves "piecemeal." In addition to selling their particular skills for a given duration, nannies and au pairs tacitly hire out more personal dimensions of themselves and of their heritage. Workers who accentuate these characteristics and demonstrate a willingness to transmit them to the children in their care better their chances for securing coveted nanny-only jobs.

CONCLUSION

The use of ethnic logics leads mothers to reduce nannies to a few essentialized characteristics rooted in ethnicity, age, or national origin, rather than regarding these caregivers as complex or evolving individuals. Mothers referred to nannies as "the quiet one," the "outdoorsy one," or the one who was "good at arts and crafts," and, based on these characteristics, judged the nanny as adept (or not) at meeting the presumed needs of children in a given age group or developmental stage. Objectifying their nannies allowed mothers to retain control. By reducing their caregivers to a set of childrearing traits, mothers could feel that they were managing how their children's needs were being met. And, in tailoring their nannies' traits to their children's developmental stages, mothers fulfilled the responsibilities assigned to them by the ideology of intensive mothering: they conscientiously consulted the experts to learn what types of care were considered appropriate for what ages, hired others to deliver that age-appropriate care, and then replaced or supplemented the providers when the children moved into the next developmental stage. In this framework, the nanny is not so much a person as she is a tool in the mother-employer's overall childrearing strategy.

Managing a Home-Centered Childhood

Intensive Mothering by Proxy

I interviewed Mary Anne, a thirty-four-year-old scientist, in her downtown apartment on her "special day"—a Friday, the day she and Jennifer, her two-year-old daughter, spent together. Mary Anne had arranged a four-day workweek so that she and Jennifer could have this extra time; they spent it running errands, going on outings, and taking art, dance, and "play" classes together. In addition to being special-day activities, these classes were part of a strategy Mary Anne had devised to compensate for what she viewed as her nanny's shortcomings.

Initially, Mary Anne had considered herself lucky to find Esther, a sixty-four-year-old Asian immigrant: not only had Esther been a successful nanny for more than ten years but she also had been a physician in her country of origin. This, Mary Anne felt, was a "a big help," since it had originally increased her level of comfort in leaving her infant daughter in Esther's care. When I asked about Esther's medical credentials, however, Mary Anne's response was to describe her nanny's "level-headed" handling of a previous employer's sick child:

> The child she had taken care of before . . . the younger son was actually quite ill. He had some congenital problem. And he kept having fluid build up, and he would start choking, and she would have to aspirate him. And she would handle real medical emergencies with him many times, so I felt really comfortable that, you know, if anything really did happen with Jennifer, I think she would be really level-headed and have some medical background, know how to handle it. And the fact that I work very close by, I mean, I could easily run home.

Mary Anne reduced Esther's professional credentials to "some medical back-ground" and ultimately focused on the fact that her own office was near enough that she could "run home" herself, should an emergency arise. This lack of rec-ognition of her nanny's medical expertise may have been unconscious, but it had material consequences. Esther's paycheck was among the lowest of the women I interviewed.

Mary Anne emphasized that she had prized Esther's maturity, patience, and experience when Jennifer was an infant. At the same time, she noted that "as a newborn, [Jennifer] was fairly easy to take care of," suggesting that her nanny's assets may not have been crucial. Esther, however, viewed her charge's early months quite differently. When she and I met, she told me about the value of patience with a newborn like Jennifer:

> All I remember is me rocking the chair—the baby was just an infant. Crying, crying, crying, and crying. And I was every day rocking this chair and singing at the top of my voice, "Rock-a-bye baby, on the treetop" [laughing]. . . . Oh my goodness; it was just nonstop. And that rocking chair is still there [laughs]. And now sometimes I told her, I said, "Oh my goodness, Jennifer, wow. You cried and cried, and cried and cried, and cried and cried." [laughs] And she likes that. She likes to hear when she was a baby—and she'll crawl up on the rocking chair, and [say], "Esther—Rock! Rock!" [laughs] She's a very intelligent girl.

When I asked if she had ever thought of leaving her job during these early days, she responded somewhat ruefully, "I almost did, but by that time I got attached to her." I asked, too, if she had ever talked to Mary Anne, or to Mary Anne's husband, Alan, about Jennifer's crying. "Well, they're not home," Esther explained. "They're not home. Basically, it was like, uh, I brought her up. Same thing with the other babies [I took care of]. Yeah, it's, um—the parents, you know, go to work, so babysitters are the ones that really get attached to the child."

For her part, Mary Anne shifted back and forth between considering her nanny a blessing and worrying that Esther was too old or too shy to do the things she and Alan wanted her to do with Jennifer. Mary Anne explicitly structured Esther and Jennifer's days. She showed me the journal in which she expected Esther to give an accounting of each day's activities; she showed me the lists she left for Esther of places they should go and things they should do; and finally, she showed me how she asked Esther to leave the leftover baby food refrigerated in its original containers. Mary Anne inspected these containers at the end of each day and then recorded what this visual check showed: "I'll write [in the log], well, you know, Jennifer ate well today or she didn't eat well." Mary Anne used a management style I call "puppeteer" management. She coordinated all of Esther's activities the way a puppeteer might control a marionette.

Even with this close monitoring, Mary Anne was concerned that Esther was no longer the best "fit" for Jennifer's changing needs:

I liked the idea of an older person, because I think that's a really good influence on the child. Now I'm sort of thinking that maybe I would like someone a little younger . . . 'cause now that she's a toddler, she's very active and . . . I think that maybe they could run around and take her out a little more. The babysitter I have is very nice, [but] she's very shy, so she doesn't take her many places where there [are] lots of people. So Jennifer isn't really socialized very well, I think, with other children and lots of people.

Mary Anne felt she had to compensate for Esther's shortcomings: "That's why I take [Jennifer] to the art class, or it used to be a play class, and then we signed up for the art class, and next time we're taking a dance class—just so that, I think, it's good for her to be around other children her age. But . . . I like the idea of an older person, 'cause she's very patient, and she was always really very caring, which is what I, especially when she was a baby, that's what I really wanted."

With Jennifer now an active two-year-old, what Mary Anne initially had valued most about Esther seemed less important. For optimum cognitive and social development during toddlerhood, Mary Anne believed, Jennifer needed a caretaker who would, in addition to taking her "many places," also teach her to socialize well with others. This was especially important because Jennifer did not seem outgoing by nature: "Jennifer tends to be a little shy, and I don't know if that is because of Esther or just, my mom and dad say that I was exactly the same, that they watch her and they say, you know, 'She's exactly how you were when you were a child'—'cause I—I tended to be a little shyer when I was younger, but she, it's hard for her . . . she doesn't really go to [pause] strangers very easily, so I'd like [the new nanny] to be someone that she really liked." Mary Anne felt genuinely conflicted about changing caregivers. Still, she had quietly begun to search for a replacement because she was worried that she might be jeopardizing her daughter's development. Jennifer seemed to be outgrowing Esther's capacities.

Although Mary Anne did not know it, Esther was aware that her employer perceived her age and mobility as a problem. She viewed the situation, though, as less a question of her physical limitations and more one of a difference in childrearing philosophies. Alan, in particular, seemed to favor an approach Esther found troubling. "Alan always wants us to go as *far*, as *far* away as possible. . . . I guess he doesn't want Jennifer just around the house. He wants her to learn things, so we're always being sent to the Museum of Science, OK? The farther we go, the happier Alan is." In Esther's view, this philosophy of nonstop stimulation, which was widely shared among the parents I interviewed, was wrongheaded. "But [Jennifer] is *too young*, I mean to excel right now, you know? What—she has to—this is my concept. A baby. She's only a baby. They are pushing her like she is, like, four or five years old. And how long is babyhood? . . . She is only two years old, and they have expectations [*spreads her arms apart*] like this, you know?" Esther did not attempt to enlighten her employers regarding the real cause of her seemingly limited mobility. But she made it clear to me that, in her mind, her age was not the issue. On the contrary, it was *Jennifer's* age that mattered. "It's too much. Sometimes it's too much. I don't mean *I* can't do it. But it's the child. The child gets tired and their parents, you know, they always like to push. Push their children, um, to the limits. And my philosophy is keep them young when they can, because there's the whole life ahead and the fun time is very short."

Esther felt ambivalent about following Mary Anne's and Alan's instructions when she disagreed with them. She also felt unable to speak up. "They don't ask my advice. I can see things, but I never say anything to Alan or Mary Anne. [Why not?] Because I don't think it's my business. I'm there just to take care of her. I'm not there as a teacher. Or as a parent. You get what I mean? Jennifer needs to have a time to relax. They're pushing her to the limit. . . . Because when she sees me, it's like, 'Oh—save me!' I mean, she's trying to relax. It's, uh—because I love Jennifer too much. I see what's coming, you know?" Still, she never voiced her opinions, and despite her reluctance, she tried to take Jennifer on many outings. She feared the consequences of acting on her own beliefs or even voicing them: "Then I'll lose my job."

Perhaps Esther *was* too old to keep up with an active toddler, or too shy to feel comfortable helping Jennifer learn to socialize. Or perhaps, as she said, she left these notions unchallenged in order to avoid a conflict about what she saw as the real issue. The important point is, although both she and Mary Anne felt emotionally torn by this central problem in their relationship, they never discussed it. And, despite Mary Anne's very real appreciation of the care Esther lavished on Jennifer, she was quietly but actively seeking a replacement. She did not view Esther as a member of the extended family who might be part of Jennifer's life indefinitely, or as a family friend, or, ultimately, even as an employee with skills of enduring value. Instead, she considered Esther as one part—the infant-care component—of an overall childrearing strategy geared toward meeting Jennifer's ever-changing developmental needs. Those needs had, in effect, stamped Esther with an expiration date.

. . .

Employers whose mothering ideologies reflected the intensive mothering ideal described in chapter 2 made up the great majority of my respondents.[1] These women firmly believed that children's early experiences significantly influence their lifelong development and that it was their responsibility as mothers to ensure that their children's needs were fully met during this "critical period." The more expertly they designed and managed all aspects of their children's care, the more confident they felt that they were living up to well-known and widely accepted cultural standards of mothering. Meeting these standards, moreover, strongly suggested that their children would suffer no disadvantages as a result of their decision to continue pursuing their careers. Thus, as chapter 4 showed, in making hiring decisions, these mothers looked for particular "types" of childcare providers, deliberately looking to match nannies' perceived traits to their children's perceived needs.

. The present chapter shifts the focus to a different aspect of the execution of delegated mothering, namely, how mothers go about managing the individuals they hired to care for their children. Most of the women I interviewed were committed to having their children raised as if they had stay-at-home mothers. They looked to nannies and au pairs as a means of replicating the care they *imagined* they would give their children if they had been at home themselves.

These mother-employers' overall childcare strategy also was designed to help them address concerns about delegating care while maintaining the all-important mother-child bond. Current childrearing ideology emphasizes the long-term positive effects of frequent mother-child interaction and, conversely, suggests the potential for difficulties later in life if early attachment is poorly executed (see chapter 2). This prospect raised fears among many of the mothers I interviewed that the hours they spent away at work might in some way harm their children. Since their positions in male-dominated occupations left these women few or no options to make adjustments on that side of the equation, they turned their attention to optimizing conditions at home. To quell their fears and uncertainties about their children's healthy development, they reinterpreted expert advice regarding the uniquely meaningful connection between mothers and young children. Substitute care became an acceptable alternative, provided the mother retained full authority and control over the caregiver—what I call "intensive mothering by proxy." This management strategy involves two interrelated components: treating the nanny as a "medium" through which a child's needs, as identified and prioritized by the mother, are fully met; and monitoring the home front.

Delegating care to a childcare provider need not necessarily be problematic.[2] How an employer delegates care, however, shapes the caregiver's job experience and may affect the care children receive. Chapter 9 explores the effects of a management strategy, used by a small subset of the study participants, in which caregivers and employers undertake childrearing as partners.[3] The present chapter demonstrates how, when caught in a vise between the competing demands of intensive mothering and a male-pattern career, they are likely to cope with the resulting strain through their management of the nanny. Just as the family is the "shock absorber" for the demands of a changing economy and workplace, childcare workers are frequently the shock absorbers for the spillover from work/ family life imbalance.[4] Furthermore, as this chapter and those that follow show, when caregivers are treated as only one aspect of an overall childrearing apparatus or as an extension of the mother, they are likely to become frustrated, and opportunities for communication and mutual enhancement between caregivers and mother-employers are reduced. As a result, children may receive lower-quality care. Moreover, employers may find that intensive mothering by proxy leaves them almost as frustrated as their care providers.

The deeply felt desire for a sense of true control and security that leads mothers to dictate and monitor what their nannies do in their absence can never be fully satisfied. As one mother lamented, "Having a child is like having your heart walk around outside of your body," and added, "It's really hard because you're never really sure whether [a childrearing decision] is the exact right thing." Despite managing their childcare providers as if they were extensions of themselves, working mothers are still faced with the hard reality that they cannot be in two places at once. For at least some part of the day, their children are being raised by someone else, a fact that left most mothers feeling vulnerable. The fear of powerlessness and lack of control mother-employers expressed was especially poignant because these women had grown accustomed to feeling in control in most areas of their lives. Paradoxically, they felt out of control in a very significant area of their lives *because* of the success they had worked so hard to attain. Striving to make certain that the "someone else" they were dependent on did the best job possible is the closest these working mothers could come to reasserting control and assuring themselves that they were meeting their maternal responsibilities.

THE NANNY AS MEDIUM

The *American Heritage Dictionary* gives several definitions of *medium*,[5] including: "2. An intervening substance through which something is transmitted or carried on, such as an agency or transmitting energy. 3. An agency, such as a person, object, or quality, by means of which something is accomplished, conveyed, or transferred. . . . 5. A person thought to have powers of communicating with . . . spirits." As practitioners of intensive mothering by proxy, the majority of mothers I interviewed (twenty-one) used their childcare providers as mediums. Eleven of the thirty mothers viewed their nannies as the "substance" through which they transmitted their wishes and effected their vision of optimal care. By creating an array of rules and scripting the nanny's day, these mothers hoped to carefully mold and direct their care providers' actions. This level of control, they appeared to reason, would allow them to meet the highest cultural standard of maternal responsibility, even while they were away from home. I term this approach *puppeteer management*. In nine cases, the mothers viewed the nanny as a medium almost in the paranormal sense. These mothers considered the nanny an extension of themselves. Their care providers, they seemed to think, were people who could and would "naturally" intuit their wishes; they were people who could and would, without direction from their employers, "naturally" make decisions that would correspond closely with the mothers' own.[6] I term this approach *paranormal management*.

These two management styles are similar to those Robin Leidner reports managers of interactive service workers as using to take control of "the service triangle" (see chapter 4). Interactive service work often takes place away from the direct oversight of the manager, so the triangular relationship among manager, employee, and service recipient (customer) must be managed in one of two ways. In some forms of service, such as that provided by the counter staff in fast-food restaurants or by representatives in customer service centers, managers train the workers to use particular scripts, thus routinizing employees' responses to customers. This ensures a consistent quality of interaction: "Would you like fries with that?" In other kinds of services, interactions with customers are simply too complex to script. In these cases, employers must rely on their ability to recruit and hire the "right kind" of persons, whom they then encourage to follow their instincts while on the job.[7]

Unlike their business world counterparts, the mother-employers I interviewed were ambivalent about their role as nanny managers. Regardless of whether they favored the puppeteer or the paranormal approach, they viewed the nanny's job as enacting the mother's will, not as an evolving activity performed by an autonomous agent.[8] Any thought of an alternative, more egalitarian approach to what was in reality the shared task of raising their children was overwhelmed by the deep need to feel in control of the home front despite being absent from it. Supervising a single caregiver gave mother-employers some sense of controlling their childcare and tailoring it to their children's needs, but, as they acknowledged, it also made them dependent on that single caregiver and therefore vulnerable to her. Most of the mothers I interviewed were acutely aware that they were transmitting their mothering beliefs and practices to their children through someone else. As Janet, a white thirty-six-year-old attorney, noted, "I feel like I do my mothering through my nanny, and I don't like it." And each act of instructing or monitoring their childcare providers further reminded them—and others—that they were mothering by proxy.

Many mothers spoke of feeling anxious about leaving their children alone for long periods of time with an employee. Amy described her concern about meeting her first au pair this way: "I can remember standing in Logan Airport thinking, 'Oh my god, I am going to turn *my* baby over to someone I've never met. This person is going to get off the plane—what if I don't like what she looks like, don't like who she is—and I've committed myself to turning this baby over to this *total* stranger.'" The sometimes heavy-handed and invasive efforts to manage and control nannies' labor (discussed below) stemmed, to some extent, from this anxiety.

Puppeteer Management Strategies

Puppeteer managers created rules, reporting procedures, and monitoring strategies in part to produce a consistent childcare experience for their children, regardless of the nanny. These mothers tended to view their nannies as interchangeable,
applying the same rules to every caregiver. Their efforts to control the nanny and
structure the workday ranged from Taylorist scheduling and rule making to more
indirect restrictions, such as limiting the nanny's movements inside and outside
the home and controlling her use of time. The most basic sets of rules applied
to the children's schedules. Mother-employers set the daily framework, including
appointing the times at which naps, meals, and indoor and outdoor activities were
to take place. Amy, explaining her use of rules, said: "Now that she [the baby] is
getting older, there are more regimented things that I want this person [the current
au pair] to make sure that she does every day. . . . I want her to be outside inhaling
fresh air every day. Like today, I would expect that they are probably outside all
day long, except for lunch and her naps. . . . Foods are very important to me. This
year, having learned from last year [with a different au pair], I was much more
specific: these are sort of the breakfast choices, these are the choices for lunch."

Puppeteer managers also often created written schedules for their caregivers to
follow, and some attempted to script caregiver-child interactions by giving specific
instructions concerning how to address their children and what kinds of language
they considered appropriate. This is how Debbie described her training regimen
for new nannies: "Just making sure they understand what I want, teach them how
I want them to treat the children, sort of doing the whole day with them there,
like how I give a bath, and—getting back to the problem we mentioned earlier
of discipline—how I suggest instead of saying, 'You will eat this for dinner,' they
say, 'Miranda, would you like fish sticks or tuna fish?' . . . Those kinds of things."
These attempts at scripting were aimed at minimizing the effects of differences
between the mother's social class, cultural background, or personal style and that
of the nanny. Children in the care of a person who sounded and acted much like
the mother she was temporarily replacing would, presumably, profit from this
borrowed cultural capital.

Mothers also set rules about socializing. For example, some expected the nanny
to arrange play dates. This could cause conflicts, though, if the nanny felt more
comfortable arranging get-togethers with her friends and their charges rather than
with her employer's friends and their children. Carol expressed her concerns over
this dilemma: "I guess the worst of our concerns is they're not hanging around
with our friends' children, they're hanging around with children of other au pairs.
We don't really know the families that well. . . . And there have been some things
coming home, attitudes and stuff—killing and shooting and war games—and stuff
that we're not real happy about." Some mothers felt strongly that their nannies

should not socialize at all, and they made this an explicit rule. More often, puppeteer managers allowed socializing with other caregivers' charges, provided they had an opportunity to first screen the prospective playmates and their caregivers. Unfortunately, this seemingly reasonable proviso could result in no socializing at all. Parents often were not home enough, or at suitable hours, to meet the prospective playmates. So, whether by rule or by default, many nannies found themselves restricted to the house, isolated and deprived of contact with other adults.

A consistent theme among rule-making mother-employers was the assumption that while she was at work the nanny was on her employer's time. Nannies who worked for mothers who relied on a puppeteer management strategy were expected to limit their activities to those sanctioned by the mother, taking neither breaks nor "personal time." Although many mothers included running errands like grocery shopping in the nanny's job description, they often did not want the caregiver to do such chores while with the children. And they certainly did not want the nanny running her own errands while she was "on the clock": "I told her that I don't want her to run any personal errands with the baby. . . . I know a lot of the au pairs do that, and she asked me if she could take the baby to Lechemere to buy a stereo. And I told her, 'You get a day and a half off a week, you get every evening off, the stores are open late. I just don't like that. I don't do that, and I don't want you to do that.'" Distinctions such as these, between what was appropriate for on-duty time and off-duty time, and between what nannies could do with the children and what had to be saved for days off, reflect the clear difference mother-employers perceived between a nanny, who is an employee and thus is on her employer's time clock, and a stay-at-home mother, who is an autonomous agent, on her own clock.

This division of labor points to the further distinction between an at-home mother, who has no choice but to do errands with her children in tow, and a professional-class working mother, who delegates these tasks to others. Intensive mothering by proxy permitted sorting the various activities of a stay-at-home mother into discrete categories. That achieved, employers could then ensure, by carefully scheduling and distributing the components of at-home work (including, frequently, hiring others to do the non-child-related tasks), that their nannies' energies were expended primarily on the children. Perhaps because they were beguiled by the elegance of these rational and efficient-looking schedules, or perhaps because they simply lacked firsthand experience, the mothers in this study blithely imposed rules on their caregivers that they themselves would have been hard pressed to follow had they been the ones at home all day with small children.

Rules related to the use of a car were among the thorniest. Sometimes puppeteer managers sidestepped potential scheduling disputes by not allowing the nanny any access to a car. This was especially frustrating for nannies who worked in areas with no public transportation; they became virtual prisoners in their employers' homes for up to twelve hours a day. Especially in the suburbs, however, many mothers did want their nannies to drive children to activities. These mothers allowed use of the car, but because they also wanted to maintain control over where nannies took children, they imposed various limitations. As Amy explained, "But, nor do I expect her—you know, I don't want her taking long car rides with the baby and, you know, going hither and yon with the baby. I mean the idea of the car, and the baby and the car, is around the house, you know—not driving to Vermont." Likewise, mothers who lived near public transportation limited their nannies to certain bus lines, or certain areas of the city. This, in their view, made it possible to simultaneously encourage the horizon-broadening outings they approved of (e.g., trips to the Children's Museum, the library, the park) and discourage any impromptu adventures that might expose their children to undesirable places or people. Jessica managed Anabel's mobility with a set of general rules:

> If she goes just around to the local park here, then she doesn't need to call or leave a note, because if I come home and she's not here, that's going to be the first place I'll go, and I'll find her there. But if she goes somewhere else, then she has to either call or leave a note here, so that I don't go into a panic. [*laughs*] And she also asks ahead of time if she's planning to take her to some place that she hasn't been before, like if it's somebody's house, or to the mall, or to take the T [subway] or something like that. I'm very open to pretty much wherever she wants to go, as long as it's not going into, like, a dangerous part of town or something like that.

Anabel did not find these rules unreasonable. They were more flexible than those of most puppeteer managers.

Some mother-employers used the allocation of space within their homes as an implicit or explicit means of control. For example, some preferred that live-in nannies not play with the children in their own suites. Rather than saying this directly, they asked the nannies to keep to other floors or areas of the house, ensuring that the children were cared for in their space and not in the nanny's space. One mother rearranged the furniture to make it inconvenient for her au pair to use the playpen, a practice of which she did not approve. Similarly, employers of live-out nannies used restrictions on the use of the car to avoid having to confront the more sensitive problem of instructing nannies not to take the children in their care to their own homes.

All of these rules were designed to protect employers' children by minimizing the impact of the nanny's personal style and limiting her autonomy. By imposing a broad array of rules, these mothers hoped to control—in advance—all the day-to-day decision making that occurred in their absence. Rather than relying on her own judgment, the caregiver was expected to carry out decisions the mother-employer had already made. This approach, unfortunately, tended to reduce caregivers to interchangeable cogs in their employers' larger childrearing system. It also transformed their work from potentially meaningful and creative interaction into a frequently tedious, scripted channeling of their employers' childrearing beliefs and practices.

Paranormal Management Strategies

The second strategy mothers used to control the home front was to employ a nanny who would not only meet the ethnic logics criteria described in chapter 4, but also act as an extension of themselves through a presumably intuitive connection between mother and caregiver. In these cases, questions of control were front-loaded into the process of selecting the caregiver. These mothers believed that hiring the right person would allow them to relinquish control over day-to-day decision making around play dates, naps, and food. They could simply trust that the nanny's judgment would mirror their own. Leigh's comments perfectly capture the essence of this approach: "Some parents say that they tell her . . . she can't do this and she's gotta do that and this is where the kids are supposed to put their boots, and we like to sit down at the table, and they've got to do this and they've got to do that. My feeling is the complete reverse. If this girl doesn't have the common sense to pick up intuitively how we treat our children, what we expect from them, if she hasn't picked that up in a couple of weeks—then she's a hopeless case." In making their initial hiring decisions, all of the mother-employers I interviewed put a great deal of thought into the type of nanny characteristics they considered essential for ensuring that their children would receive the best possible care (see chapter 4). Only paranormal managers, however, converted their hiring logics into an ongoing management strategy.

Most of the mothers who practiced this form of management sought some reason to feel comfortable with the caregivers they selected and to believe in these women's ability to "pick up intuitively" how they wanted the children raised. Some achieved this by hiring women of the same ethnic or national origin as themselves; others concentrated on finding caregivers whose values, beliefs, or other important characteristics seemed reassuringly familiar—the same as or very similar to their own. Hiring a person who was "like them," or who reminded them of another well-trusted individual, led these mothers to expect that their caregivers would intuitively know and then automatically carry out their wishes.

As Debbie said of her first au pair, "Annika was a lot like me. . . . I mean, I'd much rather sit down and read a book or something, and she was a lot like that." Finding similarities in interests and worldview led this mother to see similarities in childrearing style as well: "Somehow Annika knew exactly what I wanted." Debbie's second au pair, Ulle, was not "like her"; she did not like to read and instead preferred to go out with friends. This difference prompted Debbie to conclude that Ulle needed a puppeteer management style rather than the paranormal strategy she had favored with Annika.

Often age—at both ends of the spectrum—served as a proxy for trustworthiness. Although some mothers spoke of the extra-nurturing qualities of older women, others preferred the malleability of younger caregivers. A mother who had hired a twenty-year-old au pair praised the caregiver's implicit modeling of her employer's childrearing practices: "That's one of the things that I really like about having someone young. . . . She's been so interested in wanting to care for him the way I want him cared for. . . . She hadn't taken care of a newborn before, so there were weeks she was trying to mimic everything I did for him." The same mother added that she would not likely hire an older nanny, because older women would not be so malleable: "I think an older person, say somebody who is sixty and has raised kids of her own—'No, this is the way I do it.' I mean, I've got enough of that with my mother and my mother-in-law. . . . I just couldn't deal with that every day."

The defining advantage of paranormal management is that it eliminates the need for explicit instructions or discussion between caregiver and employer. As Naomi said of her "Jamaican voodoo" nanny, "You know, by the end, there was complete understanding. You didn't even have to say things to each other. She knew what we wanted. We knew what she wanted." Because this nanny had moved on to another job at the time of our interview, I was unable to interview her to find out whether she agreed that they had achieved "complete understanding."

To increase the likelihood that an intuitive connection would emerge from the start, several paranormal managers hired nannies whose ethnic backgrounds were similar to those of women who had cared for them when they were young. For example, Janet had grown up in Poland with a Polish nanny and she hired a Polish immigrant to care for her own children. Similarly, Suzanne was raised by a nanny from the Caribbean and hired a Caribbean caregiver for her daughter. Alicia hired the daughter of the Venezuelan woman who had cared for her as a child and, as a result, got the childcare services of both women, as well as a sense of security in knowing how her children would be treated. Linda, a white thirty-nine-year-old attorney, took this strategy to its logical limit, hiring her own childhood nanny, a now quite elderly African American woman. Unfortunately, instead of being able to intuitively trust Josephine, Linda found herself in the awkward position of having to hire *another* nanny to care for both the children and the aging nanny. She then spent most of her time arbitrating arguments between the two nannies.

Paranormal managers differed from their peers in that they extended the logics of similarity or enhancement that most employers used in hiring a nanny or au pair and applied these criteria to management. They eschewed the minute rules and daily lists that most puppeteer managers relied on as their primary management tools. Once they had found the right woman for the job, paranormal managers felt they could let go of day-to-day control. The caregiver would "just know" how to do things "their way."

MONITORING THE HOME FRONT

A new set of challenges arose after mothers had devised and communicated rules and guidelines concerning their children's care. If a mother is away from home for ten to twelve hours per day, how can she be sure her desires and directives are being implemented? One mother-employer expressed the dilemma this way: "You know what was always a concern? About whether there would be a different face when you were around than when you aren't there. And I think that's the reason that I don't tell the nanny my schedule, and I just pop in and see how things are going. And I think that that's just a concern in the more global sense—someone you don't know taking care of your child. But it's not [a fear] that is so, you know, overpowering that I can't do it." The employers I interviewed sought surveillance strategies that would give them sufficient knowledge about daily home life to feel secure enough to be able to go to work without overwhelming anxiety. Although these mothers repudiated the idea of using a video camera to monitor their caregivers, they did rely on a wide array of low-tech monitoring strategies, ranging from "the unexpected drop-in," to the "body check," to reports furnished by older children, housekeepers, and strangers.

The "unexpected drop-in" involved having a member of the family or a trusted friend stop by unannounced to check on the nanny's activities. This was the most commonly used monitoring strategy. One mother asked her husband, who was self-employed, to stop home for lunch and then give her a report: "So you come in and, you know, either you hear them playing, or you hear music going or, you know, [the baby's] asleep and she's watching some TV." This mother explained, "The fact that we've been able to do that has enabled us to be more comfortable."

Mother-employers with some flexibility in their work schedules sometimes made their own "drop-in" calls. Mary Anne recounted the following incident as evidence that she and her nanny did indeed share the same childrearing approach: "One time, I came home early and Esther didn't know I was home. So I heard her . . . coming in with Jennifer and I heard her say [*laughs*]—because I guess Jennifer bit her on the nose [*laughs*], and I heard, 'No, Jennifer, don't bite Esther!' So it was funny to hear her, how she reacted to something. . . . And then Jennifer didn't want to come in the house, and she was like, 'Well then, just stay out in the hallway.' [*laughs*] And [I thought], 'I can see myself saying that.'" Eavesdropping was the ultimate "drop-in." Mothers who listened at the door felt that they were privy to an unedited portrayal of nanny-child interactions. In this case, Mary Anne had no illusions that Jennifer was perfect or always an easy child, and she was reassured that Esther responded as she imagined she herself might when faced with a recalcitrant toddler. Other employers relied on reports from strangers. Suzanne explained, "I or my husband will take Lindsay to the park sometimes and meet with mothers of children who Lindsay plays with in the park, and they have all spoken very highly of our nanny."

Mothers also relied on the "body check." They assessed how the children were dressed, fed, and bathed to gauge good care. Amy, who was explicit in her approach to the body check, described her monitoring philosophy this way: "And I'll be honest, when I give her a bath at night, I look for bruises, you know, I want every mark on her body that I notice accounted for, and I'll ask for that.—'There's a scratch on her leg. How'd she scratch her leg? There's a bruise on her arm. What happened to it?' It doesn't, you know, it's not very often that that happens. [Au pairs] are probably better at preventing bruises and scrapes than I am, because they know I'm going to ask about it." The body check was both a way to determine if the child was unharmed and healthy and a way to test the nanny's honesty. If the nanny reported cuts and scrapes without being asked, the mother could feel at ease in trusting her.

For example, Naomi, a physician, explained how her nanny, Yvonne, allayed her remaining fears about how much she cared for her children when Naomi's five-month-old slipped in the tub and cut her lip. Yvonne, in tears, phoned her immediately at the hospital where she worked, and Naomi rushed home:

> And I came home and Yvonne had her, and she was just, like, holding her like, "How could I do this to you???" and at that moment I think if I ever had any question if she adored my child, that question left. And for me that was actually wonderful, to see that she cared so much. And so I just checked [the baby] and she seemed fine, and I said OK and, you know, "Thank you so much for calling me, and you did absolutely the right thing." . . . I got right back in the car and went back to work. You know, didn't give her the rest of the day off or anything like that.

Naomi perceived this situation as a test of whether her nanny could handle a crisis and of how honest she was. Yvonne scored a high pass on both counts, and Naomi conveyed her trust by returning to work and leaving Yvonne in charge. She noted: "And I think that made her feel more comfortable that if things happened, I wanted to know about them. There wasn't going to be recrimination, um, because I think one of the hardest things a parent does is let go and let someone else be responsible for their child's safety. It's a very hard thing to do."

In families with older children, mothers also relied on these youngsters' accounts of the day and of the nanny's treatment of them. This approach could be unreliable, though. Naomi told me about a situation that developed right after Yvonne, to whom her three-year-old daughter Sasha had been strongly attached, retired and was replaced by a twenty-six-year-old Caribbean nanny, Carla. Naomi did not have the sense of "perfect understanding" with Carla that she felt she had shared with Yvonne. Furthermore, Sasha was unhappy about the nanny turnover. She felt that Carla loved her younger brother, Nathan, more than she loved her.

A major family dilemma arose when Sasha and Carla's strained relationship was further complicated by Sasha's use of the phrase *shut up*.

Apparently, Sasha learned the phrase by listening to Carla command the family dogs to stop barking. Naomi reacted strongly, asking the nanny never to use those words around her daughter. This rebuke was followed by reports from Sasha that Carla was telling *her* to "shut up," which prompted another sit-down with Carla, who insisted that although she never told Sasha to "shut up," Sasha frequently uttered this phrase to her. Naomi was left with the delicate problem of deciding whom to believe: "Sasha's only three and a half. It's tough—and I don't want to be one of these, you know, 20/20 families who set up a little video camera and watch everything going on. I don't think that's right, and actually I don't think it's necessary. And I suspect that Sasha did kind of make this up, because we made such a big thing of it when she said it."

Naomi's dilemma reflects the difficulties working mothers faced when they were caught in a nanny-child conflict about which they could never ascertain all the facts: "It creates an interesting difficulty with childrearing and loyalties, because you don't want to undermine your—you don't want your babysitter to think you don't trust him or her; you don't want your child to think that bad things that are happening to them are just fantasies and they should bury them. It's very tricky." Naomi admitted that she wished that her new nanny "swooped her daughter up and covered her with kisses," but she also said that she felt secure that Carla did care about Sasha. In the end, Naomi relied on her own version of the body check—she focused on how Carla dressed Sasha. "I know that [Carla cares]," Naomi said, "because sometimes I'll come home and she'll have her—like if I need to take Sasha somewhere, I'll come home and she has Sasha just dressed beautifully, like a little angel. And I don't think you do that for a child if you don't care about them."

In addition to these common monitoring techniques, puppeteer and paranormal managers each had specific styles. For example, puppeteer managers relied more heavily on lists, logs, and other systems of reporting than did their paranormal counterparts. Like Mary Anne and other puppeteer managers, Debbie relied on a log of the day's activities to help her monitor the home front. Debbie explained, "I did up a sheet that she has to fill out every day saying what the baby did, what games they played, who visited . . . and that way I get to have a window onto the day. I mean she could lie, but she doesn't."

Nannies often were aware of these monitoring techniques and found them intrusive. Most expected some initial monitoring but hoped that once they had proven themselves reliable, they would be granted a degree of autonomy and trust.[9] Understanding this, some mothers tried to balance their need to restrict their children's movements with their nannies' need for some adult interaction. Suzanne, for example, generally did not like Violet to take her daughter on the subway or far from home, but she did encourage Violet to socialize with adults in the local parks and to visit other nannies in the homes where they worked: "I think that it's important for *her* [Violet] also to be able to interact with other people. I mean, being with a one-year-old all day long, you know, it's trying for me sometimes. I like when she goes to the park and makes friends with the other nannies or the other mothers. I think that it also sets a good example for Lindsay to sort of socialize with the other kids. And she has a—both the nanny and Lindsay have a whole set of friends at the park."

Unlike some other mother-employers I interviewed, Suzanne was able to imagine herself in her nanny's place and realize that her need for adult interaction and stimulation would probably be similar. In this instance, she did not see Violet as a tool that she deployed, but rather as someone like herself. At the same time, Suzanne recognized Violet's needs as legitimate in part because they coincided with her view of Lindsay's need for socialization. Nannies' basic human rights were not, unfortunately, likely to be recognized apart from the developmental needs of their charges. Finally, although only ten of the thirty employers I interviewed deliberately restricted caregivers' movements, these restrictions speak to a more common phenomenon: employers viewed their caregivers' time, energy, and personal loyalties as extensions of their own.

THE CONFLICTS AND COMPLICATIONS
OF INTENSIVE MOTHERING BY PROXY

Working mothers' desire to provide their children with a home-based upbringing that met their own individually and culturally shaped expectations created problems both for themselves and for their caregivers. Mothers wanted to feel that their children were safe and were being cared for "their way." For some, trusting in the "type of person" they believed their nannies or au pairs to be was sufficient. Alicia, for instance, based her trust in Leticia not on open, two-way communication but rather on Alicia's sense that she knew this childcare provider's basic qualities. "At least she lets me believe she does things the way I ask her to! [*laughs*] Every once in a while, you know, you toy with that—put the video camera up here and let's see what they do. [*laughs*] But she's a very honest person. She's a very humble person . . . and I don't think—she doesn't really resist what I tell her—or ask her." Other mothers wanted more details about what went on during their absence—but not so much information that they would feel threatened or envious. A "window" on everyday affairs could make it painfully clear that the child had a separate life, full of activities, relationships, and developmental milestones of which the mother was not a part. This is why Amy, for example, chose not to ask for a report:

> I sort of have a picture in my mind of what they do when I'm not there. I think it would be much more difficult to see it written down every day and see all of these

things that [the baby] was doing that I wasn't there to do. Where I know it, psychologically, but I don't have to see it on a list every single day that these are things that she's doing that I have no part in. Plus, I think it's an imposition. You know, it's hard to write down, you know, "played outside," or "had lunch and this is what we had for lunch," so I just didn't go down that road.

Many caregivers readily agreed with Amy's supposition that employers' monitoring strategies were "an imposition." Although the mothers I interviewed tried not to alienate their caregivers, those who relied on intensive mothering by proxy were the subject of many nanny complaints (see chapters 7 and 8). Not surprisingly, nannies and au pairs were most vocal about puppeteer managers. They argued that in curtailing their freedom and denying their autonomy, these employers showed a lack of respect for their childcare providers' skill. Some worried about hidden cameras and wondered whether their every move was under surveillance. Many were aware of the body check and were careful to look for scrapes, bruises, or ill health as soon as they came on duty, and to report anything out of the ordinary immediately. As Anne, a Jamaican nanny, noted regarding a rash that had developed because of a zipper that irritated the baby's skin during the night, "I told [the mother], 'I just want you to know that it didn't happen with me.'"

Similarly, employer restrictions on mobility frustrated caregivers. Ronda described her reactions to these limitations this way: "I felt closed in, like I was in a matchbox, and I don't like to feel like that. . . . She didn't want me to walk to the playground. She drove me to the playground one day. And then she felt that park had so much sun we left that park and went to a park that had no kids in it but just me and her son and her. The other park was filled with kids, but just because it was sunny, she didn't want him to stay there." Ultimately, Ronda concluded, "For somebody to be breathing down your back or over your shoulder every second. . . . I understand she wants to come and see how I am with the child. But, 'Oh, no, take him over here . . .' 'Oh, no, don't take him on that.' No, I felt like in that case . . . 'Bring him yourself. What do you need me for?'" She quit.

Isolation is more than frustrating for caregivers. It is also potentially dangerous.[10] Research suggests a connection between the treatment of nannies and the treatment of the children in their care. "Hired caregivers who get little emotional replenishment themselves, who may be with young children for ten to twelve hours a day, can have a particularly hard time summoning the energy to actively engage with children."[11] April noted this relationship. In describing employers' bans on socializing as "one of the terrific disservices that parents do with nannies," she pointed out the negative consequences for children whose care providers are deprived of regular adult contact: "If you're miserable, and you're depressed because you haven't talked to a single human being except for [the mother-employer] at lunchtime, then you're not going to be able to do your job as well. You're not going to be as relaxed, and the child definitely picks up on that." Isolated caregivers are more likely to maltreat children, not only because they lack critical social supports but also because they lack important social controls. Several nannies and au pairs mentioned monitoring other caregivers at playgrounds and social gatherings. One reported a fellow au pair to her employer after seeing her spank a child in her care. Ironically, then, mother-employers who impose tight restrictions on their caregivers in order to secure the safety of their children may instead be creating conditions that put their children at risk.[12]

Finally, employers who deny their caregivers basic freedom of movement place them in a position that they themselves would be hard-pressed to tolerate. Hertz points out that "cloistering wives in the home is unthinkable for dual-career couples."[13] Being cloistered in the home is unthinkable for just about anyone— including at-home mothers, who generally vary their days with errands, visits to friends, trips to parks, and other activities.

The nannies and au pairs I interviewed also faced communication problems. Those who worked for puppeteers complained about getting instructions via notes and having to leave replies via the journal or noontime check-in phone call. Face-to-face, open-ended conversations about the children were no more common among those who worked for paranormal managers. Although most caregivers in these situations felt that their employers basically trusted their judgment and gave them a good deal of freedom, the very lack of feedback made their autonomy, and the trust it implied, seem hollow. Some wondered if their employers really cared about what went on during their working days. Elsa, a twenty-year-old Swedish au pair, described the challenges of a job caring for a school-age boy with severe ADHD. He was often out of control and abused her physically. She explained, "I tried to talk a lot about the boy . . . and then after a couple of months she [the employer] said, 'Oh, but you can do this and try to do this.' I said, 'Why didn't you tell me that when I came?' She said, 'You should have understood. You should have realized yourself what to do.' " Lura summed up caregivers' feelings about the importance of communication: "I think that's where a lot of problems happen is when the nanny is not sure about something, she's afraid to ask and the parents are afraid to say something. And if you can't communicate, you should put them [the children] in daycare. I mean, if you can't communicate with the person—notes don't do it! [laughing] That's basic communication. And tell them thank you once in a while."

Like limiting autonomy and mobility, failing to establish good communication could have care-related repercussions. Occasionally, mother-employers who used the paranormal management approach were surprised to find that they had misjudged a caregiver's childrearing skills. One mother, for example, found that although her caregiver had excellent references, came from a family similar to her own, and had laudable "family values," she was nonetheless severely bulimic and emotionally disturbed, and therefore had to be replaced. Similarly, Caroline, an African American mother, found that common ethnic background did not always equal common values when she discovered that her caregiver was taking her children places she considered dangerous.

Clearly, intensive mothering by proxy does not challenge the belief that children need a full-time mother at home. Its overarching goal is to ensure that children receive the care their mothers imagine they would provide if they were present. What most mothers fail to perceive is that this goal, however dear it may be to them, is not necessarily the same as providing the safest or the highest-quality care for their children.

CONCLUSION

All the effort mother-employers who practiced intensive mothering by proxy devoted to turning their caregivers into extensions of themselves and to monitoring their children's days resulted in a home life for their children that, by definition, did not include the mothers. This left many sounding wistfully out of touch with what happened during their children's daily lives. Suzanne described a common incident that served as a poignant reminder that her baby had a life that did not include her or her husband: "The other day my husband was in a supermarket with Lindsay and some woman that he had never seen before comes up and says, 'Hi, Lindsay.'" This disconnection reveals that no matter how diligently Suzanne—or other mother-employers—might conduct home-front monitoring, they have very little real control over what goes on at home. Ultimately, their absence makes them vulnerable, dependent on their caregivers to be worthy of the trust they placed in them.

At the same time, the entire childcare edifice that allowed mothers to leave their children behind each workday required that they not inquire *too* closely into their caregivers' trustworthiness. As Amy noted, "I thought about it when they did that whole big series on the abuse and all of that sort of stuff, and then—once again, you want to know, but . . . I can't quit my job and stay home. The other part of me has to believe—and this is because I have to be here [at work]—that somehow I would know if my daughter wasn't happy."

To feel sufficient confidence to leave their children in others' hands, these mothers fell back on the foundational principle of intensive mothering—a mother just "knows." Joan put it this way: "If something was not right, you know, I really think you could tell. I think you could tell just by the child's behavior. You know, I just kind of believe that you could, even if they can't talk—sooner or later, something would show, I think [*pause*], so." Ironically, this notion—that the umbilical connection is sacred and permanent—is one of the least demonstrable tenets of intensive mothering.

For the employers who used intensive mothering by proxy, attempting to manage and observe a home life that was by design independent of them created a series of painful paradoxes. They had hired a nanny or au pair to have one person, who worked under their supervision, caring for their children in order to produce an approximation of an at-home mother. This, they expected, would allow them to feel more in control of how their children were being raised. Instead, they often felt less in control of the home front and more vulnerable to the person they had employed. Furthermore, intensive mothering by proxy did not ease any of the burdens imposed by blanket accountability. Working mothers felt responsible for everything that occurred inside and outside their homes during their absence, and how those activities or relationships might affect their children over time, as they grew into adulthood. By the very nature of how they had framed their caregivers' place in their children's lives, employers who believed in intensive mothering often felt inadequate both as mothers and as supervisors, and anxious about the "home-centered childhood" they had worked so hard to create.

6

Creating Shadow Mothers

According to both Joan and Melanie, theirs was a successful relationship. I interviewed each in her own work domain: Joan in an upper-story corner office in a glass-tower office building overlooking Boston Harbor; Melanie in Joan and her husband Bill's tastefully decorated flat. The two women spoke of one another in glowing terms. Each was pleased with the way they had worked out their division of labor, each was pleased with Bill's contributions, and each doted on one-year-old Charlotte. They were among the most satisfied of the mother-nanny dyads I interviewed—and yet, there were "lines of fault"[1] and areas of unarticulated tension in their relationship.

Joan came to mothering in her midthirties, after first having devoted herself wholly to her corporate career. She had not planned to have children; a second marriage, at age thirty-five, to an egalitarian husband changed her mind. Having found in Bill a husband who had "done a really good job in terms of breaking some of the traditional boundaries down," made the possibility of starting a family attractive. After years of assuming that motherhood was out of the question, Joan found that being a mother came very "naturally" to her, and she loved it: "It's the best thing I've ever done. You know, I can't believe that I waited so long. . . . I mean you know, it's like all these kind of maternal instincts that I never *ever* thought existed all just kind of bubbled up, and, I have to tell you, it's all been totally natural. It hasn't been a struggle at all. You know, in terms of integrating her into the kind of 'light of my life' kind of thing. It's been kind of easier than I thought it would be in that kind of way."

She and Bill realized they needed the perfect nanny to make their busy lives possible. They found her in Melanie, a white twenty-four-year-old with a degree in early childhood education, who had worked briefly as a preschool teacher. Plus, Joan pointed out, they approved of Melanie's upbringing, "her family values and stuff like that, you know, were nice. I mean, she's close to her parents—she has a nice family." Joan joked to me that she felt so relieved upon meeting and interviewing Melanie that she promptly went into labor: "Melanie came, we met her, and we really liked her. She left, my water broke five minutes later, and I was in labor. I mean that was exactly how it went [laughs]. And so, that was that, and I had the baby that night."

For her part, Melanie had been frustrated by the administrative politics she found in her preschool teaching job; she wanted greater autonomy and authority. So, in looking for a nanny job as transitional employment while she contemplated going to graduate school, Melanie knew that she "wanted the family to trust me and, you know, to give me authority, and not be questioning me and checking up on me all the time." She appreciated the fact that Joan and Bill recognized and valued her expertise. "I told them my experience and what I was looking for, and the interview went really well. They kind of gave me the impression, 'You sound more experienced than we do. You sound like you've been around children a lot more than we have.' This is their first child. So I think they took my degree [in] early childhood [education] and all the experience that I have had with children— they took that seriously." Seriously enough, in fact, to pay her top dollar for her fifty-hour workweek and to provide fringe benefits, such as health insurance, sick pay, vacation pay, and bonuses. She was among the top-earning nannies in this study, and she was very happy in her live-out job.

As was true of most of the nannies I interviewed, however, there was more to Melanie's job than childcare. She also performed mother-care. As a first-time mother whose responsibilities as a vice-president of corporate relations placed fairly rigorous constraints on the time she was able to spend with her baby, Joan sometimes worried that she would lose her position as Charlotte's primary care-giver. She needed Melanie's help to feel secure in that role. Like other first-time mothers I interviewed, Joan seemed to have a fragile sense of her capabilities and status as a mother. Like Suzanne, Jessica, and Joyce, she voiced concern over how much "face time" she had with her baby. She wondered whether Charlotte knew that she was "the mother." Joan described a particularly trying time: "For a while, and I don't remember how old Charlotte was, maybe six months old, she was really, really preferring Bill to me. Everybody I told said, 'Wow, that's unusual. Usually they prefer the mom.' Oh, thank you for that reinforcing comment. [laughs] It was like Bill would walk in the room and she'd cry until he picked her up. Bill would walk out of the room and she'd be just devastated. . . . She went through a couple of weeks where nothing would do other than Bill, Bill, Bill." Melanie noticed this, too, and expressed her concern about this phase in her interview with me: "When the dad left for work, [the baby] would start to cry, and I could tell that it bothered the mom. And it was like, 'Oh, dear God, don't let that ever happen, that she cries when I leave.'"

That was Melanie's biggest fear—that sometime in the future the baby would start to prefer *her* to Joan in the same way she had seemed to prefer Bill to Joan. In addition, Melanie felt that it was her responsibility to alleviate the "Bill" situation, and she took steps to do so. Joan described one intervention this way: "Melanie came down with [the baby] to my office one day and brought me flowers. I mean, I thought, 'Isn't that funny that she would see that?' Because I never said anything because it felt awful. There wasn't anything Melanie could do or I could do, and it was just this awful thing, like all of a sudden my baby doesn't like me. She figured it out, and I thought that was incredibly sweet." Beyond this "incredibly sweet" effort to soothe her employer's wounded feelings, Melanie also marshaled expert evidence to reassure Joan that she really was the most important person in Charlotte's life. Joan recalled: "Then one day I came home from work and she had found this article in one of the baby books about how they go through periods where they prefer one or the other, and I said, 'Yeah, I know. I've read it.' And we began to kind of talk about it a little bit. I just thought that was so perceptive—not that it would have taken a rocket scientist to see what was going on, Cameron, I mean, come on, to see what I was feeling—but it was a nice thing."

For her part, Melanie thought it was normal that the baby would switch from parent to parent, especially since they both were active in raising her. Nevertheless, she joined her employer in framing the incident so that it did not undermine Joan's status as Charlotte's primary parent. Melanie recalled, "We read those children's book things . . . on what to expect in the first year. And basically, in [the book] it said that sometimes they'll give the parent who's most involved in their raising the hardest time by going to the other one. So that was sort of how the mom justified that the baby was going for the dad, because she was kind of testing the mom or something." Interestingly, in her version of the story, Joan presented this "justification" as having been supplied by Melanie. Either way, both understood that explanation as the one that everyone in the family would stick to. And both understood it to be an ongoing part of Melanie's job to create and/or maintain these "mommy-centric" narratives.

Another part of Melanie's job was to "read" Joan, and to be cognizant of her likes and dislikes. Most important, she needed to be aware of the line between her connection with Charlotte, and Joan's connection. For example, it was important to Joan that Melanie respect certain boundaries concerning what she should and should not do with the baby. These were not so much safety rules as guidelines regarding what Joan viewed as mother-only tasks. Joan did not present Melanie with a list of do's and don'ts. Instead, she offered timely cautionary tales:

I'll come home with stories that I've heard from other people at work—about their nanny situation—and I'll talk to Melanie about it and I'll ask her what she would do in the same situation. . . . One of my best friends, her nanny took her little boy to the circus one day. She came home from work and . . . [the nanny said,] "The baby and I went to, you know, Big Apple Circus today." And Mary said it just kind of—she was *devastated*. Because it was something she really wanted to do and the nanny never asked, because she was probably thinking it was great, she was entertaining the baby. And I just kind of relayed the story to Melanie, with the thought that she should get the fact that she should call me if she was thinking about doing something like that.

Melanie got the message. When I interviewed her (about a week before interviewing Joan), she told me a story that conveyed her understanding of these implicit boundaries. "I don't want to step on her toes and do something with Charlotte that they would want to do with her first. So I'll call and see if she minds or if she would rather do it with her first. . . . Like silly things, like go to the Swan Boat Ride. Stuff that at this age doesn't really matter, 'cause she [Charlotte] won't remember, but, you know, in their hearts—I don't know if they'd rather do it with her."

Furthermore, on occasions when implicit boundaries were crossed inadvertently, it was Melanie's job to smooth over the rough moments. One day, as she was getting ready to leave, Melanie's biggest fear materialized—Charlotte began to cry. Although Joan did not mention this incident during the interview, it was prominent in Melanie's story. She viewed this as the only incident that had ever caused explicit tension between them. The day Charlotte cried at her departure, Melanie believed that Joan was angry: "When I was leaving she just . . . kind of, like, left the room. And she usually makes a big deal when she says goodbye. Like, she says, 'OK, Charlotte, let's say goodbye to Melanie,' and she didn't that day. I could just tell from her face and her—like she was sort of tense and not her usual self. And she wasn't even herself with Charlotte either, so. Like she didn't say anything to me, but it was what she wasn't saying that—I got the picture." Melanie believed that in Joan's eyes, Charlotte's innocent transgression of the boundary between mother and not-mother was somehow Melanie's fault.

She recalled being "kind of actually a little mad that she reacted like that, because it wasn't my fault." Nonetheless, the next day, they patched things up:

I talked to her the next day and she apologized and said that she had had a bad day and, you know, whatever happened that day at work and, you know, she apologized and stuff like that. So I told her what I was feeling and how I didn't want—that it's bound to happen—and that I was sorry that she was having such a bad day. And she kind of just said, "Well, I guess it makes me happier knowing that she doesn't want you to go versus being psyched that you're leaving and crying when you came." So I guess that's true, and that sort of is expected, I think, of a baby who I spend so much time with, that she's gonna react like that with me. So that was one of the major things that I was, like, worried about, and it happened and I didn't know how to react.

In resolving this small conflict, both women engaged in complex emotional and interpretive work.[2] Each of them had to decide whether to acknowledge the incident, how to interpret it, who was at fault, and how to resolve it. Joan began by deflecting attention from the boundary transgression and focusing instead on having brought home the tension from a "bad day" at work. Melanie pressed the issue of Charlotte's tears and tried to normalize the event as something that was "bound to happen." In the end, they settled on an interpretation that highlighted how well Melanie was doing her job. Melanie still felt the sting, "but then I understood her completely also. I could see both sides." At a deeper level, though, it was evident that this incident represented a rupture in the seamless orchestration of family life that Melanie and Joan tried to achieve.

In addition to revealing some of the tensions that underlie even the most successful childcare relationships, this incident also makes clear the extent to which Melanie's job included sustaining her employer's image as the primary caretaker. An unspoken part of Melanie's job description, but a major component of her role as not-mother, entailed restabilizing a view of family life that corresponded with intensive mothering ideals, even when this view contradicted lived experience.

· · ·

"One thing that parents really have to understand," Lonehl, who had thirteen years' experience as a caregiver, told me, "is that the children are going to love their parents regardless. The older they get, nobody can take the place of mom or dad. No matter how much we take care of them, they are still going to love mom and dad." Experienced mothers concur with this view, and research provides additional support. One of the most striking findings of the National Institute of Child Health and Human Development's longitudinal study of mother-child attachment is that the higher the quality of childcare, the more the children feel securely attached to their childcare providers and the more securely they remain attached to their mothers.[3] Paid caregivers may be beloved companions, but they do not replace parents. As Lonehl put it, "We're not there to take over like we're their mother or anything like that. We're just there to help them."

Most of the mother-employers I interviewed, because they were profoundly affected by competitive mothering ideologies and because their children were still very young, did not fully understand this. They were more influenced by the ideal of intensive mothering, which portrays a child's capacity to relate to adult caregivers as a zero-sum attachment. This means that the presence of any other loving caregiver (except, in some limited cases, the father), can infringe on or even threaten the integrity of the mother-child bond. It also means that questions concerning how to share mothering tasks, and how to interpret this delegation, can become highly charged. Chapter 5 explored mothers' need to create and manage a particular division of labor between the childcare worker and themselves. This chapter considers a different but closely related problem: mothers' efforts to define, for themselves and for the care providers they hire, what that division of labor *means*.

A mother's expectation that her nanny care for her children and love them as she herself would frequently collides with her own desire to be the primary caregiver and with her belief in the ideology of intensive mothering. In addition, a mother's desire to control her children's care can conflict with a nanny's need for autonomy and her wish that her employer appreciate her expertise.[4] These tensions led many of the mother-employers I interviewed to want a "shadow mother," an extension of themselves who would stay home *as if* she were the mother, but who would vanish upon the *real* mother's return, leaving no trace of her presence in the psychic lives of the children they shared, and making no claims to mothering knowledge or skill.

CHILDCARE AS SHADOW LABOR

Ivan Illich coined the term *shadow work* to refer to "that entirely different form of unpaid work which an industrial society demands as a necessary complement to the production of goods and services."[5] Often termed reproductive labor, or "women's work," shadow work is devalued, frequently invisible, and usually unpaid. Arlene Kaplan Daniels, expanding this definition, argues that reproductive labor is "invisible work," in part because our commonsense understanding of what "counts" as work obscures work that is unpaid, work that takes place in the private sphere, and interactive work that is traditionally performed by women.[6] Thus, much of the work mothers do, and much of the work that they then delegate to caregivers, does not count as labor.[7] Hidden in the home, caregivers' work is conventionally understood as being performed out of love, not in exchange for wages.

Conceptual distinctions between productive and reproductive labor, labor for money and labor for love, and market work and shadow work all devalue tasks not easily commodified or understood as part of an economy based on the exchange of goods or services for a fee. Not surprisingly, reproductive labor has a long history of being undervalued, despite the fact that cooking, cleaning, childrearing, and caring for other family members are tasks essential for sustaining human life. Moreover, it is this labor that creates and maintains families as social groups and the home as a source of nourishment for individual family members so that they can move out into the "productive" realm of economic and civic life.[8] Yet those who perform these vital services often go unrecognized and unrewarded. Furthermore, if they are paid workers, they are often viewed as a poor substitute for the mother or housewife conventionally expected to perform these tasks.

Childcare is pushed further into the realm of shadow work by the common tendency to view reproductive labor—"women's work"—as the simple enactment of innate propensities. In other words, the work of the home involves doing what "comes naturally" to women. It requires neither skill nor effort. Women are expected to be "naturally" empathetic; nannies are expected to "naturally" love the children in their care. As Daniels argues, categorizing capacities and actions such as these as instances of "natural" human behavior obscures the effort entailed in producing them and, as a result, further undermines their perceived value.[9] And, as discussed in chapter 3, caregivers often are denied the basic workplace rights accorded to most unskilled laborers.[10]

Mothering is a particularly paradoxical form of shadow work because, unlike other forms of housework, it is simultaneously demeaned and celebrated. Politicians and childrearing experts routinely refer to the work of raising young children as the most important job in the world and as women's sacred mission. In the mid-nineteenth century, when motherhood was first deemed a sacred calling in the American popular imagination, white middle-class women were able to fulfill this calling by delegating other household tasks such as cooking and cleaning to servants. This practical division of labor was made possible through a conceptual split that apportioned the "spiritual" aspects of the reproductive labor of the home to white middle-class women and the menial tasks to women of color and working-class women.[11] This split fostered the notion of domesticity that gave white women's mothering a moral purpose and the home the aura of a sacred haven.

Dividing the work of the private sphere into spiritual and menial labor, and assigning race and class attributes to that division, perpetuated racial and class hierarchies among women and sustained the devaluation of women's work in general. As chapter 3 explains, under stratified reproduction, such hierarchies continue to structure the labor market for domestic workers. A twenty-first-century version of the spiritual/menial division of reproductive labor allows one class of women to enter the workforce and maintain the spiritual aspects of motherhood while another class of women is paid low wages to fill in for them at home, performing the menial mothering tasks of daily interaction with children. Working mothers themselves also reinforce the spiritual/menial split by defining spiritual motherhood as designing and supervising the childcare apparatus, by defining the time they spend with their children as "quality time," and by retaining primary-parent status regardless of how responsibility for care is distributed in practice.

Because intensive mothering is now the norm, however, the division of housework into the spiritual and the menial generates substantial tensions. Delegating mother-work to a paid employee strains the spiritual/menial split because it is precisely those tasks associated with menial motherhood—feeding, holding, disciplining, and the like—that are defined as constituting the bond between mother and child deemed essential to good motherhood. How, then, do mothers who work outside the home combine delegating the menial tasks of mothering and yet maintain spiritual motherhood in the form of primary caregiver status? And what delineates the boundary between themselves as mother and the nanny as not-mother?

Part of the answer, as chapter 5 shows, lies in defining the childcare provider as the medium through which a mother's childrearing beliefs and practices are transmitted. A nanny is viewed as an extension of her employer's mothering practice, not as an individual with her own particular relationship with the children. As this chapter will argue, visible signs of a unique nanny-child relationship are specifically avoided or downplayed by both employer and employee because this kind of bonding is understood as a violation of the caregiver's responsibility to act only as an extension of the mother. As the employer, it is the mother's prerogative to set the terms of the nanny's work, including the "feeling rules" associated with the day-to-day activities of caring for children.[12]

The mother-employer has an additional priority, however. She also seeks to ensure that the nanny's daily practices do not infringe on her status as primary parent. Like Jessica, who wanted Anabel to love and adore baby Sammy when Jessica was absent but fade into the woodwork the moment she, the *real* mother, returned, most of the mothers I interviewed created implicit and explicit expectations that the nanny be someone who would be an extension of the mother-employer's practice but not threaten her primary-parent status. The demand for self-erasure, for instantaneous turning on and off of emotions, and for ensuring the bright demarcation between mother and "not-mother" are particularly troubling aspects of a job composed of many other unacknowledged, labor-intensive tasks and problematic expectations.

Working mothers and the caregivers they employ jointly create a symbolic order that defines the meaning of their division of mother-work so that it reproduces a culturally approved image of motherhood. The work both parties undertake to create and sustain shadow motherhood falls into three main categories: rendering the nanny invisible in family life, enhancing maternal visibility, and patrolling the mother/not-mother boundary.

ERASING NANNIES

A nanny's physical presence or absence, and her engagement with or disengagement from the children, are important forms of "boundary work" that help create and sustain a distinction between parents' work and home lives.[13] Because the nanny's presence signifies work time, or the antithesis of family life, many mother-employers devised strategies and rules to reduce or eliminate overlap between "nanny time" and "mommy time." For example, Suzanne chose live-out care as a way of preventing the possibility that her workday would extend indefinitely, blotting out her time with her daughter: "We've talked about having somebody live in, but I'm almost hesitant to do that, because that would—like right now, there's some structure that, artificially or not—there is this sort of time in my mind when I'm really shooting to try and be home. And I think that that would sort of like—*blend out* if I had somebody . . . here all the time." With a live-out care provider, Suzanne could protect the important boundary created by the end of her nanny's workday.

For other mothers, the caregiver's arrival and departure became a poignant reminder that they were not the only mother-figure in their children's lives. Jessica, for instance, regretted the loss of her "special time" with her son, an inevitable occurrence at the close of each weekend, when the family's au pair returned: "She's out of here for the weekend, but she comes home on Sunday nights. Sometimes she'll be home at like, six, and I'm so sad that she's home, because it means my special time with him is over. And it reminds me that I have to leave him. It reminds me that he's going to be so excited to see her. That, um, now he's not gonna want me, he's gonna want her." To avoid such tensions, many mothers tried to keep their childcare workers waiting in the wings until their services were required.

This desire that childcare workers should become invisible when the mother-employer was at home left some nannies feeling excluded and unwanted. They balked at being asked, however implicitly, to assist in demarcating the line between "family" and "not-family" by defining themselves out. The pressure to give families private time was especially troublesome for live-in workers since, unlike other caregivers, they did not have separate homes and families to return to at the end of their workday. The au pairs in this study, for example, were young and far from home. With the encouragement of the U.S. State Department, they considered themselves part of a "host family" and often viewed their employers as surrogate parents (see chapter 3). This made performing the extra work of vanishing to help create "family time" emotionally painful. Referring to her employer, one au pair lamented, "I always get the feeling, 'Oh, she's going out. Yippee!'" Another explained, "I only get the meals that I work. . . : I hardly ever get dinner 'cause they're home before dinner. . . . Basically, they don't want you to disturb them when they're home and you're not working because, you know, they want to spend time with the kids."

Employers also rendered nannies invisible in depictions of the family. Although many working mothers, especially those employing live-in workers, referred to the nanny as "one of the family," in all my visits to employers' homes, I never saw a photograph of the nanny and the children on display. This omission was striking in two ways. I looked at many family pictures; some mothers showed me albums; in other cases, I saw portraits of the mothers, their children, and extended kin prominently exhibited. In every instance, the nanny was conspicuously absent. In contrast, when I visited nannies in their homes or in their living quarters within their employers' homes, photographs of children currently and formerly in their care were highly visible. Generally, nannies had one set of photos of their biological kin and a second display area for photographs of their "work children" and their employment families. In other cases, pictures of the two sets of "kin" were intermingled. These photographs and family portraits represent a striking distinction between the displayed importance of the nanny-child relationship from the divergent perspectives of mother and childcare provider.

Detached Attachment

Nannies often lament that their importance in the children's lives goes unrecognized and unrewarded (see chapter 7). Beyond accepting this reality, they also are expected to help render their attachment invisible. The nanny's job requires that she perform acts of self-erasure by following what Margaret Nelson calls the "detached attachment" rule.[14] This is one of the "feeling rules" that structure the emotional labor of paid childcare.[15] The detached attachment rule is meant to ensure that the caregiver displays enough warmth and affection to make the child feel loved and the employer satisfied with the quality of care, but not so much warmth and affection as to risk leading the child to become overly attached, or seeming to undermine the parent's central place in the child's affections.

Detached attachment is really three rules in one: the first is a mandate to love the children in one's care and to form a stable bond with them, just as a parent would. The second is a requirement that the caregiver simultaneously love the child *and* maintain some emotional distance so that she can prepare them both for their eventual separation. The third is a demand that the childcare provider not usurp the mother's position as primary caregiver, regardless of how much time she might spend with the children or the strength of the bond between them.

Detached attachment is an unusual form of emotional labor. Most feeling rules require displaying an emotion one does not necessarily feel at the time. Store clerks or bank tellers, for instance, muster a cheerful-sounding wish that their customers "have a nice day" at the close of each transaction. In other jobs, where what Arlie Hochschild calls "deep acting" is required, workers must first "work up" and then display feelings that they would not ordinarily express in a work context.[16] For example, nursing home workers may try to make their workdays more bearable by imagining the patients in their care as elderly relatives. This type of service work, however, requires only "the performance ... not the development of genuine human interpersonal connections."[17]

Childcare, in contrast, does require forging genuine emotional attachments. Nannies and au pairs generally agreed with the common interpretation of this job requirement as not-work: they described loving the children in their care as being easy, natural, and fun. Like Miriam, a white college student who worked as a full-time nanny during the summer and part-time during the school year, most care providers likened these relationships to falling in love. When I asked Miriam for examples of times when taking care of her employer's two-year-old twins made her feel special, she offered the following: "Like when they would show love back to me. Like when they would call me 'Mimi'; when they would be happy to see me; when they would want to be picked up and held; when they wanted to dance. There were just all these things, that it's like a romantic relationship, you know? When I could see that they were assimilating things that I taught them." For most nannies, "attaching" did not seem like work. The labor involved in detached attachment lay below the surface—figuring out how to manage the *degree* of attachment, how to make it acceptable to the mother, and how to prevent it from adversely affecting the children in the long run.

Regardless of the work involved, creating and sustaining attachment provides an important source of emotional nourishment in a job with few other rewards. Ronda, the African American nanny who worked for Mary, said she "love[d] coming to work. There is not a day I get up and say, 'Ohhhh, I don't feel like going.'" With obvious delight, she described her good-morning ritual with Molly, the three-month-old child in her care: "[I come in and say,] 'Good morning, good morning, Molly. How is my little princess?' And she hears my voice and she's trying to see where I am. And she's looking and looking. And I'm like, 'I know you hear me.' And she's looking and looking, and then she just starts smiling. . . . She pays a lot of attention to me. . . . We have fun together."

Less frequently, creating attachment sometimes required a deliberate working-up of feelings and a generous willingness to look beyond the child for the source of his or her unpleasant behavior. Not all children are easy to love. Some nannies looked after children with behavioral problems and/or developmental disabilities. Others, when faced with children who kicked or bit them (or mistreated other children), found that their employers expected them to simply put up with this behavior. Still, most caregivers managed to find a way to love even the most trying children. Corinne, a twenty-eight-year-old Kenyan immigrant with five years' childcare experience, described her approach to the "just really spoiled" three-year-old girl she cared for. Kirsten seemed intent on making each day miserable, but Corinne forced herself to love her anyway. She attributed Kirsten's disagree-ableness to the parents' shortcomings: "All these horrible things, and you look at it and think, 'She's not bad, it's the parents. It's not her fault. It's the parents' fault.' And I really feel sorry for a kid like that." Although Kirsten repeatedly mistreated Corinne, Corinne reinterpreted their relationship as one of pity, in which Kirsten's parents, an Asian American fashion designer and a white physician, had created a monster through their poor judgment. In cases like these, the "attachment" aspect of detached attachment was hard work and required creative interpretation.

Many nannies, as the next chapters will show, are firm believers in the ideology of intensive mothering; yet as workers they also understood the need to provide financially for one's family. Thus, many simultaneously disapprove of and accept their employers' decision to work outside the home. They therefore interpret their attachment to their employers' children as helping to compensate for the parents' absence.[18] Esther, for instance, saw herself as the guardian of the home and of Jennifer's well-being. Like most caregivers I interviewed, she believed her role in the life of a child whose mother is "never home" was crucial. She pointed out that children may have little opportunity to bond, "because mom is not home." That, she felt, was "why Jennifer is attached to me."

This same possibility seemed to haunt mother-employers, as well. In some cases, the employer-initiated demand for detachment, though rarely explicitly stated, reflected the mothers' view of caregivers' involvement with their children as threatening. Amy, for example, was both irritated and dismayed by the degree to which one au pair had bonded with her child. "The last month with our first au pair was *very* difficult for me. I mean, I would come [home] from work and she would be *crying* because she realized that her time was coming to an *end,* you know, she was having a very difficult time with the fact that she was going to be replaced. . . . She said to us at one point, 'I can't imagine anyone taking care of the baby but me.' And I was, like, 'Hello? *I'm* her mother.'"

Lonehl, though, believed that employers like Amy were mistaken in their demands for detachment. In her opinion, working mothers needed to recognize and accept the implications of the imbalance in the amount of time they spent with their children as compared to the nanny's investment: "I'm there from eight to eight sometimes. So, that's attachment right there. I mean, they're kids. They're gonna attach with who's with them the most. No matter who it is, the grandmother, auntie, a nanny. I mean of course the jealousy is going to be there, but I mean they're working moms. They want the career and the home life. They can't have it all equally."

Some employers enforced the detached attachment rule explicitly as a way of securing family time and privacy. Christine, a twenty-one-year-old white nanny from Boston, described her employer's behavior as an effort to distance her: "When I was off-duty, I was off-duty, and Elaine [her employer] thought it was strange that I would want to spend time with the baby on weekends. She would say, 'Well, I'm sure you have more important things you could be doing.' But I wanted to be with [the baby]. It was kind of like she was pushing me away." Other mother-employers said they encouraged detachment because they did not want to exploit their nannies by letting them work during their time off.

Regardless of their employers' motivation for demanding detached attachment, it was up to caregivers to devise ways to meet this expectation. Most nannies and au pairs enacted the rule by demonstrating attachment when they were alone with their charges, and displaying parent-approved levels of detachment when they were in the presence of their employers. Esther summed it up this way: "I always try not to let the parents, uh, um—see that we are too affectionate? Because I don't know—I don't know whether they have any feelings that maybe I love her more than I should? I don't know." These remarks, along with Esther's description earlier in the interview of her relationship with Jennifer as "not uh—that, that—uh, close. I mean it's close enough," reflect the anxiety and confusion expressed by many caregivers about the line between "attached enough" and "too attached." Generally, the nannies I interviewed developed a level of attachment that they found emotionally satisfying, and that they believed would be beneficial to the children, but they were also careful not to let their employers see the depth of that love.

Since they faced a predetermined end to their relationship with the children, au pairs in particular used the detached attachment rule to try to reduce the pain of eventual separation.[19] Past experience also tempered nannies' level of attachment. Lura, a veteran nanny of eleven years, said that after her first experience, she learned never to get so attached. "I think it's because you don't let yourself. Because you know how hard—how much it hurts when you have to leave them. And so you love them, you know, and you get, you get attached to them some, but you don't, you don't let them get wedged right into your heart. . . . So, you treat them like your own, but you don't love them like your own. And it's hard to do." Cassie, a twenty-seven-year-old white working-class nanny from Boston, added that summoning the courage to love the child in the second family she worked for took time: "I really didn't grow attached to her until a year ago. I kind of kept myself at a distance, not on purpose, but subconsciously I did, because I didn't want to go through that hurt again. It took a long time for me to get over Kimberly [her first employer's child]. I still miss her, but I'm starting to feel almost the same about Lynn as I did about Kim."

Others spoke of holding back certain core aspects of their affection in the hope of protecting both themselves and the children in their care. Margaret, a twenty-four-year-old British au pair who was working for her third family when I met her, said: "You try not to think about it, and you fool yourself into thinking you're gonna be with them for a long time. Um. It's never made me not give 100 percent of myself, and as much of my friendship and my love and my caring, rather than my more emotional, personal self. It's never stopped me doing that. But you know, you go into the job knowing of course you're gonna leave someday. It's hard." Detached attachment thus required an emotional balancing act: if caregivers did their jobs too well, loved the children too much, they were bound to suffer at separation. If they protected themselves, they worried that they were depriving the children of love and failing to do their jobs. In the end, most gave in to their own desire for attachment and hoped for the best.

Protecting the *children's* feelings, in contrast, was never left to chance. Most childcare providers saw finding a way to separate from the children as painlessly as possible as a critically important aspect of their job. Valerie, who had only a few months remaining on her contract, described her separation plan this way: "Within the next couple of weeks, I don't want to get too attached—or, I am already attached, but try to slowly break that attachment without them realizing it. Like before I used to give them hugs all the time for doing something good. Now it's just only when I see them in the mornings and maybe when they come home from school. I'm doing it [separating] gradually." A gradual approach was of little help with very young children, though, as April learned when she tried to prepare Zoe. Since she knew that Zoe did not understand the concept of future time, she waited until shortly before her departure date to break the news. Still, April admitted ruefully, "She certainly didn't grasp the angst of the situation. I would try and tell her, and then she would be, like, 'Can I have a snack now?' [laughter] And I would think, 'No, you don't understand! This is going to be very trying emotionally.'"

Even if, as in this case, children were not old enough to recognize the impact of an impending good-bye, caregivers still felt the need to prepare children for their absence. For the most part, they did this work unaided, since many parents did not recognize a nanny's departure as a significant event. Even in leave-taking, they were to leave no footprints.

ENHANCING MOTHERS

The image of the good mother stood like a religious icon at the center of the childcare employment relationship. Both mothers and nannies paid homage to the mother's sacred status by enhancing her real and her abstract place in the child's daily life and by maintaining the boundary between mother and not-mother. A separate set of childrearing tasks was reserved for the mother and these tasks were assigned a special status; children's developmental milestones were not given significance until the mother had witnessed them; and the child's day was engineered to ensure that high-quality family time began at the mother's homecoming. The nineteenth-century split between the spiritual and the menial aspects of motherhood lives on among today's in-home caregivers. Shadow motherhood, as this section will show, involves a great deal of interpretive work aimed at symbolically separating the sacred realm of the maternal from the mundane tasks of the caregiver.

Engineering Quality Time

Mothers made the most of the time they had with their children by ensuring that it was "quality time." For example, Suzanne, explaining that "[I] need to feel like I'm getting a lot of face time and bonding time with my daughter," said that she appreciated it when her husband suggested, "Why don't you go and play with [the baby] while I clean up?" As stated in chapter 2, "face time" was significant for many mothers not only because they wanted to be with their children but also because they wanted images of their faces securely fixed in their children's imaginations. Finally, as believers in the ideology of intensive mothering, the mother-employers I interviewed were convinced that their children deserved and required—at all times—a consistently present, focused, and attentive caregiver. Nannies made it possible to achieve this ideal. Jessica described how rotating shifts of nannies and parents could guarantee a high-quality childhood: "He [her son] has Anabel [the au pair] all day, and I think because he sleeps five hours a day, she's 100 percent energy with him when he's awake. And then at night when we get home, we're so excited and energized to see him, he has Mom and Dad at that same peak performance." Mothers often mentioned the "peak performance" concept when they compared their current childcare situation with what it might be like if they stayed home: better the child should have multiple caregivers at peak performance than only one who might be burned-out or bored.

Mothers also wanted to ensure that the highest of high-quality time occurred during *their* shift. Much negotiation and behind-the-scenes work on the part of the caregiver went into producing the picture-perfect parent-child reunion at the end of the workday: the child waiting with excited anticipation for family time to commence, having been reminded that "Mommy and Daddy are coming home," having been helped into fresh clothes, and having already been fed dinner. Preparing for evening quality time took effort on the child's part, as well, which was one reason mothers and caregivers periodically clashed over this aspect of the day. One mother-employer explained her nap strategy this way:

> Scheduling of naps and deciding when the baby should or shouldn't have a nap was something that became an issue. See, the baby can take one nap during the day and be fine until about five o'clock when the au pair's done. If she *doesn't* have *two* naps, her miserable time is not while the au pair is taking care of her. Her miserable time is between, you know, six and eight-thirty, when *we* get her. . . . [O]ur time with her in terms of quality was horrible because she was so upset and tired that we couldn't enjoy our period of time with her.

To resolve this dilemma, she instructed her au pair to wake the baby after one hour of her morning nap so that she would be tired enough in the afternoon to take a second nap. She acknowledged that implementing this policy might be a hardship for the au pair: "I mean, it's tough to wake up the baby. She's cranky when you wake her up, but it's important so that she'll take her second nap. It wasn't acceptable to me to work her schedule so that it was shortchanging me . . . and it would really upset me when, um, the arrangement worked out so that she would miss her second nap, and I would get the lousy time of the day with her." Quality time, as this example suggests, may not occur naturally. And when it does not, it may become part of the caregiver's shadow work to ensure that the child's "lousy time" occurs on her shift, not her employer's.

Other mother-employers defined quality time in terms of whether they would have to struggle to get their children to bed. Rather than engineering the day so that children would be perky and alert in the evening, in these situations, caregivers had to keep children awake so that they would go to bed readily at night. Christine's employer instructed her to prevent three-year-old Courtney from taking naps for just this reason. Christine resented the no-nap policy, not only because it meant that she had to work twelve-hour shifts without a break, but also because she felt she was not able to do what was best for the child in her care: "I think Courtney really needs naps. Especially on days when she goes to school, she comes home exhausted. She falls asleep in the car. She falls asleep eating her lunch, and I have to get her an activity to keep her busy. . . . Whenever she's cranky, [the employers] blame it on either she's hungry or she needs an activity, not she needs a nap. So she eats all the time, and she's constantly driving me up a wall because I have to find things for her to do all the time, and you just run out of things."

Marisol, a forty-three-year-old nanny from Nicaragua, reported similar concerns. Her employer wanted the baby to be asleep when she got home so that he would wake refreshed after she had dinner: "But what I didn't like about her was that she would get angry if the baby was not asleep by the time she came back home. Two things I know are bad: to force a baby to go to sleep or to eat. I have been told by the pediatricians that it's harmful when you force them to eat or sleep. You can traumatize them psychologically, but she wanted me to force him." Marisol said that she simply did not do what her employer asked, "because it's harmful [to the baby]." Other nannies also reported having to choose between obeying specific directives and following their own sense of the children's needs.

As these examples of struggles over engineering quality time suggest, the central problem faced by all the parties is a misalignment of competing concepts of time. Mother-employers must contend with the constraints of the "industrial time" that structures their work lives, while nannies adhere to "baby time," in which the day is paced by their perceptions of the children's needs.[20] Since workplace time schedules typically are rigidly defined, many of the working mothers I interviewed needed to fit their family time into the evenings. The relative brevity of family time and the fact that its scheduling was in important ways determined by forces outside the mothers' control heightened their frustration over unexpected changes in the home time schedule. Joan, for example, recalled her annoyance one evening when she came home to find one-year-old Charlotte asleep at six o'clock. She confronted Melanie about this failure to adhere to the regular agenda:

Melanie said, "You know, my philosophy is that I go with Charlotte's needs. And she was really tired and really cranky and this is not the normal thing, but for some reason she wanted to go to sleep. So I let her." . . . I said, "Well, you need to understand what is going on with me. When I come home and she's sleeping at six o'clock, I know she's going to wake up at seven. And then I'm going to be up with her all night, and I have a big meeting at seven thirty the next morning. That is what I'm going through."

In this case, Joan felt that the demands of her work schedule ought to have had priority over her daughter's sleep schedule.

Hochschild uses the distinction between family time and industrial time to contrast the experiences of at-home and working mothers. She describes at-home mothers who perceive themselves as building "spacious temporal castles" around their children's lives and who perceive working mothers as time-keeping "prison wardens."[21] Yet the mother-employers I interviewed were not "prison wardens." Precisely to avoid regimenting their children, they chose a one-on-one caregiver over a daycare center that would impose its own routines. And when they were home, they consciously shifted into the relaxed pace of family time with their children. It is ironic, then, that many of these same mother-employers did not hesitate to impose an industrial time schedule on their nannies and, by extension, on their children, in order to create the possibility of family time for themselves, or in order to accommodate their own industrial-time-based work lives.

Mothers and nannies also engineered quality time by enacting a "dirty work/ clean work" division of labor.[22] Nannies often found themselves in the position of disciplinarian or rule enforcer in their employers' families, because parents did not want to taint quality time with disciplinary battles.[23] Some felt that they had been "set up" by overly lenient parents who absented themselves and left the caregivers in the role of enforcer. Lonehl described what seemed to be a typical scenario: "Say the child's disobedient and don't listen to them. They think you're going to come in and make the child listen to them, when actually the child starts to listen to you and still don't listen to them. They kind of want you to enforce the rules, and they don't. So, I mean, it doesn't work out that way. You have to work at it together."

Still, mothers who were rushed to get out the door to work in the morning, or who were exhausted after a long day at the office, had good reason not to engage in battles of will with their children. As Christine pointed out, "[Courtney's] mom's always saying, 'Well, I'd rather not have a big confrontation with her this morning, and I've got to leave for work,' and instead of arguing with her for a few minutes, they just let her do what she wants to do." The work of creating quality time could leave nannies feeling like the custodial parent in a divorce decree: they did the unpleasant work of parenting, while their employers were on hand for weekend outings and special events. Mother-employers generally agreed with this assessment, although not with the value judgment nannies attached to it. Jessica spoke for many mothers when she said that she had hired an au pair precisely so that when she was home she could be "100 percent baby-focused."

Mother-Only Tasks

Finally, mothers enhanced their maternal profile by choosing specific tasks to designate as "mother-only."[24] The fact that certain events were likely to occur on the nanny's shift, or that her shift might be longer than the mother's, could be offset by the fact that only the mother could or should perform certain childrearing tasks. Breastfeeding is the most commonly cited example. Leigh, as a physician, might have been expected to stress the inherent nutritional or emotional value of breastfeeding. Instead, like other mothers who mentioned this task, she emphasized its symbolic importance as a marker designating her as the mother: "This is the only thing I can do that the au pair or the nanny can't do. We had a nanny at the time who came in every day. She can do everything else. She can care and bond with him. This is the one thing I can do. And it was a little mental game that I played [*laughs*] with myself. It's like, 'Baby, I really am your mom, because I'm the only one who can do this.' . . . And I think it helped me. It helped me deal with the fact that somebody else was home with them."

Other mothers chose bathing, bedtime rituals, or breakfast preparation as their designated task. Aside from breastfeeding, the nature of these restricted tasks was unimportant. What was crucial was that they were sanctified as mother-only, and that the mother-only restriction was strictly observed. Joan explained that Melanie "[never] gives the baby dinner. We [Joan and her husband] always have dinner together and then we do the bath. So that dinner and bath is always our stuff." Suzanne went further in defining mother-only tasks. She excluded her husband as well as their daughter's nanny. "I *always* get her up. [Not your husband, but you?] Yeah. She always calls for me, and . . . I've tried to make it the rule that I am the first person that she sees."

Pat described a typical conflict concerning a mother-only task. She had chosen bathing her infant son Timmy as her designated ritual. ("This was what *Mom* wanted to do, where my ego was.") And she had asked Dagmar, her nanny, not to give him a bath during the day. Then, after an unexpectedly long day, Pat arrived home so late that she missed even seeing Timmy, let alone bathing him. Feeling "mad at" herself and "mad at the world," she apologized to her nanny: "And I come in, and I'm like, 'Oh, I'm sorry, Dagmar. I didn't get Timmy bathed.'—She said, 'That's OK. I bathed him this morning.'—So then I was *really* mad." But after a "good cry and a drink," and some serious thinking, Pat realized that, "the whole reason I'm upset is because I made the decision that that's what a mom should do, OK? Because that's what my mom did."

A little more thought brought her to two conclusions: failing to bathe her son did not make her "a bad mother," and Timmy did, after all, get his bath that day, even if she had not been the one to bathe him. These insights, Pat said, led her to decide to "disassociate my beliefs of what a mom should do with an infant and what a nanny should be doing with an infant, because I will always be the children's mother, no matter what. And they will always be the children's nanny. And the children may develop the same or similar or very, very close relationships with them. But I'm *always* gonna be their mom. And at that point, what we call my 'bathing thing' was over."

Pat's solution is significant for several reasons. In consciously opting for a commonsense approach to her child's actual needs, rather than his idealized ones, she broke free from the constraints of an ideology that had created emotional and cognitive stress. Her assertion that she would *always* be the mother, regardless of who gave the bath, represents a shift from the notion that the only mothering practices that "count" are those performed by the mother herself.

PATROLLING THE MOTHER/ NOT-MOTHER BOUNDARY

Most of the mother-employers I interviewed, particularly those who practiced intensive mothering by proxy (see chapter 5), worried that their children, especially the youngest ones, might not remain securely attached to them and would come to relate to the nanny as a substitute mother. They were, therefore, deeply ambivalent about how to interpret signs of attachment between caregiver and child. As Suzanne remarked, "Just this week, actually, when Violet left, Lindsay cried. And on the one hand, it hurts me that Lindsay is—[*pause*]—I like it and it hurts me that she's so attached." "I like it and it hurts me" aptly captures this widely shared dilemma. Most of the mother-employers I interviewed wanted the security of knowing that their children were well treated, but they feared being replaced in their children's affections. Carol recalled an incident in which her youngest child, after a fall, sought solace from his au pair even though she, Carol, was standing nearby. She admitted that his choice hurt her but said it was "better that than the opposite. But if it happened too often—I mean if it happened all the time. . . . It's the same thing with your husband, though. When the kids, when they move back and forth in their affections. It's good. It's a healthy thing." Carol normalized the children's attachment to their au pair by framing it in terms of their attachment to their father, as opposed to attachment to a substitute mother. Unlike first-time mothers Suzanne and Joan, Carol had the advantage of experience. As the mother of three children, she had learned that no matter how much it might hurt her to occasionally be second choice, she preferred that to leaving the children with a caregiver they did not love or trust.

Mother-employers frequently pressed the concept of attachment into dual service. Several mentioned the importance of their being the child's "special person," or noted that their child was very "mommy identified." These remarks established that they had achieved the primary bond required of a "good mother."

They then went on to describe the child as "adoring" the nanny or being "very bonded to her," thus establishing that they had also provided a nurturing substitute in their absence, another sign of being a good mother. Yet, believing in the importance of both types of attachment left these mothers in an ongoing emotional dilemma. Asserting the concept of "primary" and "secondary" attachment roles helped reduce some of the strain.

Caregivers were expected to defer to their employers not only in matters of day-to-day decision making (as discussed in chapter 5), but also in role differentiation. So, for instance, Joan praised Melanie's awareness of and sensitivity to "the fact that I'm the mom and she's not the mom. . . . [S]he's pretty deferential to me when I'm there. That I'm kind of the primary person and she's the secondary person." Ensuring that the status boundary between the mother and the caregiver was clearly delineated not only was essential—it was, as Joan suggests and as all the nannies and au pairs in this study confirmed, also a responsibility that fell mainly to the caregivers.

First-time mothers, especially, wanted to feel confident that their babies clearly recognized them as the mother. For example, Joyce spoke of her discomfort when her husband asked her if she thought their eleven-month-old infant knew the meaning of the visual distinction between her, his Afro-Caribbean mother, and Stacy, his white nanny. "He said, 'Well, I think he can see the difference, but does he know you're his mother?' And I said, 'Sure he does.' I don't know if that's true, but he probably does. [*pause*] But she does spend more time with him than I do. . . . I think he knows there's some difference. He may not have figured it out yet." Regardless of whether the baby truly understood the distinction between the women who cared for him, the family's smooth functioning required that all parties tacitly agree to act as if he did.

Once children were old enough to begin talking, the importance of establishing and maintaining the distinction between mothers and nannies grew significantly—for the adults. This distinction seemed to have little meaning for some of the children, however. For example, Christine recalled a period of tension when her youngest charge, Zachary, was learning to talk: "There was a while when Zachary thought I was his mom. . . . Elaine got all happy and excited when he started saying 'mama,' and he said it on a weekend. And when I got there on Monday it was the big thing, 'Zachary says *mommy* now.' Well, he says it to me too, so I don't think he knows. . . . Zachary's going both ways now, sometimes he wants me, sometimes he wants her, and sometimes he even wants [his dad]—[his dad] can't understand it because [he] doesn't think Zachary even knows who he is."

The word *mommy* and its usage were considered critical symbolic markers of whether the boundary was being adequately maintained. Anne considered it an integral part of her job to teach her charges to use the words *mama* and *dada* correctly: "I try and teach the child, when I see they start calling me 'Mama,' I will teach them, 'No, I'm not Mama. I'm Anne,' and I start teaching them my name. And then I let them call the mother 'Mama,' you know? I'm Anne. I just switch it around for them. But at first, they are a little confused. Just like they feel they can call everybody 'Dada,' you know? You can be a female and they call you 'Dada.' [*laughs*] So they are a little confused." As Anne discovered, however, even careful coaching does not necessarily produce the desired result:

> They *still* call me "Mommy." Right in front of the parents. And I know—I know, because every time—well. They know Gail [Anne's employer] is different. They know Gail is their mommy or whatever, but they can call everybody else's name—and you know, every time they call me "Mommy," I say, "It's Anne, Anne." But to them it's "Mommy, Mommy." You know. And sometimes Gail said, "Oh—that's so nice. You know, if you weren't taking good care of them, they wouldn't call you Mommy." You know? She kind of laughed it off. Now some people would fire me a long time ago because they would say I'm trying, whatever—and this child shouldn't be calling me "Mommy," because I'm Anne.

As Anne indicates, the nannies and au pairs in this study were aware that they could lose their jobs if they failed to adequately maintain the mother/not-mother boundary. Some had been fired by previous employers for just such a failure. In contrast, some mothers, like Gail, viewed a young child's name confusion as a sign that the nanny was doing a good job, provided the nanny took pains to correct the mistake.

A child's innocent violation of the mother/not-mother boundary could make the caregiver feel guilty if the misuse of *mommy* seemed to indicate the display of a preference for the nanny over the mother. April gave this example: "Sometimes Bonnie seemed in a rush for me to get out of there. And she'd get *very* miffed if Zoe would choose me—like she'd want me to carry her, hold her hand, or whatever—Bonnie would get very upset about it. You couldn't help but notice, because her facial expression would just go down." Not only did the nannies I interviewed often feel responsible for these largely unavoidable transgressions, they also felt it was their duty to restore the mother to her rightful place as primary caregiver. Even April, who disliked her employer and found her difficult to work for, felt she should intervene to shore up the mother/not-mother boundary: "Typically, no matter how much I was fed up with a lot of things that Bonnie did and a lot of ways she treated me, I would still feel bad for her. I felt, like, 'No, come on, Zoe, it's your *mom*.' And I'd feel terrible."

Mothers and caregivers colluded to further enhance the mother's status through a selective definition of childhood milestones. Typically, a developmental milestone did not "count" until the mother had witnessed it herself, as Leigh explained: "I remember coming home from work and the nanny said, 'He took his first step.' And I'm, like, that's great, I'm really happy for her. But in my mind, he had *not* taken his first step because I hadn't seen him take it. When he took his first step and I saw it, *that* was the one that went down in the baby book. Spiteful of me? I don't know whether that was selfish or not." Childcare experts reinforce the validity of this view, suggesting, for example, that childcare providers avoid telling parents about important firsts that occur in their absence and instead drop hints, such as "I bet she's going to walk any time now."[25] Many mothers appreciated this sleight of hand. For example, Pat noted: "You know, Dagmar saw Timmy take his first step. But instead of her telling us, she was so considerate, she just waited. And after we had seen it a couple times, I said, 'Well, how long has he been walking?'—not being stupid to think that he'd only done it on my time. And she just said, 'Oh, about a week. But I didn't want to tell you.'" Whether they chose not to recognize a "first" that occurred on the nanny's time or preferred to find out when the event had initially occurred, most of the mothers I interviewed tracked developmental milestones by shift—and they viewed developments that occurred on their "watch" as more significant. Nannies and au pairs were keenly aware of this distinction. Most told me that they would either not tell parents about these events, like the nanny who noted, "I just let her see for herself so she can be happy," or else cross their fingers and hope that every milestone occurred on a weekend or during the evening.

CONCLUSION

The work of shadow motherhood has very little to do with the actual quality of childcare or with the work of caring for children. Aside from breastfeeding, childcare workers could and did perform all the same mothering tasks at-home biological mothers undertook. So, in the households of mother-employers, the distinction between mother and not-mother must be consciously created and continually monitored. Moreover, it is a particular portrayal of shared mothering that mother-employers and caregivers collaborate to establish and sustain. This co-care is created within the context of a dominant cultural ideology that values only intensive mothering performed by the biological or adoptive mother, not by a hired provider. As a result, mothers and nannies perform an extra dimension of shadow work designed to mask the fact that their mother-work is, in fact, shared. It is a distinctive feature of the labor of shadow motherhood that this work is not in the service of either the children or the family as a whole. It is work in the service of ideology—the tenets of intensive mothering and the ideal of the self-sufficient nuclear family.

Ironically, although shadow mothering reinforces an idealized image of motherhood, and seeks to assuage mothers' feelings of inadequacy with respect to this image, it does not necessarily serve mothers' interests. By creating and, with their caregivers' help, maintaining rules that define a boundary between mother and not-mother, the mother-employers I interviewed reinforced the commonplace belief that children in nonmaternal care are somehow deprived, regardless of the quality of that care. Thus, these mothers unavoidably (though unintentionally) bolstered a belief system that often made them feel guilty and unhappy—and frequently caused similar distress among their care providers. It is important to note, however, that in their efforts to enforce what they saw as a necessary and appropriate division of labor, the mothers were not being arbitrary or deliberately inconsiderate. They were trying to relieve some of the intense pressure exerted by their simultaneous commitment to the principles of idealized mothering and the inflexible demands of their male-dominated occupations. Most had very little maternity leave or access to family-friendly work schedules, such as part-time work or flextime. As a result, they often felt painfully disconnected from what went on at home during the day. They relied on their childcare providers to help them strengthen their sense of being the primary caregiver within their own families.

Nannies and au pairs faced more and different difficulties than those that confronted their employers but, like their employers, these women also frequently acted against their own best interests. Shadow motherhood required erasing, or at least detaching from, those aspects of childcare that were the most meaningful to them. Yet, for the most part, they colluded in this self-erasure rather than resisting it. As chapters 7 and 8 will show in greater detail, they did so because, like their employers, they believed in and adhered to the tenets of intensive mothering. And, like their employers, those beliefs led them to act and feel in contradictory ways. On the one hand, they concurred that the biological mother *should* be the primary parent, and thus they worked to reinforce that image. On the other hand, they believed in the value of bonding, of their own bonds to the children in their care, and of the grounded knowledge that emerged from those bonds, and they resented being defined out of the family realm. Most longed to have their skills, including their ability to forge strong and meaningful connections with the children they took care of, acknowledged and valued by their employers. The next chapter explores this quest for "third-parent" status.

7

The "Third-Parent" Ideal

In looking back on my interviews with Jane, a corporate vice-president, and Sarah, her nanny, I was struck by how differently each perceived the life they shared. The two told very different stories—what amounted to "hers and hers" accounts of their lives together. It was difficult to believe that Jane and Sarah were describing the same family, the same children, or the same employer-employee relationship. Even the house seemed to be different depending on which woman I was interviewing.

For both interviews, I came into the house through the kitchen door—the "servants' entrance." When I interviewed Jane, the door was opened by Jane's husband, Peter, who was busily preparing the children, eight-year-old Brian and two-year-old Matthew, to go outside and shovel snow from the driveway. After Peter and the boys bundled themselves into their winter gear, Jane and I carried cups of tea to the family's spacious, elegantly furnished living room and began our "front-of-the-house" interview. For Jane, the kitchen was a place traveled through—it was where people came in and got ready to go out, where refreshments were prepared and taken elsewhere.

When I returned to the house several days later to interview Sarah, she and I never left the kitchen. This was Sarah's "back-of-the-house" living room, and it was here, seated together at the counter, that we had our interview. I visited Sarah at the house three times, watching her make lunch, arrive and depart for various errands, prepare dinner, wash dishes, play with Matthew, and interact with various repairmen. I never saw her enter the front rooms or use the front door or front stairs. Her world was limited to the kitchen and to the back stairs that led from the kitchen to the boys' rooms and then up to the third floor, where her room and the playroom were located.

Much as Jane and Sarah differed in how they experienced the space they both lived in, they also diverged in their conceptions of the children, the nanny job, and each other. Jane told me that her general preference was for a nanny to "feel that [the nannies are] part of a family and that we do things together and that we help each other out, versus that I sit in the living room while I expect them to take care of me." She viewed Sarah as being very close to the family, noting that the boys were more attached to Sarah after a few months than they had been to the previous nanny after almost a year. And Jane mentioned that, unlike the previous nanny, Sarah cooked and ate dinner with the family.

Sarah, in contrast, felt that her relationship with the family was uncomfortably distant. She told me that she had considered leaving, but she did not have any other employment options lined up and she was reluctant to break her one-year contract. Also, she liked Brian and Matthew: "And that's who I deal with most of the time. Jane and Peter I see ten minutes in the morning and ten minutes at night, and then I'll either go out or leave and go to my room. And they're nice to me. It's just hard coming from Dan and Karen's [her previous employers], where we would just talk, just because. Here it's just really forced. I think it's just hard for them to let somebody in." She added, "Here I don't cook. I also don't eat with them. I ate with Dan and Karen—here I don't feel comfortable enough to eat with them, I guess." These statements directly contradicted Jane's version of their relationship.[1]

The views Jane and Sarah presented of Sarah's duties and what tasks family members were responsible for doing also diverged. Jane saw Sarah's job as primarily caring for the children and "helping around the house." She told me she did not want the job to be a "housekeeping job with some kids on the side." She expected Sarah to do the family's laundry and ironing, to straighten up the house daily (including cleaning Matthew's room and supervising Brian as he cleaned his own), and to do a thorough house cleaning twice a month (for which she paid Sarah extra). Jane's depiction of Sarah's housekeeping responsibilities was couched in a language of mutual respect, and of fairness and reciprocity ("I don't want someone to feel like a maid. . . . I will say, 'You're part of the family. I will do your dishes; I expect you to do mine too.'")

This vision of a family whose members all pitch in to do their share of the work did not align with Sarah's daily experience. Sarah told me that she *did* feel like a maid. Describing how challenging it was to teach Matthew to pick up and put away his toys, she noted ruefully that his parents "don't make him pick up anything. Of course, they don't pick up anything either [*laughs*]. Neither does Brian." According to Sarah, the notion that Brian cleaned his room and made his bed was a family myth: "It's usually a mess. Sometimes I leave it . . . but sometimes I just can't stand it and I have to do it myself. But they don't make him clean it up."

It was up to Sarah to choose between doing battle with the children over their chores or doing them herself.

Differences in how Sarah and Jane perceived and reacted to the children's behavior made it seem as though they cared for different sets of boys. Jane's son Brian always made his bed and cleaned his room; Sarah's charge Brian rarely did, and usually responded to her "Is your room clean?" questions with "Yeah, clean enough." Sarah described Matthew as a "big-time whiner"; generally, she told him that he could either "talk normally or go to his room." His parents, she said, "just listen to it. I don't know how they stand it, but the kid just whines all day on Saturday and Sunday."

Sarah may have viewed the boys' behavior more negatively than Jane did in part because her job required that she be the "dirty-work parent" all week. The drudgery of mothering fell to her: the cleaning, laundry, and ironing; the daily conflicts with the boys over discipline, chores, and naps. Jane, in contrast, did most of her mother-work on weekends, when there were mainly fun activities, such as family outings, and lots of playtime. Weekends did not include naptime for Matthew, for instance. According to Sarah, this meant that he was "tired the rest of the week." Jane had a different perspective. She described Matthew as a child who "needs a lot of sleep. . . . He still naps two, three hours per day." She never mentioned a difference between his weekend and weekday schedules. Jane's share of the mother-work seemed to consist mainly of the joy of having children with little of the irritation (in this, her role was similar to that traditionally filled by fathers).

In thinking about why Jane and Sarah gave conflicting accounts of the life they shared, I realized that the two women had different sets of needs and different agendas for divvying up the work of mothering Matthew and Brian. Jane wanted an extension of herself—a shadow self. She wanted someone who would stay home while she was at work and perform the tasks she would perform if she were there. And she wanted that someone to fade into the background when she returned home. "If I'm home," she told me, "I like to be in charge of the situation. And I like my kids and I like playing with them, and I don't need to hire somebody else to do that. . . . [I]f I'm at work, then someone else is responsible. And I don't want to have to worry about it." In practice, not worrying about the home front meant controlling it. The boys had a rigid schedule of activities that Sarah was expected to follow. In addition, Jane left her lists of chores to be completed. Jane pointed out that she appreciated "if [Sarah] can get some basic prep work done for dinner, that means as soon as I get home, I can take over and finish up." The sense that she had little autonomy, and was essentially a second set of hands who did the "prep work" for the commencement of real family life, irritated Sarah. Her previous experience as a nanny had involved both more responsibility and more freedom, and she resented her limited autonomy and authority. She said, "Jane and Peter like to run their house themselves, which, I mean, is understandable, but I don't like to have the restrictions at all." Working for her previous family had been "super—they were the best and we were just one big family. Jason had three parents instead of only two." Sarah hoped to achieve a similar relationship with Matthew and Brian. She wanted to be their third parent, not their "shadow mother." The first few months in her new position had left her discouraged, however. She said that, despite her reluctance to break her year-long contract, she planned to leave before it ended.

. . .

In July 2005, when a Manhattan building collapsed, a nanny risked her life to save the baby in her charge. The New York Times's coverage of the story reported: "It bewildered some rescue workers . . . to realize that the tiny child buried beneath a building that had just collapsed on Broadway, the one Brunilda Tirado had been calling for desperately—'My baby! My baby!'—was not Ms. Tirado's child at all. But scores of her fellow nannies, who spend their days caring for other people's children, were surprised by their surprise."[2] A nanny interviewed for the story explained that Ms. Tirado's actions were normal: "These children are your babies because you are their parents all day . . . and when I go out the door, they become their parents' again."[3] The nannies who participated in my study were incensed by the kind of "bewilderment" reported in this and similar stories. It made them angry that women who failed as caregivers made front-page news, while those who were deeply attached to the children they took care of, like Ms. Tirado, were viewed as aberrations or were simply overlooked.[4] Like the nannies quoted in the New York Times, they were strongly attached to the children they looked after; they often referred to these youngsters as "theirs," and to themselves not as substitute parents, but as "third parents."

The fifty nannies and au pairs I interviewed had no interest in being the "shadow mothers" their employers desired. Instead, they tried to redefine their work in a way that dignified it.[5] For many, this meant identifying with and defending a mothering model; nannies argued that maternal care at home was best for young children, and that through their work they were approximating the ideal form of childrearing. For a few, primarily caregivers who were white and came from middle-class backgrounds, it meant aligning themselves with a teaching model as a way of "professionalizing" their work.[6] Most of the nannies I spoke with selected elements from both models as they struggled to attain third-parent status.[7]

During interviews, caregivers consistently articulated the same basic desires: autonomy and recognition for both their skill as childcare providers and the value of their attachment to the children in their care. They wanted a degree of autonomy in their jobs. That is, they wanted to be viewed as individuals performing a distinct role in the family, not as nearly invisible extensions of the mother. They wanted recognition for their skill as childcare workers, and they believed that they should be treated as skilled workers. Last, they wished that their employers would value the deep attachments they formed to the specific children in their care. They felt that the amount of time and energy they invested in their employers' children gave them a degree of expertise, not only in childcare, but in the care of *particular* children. When they spoke of wanting to be the third parent, nannies and au pairs meant that they wanted to be a valued, if transient, member of the family team in raising the children. They were not seeking literal parental status. Lacking a socially acceptable term for individuals who love young children for pay, however, they fell back on the language of parenthood.

This chapter explores the third-parent ideal by focusing on the three work characteristics identified by caregivers as most important to them and explaining why these basic job-related desires were so infrequently met.

AUTONOMY

For the nannies and au pairs I interviewed, the wish for recognition as mother-workers started with a desire for the basic level of autonomy, respect, and acknowledgment of personhood that is accorded most adult employees.[8] These needs conflicted directly with those of their employers (see chapters 5 and 6). Mother-employers wanted to monitor and control the home front, and they wanted to have nannies act as extensions of themselves rather than as autonomous caregivers.[9] These desires could lead to the imposition of rules focused so exclusively on the child that their potential impact on the caregiver never came into consideration. For example, when Kristina, a Scandinavian au pair, complained of the indignity of being tethered to the house for twelve hours a day, she noted that her employer's concern was limited to the perceived needs of "the baby": "Because they think, when I just have the baby, where can I go with a baby? He doesn't need to go anywhere."

Shadow motherhood requires that the caregiver protect the mother's primary-parent status. In some extreme cases, this resulted in restrictions that made a nanny superfluous. Marjorie, a twenty-five-year-old British au pair, described her experiences with a highly controlling previous employer this way: "I could only go around the block. I couldn't go anywhere else with the child. I couldn't get the baby dressed in the morning. She wanted to do absolutely all that. She wanted to prepare his formula. . . . Bath times she wanted to herself because obviously she thought she was missing out." The baby also slept for long blocks of time each morning and afternoon, so Marjorie felt she had no job: "I felt completely useless because I couldn't do anything." This story is unusual in that few nannies had to contend with the problem of too little work, but it is also representative in that most nannies felt they were deprived of the childcare tasks that they considered most meaningful and fulfilling.

Some complained about employers who gradually added more and more housework to the list of their job responsibilities without acknowledging how these additional tasks might affect the quality of childcare they were able to provide. Caregivers wanted their employers to understand that housekeeping needed to be scheduled separately from childcare, and that it required extra pay. Chantal told me that when her employers started squeezing in extra work for her to do during the baby's naptime ("as the baby's asleep, you can iron these shirts"), she found the new demands difficult to meet. Implicit in her frustration is the nanny's sense of the hierarchy of domestic work and the fact that housework was generally not in their contracts, but also her allegiance to intensive mothering as a work ethic. The baby cried when she put him down in his crib, so she preferred to let him sleep in her arms. "He's screaming and crying and I don't want to leave him there like that, so I don't do the laundry," she said. Other nannies did not mind cooking or cleaning *if* they were able to schedule it around the children's needs and *if* they were paid extra for doing this additional work.

Nannies also resented the loss of autonomy that resulted from employers' constant monitoring and scripting of their activities (see chapter 5). Most nannies expected parents to give guidelines and to suggest play dates or activities. But once they had received the general parameters of their workday, caregivers wanted to work without constantly having to report on how the work was proceeding. Lura spoke for the majority when she described her feelings about the midday check-in phone call: "But if I was changing his diaper, I wouldn't leave him on the changing table, so I wouldn't answer the phone. She would run home if I didn't answer the phone 'cause she was only a couple blocks away. 'Oh my god. You didn't answer.' . . . And I said, 'I was changing his diaper. I'm not gonna leave him laying on the changing table to answer the phone. He could fall off and hurt himself.' . . . [A]fter [I explained] that, she would wait five minutes and call back again. That was just really hard." Lura could identify with her employer's desire for knowledge and long-distance involvement, "I don't blame her. . . . I would want to know, too, if I was working." But she also believed that if a mother chose to work, she should accept the reality of another individual in charge of her home and her family during the workday.

The desire for autonomy and recognition as skilled workers made the "journal requirement" seem especially burdensome to most caregivers. Ten of the employers I interviewed explicitly stated that they expected the nanny to keep a detailed journal of the day's activities with their infants and toddlers. Chantal described what her employer wanted her to write down concerning the two children in her care, ages one and two: "What we played, what we ate, what he didn't eat; if they slept, how long; if they were angry. . . . Look, when you come here from another country, it seems like she's just crazy. . . . I thought no, she doesn't trust me. [Eventually], I said, 'Look, I don't have time.' Listen, how am I going to remember little details. If they cried, if they fell, if they ate, how many sips of milk or juice [*laughs*]. So I said to myself, 'Why am I going to do this if I never did it with my own children?'" Of course, the fact that they were *not* her children was precisely the point of contention. Chantal wanted to be treated like a second mother to the children, with the autonomy and trust that this status entailed, but her employer wanted to supervise and to experience, even at a distance, the details of her children's upbringing. Both women's desires were understandable—but not compatible.

April, who was a bit more understanding of her employer's needs, said, "The main function of the journal was for her to make up for the fact that she wasn't around, so that she could see what had happened. Maybe Zoe said a word that she hadn't said before or things like that. But to also write down what Zoe ate just so Mom could keep a running check on whether she was getting enough food, enough of certain nutrition, that kind of stuff." As a college graduate with a Bachelor's degree in creative writing, April said laughingly, "I could definitely write," but the repetitive nature of life with a toddler challenged even her creative capacities, and April ultimately became frustrated with the effort needed to make the mundane exciting or, as she put it, creating an image of "Zoe's big day": " 'She just blew her nose!' [*laughter*] Some days, when you're working with a toddler, she'd go off and have her nap, and then you'd go to the journal and say, 'Goddamn it, she did the same thing today that she does every day because she's a toddler and they do the same thing every day!' [*laughter*] Sometimes I felt that I had to literally make up stuff to make it sound interesting because there really wasn't anything new."

Writing the daily report was more than simply tiresome and time-consuming. For most nannies, it was a concrete expression of nonpersonhood, a regular reminder that nannies were to act as their employers' hands, eyes, and ears in the home. The caregivers I interviewed rejected this characterization. They did not see themselves as mother-extensions. They were the third parent, the one who stayed at home while the other two were away at work. They lacked the autonomy and the resources to make this view of their employment a reality, however. Helene described a typical dilemma. "It was one of those days when we had all these activities. I didn't know what to fix for lunch." She had been given neither the time nor the funds to shop for groceries, so she offered the children the frozen dinners that were on hand. "The next day I got a note saying not to use the frozen foods because that's for them on the weekends. Basically saying, 'That's our convenience, not yours.'"

CONTESTED DEFINITIONS OF KNOWLEDGE
AND SKILL

The third-parent ideal also meant that nannies wanted to be recognized as skilled childcare workers. Yet, one of the most striking findings that emerged from my interviews was how rarely mothers mentioned the nanny in response to the question "whom do you ask for advice regarding your child?" Relatives, friends, pediatricians, and advice literature all figured prominently, but in mother-employers' responses, the person they employed to spend up to sixty hours per week interacting with their children was almost never included in the list.[10] The nannies and au pairs saw themselves as bringing their abundant childrearing skill, knowledge, and hands-on experience to the aid of parents as well as to the care of children. They wished that their employers would consult them about questions of discipline and care, invite them to come to parent-teacher conferences, or bring them along on visits to the pediatrician. They wanted their expertise to be acknowledged and respected.

This was not an unreasonable expectation, given that in advertisements and during interviews with job candidates, employers typically emphasized their preference for childcare providers who were experienced and, ideally, who had training in early childhood development. Yet, once having located and hired these skilled workers, mother-employers rarely consulted them. Many of the caregivers I interviewed expressed frustration that their suggestions were rarely heeded and their observations concerning the children discounted. Their employers expected them to accept a new definition of themselves, in which they were the childcare novices and their employers were the experts. As one nanny remarked, "Sometimes I feel like they don't *listen* to me. Like when the kids are having a problem and I mention it to them, sometimes I feel like it goes in one ear and out the other because they just don't want to hear it."

Whose Knowledge Counts: Effects of the Management/Worker Division of Labor

There are several reasons why employers may not want to hear what their caregivers have to say. One is related to the division of labor. Typically, in the management/worker division of labor, the person with the most hands-on experience with a given task is not the one who makes policy. Paid childcare is no exception. The separation between "head and hands" or "conception and execution" was a key reason why it was so difficult for nannies and au pairs to gain recognition for the very real skills they brought to their job.[11] Hands-on experience is a crucial source of knowledge in childcare; this type of work is resistant to general rules and abstract theories. Often the mother giving instructions had no concept of how the work got done. As Sarah remarked of her first employer's instructions, "She'd tell me to do all of these things but then not give me enough time to do them. . . . [S]he had never done these things [herself] enough to know what it took."

Nannies spend as many as sixty hours per week caring for one or more children. Through daily trial and error, they discover what works and does not work with their charges. And, like childcare workers in other settings, over time, nannies and au pairs learn that what worked with one child may not work with another, and that what worked yesterday will most likely fail tomorrow.[12] Their employers have little opportunity to acquire this level of grounded knowledge and thus can be frustratingly ignorant about the difficulties of caring for young children. For instance, Miriam, a twenty-two-year-old white college student, often felt that she was the only one in the household who really experienced the "everydayness" of life with the family's two-year-old twins. Her employers' "hour or hour and a half of being with the kids" left them living in a "bubble" in which life with the children was always easy. Miriam concluded, "I don't think the parents really believed that, but I also don't think that they would want to be shown that it wasn't so." In Lura's case, the employer's lack of experience led to the mistaken perception of a normal event in a child's life as a major emergency, and as an indication of poor care on the nanny's part. The baby in Lura's care had a cold: "And the one day when I had to suck the stuff out of his nose, of course he screamed, and she, the neighbor, called [the mother] at work and said she could hear him crying. So [the mother] came running home, and I'm like, 'You know, he's gonna cry when you do that. They don't like it.'" For the nanny, the task was unpleasant but normal; for her employer (and perhaps for the employer's neighbor), it was a crisis that warranted immediate intervention.

In addition to creating mistrust and misunderstanding, a division of labor based on the assumption that the worker has no knowledge or expertise can result in unintentionally denigrating behavior by employers. Most of the nannies and au pairs I interviewed were proud of their expertise as caregivers, whether that came from formal training, previous jobs, or having been mothers themselves. Having to listen respectfully to a long recital of instructions was trying, at best. As Rosa explained, "It was so tedious because even the most basic thing, they thought I didn't know how to do it. In other words, you know, I couldn't discuss it or say, 'Look, I have two daughters. I know what this is all about and I know how to manage a home.'" Tedium gave way to a sense of injury in some cases, such as when the knowledge the mother transmits came from the nanny in the first place: "Well, she had a second child and she stayed home for a year after she was born. And that—that was a *little* harder, because everything I had taught her with the first one, she was trying to reteach me with the second one. It wasn't like, pushy, but she would say things, and I'm like, in the back of my mind I was just thinking, 'I taught *you* that.'"

Whose Knowledge Counts: Effects of the Ideology of Intensive Mothering

Another reason why mothers, and especially first-time mothers, may not seek or even accept advice from their caregivers is because they cannot afford to do so. The logic of intensive mothering assumes that a good mother must be the most knowledgeable person concerning her own children and their needs. Indeed, the ideology of intensive mothering makes mothers morally responsible for knowing more than caregivers about the day-to-day lives of their children. This impossible-to-meet cultural demand radically reduces the chances that mother-employers will consult the women who care for their children for advice that might make the childcare situation more effective. Rather than being pleased by the prospect of drawing on a caregiver's expertise, a mother-employer may feel threatened by evidence of another person's thorough knowledge of her child.

In my study, even first-time mothers tended to have fixed ideas. April, for example, commented that her employer would "occasionally ask my opinion on certain things, but for the most part she pretty much had her mind set up on how to take care of Zoe and what she wanted done and what she didn't want [done]." Among the mothers I interviewed, fourteen of thirty had no experience caring for a young child prior to the birth of their first, and had never cared for younger siblings or any other children.[13] Nevertheless, they discounted or ignored the wealth of information their childcare workers, most of whom had been raising children all of their lives, had to offer. Instead, they tried to cope with the insecurity created by their lack of experience and their lack of control over the day-to-day aspects of their children's care by turning to advice books. They were reassured by the universal "laws" of childrearing they found in these volumes. The dictums of experts became the basis for detailed rules, which these inexperienced mother-employers then imposed on their caregivers.

In defining what constitutes adequate childrearing knowledge and who could legitimately possess it, employers unintentionally reinforce the historic trivializing of women's work in general and fortify the notion that only biological mothers can know their children. The concept of shadow motherhood assumes that nannies and au pairs do not and should not develop the kind of unique, intimate knowledge of the children in their care that their "real" mothers possess. The caregiver is intended to be a permanent understudy, not an actor in her own right. In most cases, the nannies I spoke with had been subtly advised to keep their opinions to themselves. Those who did impart information did so gingerly. Cassie was concerned that the baby in her care was developing too slowly, but because Lynn, her employer, a first-time mother who "didn't really have experience with other children," did not view her as an authority, Cassie was careful to provide key information cautiously. Lynn remained unaware that she was being taught or that Cassie was intervening on her behalf: "I used to go along with them to the pediatrician and I would either ask the doctor, or I would ask Lynn, 'Maybe you should ask the doctor about this?' Things like that." Lynn also remained unaware of the depth of her nanny's knowledge, as the need to protect her employer's sense of mothering expertise led Cassie to deliberately hide her own.

Whose Knowledge Counts: "Book Parents" and "Natural" Nannies

Finally, employers may fail to recognize the expertise of nannies and au pairs because their occupation carries little status. The low market value of caregiving work defines the knowledge that emerges from such work as of similarly little worth. Parents operate on this belief when they consult advice books instead of their nannies for information concerning their children. The mother-employers I interviewed tended to characterize their caregivers' knowledge as "instinctual" and thus of lesser value.

Childcare workers traced their knowledge and skill to a very different source. They invoked the "rationality of caring," in which knowledge is derived neither from rules and theory nor from instinct and innate capacities. Rather it is grounded, experiential knowledge, "dependent both on practical experience in caregiving work and on personal knowledge of the child in question."[14] While their employers paged through books, the nannies drew on their own "motherwit," the knowledge gained from experience, common sense, and direct interaction with individual children.[15] Caregivers vigorously championed the value of this form of knowledge.

In the playground culture of childcare workers, accusing an employer of "book parenting" was one of the greatest insults possible. Nannies and au pairs referred derisively to their employers' reliance on childrearing manuals in part because they felt that, as childcare practitioners, they offered their employers a wealth of knowledge that was ignored. Lonehl underscored this point: "The books a lot of parents go by—especially, like, first-time parents, you know, they follow it directly. And you tell them you can't follow it directly. You have to look at how the child is and feel it from there." Sarah recounted an example of a collision between book knowledge and grounded knowledge that she experienced while working for one of her first employers, who were, as she put it, "book parents, big time":

> They had read this book that said you shouldn't say "no" because it stunts the curiosity of your child. And so they were like, well, we don't want to do that, so just don't ever say "no" to him. And so it got to the point where he was just doing anything. You can't tell him not to do it, you can't tell him "no," so what they wanted me to do was just take his hands away or put something else in his hands or whatever. But if the kid's playing with the light socket, you have to say "no," you have to move him, he has to learn. So I just finally—when they weren't there, I would say "no" to him because otherwise the kid's just not going to learn. So he said the word "no" to [the parents] once. And they said, "Where did he learn the word 'no'? We weren't supposed to teach him the word 'no.'"

In the end, Sarah was able to explain to her employers why banning "no" was not a good idea, and they were able to hear and accept her advice on this issue.

Ida was less successful. A thirty-eight-year-old nanny from Trinidad with more than a decade of childcare experience as well as her own experience as a mother, she was frustrated in her efforts to help her employers clear up their two-year-old son's frequent cough. Ida believed that the parents' habit of giving the boy cold milk, taken directly from the refrigerator, when he woke in the night stimulated the production of mucous that "goes right down in your chest and gives you a cold." She offered her theory, but the parents ignored it. Ida explained that the boy's mother "reads a lot of books about childcare and stuff," and that even when they asked her opinion, the parents "don't listen to me. They just [do] their own thing, or she reads in her book and she will see something else, something to try." Voicing a complaint shared by most of her peers, Ida said, "If you didn't go to school, you don't know, even though they have you in their own house, all of a sudden you know nothing. They asked me what my training is. I told them I am a mother and so far my child has turned out fine." Like most nannies, Ida agreed that first-aid training and CPR were necessary for anyone who spent time with children, but beyond that, "you have to understand the child."

Generally, the caregivers perceived book knowledge as less reliable because it was one step removed from hands-on experience and common sense. Moreover, books could not address the unique characteristics and needs of individual children. Anne echoed the sentiments of most of the nannies I interviewed when she asserted, "If somebody has to go into a book, *Know How to Grow Your Child*, I don't think they should have [a child]—I think these things should come up naturally. I don't know how any book can prepare you for a child coming into your house. Because all the books that's been written and all the people who have had children have not dealt with this child who is coming into the world. This is going to be the first time you're going to have this experience with *this* child." Lonehl agreed: "A lot of these parents read all these books, how to do this, how to do that. A lot these people don't even have children that write these books! So, I mean, give me a break! You have to have experience more than the knowledge. You have to *be* there, not just the book-smart, you know, the actual being there. . . . You have to see how the child is. Each one is their own individual."

In their struggles over what kind of knowledge "counts," caregivers and mother-employers reinforced a male-female binary opposition that is deeply embedded in Western culture. This dualism views mothering as a "natural" female attribute, rooted in biology and involving "strong emotional attachment and altruistic motives."[16] Employers relegated their caregivers to the "female" role in their relationship by aligning caregivers with nature and innate propensities. For example, when I asked Joan if she felt that she had learned from her nanny, Melanie, about childrearing, she replied, "Maybe a little bit. I think that in some ways I am more the research, data-gathering type of person. I read everything. When I was pregnant I must have read five books about being pregnant. When I can't control something, I have to at least understand it [*laughs*] . . . whereas Melanie is more instinctual. I think that she's going to be a great mom. She wants to be a mom, she's very intuitive, very intuitive. She's a natural. Although she is trained in it, to her, I think, it is totally natural." Joan acknowledged Melanie's training in early childhood education and her skill in childrearing, but she nevertheless attributed Melanie's present and future success to her instincts and natural inclination toward caregiving.

Melanie recognized that Joan liked to do "data gathering." But, in her view, Joan substituted book knowledge for experiential knowledge: "She actually reads [child development books] monthly. Like, Charlotte is ten months, so she'll read what should happen at eleven months and kind of see what to expect. So she reads them a lot and tells me, 'Oh I read something interesting. You should read it.'" Melanie did turn to books, but only when there was a problem that was outside of her experience: "Like when Charlotte was starting foods, I just read that section; or when she was sick, I read that section."

By viewing their caregivers as the "type of person" who finds childcare gratifying, mother-employers simultaneously defined these workers as unskilled, naturally nurturing, and possessed of knowledge that, because it was instinctual, amounted to nonknowledge. As unskilled shadow mothers, nannies were expected to confine themselves to following their employers' instructions. This interpretation of their job fell far short of the third-parent ideal caregivers sought to achieve. The effort to gain recognition and respect for the work they did led the nannies and au pairs I interviewed into a difficult dilemma. If they defined themselves as being "like teachers," this negated the nurturance and altruism that they valued in their self-image as *caring* workers. If they defined themselves as being as "like mothers," this negated the very real skills they knew that they brought to the job.[17] Worse, neither definition seemed to carry weight with their employers: most of the nannies and au pairs felt that their employers devalued their contributions on both of these levels. If they had early childhood education training, it was deemed insufficient. If they had experience as mothers themselves, it was essentialized and discounted. If they developed a close bond with and understanding of the particular child they looked after, this was perceived as a threat. When mother-employers deferred to the expert advice of best-selling authors and healthcare professionals, they were effectively rendering their nannies' childcare knowledge valueless.

ATTACHMENT

As discussed in chapters 4, 5, and 6, employers generally did not endorse caregivers' strong ties to the children. Many of the nannies I interviewed, however, were frank about the depth of their attachment. Describing her relationship to

Charlotte, for example, Melanie said, "Basically, I'm like a mom to her and I give her everything she would get from a mom." Lonehl made a similar claim: "I love children, so it's like anyone I take care of is like my own, where I treat them as one of my own—which I don't have any but—one of my own like that." After describing her feeling toward the twins in her care as "total euphoria," Miriam voiced the desire for third-parent status that was evident in the remarks of many of the nannies I interviewed. She wondered out loud, "What's necessarily so special about this biological relationship between mother and child?"

The coveted third-parent status would free caregivers from having to hide or erase their love for their employers' children. But, as the nannies were careful to emphasize, they were not trying to displace or replace the biological parents. The third-parent ideal would result in children receiving *additional* love. It was not aimed at substituting the love of one adult for that of another. British au pair Margaret spoke sadly of being fired from her second job because her employer was uncomfortable with the degree of attachment between her and the children. Margaret said that she had never intended to replace the mother in the children's affections, but only to inhabit what she perceived as her own rightful place there: "You're not there to replace the mom. That was *never* my intention. I think part of [the former employer's] problem was she thought that I was trying to do that. But you're trying to be—you are trying to be like a big sister. Somebody else, another adult that they can communicate with and just be with."

Most nannies asserted with pride that they gave the children in their care more time, attention, and stimulation than they would get if they were cared for by an at-home mother. Celine, a forty-two-year-old nanny from Trinidad, summed up how most nannies evaluated their work compared to that of at-home mothers: "Where do they spend their quality time? At Wal-Mart. When I am with the kids, everywhere I go and everything I do is for them, for their enjoyment." Like their employers, these caregivers believed in the values of intensive mothering. They worked hard to ensure that the children received nonstop quality time. Sadly, many nannies who had children themselves reported doing more with their employers' children than they did with their own.

For the caregivers I interviewed, both the experience of creating and maintaining healthy bonds with children and employers' recognition of the importance of those attachments were important sources of gratification. Children's affections were often the primary currency in the childcare employment arrangement. Even if a caregiver was well treated and well paid, she felt her work was devalued if her employer did not recognize the importance of her emotional connection to the children in her care. At the same time, most mother-employers' commitment to the tenets of intensive mothering made it impossible for them to accept the possibility that their children could form a primary bond with another woman without that bond threatening their own status as good mothers. The flawed logic of the notion of zero-sum attachment cast both employer and caregiver as failures. Each felt she could value her own contributions to childrearing only by devaluing those of the other.

CONCLUSION

Caregivers wanted to be recognized as adult workers with basic rights, and as important co-participants in the rearing of a specific set of children. They also wanted to be seen as skilled workers and given the level of autonomy that they felt was on a par with the degree of responsibility their jobs entailed. All three of these components of the third-parent ideal were equally essential to most caregivers. Most, however, did not receive this kind of recognition or the autonomy that would naturally accompany it. Many were locked into a schedule and a set of rules that had been predetermined by their employers. As Lupe noted, "The mother can change her mind and I can't." Caregivers were left with little room to adjust to the needs of the moment or to consult their own feelings or the moods and desires of their charges: "I was a nervous wreck some days with that silly schedule," April complained.

By contrast, Sarah described the autonomy and freedom she experienced at her favorite job this way: "At Dan and Karen's, when I got there they set up a house account in my name. And they just put money in it, and any time we needed anything, if the baby went to a new size of clothes and needed new undershirts, I would go out and buy them for him. . . . I mean I did everything, and I liked it . . . and having the freedom to do what you want when you wanted made it better." Sarah worked sixty to seventy hours per week and did all the housework, errands, cooking, and a host of other "motherly" duties. She viewed the loss of delineated on-duty and off-duty time and the resulting extra work she performed as a fair exchange for the autonomy and recognition she received as the "third parent" in the family.

The shadow-mother imperative is inherently self-defeating because it precludes mutual learning and information sharing, and because it is based on an assumption of zero-sum attachment. Yet the third-parent ideal has its own self-defeating characteristics. As the next chapter explains, many of the resistance strategies caregivers used involved taking on more work and responsibility in their employers' homes, not less. In the search for recognition, many assumed the role of shadow mother wholeheartedly. In these cases, striving for the third-parent ideal led to the creation of yet another fiction. Employers who wanted to believe they were omnipresent tried to transform their caregivers into shadow mothers. Employees who wanted to believe that their work was recognized and valued acted as though they were indeed mothers to the children in their care. This game of pretend, as some nannies discovered, was a fiction that could prove emotionally and financially costly.

8

Nanny Resistance Strategies

On a warm day in October in a large playground, I sat on a bench with three nannies: Anne, a documented immigrant from Jamaica; Penelope, a mixed-race former au pair from Britain; and Lonehl, a Boston resident whose family had long ago emigrated from Barbados. I recruited a number of the nannies who participated in my study by "hanging out" in the park, getting to know them, and listening to their "bitch sessions."[1] This was the third time I had spent the afternoon with this group. As we sat swapping snacks and taking turns caring for their five charges, I asked if I could tape-record our conversation. They agreed. Lonehl spoke first: "Some of the jobs I interviewed for, it's like they want you to work fifty, sixty hours a week and they want to pay you eight dollars, and they're taking out taxes. You're getting nothing and you're killing yourself being tired from the long hours. And then they want you to clean on top of it—and they don't want to pay you [extra]."

Anne broke in: "The worst story I heard, we met a girl here, she was from Africa. She was a live-in. Now live-in, you're supposed to be entitled to some free time off, but she worked around the clock and the lady only paid her five dollars an hour! Five kids and the cleaning. . . . And they were, like, high profile, too." Anne explained that undocumented immigrants like the one she described faced the worst injustices because their employers often prevented them from developing the kind of social networks that could help them. "She came to the park and we were all sitting around and the lady [her boss] saw her. And the lady didn't let her come to the park anymore. Wouldn't let her talk to us, because, you know, . . . we would have told her, 'That's not right.'" Anne added that the placement agencies "should do the same kinds of background checks on the parents that they do on the nannies, because you could wind up with some crazy people." "Uh huh, tell me about it," the others said, agreeing that crazy employers were a very real possibility.

When I asked the group about their own jobs, the responses varied. Anne said her employers paid her well and "they really go out of their way to please me. Sometimes I just think, you know, they love the children this much that they are going to make my life a heaven, you know?" But when Penelope interrupted, reminding Anne about "the beginning" of her job, she acknowledged that "when they were smaller, they were very difficult children" and that her employer did not warn her before she took the job that the babies "were just constantly crying and stuff."

Lonehl cut in, explaining, "They weren't on a schedule. [Their mother] didn't put them on a schedule." This comment led into a long discussion of the flaws of wealthy parents—their unwillingness to discipline their children, their failure to set boundaries—and how nannies generally had to make up for these lapses. Lonehl described a typical scenario that involved her employer's battles with her then three-year-old daughter: "Me and Chloe had an understanding. I'm the boss; she listens to me. She's only three years old. So [the mom] would call me and say, 'How do you get her down for a nap?'" Laughing, Lonehl added, "But I mean, she'll call me and ask my advice, which I appreciate." The conversation halted for a few minutes while Anne ministered to one of the three-year-old twins in her care, who had fallen while playing near the sandbox. Her tears blotted, the little girl snuggled happily on Anne's lap and Lonehl resumed talking.

"It's like having your own children," she said. "I mean, you can go anywhere you want to go. You're out in the fresh air. You can basically do what you wanna do."

"Well," Penelope countered, "you have to ask. Tomorrow I will take him probably to the aquarium, or maybe this or that. But if he was mine, I would probably take him a lot further, and do some things that I need to do, you know what I mean?"

Anne agreed: "The truth is, I do more [child-centered activities] with these babies than I do with mine. That's the God's honest truth."

"Mmm-hmmm. There you go," Penelope concurred, underscoring the distinction between having her own children and being on her own clock, and taking care of someone else's children and being on *their* clock.

Then, addressing Lonehl, who was now holding Chloe on her lap while the little girl munched on grapes from the snack bag, Penelope said, "But your situation is different. They come to you for advice. What I'm saying is, this is my *job*, Lonehl, and if they told me what to do with him, whether it's juice or milk or water—he's not my kid. I'm gonna do that."

"Hmmmf. I do what's right for Chloe," sniffed Lonehl.

"Yeah, well, we all know who wears the pants in *that* family," laughed Anne, implying that Lonehl ran her employer's household.

Penelope held her ground: "At the end of the day, this is my job. He's not my child. If they're going to tell me to do one thing, I'm not going to do the other, you know?"

Changing the topic slightly, I asked, "Do you find you get attached to the children?" Characteristically, Lonehl responded first. With Chloe still in her lap, she mused, "She's about to turn four, and I've been with her since she was eighteen months. And they pick up your traits so easy. . . . You know, like, when I'm joking, I'll say, 'Yeah, beat it, Chloe.' And the other day she says to her mother, 'Yeah, beat it, Ma!'"

Anne drew a distinction between the love she felt for the children in her care and her feelings about her own children. Referring to the latter, she swore, "Not even death can separate me and them. I think [my employers] respect me because of how I am about my own children."

Penelope said, "Well, how can you not fall in love with them if you like children and you're with them every day? And you know, they really can't, they really shouldn't . . . ," she said, trailing off into silence.

"What?" Anne prodded. "Get jealous of you? It shows, if the child is coming to you more, obviously you're doing your job. They should be happy, but you see, some women, I guess, don't think about that."

. . .

As discussed in chapter 7, the caregivers who participated in this study sought two types of recognition from their employers: recognition of their expertise as skilled childcare practitioners with extensive knowledge developed through experience, and recognition of the important contribution they made by forming strong bonds with the children in their care. Their employers, however, often ignored their advice, were dismissive of their expertise, and felt threatened rather than pleased by the degree of attachment they forged with the children. The childcare workers described in this chapter therefore worked in what I call a "recognition deficit," meaning that they received little or no recognition or validation for the aspects of their work that they most valued.[2] This prompted many of the nannies I spoke with to engage in various forms of resistance. Some forms were overt, like leaving the job or confronting employers. Actions like these were less available to nannies than to other types of domestic or childcare workers, however, because of nannies' greater dependence on references and because of their devotion to the children in their care.

More often, nannies used covert forms of resistance, such as secretly breaking rules they perceived to be unreasonable. Many indulged in forms of wishful thinking, such as imagining that their impact on the children would be lasting no matter how brief their tenure. Perhaps most detrimentally, when nannies could not achieve the goal of third-parent status, they often compensated by overachieving: they threw themselves into enacting all of the ideals of intensive mothering. They conducted covert "competency contests" with their employers in which the goal was to "out-mother the mother." They were determined to demonstrate, at least to themselves, that they could care more, be present more, and, in some cases, sacrifice more for the children than their employers could.

The work ethic of nannies and au pairs and their employers' needs inevitably collided. Market conditions and other structural aspects of childcare providers' jobs contributed to this conflict (see chapter 3), but so too did the competing cultural demands the mother-employers struggled to meet. To succeed simultaneously in their male-pattern careers and in their role as intensive mothers, they had to juggle the very different and sometimes incompatible sets of expectations associated with the two realms (see chapter 2). The nannies' work and home lives were in closer ideological alignment: they embraced most aspects of intensive mothering in both worlds. As a result, they often compensated for their employers' seeming inability to mother the way the nannies believed they would if they had similarly ample financial resources. Viewing their employers as falling short of the "ideal mothering" mark only increased the caregivers' frustration that their own devotion to the children of their employers was undervalued, unacknowledged, or misunderstood as a threat.

The forms of resistance nannies engaged in directly countered the anger, frustration, and sadness they felt at not being recognized as individuals who were making a unique contribution to family life, at being forbidden autonomy, at being refused the dignity of having their work perceived as skilled, and at being denied the gratification of recognition for their value to the children. In response to the denial of their personhood, they quit; in response to their lack of autonomy, they made their own rules; in response to the denial of their skill, they engaged in competency contests; in response to the demand that they hide their attachment to the children in their care, they tried to make a lasting emotional mark in the children's lives.

THE DIFFICULTIES OF OVERT RESISTANCE: QUITTING BEFORE THE CONTRACT ENDS

Other studies of nannies and domestics have found that often when these workers are dissatisfied, they simply quit. They may leave abruptly after a "blowup" with an employer or, less dramatically, they may call in sick one day and never return to work. These studies, though, included women in a range of employment situations—some worked for at-home mothers; some were housekeepers whose responsibilities included childcare "on the side" when school-aged children returned home in the afternoon. The nannies and au pairs I interviewed worked full-time caring for infants and preschoolers in their parents' absence. Those who are entrusted with all-day care of very young, vulnerable children typically must have impeccable references if they are to find future employment. Unlike maids, housekeepers, and mother's helpers, these caregivers also tend to develop ties to the children that may keep them in jobs they otherwise would be likely to leave.[3]

Of course, sometimes poor working conditions can force care-workers to break both emotional and legal ties. Among the women I interviewed, when quitting was the only option, the native-born nannies and documented immigrants had the easiest time finding new jobs. If they had good references, good English, and working papers, another job was usually just around the corner. Au pairs faced greater difficulties because, locked into a one-year contract with a particular agency, they were limited to families already enrolled with their host agency, and most families were reluctant to take on a "tarnished" au pair or one with less than one year remaining on her visa.[4] Undocumented immigrants had the most limited options, given that they were restricted to word-of-mouth referrals and that many employers preferred not to hire them for childcare-only jobs. The worst employers were notorious for preventing their undocumented nannies from frequenting the more popular parks and playgrounds for fear that they would learn of new job opportunities through the local nanny network.[5] Some undocumented nannies described employers who threatened to report them to the U.S. Immigration and Naturalization Service, which might deport them. Faced with few options and dire threats, they often stayed in unpleasant jobs.

Most unhappy caregivers, however, stayed in their miserable jobs because of a combination of worry about references and guilt about abandoning the children. The task of summoning up an explanation for leaving that was at once reasonable and inoffensive enough to insure a good recommendation could be daunting, as April reported: "Well, the nanny before me said that she was being stalked by her boyfriend. I don't know. I hypothesized many times over the course of my job that this may have been a fictitious way of comfortably leaving the job. I questioned my own ability to make such a story up [laughs]. 'Being stalked' is out now, and I guess 'life-threatening disease' is going to have to go on [laughs]." Despite her cynicism, April, like other nannies, was ever-conscious of the fact that she was dependent on the goodwill of former employers for future jobs. Most tried to maintain civil relations even in departing.

COVERT RESISTANCE

Not all the nannies I interviewed disliked their employers or their employers' husbands. In fact, twenty-eight of the fifty caregivers said that they liked some of their employers, or at least grew to like them. But when a relationship went sour, or when it was unpleasant to begin with, the power dynamics inherent in the domestic service relationship made it difficult for nannies to confront their employers directly. Most disgruntled nannies and au pairs did not quit. They stayed in jobs that made them unhappy and coped by using subtle forms of covert resistance.[6] Derogatory comments, mockery, gossip, and caricature carried out "behind the scenes" are common resistance strategies that individuals with little power rely on in order to maintain a sense of self-respect.[7] Nannies and au pairs resorted to each of these from time to time, as bitch sessions in the park showed.

Retaliating through Talk

Local parks and playgrounds and meetings provided impromptu forums for bitch sessions in which caregivers compared notes about their employers' parenting styles, housekeeping habits, and personal foibles. Au pair agencies also arranged more structured meetings that performed the same function—gatherings hosted by local coordinators at which au pairs could share stories and provide mutual support. Whether scheduled or spontaneous, however, caregivers' get-togethers served a purpose beyond airing grievances. They helped keep nannies in their jobs. Julie explained that "we get together and complain about our bosses and our kids and after you do it you feel so much better. We have [au pair meetings] once a week and then we can go on for the rest of the week."

These meetings served the dual purpose of providing recognition for how hard childcare providers worked and reassuring them that no matter how difficult they found their job, there was someone else who had it worse. Every get-together provided a chance to talk about or listen to a tale about a true "nightmare" employer. The horror stories recounted in these discussions almost never involved nannies who were present. They usually were about a nanny the speakers had heard of or, sometimes, had met. The bitch sessions invariably concluded with the nannies deciding that no matter how unreasonable their employers might be, compared to others, *they* were the lucky ones and thus were better off staying in their current jobs. Still, they found covert ways to retaliate, which made bad jobs bearable.

Retaliating through Subterfuge

Some nannies engaged in subterfuge as a form of covert retaliation. Pilar, a twenty-one-year-old immigrant from El Salvador, for example, complained that her employer tried to prevent her from eating food she prepared and served to the children. Pilar recalled her dismay when each day she would arrive at her employer's home to find that whatever she had eaten for lunch with the children the day before was now hidden: "You sit with their kids ten to eleven hours, but if you eat something today, they hide it tomorrow." One day, one of the children had a play date. Pilar wanted to offer snacks to the children, but she could not find anything suitable. When she asked where the snacks were, the boy she was taking care of replied, "My mom hid [them] away from you." So she told the children there would be no snacks that day. Then she resolved to eat just a little bit of everything each day, reasoning that if the mother continued to hide the food that Pilar had eaten, the family would eventually have no food in the house.

Retaliating through Breaking and Remaking Rules

Nannies and au pairs who perceived their employers' guidelines as arbitrary, unnecessary, or unfair often resorted to covertly breaking the rules or to making their own. Even the most careful rule-breaker risked the possibility of getting caught, however, so having a defensible excuse at the ready was important. Christine circumvented her employer's no-nap rule by letting Courtney sleep while she drove her around in the car. Dozing in a car seat, Christine rationalized, did not really constitute an official nap. Scandinavian au pair Kristina finally broke the no-car, no-socializing rule her employer imposed by walking with the baby into town or over to a friend's house. She confessed somewhat guiltily, "I have started to know another au pair in the neighborhood, and so I just go and see her." When I asked if her employer knew this, Kristina said no. She said she felt especially bad about these visits because the child the other au pair cared for was one year older. This made the idea that the socializing was "for the good of the children" a dangerously weak excuse. Nonetheless, Kristina continued her secret visits, relieved at last to "have a grown-up of my own age to talk to."

When they chose to ignore their employers' rules, nannies had to make complex calculations, weighing a prohibition they perceived as unfair or unrealistic against the fear of getting caught and against their own sense of what constituted good childcare. Valerie described this mix when she explained her approach to the "no snack after 3:30" rule. Although she hoped to avoid spoiling the children's appetites for dinner, she sometimes broke the rule because she could never be sure what time the parents would be home for dinner. Meanwhile, the "children were starving. . . . The kids are, like, 'Valerie, I'm hungry, I'm hungry.' If I tell them, 'dinner's soon' and then they come back in five minutes, then I know they're really hungry and I'll give them something, but I make them have a glass of water or something to fill them up, 'cause I know if their mom found out they had half a cookie, she might freak out."

Sometimes nannies disciplined the children in their care, even when they knew that the parents might not approve. After growing tired of trying to get Kirsten's parents to discipline their disrespectful three-year-old, Corinne took matters into her own hands:

We were walking home and we're talking and then I happened to say that something was smelling really bad. And [Kirsten] said, "It's you." And I said, "What did you say?" She said, "I didn't mean it." I said, "Kirsten, what you said was wrong. I'm not going to take it. In your room. I'm not going to talk to you. Let's just go on home." So on the way home, she's getting tired and complaining, "It was a joke." I said, "I don't take that kind of joke. You do *not* insult *anybody*." And she's walking and complaining. I said, "Complain all you want. People can see." She doesn't like to be embarrassed. So finally she gave in and [said], "I'm sorry." Then I carried her home and she fell asleep. I didn't tell her parents that. It's, like, because I figured, "Hey, she learned her lesson with me. She was never going to do that again."

In disciplining Kirsten, Corinne was both setting a limit concerning the type of behavior she would accept and compensating for what she perceived as the poor upbringing provided by the child's parents. The latter could have serious long-term repercussions, Corinne pointed out: "If she doesn't learn how to act around people, she'll never have any friends."

Although some might interpret the conflict Corinne described as a form of racist devaluation of the nanny, Corinne did not view it as such. Among the caregivers I interviewed, women of color such as Corinne were no more likely to be poorly treated in their jobs than white women were. Generally, children's behavior toward their caregivers was based on the children's age and on subtle signals transmitted by parents concerning acceptable and unacceptable behavior. Undocumented immigrants, however, were less likely than other nannies to risk making their own rules because they had so few employment options. Corinne had working papers. She left this job not long after the incident she described, and she found a better position despite Kirsten's parents' refusal to give her a positive reference. Kirsten's next nanny would become the child's eighth caregiver in three years.

Setting limits concerning what rules they would and would not follow was one way nannies and au pairs tried to establish a sense of personal dignity and autonomy on the job. All rules were not equal, however. Some could not be broken. All of the caregivers I spoke with were very clear about these distinctions. For example, a few nannies mentioned that they had been brought up to believe that spanking was an acceptable form of punishment, and they indicated that they probably would spank their own children if they felt the situation warranted that. The same nannies were also adamant that in disciplining the children in their care, they would never use a method that did not have the parents' explicit approval. They recognized their employers' right to set certain policies concerning childcare, and they followed these whether they personally believed in them or not. If the parents believed in "time-out," for instance, then time-out was the disciplinary method the nanny would use. In my many hours of observing nannies in homes and parks, I never saw anyone physically discipline a child.

Caregivers were torn between trying to find dignity in setting their own rules and their competing desire for belonging and being recognized as a family member with a special role to play and with specific rights and responsibilities consonant with that role. They wanted to behave like stay-at-home moms, acting in response to the children's varied and spontaneous needs rather than adhering to a rigid employer-imposed schedule. Usually, nannies and au pairs described their wish to break the rules, impose new ones, or depart from a schedule as being for the children's benefit rather than their own. Yet, for both caregivers and their employers, more was at stake. Most parents were unable to forgo drawing up detailed rules or daily schedules since to do so would mean surrendering their sense of being in control of their children's care (see chapters 4–6). Nannies could not always follow the rules or adhere to the schedules because to do so made them feel trapped, undercut their dignity as adult workers, or violated their sense of appropriate care for the children.

COMPETENCY CONTESTS

The primary way in which caregivers (and other domestic workers) maintain a sense of their own worth is by developing a fine-tuned "consciousness of the other" that acts as a buffer against both specific and generalized pressures to assume a subordinate position in their employers' households.[8] When their employers refused to recognize them as skilled workers, nannies and au pairs engaged in overt or covert competency contests. They used their intimate knowledge of their employers' lives, and specifically of their parenting techniques, as a framework within which they reinterpreted their own work and defined their self-worth. For nannies and au pairs, consciousness of the other generally involved a contest over which adult—the caregiver or the mother-employer—had the superior parenting skill. Sometimes these competency contests were conducted secretly, with only the caregiver keeping score; more often, they were fodder for lively discussions at playgrounds and parks.

Nannies and au pairs valued and dignified their work by contrasting themselves with their employers. Helene complained that her employer never called to warn her when she would be late, and she never paid her overtime. In Helene's view, this was more than an inconvenience, more than a denial of adult autonomy, and more than financial exploitation. It was a violation of basic principles of good mothering. Her employer would arrive home so late that "the kids would be in bed." Helene was distressed by this behavior. She concluded that this mother "probably [was] having an affair. . . . I hate to say it, but what could she possibly be doing that much?" A workday that extended until 10 p.m. would not have seemed either surprising or suspicious to most of the mother-employers I interviewed. Their nannies, however, saw this degree of commitment to work as clear evidence of a lack of maternal devotion.

Most nannies judged some if not all of their employers as helpless and incompetent. Sarah was typical in her complaint that her employers spoiled her hard work during the workweek by not following through with agreed-on childrearing strategies on nights and weekends. "I spend so much time with them," she said, "but no matter how much time I spend with them, it's corrupted every night, you know? It just goes backwards." She described her struggle to potty train Matthew: "They want me to do it, but they don't help me with it at all. So I work with him all week, and on Monday it turns out that all weekend he hasn't used the potty at all, he hasn't worn training pants at all, and he's been in a diaper all weekend, because they don't want to take the time to help him. So I have to start from scratch." Unlike her employer, Sarah was willing and did in fact repeatedly "take the time to help" the children. In making this observation, she gave herself the recognition she was denied by the family. In addition, through comparison and consciousness of the other, she was able to define her work as skilled, and to see *herself* as the expert concerning her employer's children.

Class differences played a role in how caregivers viewed their employers, and the nannies I interviewed were aware of this. They diffused their resentment over having their views ignored or devalued by categorizing all those who employ in-home caregivers as a certain "type." For example, Lonehl said that she had never had a problem with an employer herself, but in general she had little respect for the class of parents who hired nannies: "All these professional people, they want to have kids, and to me it's just for the—what is it called—like the picturesque family, the two-point-five kids, the—you know—two cars, two fish, three dogs, whatever. And then they hire someone to come in and take care of their kids." Competency contests rooted in class-based differences often took the form of a statement of class pride. Nannies and au pairs would insist that no one from their family, or from their socioeconomic background, would need hired help. Recalling her family life in Jamaica, Anne said, "My mother had six of us. And she did a damn good job . . . raising us by herself while my daddy was over here making money." Lonehl pointed out that although there were fifteen children in her family, "You know, my aunties and them, they never hire nobody. And then these people with one and two children act like it's, like, hell to raise their kids, so they bring a nanny in and want the nanny to do everything."

The most common form of competency contest involved caregivers pointing out that the children behaved better for them than for their parents. Generally, they did not interpret the difference in behavior the way childrearing experts frequently do: that is, that children display their frustration over parental absences by misbehaving when their parents return home. Nor did the nannies accept the other traditional explanation, that children are more relaxed with their parents and thus feel free to act out more. They simply viewed themselves as more skilled at childrearing. For example, Rosa described with pride how she got the three-year-old in her care to eat a full meal when his mother could not: "I gave him anything. That is, his dinner, which was chicken, rice, and a salad. There was no problem. He ate everything. When his parents came . . . 'No, I don't want that!' If there was chicken he wanted meat; if there was meat he wanted chicken. In other words, everything that was the opposite of what we had on the table, and because his mother wanted to please him, she would try and make six different things. [*flabbergasted tone*] She would show him all six things."

Like many other nannies, Rosa perceived her employer as too lenient. Moreover, like Sarah, she found that her employer's poor childrearing skills effectively undid the good work she did with the child during the day. "This would hold me back and ruin what I had tried to do beforehand . . . and I would tell her, 'This is not right, Margo.' At first I didn't say anything, until afterwards, with time, I told her it wasn't good. That he did it just to get her attention." Although this employer never listened to her advice, Rosa told me with obvious satisfaction that at least, "She doesn't [tell me what to do] anymore [*laughs*]. . . . When she realized that maybe he ate better with me than her, or that he expressed himself better, or that he just was better with me, he didn't get upset or have a temper tantrum, she stopped supervising me." Her employer's reversal served as de facto recognition of Rosa's superior childrearing abilities.

Most nannies argued that they were more consistent than their employers. As Colleen said, "I stick to my word." This split between the lenient parent and the consistent nanny may be rooted in the childcare division of labor, since that assigns the "dirty work" of childrearing to the latter and the "fun time" to the former (see chapter 6). Melanie, who was unusual in her accepting attitude toward being given the role of disciplinarian, pointed out that parents' limited time with their children made them feel "guilty" and thus reluctant to "get mad and mean it." They did not want the precious hours they had with their children to be spent fighting with them: "I think it's easier for me. . . . I don't mind if that's the way it ends up. I think for them, they're going through all their guilt of working, guilt of not being around, so I don't think they really want to be disciplining her. Plus, I think also they're just too nice. I don't think that they know how to discipline and mean it—like, get mad, you know, and mean it. . . . [I]t might be easier [for me] because I've done it as a teacher, I've done it as a babysitter." Practice, Melanie suggested, makes perfect. As the primary (and sometimes the only) rule enforcer in a family, nannies quickly gained expertise as disciplinarians. In childrearing competency contests, they touted their ability to discipline effectively as a sign of their skill, and they often accused employers of hypocrisy concerning discipline and limit setting. "They [parents] want you to come in and do this," Lonehl said, "and when you have to set limits—you know, watch TV all times of the day? No, I don't think so!—and then they say, 'No, don't make the kids upset,' and this and that. But kids want limits. You let them do whatever they want, they feel that you don't care. They need limits, period. No matter what, they need [consistent limits]." Although most nannies resented being cast in the bad-guy role, they relished the sense of authority and expertise that came with effective limit setting. By being the weekday parent, they acquired superior skills and they had the satisfaction of knowing that they, at least, were not hypocrites when it came to discipline.[9]

Framing competency contests in terms of the parents' shift versus their shift was another way in which nannies and au pairs sidestepped direct confrontation over parenting decisions they disagreed with and lax approaches to children's behavior problems. Like their employers, caregivers divided childcare into shifts, and if there was no two-way communication and consensus concerning day-to-day childrearing issues, they were determined to at least protect the smooth flow of their own shift. Pilar explained this strategy when she noted, with some resignation, "Look, in my presence the girls were always well behaved. When she [the employer] came home, it was no longer my responsibility."

Some caregivers also actively worked to compensate for what they perceived as their employers' inability to meet their children's needs. For example, Elsa, a twenty-year-old au pair from Sweden, found herself in the middle of her employers' divorce midway through her year as the family's au pair. She stayed in the family home with the three older children and their father, Robert. Our interview, however, took place at the new home of Shelly, the children's mother, where Elsa spent her days off. She explained that she missed the baby, Marisa, who lived with Shelly, and that she wanted to be available for the older children if they needed to talk. She said she had told Robert that she had decided to use her free time this way "because I love the kids and I want to spend time with her [Shelly]." Elsa admitted that her friends think she is crazy ("It's your day off and you visit your kids!"). But she defended her decision, citing a combination of self-interest (she got to be with Marisa) and a job-related sense of responsibility for protecting the well-being of all the children.

Not surprisingly, Elsa's decision to work in both households created problems between her divorcing employers: "He told her, 'Elsa is on my side.' And she said, 'No, she's not. She respects me.' But I'm on the kids' side, and they [the parents] know it. They know that their problem, the whole thing about the separation and the divorce, is their problem. I just want to make it easier for the kids." For Elsa, protecting the children's well-being went beyond her normal workweek, and beyond her typical duties. At the time of our interview, she was helping both parents interview and hire a new au pair who would take her place when her year in the United States ended.

Childcare experts generally frown on caregivers' strategies of resistance. Ellen Galinsky, for instance, has argued that engaging in covert or overt competency contests is a form of discrimination: caregivers are exhibiting a "parentist" attitude that censures employed mothers as women who have abandoned their children.[10] It is important to note, however, that nannies and au pairs did not engage in competency contests in households where their contribution was recognized. These and other forms of resistance came into play only when the caregiver's skill and value to the family was ignored or denied.

WISHFUL THINKING

When they could not engage in the types of competency contests described above or when doing so did not fully assuage their feelings of anger, frustration, and sadness, the nannies and au pairs I interviewed often fell back on wishful thinking. Much like the child in the Dr. Seuss classic, *If I Ran the Zoo*, they fantasized about how they would run the household if the children really were theirs. Valerie day-dreamed about more flexible, spontaneous days: "I'd have a more liberal freedom with the kids. Like, um, play when they want to play. Eat when they want to eat. No rigid schedule, which they have. Everything is done on this little timeline. It's not their timeline. I'd let them have their timeline. But, ah, I mean, it's like I'm surprised the mother doesn't schedule bathroom time! [*laughs*] It's like, it's funny . . . but it's like you can't say anything to them [the parents] because that's the way they are."

Other nannies wished that parents would be more involved in childrearing. Peggy, a thirty-year-old white nanny who had worked for the same family for four years, routinely took the children to all of their many enrichment activities. She thought not only that the children should take far fewer classes but, more important, that the *parents* should be the ones to accompany their children: "I think there are places where moms and dads should be, not childcare workers." Similarly, Miriam spoke for most of the nannies I interviewed in wishing that parents who could not be directly involved in the daily lives of their children would at least express an interest. "I would have wanted them to ask more about the girls' progress, like what turned them on that day, how I felt. . . . I was notic-ing all these exciting changes and having this beautiful experience and they didn't really know about it. They didn't really know much about their kids either. They knew what they saw, but I would have liked them to ask me things about them." The desire that all aspects of childrearing be more of a shared endeavor was the most frequently expressed wish, especially among younger nannies who did not have children of their own to dote on.

Wishful thinking took other forms as well. Some nannies and au pairs found satisfaction in the belief that they were leaving a lasting legacy with the chil-dren in their care. Others internalized the intensive mothering ideal and then saw themselves as embodying that ideal, providing children with all the stimula-tion, interaction, and attention that, in their opinion, the biological mothers were failing to supply.

Leaving a Legacy

Caregivers often found it difficult to adhere to the "detached attachment" rule (see chapter 6). They coped with the tensions caused by having to render invisible the rewarding and important bonds they formed with their charges by focusing on having a lasting, positive influence on the lives of the children in their care, even if that effect was unrecognized or denied by their employers. The impressionable nature of young children helped bolster the caregivers' hopes that all the effort and love they provided now would shape the children's lives in the years to come.

Lonehl planned to stay in touch with three-year-old Chloe long after she had stopped being her nanny. The fact that Chloe had picked up some of her traits acted as a kind of insurance policy, protecting their bond and the lasting impact of her work. Like many nannies, she viewed her work as "structuring," or providing a psychological foundation for later stages of life. And, like most of her colleagues, she believed in the permanence of early childhood experiences in effect, if not in memory. She took comfort in the notion that, regardless of how long she and Chloe remained in contact, the foundation she had created in the first three years of Chloe's life would endure: "You can't help but get attached to them, especially if you love kids. The attachment's gonna be there. And then, when you see them grow older and they're doing really well, you're proud, you know? You're happy that you structured some of that when they were younger." Fiona, a thirty-year-old nanny from Ireland, shared this perspective: "It's really rewarding to see the kids when they're growing and to see that the lessons that you taught them, as well as the ones their parents taught them, are working. Even something as stupid as tying their shoe laces. You know? Even something like that. You taught them to do that and you look at them now, five to six years older, and they can do it themselves. And it's like, 'I taught them to do that. Without me, they would never know how to do that.' The rewards *far* outweigh the [pain of] leaving."

Most of the nannies and au pairs I interviewed continued to correspond with former employers in the hope that they would not be completely forgotten and their time with the children erased. Interestingly, the onus of keeping in touch seemed to be largely on the nanny. Fiona, for example, said, "There's the telephone, there's mail service, and there's transportation. I can write. There's no excuse for me never to stay in touch." Most of the nannies I interviewed had photos of all the children they had cared for, and they attempted to stay in touch with all of them. Some were prevented from doing so, however, by parents who preferred not to have reminders of previous caregivers or who required that ongoing interaction occur only on their terms.

The difficulties caregivers faced in their efforts to be a lasting influence in the lives of the children they had cared for could be formidable. Moira's dilemma is a case in point. An immigrant from Ireland, she had lived with her employers when their son Nelson was a newborn. After a few years, she moved out in order to live with her boyfriend, but she continued to care for the child on a live-out basis. She received her green card about the time that Nelson was ready for kindergarten. She decided to change careers and work as a travel agent, but she wanted to remain in contact with Nelson. Her former employers valued Moira's relationship with their son and recognized that it would be healthy for him to continue to have a relationship with her. It seemed a perfect ending. But Moira's former employers wanted her to maintain contact on their terms: they wanted her to babysit for Nelson one night a week. Moira did not want to make that kind of commitment. Moreover, she was insulted by her former employers' seeming failure to grasp the fact that she had a new career and was no longer a domestic. They continued to "treat me like a servant," she said. Moira had envisioned a very different scenario. "I had hoped to have him over, like, once a month to play—take him to the zoo, that sort of thing. But on *my* schedule—not working for them." When I asked if she had raised this option with her former employers, she replied, "No, because they might just cut me off altogether."

This conflict, or misunderstanding, captures the frequently mismatched views of parents and nannies regarding the nannies' ongoing role. Nannies hope to remain important in the lives of the children they care for, even after they have moved on to other positions. In a different context, the fact that healthy emotional attachment prompts a desire for ongoing contact would not be problematic. In childcare work, however, a different dynamic prevails.[11] Ellie's comments address the crux of the dilemma: "The mother has a big power and she knows it. That power [is] that you love their child so much, and she knows that you're going to come back the next day. That's a very big power, and that's not uncommon among the nannies I've spoken to. You take care of a kid for two years, you watch them roll over for the first time, walk the first time, talk for the first time. And then when things get bad [with the employer], you can forgive more easily—or forget, I guess; I don't know about forgive." In Ellie's view, no matter how much she might resent the employer, she was bound to the child, both during her employment and after she had left. In both situations, her access to the child was controlled by the mother.

Of course, even when former employers do not erect barriers, caregivers frequently are unable to maintain contact. This is especially likely if, as is nearly always the case with au pairs, they return to a home far away. Most gradually—but sadly—relinquish the hope that they will have left a significant, lasting mark in the lives of their young charges. One nanny said of her experience, "When he [a seven-month-old] got a new nanny—all he did for the first week was cry. . . . But I mean, he'll never even remember it. I was gone a month, I came back, and he had no idea who I was. It kind of hurt at first, but then I understood—he didn't recognize me at all. But [the new nanny] is good with him, and I trusted her [*pause*] to take care of my baby." Although this caregiver referred to the baby as "mine," he clearly was not hers. She moved through his life at a stage when he was too young to form a lasting memory of her.

Another nanny, who had taken care of a toddler, described a similar sense of loss when she left the family. She indicated a bittersweet awareness that this child's memories of her probably would not last long: "It was tough, because when they're so young, they're probably not going to remember you and it's almost—in some respects you're putting in all this energy into something that you're really not sure will pay off. But it's neat when you say a word one day, and the next day they say it spontaneously. They don't even have to remember that I taught them that word." In their efforts to leave a lasting mark in children's lives, caregivers are willing to settle for small victories, like being able to lay claim to teaching a word, or to overseeing a learning milestone, or perhaps to passing on one of their own gestures.

Being the Mother behind the Mother

A second form of wishful thinking common to caregivers involved trying to embody all aspects of the intensive-mothering ideal and viewing themselves as the only person willing, or able, to fulfill that ideal. In this sense, shadow motherhood took on a new meaning. Nannies not only worked in the shadow of the real mother and propped up her image, they also attempted to fulfill the children's perceived needs according to an ideal that the actual mother could not meet, given that she worked outside the home. The tacit agreement behind shadow motherhood implies that the nanny's job is to help the mother-employer fulfill the intensive-mothering ideal, or at least help her look as if she is doing so. So, in playing the role of the "real" mother, whether in action or in imagination, nannies directly contradicted the unspoken rules of the work arrangement between themselves and their employers.

Many caregivers depicted themselves as being able to give children the benefit of consistent attention and the leisurely pace that an idealized at-home mother might provide. Nilda told me proudly that one of her former charges phoned her to make a request: "I want you to make that cream of wheat for me with the little bit of brown sugar in it. I want you to come give me a bath and wash my hair." Nilda asked, "Doesn't your mother do it?" Her caller replied, "She doesn't have time." Nilda's pride in the gift of time and cream of wheat points to one of the ironies inherent in the third-parent ideal. By holding intensive mothering as the standard, caregivers were implicitly negating their own position. If there can be only one primary caregiver, they surely were not and never would be that person, no matter how much time and energy they might invest.

Like many of her colleagues, Nilda viewed herself as the embodiment of much-needed continuity in a child's life. Although on a daily basis this might be the case, in the long run it is not. The average nanny job among the women I interviewed lasted 2.5 years,[12] and most nannies I interviewed cared for children younger than three. Thus, the likelihood of the nanny being remembered, much less providing psychological continuity in the children's lives, was slim. Still, that possibility was enough to motivate nannies like Valerie, who opted to stay in a job where she received both low pay and poor treatment. She knew she could get a better job elsewhere, but her commitment to intensive mothering compelled her to sacrifice her own interests in favor of the children's.

She explained, "It's a heartbreak, because the youngest one says, 'You're gonna stay with us forever and ever. I'm not gonna let you go.' And in my mind, I'm thinking, 'Well, I might be quitting.' And I hate to do it to them." But she felt that she already had stayed too long, and the poor treatment she received from the father was getting worse. "People tell me you can't stay in one place just for the sake of the children," she said, "because you have to be happy yourself." Valerie's strong desire for "continuity between the kids and me" compelled her to ignore her best interests and remain. She could not be sure that she would be able to see the children again if she left on bad terms. April, too, cited continuity as an important reason why she stayed with Zoe's family, despite an unsatisfying relationship with her employer: "I really loved Zoe. I felt a great deal of sympathy for her, having the confusion between constantly not knowing who's going to be around. So I wanted to stick with it for her sake."

Sometimes nannies will make this kind of sacrifice because they view themselves as the *true* guardians of the children's well-being. Putting the children's interests ahead of their own can become an extension of the ongoing competency contest between nanny and mother. When caregivers embrace the image of the ideal maternal figure as self-sacrificing, the stage is set for ongoing, unacknowledged games of "who can forfeit the most for the children." For instance, Julie had been planning to leave a job she disliked intensely. Then her employer announced that she was pregnant with her fourth child: "I was there for two years only because she got pregnant with Gabriel, and I didn't see the point in the three [other children having to adapt]—they were all really insecure, and I didn't want to see them have to get used to a new nanny and then get used to a new baby brother. So it was just easier to stay and let them get used to Gabriel before I left." Although Julie's employer neither asked for nor recognized her sacrifice, Julie used the logic of putting the children first as evidence that she was more concerned with their needs than their mother was. In so doing, she both claimed her value to children and aligned herself with a childcare worker's version of intensive mothering. Julie defined herself as the *real* mother in the family, at least to the three older children in her care.

Even caregivers who are happy with their working conditions often find themselves making plans around the children's developmental needs and putting those needs first. For example, Melanie planned to return to graduate school to get a degree in occupational therapy. When I interviewed her, she was trying to decide when she would enroll and how to balance her need for career advancement with her perception of Charlotte's need for her: "I thought of maybe going back to school when she starts school—not like kindergarten, but like, if she starts, like, a three-mornings-a-week-type [preschool] program. But then they want to have another baby, like when she's two or two and a half, so then that wouldn't work, so . . . probably when they have a new baby, I'll leave, I think. But if I absolutely love it, then I will stay."

Ultimately, when her one-year contract ended, Melanie decided to go back to school. It is not clear whether she had tired of the job she had loved so much or whether personal considerations or family pressures led her to value her future plans over her attachment to Charlotte. What remains significant, however, is that calculations of working conditions, salary negotiations, and issues of job mobility all take place within a logic that places children's needs first, even when those children are not one's own.

INTENSIVE MOTHERING AS WORK ETHIC: THE RACE TO THE BOTTOM

Pay and recognition often—but not always—went hand in hand. Those whose work was viewed as skilled and whose attachments to children were valued (see chapter 9) also were the highest paid among the childcare workers I interviewed. Those who received the lowest pay also generally were the least recognized. These workers also were most often expected to do work that was outside their contracts. Most of the lowest-paid, least-recognized workers were unable to change jobs because they were undocumented immigrants, they were au pairs dependent on an agency for employment, or they were so committed to the intensive mothering ideal that they were immobilized by feelings of guilt over the idea of "abandoning" the children in their care.

Most of the complaints among caregivers, however, concerned not low pay but lack of recognition. This may have been because the majority of the workers I interviewed were able to move to better-paying jobs when and if they so chose. It was the combination of attachment to the children and desire for recognition of the value of that attachment that kept many tied to the same families for longer than they would have stayed at a less emotionally fraught job. They embraced intensive mothering as an ideal just as fervently as their employers did, seeking to build strong bonds with children, to be knowledgeable about and responsive to their needs, and to be a consistent, loving presence in their lives. When they were denied recognition as "good mothers" to the children in their care, they often responded by working even harder, determined to prove themselves "better mothers" than the women who employed them.

Using the intensive-mothering ideal as a work ethic, and indeed as a form of resistance, resulted in several paradoxes for childcare workers. The most common of these involved caregivers' willingness to trade fair pay for recognition. The emphasis on self-sacrifice that is part of the intensive-mothering ideal often produced a race to the bottom for nannies as they gave up more and more of themselves and their rights as workers in order to prove their worth as caregivers. Since caregivers already were disadvantaged by the vast differences in class status between themselves and their employers, the race to the bottom was one caregivers were almost certain to "win."

Sarah's experiences exemplify the lure of trading pay for recognition. During our initial interview, she said that she was so unhappy that she doubted she could manage to complete the remaining six months of her year-long contract. Four years later, I interviewed her again. She was still in the same job, but now she felt much happier with her situation. She explained that several months after that first interview, she had announced her plan to leave and had secured a job at a daycare center. Matthew, the toddler, was unhappy about the coming change: "He was turning into, I don't know, somebody else. . . . All of a sudden he was a baby again, and he needed me to do everything that I hadn't been doing for him. And the only thing that we could figure out was that he just really didn't want me to leave and . . . [the employers] decided that if I wanted to stay, they'd still pay me as though I was full-time, even though I was only working part-time. So I decided, 'Hey, I can't beat that!'" Matthew's response to Sarah's imminent departure shifted the dynamics of her relationship with her employer. In theory, Jane's explicit recognition of the value of the bond Sarah had created with Matthew strengthened Sarah's bargaining position, since she could use the child's attachment to her as leverage in negotiating better pay or improvements in other aspects of her job. In reality, Sarah did not receive a net raise in pay or a work reduction under the new arrangement. She moved from a live-in situation in which she was paid $300 per week plus room and board for a sixty-hour workweek, to a live-out situation in which she was paid the same amount for a forty-five-hour week, minus the room and board.

Furthermore, her new live-out job was a split shift. She worked from 7 to 10 a.m. and from 1 to 6:30 p.m. Nevertheless, Sarah counted this new arrangement as a victory because her importance to the family was openly recognized: "Jane actually said, 'We'll do what it takes to keep you here because we really want you here.' And she was very nice about it, and she really made it seem like she wanted me here. Not anybody, but *specifically* me." Sarah effectively took a cut in pay in exchange for her employer's willingness to *recognize* her and the importance of her work.

Nannies and au pairs used the logic of self-sacrifice when they explained why they accepted a lower rate of pay than they felt they needed. Margarita said that she had accepted less money from her most recent employers because they were "factory workers and could not pay. . . . One has to consider the family's situation." Her first employer had paid her $250 per week for a live-in situation; in her most recent job, the pay had been $100 per week for live-out work. "Well," she said, rationalizing, "something is something, right? And that boy also had a great deal of affection for me and I for him. He even sang to me [*laughs*]." In Margarita's economy of caring, this child's songs were worth the loss of $150 a week plus room and board.

The same attachment that can lead caregivers to take a reduction in pay in exchange for a song also gives them a sense of superiority as caregivers, a sense that even if their employer does not value their work, the child does. Yet strong ties to a child also leave caregivers emotionally vulnerable and potentially unable to negotiate effectively on their own behalf. Ironically, the same attachment that can lead employers to offer nannies incentives to stay on for a period of years can also lead nannies and au pairs to sacrifice too much. They trade fair wages and decent hours for the chance to stay with children they love and for the satisfaction of having their shadow labor acknowledged.

The nannies I interviewed considered childcare deeply fulfilling work and they viewed their occupation as carrying a high moral value. Most enjoyed raising the children in their care; they did not perceive the work involved as inherently degrading. Few felt an allegiance to their employers, but almost all felt bound to the children and to the third-parent ideal. In their role as third parents, the nannies and au pairs took pride in their deep understanding of the children they cared for and in the extent to which they put the children's needs first. Yet none of these women was truly a third parent. And none had any likelihood of seeing her work come to fruition, much less any right to maintain a long-term connection.[13]

CONCLUSION

Nannies and au pairs often sought not to reduce their childcare responsibilities but to increase them and, more important, to gain recognition for them. Their professionalization project entailed reframing their work as skilled labor, and redefining themselves as third parents and as valued team members rather than as mother's helpers. Ironically, allegiance to the intensive-mothering ideology led them to forgo viewing their work as an exchange of wages for services. Instead, they viewed it in terms of love and self-sacrifice. As a result, in negotiations with employers, they often neglected their own interests as workers.

This professionalization project also involved them intimately in renegotiating the division of mothering labor and the meanings associated with it. Struggles over domination and resistance, fair wages for fair work, and market versus family norms are all anathema to the ideal of good motherhood. Therefore, in attempting to redefine the meanings that frame both their work and their negotiations with their employers, nannies and au pairs used this cultural ideal as a bargaining tool, as a form of resistance, and as a higher authority to which they could appeal in negotiations with employers. Ultimately, however, they capitulated to this ideal, and it both shaped the contours of their work and constrained their attempts to change them.

Like the mother-employers discussed in chapter 5, caregivers' strategies for dealing with the conflict between a cultural ideal and their own work arrangement involved creating a fiction in which they were more present and permanent in the lives of the children in their care than they actually were or could ever be. Just as mothers who espoused the intensive-mothering ideal undermined their own positions as mothers who worked outside the home, caregivers who viewed intensive mothering as a work ethic contributed to the exclusive definition of intensive mothering that led to their own devaluation, since that definition held that there could be only one primary caregiver. Rather than working with their employers to create a new ideal that involved multiple parenting figures, they too fell prey to the game of zero-sum attachment that intensive mothering implies. If the only way that each party can value her own contribution to a mutual endeavor is to devalue the other's contribution, each participates in a downward spiral of diminishing recognition. This, in turn, leads to less communication, a diminished ability to collectively solve problems, and, ultimately, a compromised ability to collectively provide care for the children.

9

Partnerships

Seeking a New Model

PRELUDE: ELAINE AND CHRISTINE

When I first met Christine, she was twenty-one years old and one of the most vocally dissatisfied of the nannies I had interviewed. She had grown up in a working-class town near Boston. After studying for a degree in early childcare education, she had worked at a daycare center and then had worked as a nanny for three years. During our initial interview, she echoed many of the sentiments I had heard from other nannies: she felt that her employers were too permissive, that they were out-of-touch with the realities of childrearing, and that they placed unreasonable restrictions on how she spent her time with the children. Moreover, she was angry that although her employers had hired her because of her education and successful childcare history, they seemed to ignore her advice.

When I asked Christine for an example of advice that had gone unheeded, she described the approach her employers, Elaine and Steve (white professionals in their midthirties), took with their three-year-old daughter, Courtney. Christine complained that Elaine and Steve were inconsistent in disciplining Courtney and failed to use "time-out" on a regular basis. As a result, their little girl was "out of control." She hit her baby brother Zachary; she hit her parents; she hit Christine. Although Christine tried to coach the couple, her efforts failed: "When I first started working for them, I was the expert because I *know*. I've worked with so many kids that I just know the typical behavior of children. And I mean, I try to tell them. At first I was the expert and they listened to me, but the more they got used to me, the less they—I don't know." At the time of our interview, Christine's frustration level was so high that she had decided to leave the job and return to the local community college to complete her childcare certification.

Three years later, as I gave a guest lecture at a local university about some of my preliminary research findings, I saw a familiar face in the audience. It was not until I read aloud a quotation from Christine that I realized who this familiar-looking listener was. After the lecture, Christine came up and thanked me for having accurately captured the frustrations of the typical nanny experience. She went on to tell me that she had returned to working for Elaine and Steve, and that everything about her job had changed since our first discussion. She was now happy with her position and grateful to be part of a family that she "loved." I was intrigued. What had caused this dramatic change?

Christine agreed to a second interview. When we met again, she told me what had transpired during the intervening years. Not long after our first talk, Elaine and Steve had asked her to stay on and had offered her a small raise. More important to Christine, they began giving her the recognition she craved, both for her skill with their two children and for her contribution to family life. "That summer Elaine started rewarding me . . . not rewarding me, but she praised me a lot. They just started telling me, 'You're the best nanny we've ever had. The kids love you.'"

The quality and frequency of communication between Christine and her employers also changed. When Christine felt that her advice was being ignored, she grew increasingly reluctant to express her concerns. Elaine helped reverse that trend by explicitly encouraging her to speak up: "They intimidated me a lot. And Elaine's a very difficult person to work for. She'd be the first to admit it. Um, [*pause*] I don't really know exactly what it was that made that all change. . . . [S]he, like, kind of gave me permission to tell them when something was wrong. She would say to me, 'You know, you're not yourself today. What's the matter? You need to tell us when something is wrong so that we know. We can't read your mind.'" Her employers also "gave [her] permission" to demonstrate her skill: "They started asking my advice. I remember that. They would say, 'Well, what would you do in this kind of situation?' And I would tell them, and they kind of thought of me as, like, an authority on the subject, maybe because of the experience I had with all the kids I took care of."

Once the lines of communication were open, Christine found that she, too, became more flexible and more open to her employers' way of doing things. Whereas previously she had seen them as overly permissive and had viewed herself as the last bulwark against household chaos, she began to modify her perspective and to loosen up with the children. In turn, Elaine and Steve became more consistent, and the three adults began to work as a team. Christine explained, "I just got flexible and they just got a little bit more strict. It may have had something to do with the books that they read. It may have had to do with seeing their children going nuts and deciding, 'We better do something now.' It may have been just by watching me. We both moved a little closer to each other. . . . Because like the discipline thing with Courtney, I started realizing that I was aggravating the situation just as much as [Elaine] was. I've learned a lot from them, obviously." As all three parties lowered their defenses and started listening to one another, they began an exchange of information and mutual learning about childrearing that benefited the whole family.

After our second interview, Christine introduced me to Elaine, who agreed to be interviewed. When we talked, I asked her to describe her relationship with Christine, who by then had been part of the family for six years. Elaine said,

> She's my oldest child! Not, not in the negative sense of the word. Um, it's been [*pause*] way beyond employer/employee. Um, [*pause*] but that's what it started with and it was just *tremendous* respect on our part for her [*pause*] professionally. What she can do, and what she did, and what she still does with one hand tied behind her back. It's awe-inspiring. Like, ah, the kinds of activities she'll do with them. Like, ah, the things she'll make with them, places she'll take them, or the way she'll coax them to do things. With me, their heels are dug in so deep they're up to their knees. Just everything. She just has a skill.

The extent of Christine's involvement with the family varied over time. Some years she worked full-time, and at other points part-time. Sometimes, even when she was not employed by Elaine and Steve, she continued her relationship with the family as a special friend who joined them every Friday night for Sabbath dinners.

During this six-year span, Elaine's life had also changed significantly. She switched from full-time to part-time employment, which in her line of work meant three ten-hour days per week, a move that she felt had made her more relaxed in general and more comfortable in her role as a mother and as an employer. She explained, "I just decided at the end of my life, how hard I worked and how many years I worked seventy hours a week wasn't gonna be the measure of my success. And that if I was gonna have the kids, I should really find a way to give them more, enjoy them more. So I decided to go to three days a week." She acknowledged that this cutback at work had cost her the opportunity to advance further, but added that the "balance" in her life now was "phenomenal." The two days a week Elaine stayed home, she explained, "I devote to me and to my kids. And it's been *very* healthy. . . . And so the experiences have been very different just because my own mental state is a lot more in check." She emphasized that having time for her children *and* for her own well-being were equally important in maintaining her newfound equilibrium.

For her part, Christine appreciated that Elaine was "more realistic" about her children now that she spent more time at home. And she defended her employer against the at-home mothers in the neighborhood who criticized moms for hiring nannies. "People who have bad attitudes about nannies are always [saying], 'The parents don't do anything. They come home and put their kids to bed and on weekends they hire babysitters to watch their kids.' And I always try to tell them, 'Yeah, there are parents like that. But when Elaine's home, she's with the kids." Although most nannies said they would not want an at-home mother looking over their shoulder, Christine seemed to enjoy the arrangement. Elaine allowed her to be in charge during her own "shift" and, now that Elaine was home more, she understood and valued Christine's work in ways she previously had not. She had more direct experience with her children and therefore became more realistic about their daily activities. No longer torn between competing identities, she also was a more relaxed employer.

In comparing Christine to the other nannies and au pairs she had employed, Elaine mentioned two qualities that set Christine apart. First, she appeared to have the potential to do more than childcare work, and Elaine encouraged her to get more education: "She's very smart. And she's a real perseverer, if there's such a word. I mean, against pretty high odds, she's pulled herself up from [pause] with no support, um, to really have come quite a long way. And we just developed a very mutually beneficial relationship. She, ah, she needed guidance and we were happy to provide it because she just melded in to become part of the family." Their guidance included mentoring Christine when she went back to college for her bachelor's degree. In turn, Christine was always there as an additional caring adult for their children.

Second, Elaine recognized and appreciated that, unlike other nannies, Christine took initiative with the children. At the time of our interview, Elaine was just finishing a year with an au pair who had been satisfactory, but "not spectacular," and she was looking forward to having Christine return for another year with the family after she had been working as a nanny in California. The level of confidence Christine inspired made Elaine feel comfortable delegating authority to her, which in turn made it possible for Elaine and her husband to relax into "autopilot": "But there's, um, there's a total and complete confidence in her with the kids. Always has been, right from the start. She's the *only* person I've left them with for a week at a time. Um [pause]. They're happier with her than they are with anybody [else]. . . . And I guess what I'm saying is that's the qualitative difference is that Christine would clearly recognize [a problem with the kids] as something that we need to know about. Not that we need to do anything, probably, because she can do it, and she will." The open communication the two women had established further deepened Elaine's trust and peace of mind. She was certain that if there were anything she or her husband needed to know about their children, Christine would not hesitate to tell them.

The great majority of the mother-nanny relationships I observed did not evolve into the kind of partnership that Christine and her employers had forged. Over time, Elaine, Steve, and Christine had moved from distrust to cooperation, from recognition deficit to reciprocal respect, and from one-way communication to mutual learning.

· · ·

My chance encounter with Christine, and the interviews with her and Elaine that followed, spurred me to conduct additional research. Among the employer-nanny relationships I had been studying, the shadow-mother model strongly dominated. The kinds of cooperative care and mutual recognition that had blossomed between Elaine and Christine appeared only occasionally, rare bright spots in a group of relationships in which employers relied on either puppeteer or paranormal management strategies, and nannies felt resentful and resistant. I wondered what characteristics were common among "partnerships," and what conditions made partnerships possible.[1] How did other mother-nanny partnerships avoid the frustration and misunderstanding that seemed to occur so commonly between mother-employers and their caregivers?

In looking back through the management styles I had observed in the first fifty-eight interviews, I noted variations in the quality of four relational elements: trust, autonomy, two-way communication, and mutual decision making. I found only two additional mother-nanny dyads in which both parties' responses indicated that all four of these characteristics worked in their relationships in a way that enhanced each characteristic: Joyce and Stacy, and Min and Li Chan.[2] In analyzing these two relationships, as well as the partnership between Elaine and Christine, I noticed structural and/or cultural features that set these women apart. Both Joyce and Min had been raised by employed mothers in cultures in which this was the norm. They flatly rejected the extremes of intensive mothering and accepted the presence of another loving adult in their children's lives as normal and natural. By contrast, Elaine's relationship with Christine changed after she had scaled back at work and had more time and energy to invest in their shared endeavor. She rejected the "intensive working" norm associated with male-pattern careers. Moreover, spending some time at home deepened Elaine's confidence in the strength of her connection with her children. This in turn made her comfortable sharing a broad range of mother-work with Christine.

Demands for shadow mothering emerged from the anxiety mother-employers felt when they were caught between intensive mothering and intensive working. I therefore hypothesized that mothers caught in the vise between the demands of intensive mothering and those of intensive working resorted to puppeteer or paranormal management strategies, and felt compelled to demand that their nannies be shadow mothers. If this were the case, then removing at least one of these pressures might open up new ways of conceptualizing the division of childrearing labor among mothers, childcare workers, and even fathers.[3]

I sought to find more partnerships by interviewing a second set of mother-employers who fell into two categories: those who had grown up in cultures where mothers working outside the home were the norm or who had been raised by mothers who had worked outside the home, thus removing some of the pressure to emulate the ideal at-home mother; and mothers who worked part-time or flex-time, thus reducing some of the pressures of the "test of manhood" at work and increasing their sense of security in their relationships with their children and their connection with what went on at home. In this second phase of data collection, I interviewed twenty-two women (thirteen employers and nine caregivers).[4] Seven mother-nanny dyads within this second sample fit the partnership model.[5] Along with Elaine and Christine and the two partnerships from the initial interviews, this brought the total number of partnerships in this study to ten.[6]

Next, I turn to a comparison of the attributes of the three management styles—puppeteer, paranormal, and partnership—used by the mother-employers in the study. Examples provided by the women interviewed in the second round of data collection show how the contours of trust, autonomy, two-way communication, and mutual decision making can promote a cooperative childcare relationship between mother-employers and nannies. The discussion then turns to an assessment of the extent to which the partnership experiences described by the interviewees confirm my hypotheses about the cultural and structural conditions that help women break the shadow-mother mold.

DEFINING ATTRIBUTES OF PUPPETEER, PARANORMAL, AND PARTNERSHIP CHILDCARE MANAGEMENT STYLES

Among the initial fifty-eight interviews I conducted, puppeteer and paranormal management styles predominated (see chapter 5). Employer-employee relationships among puppeteer managers are characterized by one-way communication, a lack of autonomy, limited trust, and an absence of shared decision making. These mothers may trust the caregiver to follow their instructions, but since trust does not extend beyond this, there is no basis for granting adult-level autonomy, no opportunity to engage in two-way communication, and no reason to make decisions jointly. In paranormal relationships, trust is assumed. These employers assume their caregivers will "naturally" make the same decisions that they would make. This assumption, in turn, removes the need for even one-way communication, shifts most decision making to caregivers, and provides the basis for a significant amount of day-to-day autonomy. The caregivers in these relationships often are frustrated by the lack of meaningful communication, however, and although they usually appreciate their relative freedom, they tend to perceive this autonomy as a form of benign neglect rather than as the logical outcome of earned trust.

TABLE 1 Management Strategies and Relational Characteristics

Relational Characteristics	Strategy		
	Puppeteer Managers	Paranormal Managers	Partnerships
Trust	Limited	Presumed	Earned
Autonomy	Restricted	Unrestricted	Negotiated
Communication	One-way	Unnecessary	Two-way
Decision making	Mother-only	Delegated	Mutual

Partnerships were the only cases in which all four elements were present in ways that satisfied both mother-employer and mother-worker (see table 1). A partnership management style involves delegating a level of autonomy based on *earned* trust and, most important, makes respect for the caregiver's particular skills clear through two-way communication and mutual learning. Mothers and caregivers also share decision making about the children's daily activities and ideas about discipline and development. The mother-employers in these relationships do not view their caregivers as extensions of themselves, nor do they view them as puppets to be directed via marionette strings. The caregivers, in turn, do not view their employers as obstacles to be worked around or resisted. Instead, each party views the other as a teammate who brings different, yet equally valuable, skills to their shared childrearing endeavor. In these ways, both parties move beyond viewing childrearing as a competitive, zero-sum game in which each party seeks recognition for the value of her own contributions through the denigration of the other. Instead, as these women reported, they came to value their differences and to learn from each other.

Since trust, autonomy, two-way communication, and joint decision making are essential aspects of partnership-style childcare relationships, each of these elements is discussed separately below, using examples described by the study participants. It becomes evident that the *process* of forming partnerships is as important as the outcome. It is likely that partnership arrangements result in more successful joint childrearing, but that remains to be studied. Unquestionably, the relational processes in these relationships resulted in less anxious mothers and more satisfied workers.

Earned Trust

The ten mother-employers who used a partnership management style established relationships with their caregivers based on mutual recognition and respect. These provided the basis for trust and a degree of autonomy in the caregivers' workday. Employers' awareness of their nannies as separate individuals whose unique backgrounds, experience, and skills deserved recognition was one source of the respect that led to trust. Min, a thirty-seven-year-old scientist with two sons, ages three and nine months, described her view of her nanny, Li Chan: "I was thinking, she's somebody if I met her in China, she could be the person who taught me biochemistry. I couldn't possibly treat her as just a nanny at home." Although several of the immigrant nannies who participated in the study had held positions of authority in their home countries (teacher, doctor, lawyer), it was only in the partnerships that these or other qualifications earned the caregiver respect *within* the nanny job. For example, as discussed in chapter 5, Esther's years of experience as a physician in China did not earn her any more respect or autonomy in her employment with Mary Anne.

Perhaps the most common foundation for these mother-employers' trust in their nannies was their view of childcare as a job requiring particular skills, and their view of their own caregiver as a professional who possessed these skills. Libby, a forty-two-year-old white executive who worked a flextime schedule, described her relationship with Grace, her thirty-year-old Scottish nanny of two years, this way: "It's also interesting to watch her. She deals with the two kids very differently, as well she should, because their personalities are very different. Grace is a real professional. It was just a huge quantum leap from what we were accustomed to in the way she operates. And she's patient, unbelievably patient, in a way that neither myself nor my husband are. She and I laugh about it, how much of it is because they're not her kids." Although most of the nannies in this study had the same level of experience as Grace, and many had more childcare education, the value of this experience was recognized only in partnerships.

Grace appreciated her employers' view of her as a skilled worker whose knowledge contributed to the well-being of their children. She also appreciated the freedom and autonomy she was given. Both she and Libby hoped that their relationship would continue until the children were in school full-time. Grace said, "I'm really happy in this job. I think both of [the parents], they definitely communicate everything about their kids. They are really open; I'm really open." The fact that they had such open communication and mutual respect not only made childcare smoother but also enhanced family life. As Libby noted, her eyes misting, "She's such a glue. I left this morning and she's sitting on the couch reading to them and they're just so happy. . . . They're happy, my husband's happy, and I think Grace is happy. What more could you ask for? I can't believe I'm crying about my nanny, but she makes our family life possible. That's what it's all about."

Trust also accrued through experience and over time. Elizabeth and Lonehl had worked together for more than two years when I met them. Elizabeth explained that, as a single mother with no backup, she needed Lonehl to be "extraordinarily reliable"—and she was. "I know she's really looking out for Chloe's interest and that Chloe's going to be safe and well cared for. And that she won't leave me hanging." She gave an example of why she trusted Lonehl completely, describing it as "classic Lonehl." Lonehl phoned to say that she had been to the doctor and was ill: "[Lonehl] called me one day and said, 'I wasn't feeling well and [the doctor] gave me some medicine and I'm resting. Would you mind if I came and got Chloe this morning and my mom watched her while I slept?'" Elizabeth was impressed with Lonehl's straightforward explanation of the problem, with the fact that she offered a solution, and that this solution would simultaneously assure Chloe's well-being (both Elizabeth and her daughter knew and liked Lonehl's family) and relieve Elizabeth of the burden of a last-minute search for childcare on a workday.

Unlike the puppeteer managers I interviewed, Elizabeth did not insist that Lonehl keep Chloe at home in Elizabeth's relatively affluent neighborhood. Unlike the paranormal managers, she did not simply assume that leaving her child with Lonehl's family (who lived in a poor neighborhood in the nearby town of Dorchester) would be fine because she and her nanny shared a "common bond." Instead, she recognized that Lonehl shared her own deep commitment to meeting Chloe's needs and this earned trusted shaped the two women's ongoing relationship. In this case, trust developed in part out of Elizabeth's respect for Lonehl's background as a daycare teacher, but also through the autonomy that Elizabeth, as a single mother, needed to offer Lonehl. As her only partner in childrearing, Elizabeth needed to trust Lonehl's judgment, and Lonehl demonstrated daily that this trust was deserved.

In partnership relationships, earned trust accrued in three ways: first, through appreciation of the skill the caregiver brought to the job; second, through increasing autonomy and seeing that the caregiver did not abuse that autonomy; and third, through two-way communication that allowed for greater mutual understanding. One might take this finding as evidence that all mother-nanny relationships would evolve into partnerships over time, but this was not the case. Among the puppeteer and paranormal relationships I observed, those that lasted more than a year did not necessarily change, or, at most, puppeteer management would evolve into paranormal management as the employer felt less anxious. They did not, however, naturally transform into the kinds of employer-employee interactions present in partnerships.

Autonomy

Employers in partnerships also offered their nannies a great deal of autonomy based on earned trust. They did not, like puppeteer managers, restrict mobility or construct rigid schedules; nor did they offer autonomy, as did the paranormals, based on the assumption that the nanny is "just like me." In fact, as will be discussed below, many noted and appreciated the differences between themselves and their nannies, but viewed these differences as mutually enhancing rather than as a threat to high-quality care. The autonomy granted in these relationships, therefore, was due, not to assumed similarity, but rather to a thorough knowledge of both similarities and differences in how the mother and the nanny would exercise judgment.

Autonomy for nannies ranged from being able to plan daily activities for themselves and for the children to being on the list of people who could speak to the doctor on behalf of the children if need be. Unlike the puppeteer managers described in chapter 5, Libby noted that Grace planned the children's activities. She explained, "Grace has a number of friends who are also nannies, so there are a lot of group activities. And she and I will talk about those." Here we see Grace exercising autonomy in planning activities, but keeping Libby in the loop. Similarly, when Libby and Rob made decisions about the children's activities, they consulted Grace: "Jaden is now in summer camp, which is a big step—Rob and I put him in there. Grace didn't say, 'Oh, do you think he should go to summer camp?' But she's very tuned in and will alert us to classes that maybe Avery might take and stuff like that, and get me the literature, and sign up. So she definitely develops activities." Unlike the mothers in the first wave of interviews who found it somewhat alarming that their children would be socialized into play groups constructed by their nannies, Libby found this to be a clear benefit of having Grace in their lives. "And it's really nice to have a natural collection of other kids that they hang out with and that they become friends with, not because they go to school with them but because they are with the other nannies. And they know Rose, and they know Fiona and Lourdes [other nannies]. It's part of their extended family." Grace agreed that it was important for her to "be able to plan things for the kids. Like their little social calendar, as well as mine." She added the refrain that was common among nannies who worked alone with children all day. "It's important for me to be around other nannies I know so that I can speak to another adult as much as the kids are around other kids. And both of these parents totally understand that." Like most nannies, Grace wanted to be in charge during her shift. "When I have the kids, like I have them from 7 to 4, they are my responsibility, so if I thought the kid was sick, I wanted to be able to take the child to the doctor's." In partnerships, this level of autonomy was allowed, not because the parents blindly trusted the nanny's judgment, but because she generally attended regular checkups with the parents and therefore knew the children's health histories.

When we asked Luz, a twenty-six-year-old immigrant from Chile, if she would like to be included in conferences with her employer's children's doctors and teachers, she responded, "I do those things with them. School, to the doctor, I go with them and their parents are there. And if, if, I stay with them . . . if they get sick . . . it's what happened to me once, it is me that takes them to the doctor, myself. I take them, I assume, let's say, perhaps the . . . the authority. They are under my care, I have to respond." When I interviewed Vivian, Luz's employer, a white forty-three-year-old executive, her concern was not that Luz arranged the children's activities but rather to make sure that she and her husband attended these appointments and events with Luz as often as possible. Her husband, for example, liked to take the children to their doctor's and dentist's appointments, but went with Luz. Other activities, Vivian said, "are [divided according to] whatever makes sense. Sometimes she's been in charge of it and sometimes we've moved it. Like baths are now in the evening, but some days it just makes sense to do it during the day."

Two-Way Communication

Mother-employers who relied on puppeteer or paranormal management styles never mentioned their nannies or au pairs in response to the question, "Whom do you ask for advice about your child?" (See chapter 7.) Partnership managers, in contrast, always mentioned their childcare worker as an important source of information and expertise. Mother-employers who viewed their nannies as skilled caregivers had no qualms about turning to them for advice. The resulting two-way exchange of information did not diminish the mother's authority or her position as the ultimate decision maker, but it did give her an important resource on which to draw. In all cases, nannies were given lessons in childrearing by their employers, some of which they appreciated and some of which they tolerated. Mothers who managed by partnership, however, also consulted their caregivers frequently and demonstrated that they valued their expertise by including them in basic decision making. From the perspective of the women I interviewed, this constant interaction and mutual learning is the hallmark of a successful employment relationship, and thus defines a partnership.

Caregivers perceived information sharing not only as contributing to the children's well-being but also as an important form of recognition of their own role in family life and, in some cases, as a creative outlet. For example, Colleen mentioned how gratified she was that her employer noticed and adopted some of her techniques:

> I think they watch for how I use humor a lot, and [then] they do that too. Like I know something that was real big at first was trying to get the kids dressed. I made up this game, "Who do you want to be today?" "I want to be Elmo." "OK. Let's find things that are red." So, things like that. Silly things. . . . So now every day, we have a theme of who we want to be. It could be the ocean. Blue shirt and brown pants, sand and water, you know? Ways to make things easier that they've learned from me. And I've learned from them, too.

For Colleen, as for many other nannies, the content of the information exchange was not as crucial as the fact that a two-way dialogue existed. Her remarks reflect several of the components of mutual learning that were important to nannies. First, her employer noticed her ability. Second, her employer not only listened to a suggestion from her but began to incorporate it. Third, her employer taught her, as well, so both parties were engaged in useful learning.

Min asked Li Chan for advice concerning how and when to start solid food because, as she said, "she has two children of her own." Li Chan explained that she, too, learned from Min: "She read a lot of books about childrearing. Sometimes I think what she said made more sense. [For example], if there would be any change in the diet we would always discuss it together." Here the "book knowledge" of the employer melded with and enhanced the "grounded knowledge" of the more experienced parent, Li Chan. This approach to sharing knowledge is vastly different from the knowledge wars described in chapter 7.

Similarly, Libby characterized her exchanges with Grace as, "What do you think?" "I don't know. What do *you* think?" She explained that her youngest, Avery, was entering a "stubborn" phase, "she's developing her own self . . . and we talk about how to deal with that." She was relieved to find in discussions with Grace that "it just happens that Grace deals with her in the same way we do." Importantly, however, in partnerships, even if the mother and the caregiver did *not* share the same parenting style, two-way communication allowed them to find middle ground.

Elizabeth and Lonehl had similar approaches to dealing with Chloe in some respects, but differed significantly in others. Elizabeth offered several examples of resolving differences in style with Lonehl:

> Lonehl is more of a disciplinarian than I am on some issues. So she'll say "No TV for a week." Well, that leaves me in a position that I'm stuck enforcing that, and I think that it's too much for a five-year-old. So we've had to talk about that and negotiate back and forth on those sorts of things, and she'll generally give on those pieces. . . . *It's like any two people involved with a kid.* You've got to back one another, but we'll talk about if I'm not comfortable with where it is. Otherwise I think we're pretty much in sync. She's a little bit more about a reward for good behavior, and I don't particularly like that. But to some degree that's all right. You find yourself, like in any relationship, compromising and deciding what the important issue is really.[7]

Shared Decision Making

All of the mothers and nannies in partnership relationships described a team approach to making day-to-day decisions about the children's lives. Elizabeth explained the decision-making process she and Lonehl used this way: "We will talk about issues with Chloe some. . . . Is Chloe old enough to do this? Should we start her on that? Is taking lessons in addition to school too much? Is she ready for that? Those are the things that we will talk about." In some cases, decision making took place between the mother and the nanny alone, but most partnerships broadened to include the father in decision making as well.

For example, Gwen, a thirty-four-year-old white professor with two daughters, Emilia and Carolina, ages two and five, explained how she, her husband, Federico, a physician, and their Guatemalan nanny, Sylvia, worked through the thorny decision to remove Carolina from her preschool and move her to another. Originally, they had chosen a local half-day co-op because Carolina "needed some preschool time with other kids and it was affordable enough that we could still afford to have Sylvia in the afternoons. This was also necessary because I was working full-time." She noted that there had been some red flags at the beginning of Carolina's attendance at the co-op, the fact that the other parents were "able to manage [financially] with only a couple of hours a day of childcare—not a good fit for us." Families who could afford daycare for "enrichment" rather than to cover much-needed working hours were likely to be of a social class that made Gwen and her family uncomfortable. And more important, Carolina, as the child of a Mexican immigrant, was the only "child of color" in her classroom.

The first sign of difficulty came when Federico had a turn working at the co-op and "was a bit shocked when the teacher asked if she could call him 'Fred' since Federico was too hard to pronounce." The second sign came when the teacher referred to Carolina as an "ESL child." Gwen noted that although they were a bicultural household, they did speak predominantly Spanish at home, so "it is true that she spoke only Spanish upon entering the preschool, but she certainly understood English." As she said ruefully, this was another "alarm bell that I ignored."

The final straw came in negotiating with the teacher about how to interact with Sylvia. "I explained to the teacher that I had to work but that she needed to communicate with Sylvia [who spoke fluent English] at pickup just as she would with me about Carolina's day. I explicitly said that Sylvia had been her sitter for two years and was like a third parent to Carolina." The teacher agreed, but Sylvia began to express concern. The teachers and other parents all ignored her when she went to pick up Carolina. By the end of the third week, Gwen said, "this was all starting to make us nervous, when Sylvia flat out said to me, 'I don't think this is a good school for Carolina. They are obviously racist against Latinos. Carolina is Latina. She needs to be at a school where they respect her, our language, and us.'" Gwen, Sylvia, and Federico discussed the situation and agreed that they needed to find a new school for Carolina, who stayed home full-time with Sylvia until Gwen arranged a new school. Sylvia ultimately took a cut in hours and in pay to facilitate Carolina's transfer to a more Latino-friendly preschool.

The preschool decision is an example of the kind of mutuality that can develop in partnerships. Although Federico had immigrated from Mexico and Sylvia was from Guatemala, the parents did not assume that Sylvia would "naturally" share their views on all things. In fact, because of the class differences between them, Sylvia was more attuned to subtle forms of racism and anti-Latino sentiment than her employers were. Because they had always encouraged two-way communication and valued Sylvia's perspective, she felt empowered to speak up when she saw Carolina being marginalized at school. They came to a mutual decision based on input from all of the adults involved, and both parents felt they had benefited from Sylvia's insight.

. . .

Relationships based on earned trust, employee autonomy, two-way communication, and mutual decision making earned the partnership label. They were also the most mutually satisfying relationships in my study. The question remains, however, why were they so rare in the first round of interviews?

WHAT MAKES PARTNERSHIPS POSSIBLE: TESTING THE HYPOTHESES

As noted earlier, my analysis of the first round of interviews indicated that the mother-employers, caught in a vise between intensive mothering and all-or-nothing careers, often felt out of control and anxious in both areas of their lives. Arlie Hochschild has noted that families are the "shock absorbers" for economic change; I argue that childcare workers are the shock absorbers for professional women's work/family conflicts. What would happen, then, if one or both of the pressures weighing on mother-employers were removed?

If mothers did not embrace intensive mothering so wholeheartedly, but instead drew on another set of beliefs about the role motherhood should play in their lives, would they no longer feel threatened by the nanny as a loving adult in their children's lives? By the same token, if mother-employers were less pressured to travel, to work fifty-hour weeks, and thus to become virtual strangers in their own homes, would they feel more comfortable with delegating care, benefiting from a grounded sense of the childrearing work they were delegating? To explore these questions, I sought two sets of women: those who had been raised by employed mothers, particularly in cultural contexts in which this was the norm; and those who worked part-time or flextime.

In the first set, I hoped to find working mothers who could draw on counterhegemonic ideals that would allow them to reframe intensive mothering so that they could combine their mothering practice more easily with demanding professional careers. In the second, I recruited mothers based on the concept of the "threshold of connection," a theme that developed in my interviews with mother-employers about their ideal work/parental leave combination. The threshold of connection is the amount or quality of time with children that a given parent feels she needs in order to feel secure in her mothering and, by extension, to feel comfortable delegating mother-work to another. Clearly, this threshold varies across parents and over time.

The threshold of connection is an important concept for several reasons. First, the literature on mother-child attachment draws only from the imagined perspective of the child. It further assumes that all children are the same in their attachment needs, and that all children need to bond with one and only one caregiver, the mother. Third, it assumes that the mother's need for connection to her child is (a) innately present or pathologically absent, (b) unchanging over time, and (c) unaffected by outside forces. In short, mother and child inhabit a bubble within which both are driven to bond successfully. If attachment is not secure, this problem is due to some pathology of the mother and is assumed to have lasting effects on the child's later development.

By contrast, I found great variation both in how much time mothers felt they needed with their children and at what age they needed that time. Some mothers felt profound grief at being separated from their infants upon returning to work. Others found infant care relatively boring, stating that they believed their children needed them more and were more "interesting" when they were toddlers, or in grade school, or even in high school. Based on these findings, it seems that the threshold of connection rises and falls throughout a given child's life, and depends on numerous circumstances, including the mother's level of childrearing experience, her comfort level with her knowledge of the child at a given developmental stage, and the other demands on her energies.

It is important to recognize that satisfying the *parent's* need for connection may be as important as satisfying the child's.[8] And parents, like children, may vary in their needs for attachment; those variations may well be perfectly normal. Finally, if the parent's needs are unmet, the tension and insecurity that this creates will undoubtedly affect the child's experience of the relationship with his or her parent and with other loving adults. I therefore hypothesized that mother-employers whose thresholds of connection were met (whether they were working full-time, part-time, flextime, or not at all) would be more secure in their parenting and thus more reasonable as employers.

In approaching the second round of interviews, I based my participant selection on these two hypotheses, seeking women who challenged intensive mothering, intensive working, or both.

Challenging Intensive Mothering: Working Mothers and Counterhegemonic Mothering Norms

When I set out to find women who had successfully challenged the intensive-mothering component of the shadow-mother knot, I had several reasons for seeking mothers of color who employed nannies. First, among the mother-employers I had already interviewed, white women who worked full-time expressed more guilt about not staying at home, regardless of whether their own mothers had worked outside the home. Second, a rich literature documents the tradition of "othermothers" and extended kin care in communities of color.[9] I wanted to see whether this tradition also held among professional-class working mothers. Finally, in looking back over the interviews with the twenty-two mother-employers in the first wave of data collection, the only employers who engaged in partnerships with their nannies from day one were Min and Joyce, both raised in cultures where mothers who worked outside the home were the norm.

In the second round of interviews, therefore, I sought out mother-employers whose own mothers had worked outside the home, particularly women of color. I found that growing up with an employed mother did not automatically cause respondents to reject the more outrageous demands of intensive mothering. Of twenty-two white mother-employers, seven had mothers who had worked outside of the home when they were children, but only three of these engaged in partnerships with their nannies. Of the eight black, Latina, and Asian mother-employers I interviewed, all had been raised by mothers who worked outside the home. Only three were in partnerships, however. The other five tended toward paranormal relationships, assuming that racial/ethnic similarity would translate into similar childrearing practices. Rather than acting as a causal factor, coming from a culture that affirmed mothers' work generally offered mother-employers a resource, a "vocabulary of motive," on which to draw in framing their own relationships to the demands of intensive mothering.[10]

For example, Gloria, a forty-five-year-old African American schoolteacher with two young children, explained her upbringing this way: "My mother worked nights, my father worked days. So to me this was normal. I realize there's an entire society of women out there [for whom] this is not normal. They don't have role models to follow, which I think kind of prepared [my husband and me] for this. . . . Both our mothers worked. We both had that role modeling and that was valuable." When her children entered school and paying for a full-time nanny was no longer feasible, she and her husband managed childcare by doing what she called the "flip-flop": "Like the flip-flop. My parents flip-flopped their work schedule. My husband and I have pretty much done that too, except he's the one who's done most of the flipping [laughter]. I mean after the third babysitter left, he stayed home with the kids and got a night job." Gloria was able to work full-time without guilt, to delegate childrearing to a nanny when the family income could support full-time paid childcare, and to share parenting with her husband when having a nanny became too expensive. She attributed the ease with shared childrearing she and her husband felt to the role modeling they had received when they were growing up.

Joyce echoed the importance of upbringing and culture of origin in the construction of maternal guilt. In response to my asking, "Do you think that in our culture in general, working mothers are made to feel guilty?" she began, "I think it depends on which culture you're talking about. Um, if you're talking about—

[*pause*]." Although she stopped short, avoiding an explicit statement of the refer-
ent, she clearly was referring to the distinction between the dominant white middle-class culture and the African American working-class culture of her childhood.

> *Joyce:* Well, let me first say that my mother was always a working mother. We
> were a working-class family and my mother in fact had two jobs. And
> she would work as a secretary during the day, and she would work at the
> post office at night.
>
> *Cameron:* So who took care of you growing up?
>
> *Joyce:* First we had a babysitter's house we used to go to and then we were in
> school, and my sister was seven years older than I was, so we would just go
> home. And we were supposed to stay in the house. I grew up in Brooklyn,
> in New York, and so we were supposed to stay in the house until—they
> came home. So, um, I was used to having a mother who worked. Almost
> all of the friends that I had, their mothers worked. And that's what you
> have to do to survive and make a living, so I mean that was normal.

In Joyce's view, her mother showed her love for her family by working two jobs.
Her absence from the home was not a sign of maternal neglect; on the contrary,
it was a necessary sacrifice. Joyce's mother provided a model of good motherhood
in difficult financial circumstances: she prioritized her children's economic well-
being. For Joyce, the normalcy of this mothering model was reinforced by the fact
that every mother she knew raised her children this way.

Later in her life, when she attended an elite boarding school on a scholarship,
Joyce was exposed to a different mothering culture:

> And that was a very different culture where some of the mothers worked, but most
> of the work was volunteerism-type work. And then I think, you know, there are
> segments of our society that do make women feel guilty for working. But I think
> that you should do what you want to do. Some people don't have a choice as to what
> they can do because it's a means of surviving. If they don't work—then they don't
> have money. But if that's what you like to do in terms of being home and being with
> your kids, and you can afford to do it, then that's fine. But I don't think you have to
> do it. I could never be a full-time at-home mother. Even if we're talking about that
> volunteerism-type stuff.

Joyce's personal experiences had exposed her to two different models of good
motherhood. Her childhood experience with mothers who worked because of
economic necessity shaped her view that the mothers of her boarding-school
peers were not really working but just doing "that volunteerism-type stuff." She
assumed these women were not meeting financial obligations, so she saw them
as at-home mothers, even though their work as volunteers regularly took them
out of the home.

Mother-employers who were raised in countries where employed mothers were
the norm also drew on their childhood culture as a resource in reframing their

relationship to U.S. mothering ideologies. For example, Min, an immigrant from China, brought an international perspective to the question of working-mother guilt:

> *Cameron:* Did you feel pressure from your colleagues to continue working after your son was born?
>
> *Min:* No, not from my colleagues. If there was any pressure, I would say there's some pressure from the way I was brought up, from my mother. Because uh—in my memory, my mother had always worked. And then when my brother and I were little, we had a childcare person live with us for years in China. Also, in China most women work. If it's not 95 percent, I would say it's 94 percent or more. . . . When I grew up, I didn't know any mothers who didn't work. All my friends' mothers worked. So for me that was just the way it was. I never thought there would be other ways. So I did plan to work before the child was born. I thought of course I would go back to work [*laughs*]. Until he came, and then I realized how difficult it was.

Min felt no culturally prescribed guilt about returning to work, but she was appalled at the lack of institutional support for working mothers in the United States. "Compared to China, the support a working mother gets is just *so* little. Just *so* little. . . . In China, every workplace has a daycare center. . . . American daycare is not at work, and it is so small, sometimes a half basement! And I would say the housing in China is much, much, more crowded compared to the United States. However, every Chinese daycare, the space is better than American daycare! [*laughs*]" Although this lack of support made her return to work difficult, it did not deter Min from continuing to pursue her career as a scientist. She explained, "I enjoy what I do at work. Also I realized that I have another life other than having children. And then my son needs to go out to spend some time with children his own age." Like Joyce and Gloria, Min challenged intensive mothering ideology by drawing both on her personal history and on a cultural context in which employed mothers were the norm.

Among the women I interviewed, those who were able to challenge intensive mothering were most likely to be women of color who came from generations of mothers who worked outside the home, and who thus could draw on counter-hegemonic models of good motherhood.[11] These mother-employers also pointed to the fact that they were more available to their children than their mothers had been to them, just as their mothers had spent more time with them than their grandmothers had spent with their mothers and their aunts and uncles. Unlike most of the white working women in my study, the women of color could point to a rising "emotional standard of living" in each successive generation. Although I would have expected the same to be true of at least some of the white mother-employers I interviewed, this trend was not so evident.

In addition, the mother-employers of color I interviewed held to the "other-mothering" tradition, further strengthening these women's resistance to the excesses of intensive mothering. Although these interviewees believed strongly in the infant-toddler version of "concerted cultivation," they had very few qualms about sharing childrearing labor with their childcare providers or with their husbands and other family members.[12] Having loving adults outside of the family providing childcare was not anomalous to these women. It was not an add-on or a detriment to their mothering practice; rather, sharing the care of children was understood as an organic component of being a good mother. This is childrearing in the "it takes a village" sense rather than the mother-only sense.

Two of the white mother-employers I interviewed in the second wave of interviews overtly resisted the demands of intensive mothering and were in partnerships with their caregivers, but for reasons that differed from those cited by the women of color I interviewed. Leah, a forty-four-year-old white attorney, grew up in a working-class home among European immigrants; her mother worked outside the home but viewed cooking and cleaning as the most essential woman's work. As Leah pointed out, "I remember my mother would ask me to help with the dishes and things in the kitchen. And my brother was not asked to do that. And I found that to be a grave injustice in ways that make me smile with amusement now. But I do remember saying to my mother, 'I just don't want to have to do all this when I grow up. And she said 'Well, *you'll see.*'" Leah's mother worked out of necessity, not by choice, and she did not view her work as the model Leah should follow. Rather, as Leah said, her mother was more attuned to the "kind of 1950s idea that women did stuff in the kitchen."

Her mother's views on domesticity ultimately clashed with Leah's hopes for the future when Leah sought to go to college. Her family could now afford to send her, but her mother thought she should stay home and go to junior college. Her father stepped in and, as Leah recounted, told her mother, "I've never said this in twenty years of marriage, but I think if she stays here and lives with us, she'll be pregnant in a year and her life will just go down the tube, and she's too smart and too talented to do that. I make more money than you do, and I'm sending her." She described her mother as being furious but ultimately giving in—until Leah was accepted at a top-ranked law school, when she started the fight again. "I remember my mother saying, 'We shouldn't spend all that money on you going to law school because you'll just get married and have a baby and you won't use your law degree.' . . . And in part, I think she probably was a little jealous, you know? Because look, I was getting to have this life that still, to me, seems like a Cinderella life. What it must have seemed like to her. So it's very poignant looking back on those things."

Leah found peace and belonging among the feminist colleagues at law school, and later in her marriage to an egalitarian husband. She explained that she came to her sense of work/life balance in the company of her law-school cohort:

> We were politically identified as feminists; we wanted to change the world. And having kids was going to be something we did, but not all we did, and not even necessarily the central thing we did. . . . We were very driven by work as a vocation. . . . And I think we married men who were good material for egalitarian relationships. We had our kids late in life [Leah was thirty-nine]. I just know a number of people like that, and I think that it was our vision of feminism [that made it work]. Not the only way to do it, but a good way to do it.

As one of the older mother-employers in this study, Leah was greatly influenced by second-wave feminism, and it provided a counterhegemonic ideology on which she could draw to chart her own mothering course. Feminism, a father who believed in her, a mother's cautionary tale, and a role-sharing husband combined to give Leah a path out of intensive mothering, and thus a way to opt out of the need for a "shadow mother" in Ellie, her daughter's nanny of four years.[13]

Elizabeth was the other white mother-employer from the second set of interviews who broke the intensive-mothering mold. She had a highly demanding job as a CEO, became a single mother by choice at age forty-two, and had a solid partnership relationship with her nanny, Lonehl, in raising her daughter, Chloe. Elizabeth's mother had been a teacher but left the workforce when the first of her six children was born. As Elizabeth explained, "When my next-to-youngest brother was almost six, [Mom] was planning to go back and teach and she got pregnant again. I was ten years old and I still have strong memories of how angry she was about that." Her mother stayed out of the workforce for another six years and finally returned to teaching. Elizabeth's mother's experience was also an influential cautionary tale. Although Elizabeth had always planned to have children, she had never planned to sacrifice her autonomy the way her mother did. And like the women of color I interviewed, she did point to a "rising emotional standard of living" for Chloe because "by the time I was Chloe's age, I had three younger siblings and an older sibling." By contrast, "Chloe is an only child and gets a whole lot more one-on-one time than I got."

As important as her mother's life trajectory was in shaping Elizabeth's need to renegotiate her view of mothering, giving birth to Chloe at age forty-two pushed her even harder to rethink her conception of family and of combining work and mothering. In her path-breaking study of single mothers by choice, Rosanna Hertz has argued that these women "develop a concept of the child care provider that is far from normative. . . . [F]or these mothers the child care provider is not invisible, but rather is part of the team."[14] As Elizabeth pointed out, her single-mom status meant that she *needed* Lonehl more, and therefore had to work harder to create a successful partnership. "There is no doubt, versus a couple, that I have a much higher need. I don't have the *give* of 'John, why don't you get home early tonight?' . . . Two parent-families don't have a clue. . . . It's easy for a two-parent family to tell you that you don't need [at least full-time] backup, but they've got each other."

Because she relied so heavily on her nanny, she needed to invest more in maintaining a working relationship with Lonehl. She also noted that she invested more in this "relational work" because she lacked a husband to play the all-important role of bad cop.[15] "[Being a single mom] makes your needs that much higher and it makes it a more charged relationship, and you don't have that third variable. You can't say, 'Oh you know, it's really OK with me but John wouldn't like it.' I can't do that."

Like many single mothers by choice, Elizabeth hired the family support she needs by building an extended family relationship with Lonehl and her family. As she put it, "Lonehl is part of the family and part of Chloe's extended family, so unless there was some ugly blowup, which I can't imagine—we've put up with each other for $3\frac{1}{2}$ years—I would expect that Lonehl and her family would be part of the extended family." As part of a small but growing group of women intentionally building families without partners, Elizabeth created family bonds where she could find them.

Elizabeth and Leah were unlike the women of color I interviewed who rejected intensive mothering due to long-standing cultural norms, or the mothers from countries where state policies mitigated the demands of intensive mothering. Instead, they rejected intensive mothering because they were on the leading edge of particular social movements that led them to pioneer new ways of combining work and motherhood and simultaneously offered them cultural resources on which to draw to support their choices.

We might expect the same from all white women whose mothers worked outside the home, but the other white mother-employers I interviewed approached mothering from a perspective driven by intensive mothering. Although seven of twenty-two white mother-employers were raised by employed mothers, they were ambivalent about their mothers' work lives. Most often, they viewed their mothers' work lives as cautionary tales. This negative interpretation did not reflect a belief that they had suffered as children because their mothers worked. Quite the contrary: most had good memories of time spent in childcare centers or of beloved nannies. In some cases, they viewed their mothers as anomalous "super-moms." Others pointed to mothers who said that they regretted lost time with their children. More often, the mother's relationship to work was interpreted in more nuanced ways by their white daughters.

Gwen's ambivalent relationship to her mother's work history is a typical example of this complexity. Her mother worked as an instructor at four colleges simultaneously, but never completed her doctorate in order to pursue a tenure-track job because it would take time away from her three children. Gwen said that she followed in her mother's footsteps by "deciding early on to screw my career in order to not have regrets about parenting. That's the decision my mom made." She said that her mom "was always exhausted, up late grading papers, and running around teaching at four different colleges and doing 'office hours' sitting on her back bumper in college parking lots." At the same time, her mother made it clear to her that she never regretted her decision to work and to hire the German nanny who made this possible: "I remember very clearly a discussion I had with my mom once when I was a teenager that was very formative. I looked at her tired self and said, 'Mom, I am so sorry that you have to work so hard all the time at all these jobs. I am sorry that you couldn't work less and have an easier life.' She looked at me and said, 'I *love* my job, honey. I could *never* have stayed home with you guys. It would have driven me absolutely nuts!'" Gwen described the conversation as "unbelievably liberating," although also a little shocking, adding a wry reference to a child's egocentric view: "What? I'm not the source of all your happiness? [*laughter*]" She said that her mother's "example of pride in her work . . . plus the fact that she was a really great mom probably has been the main reason that I have had little or no mom guilt. I want my daughters to see that in me."

But Gwen's interpretation of her mother's life is neither simple nor straightforward. Although she wanted to emulate her mother's pride in her work and to model that pride for her daughters, she simultaneously chose to "screw" her own career so that she could work part-time and flextime to avoid mother-guilt. Furthermore, Gwen attributed her mother's premature death from cancer to "a weakened immune system due to lifelong exhaustion and chemical exposures. She never could sit down without falling asleep, and she constantly sublimated her own needs to the rest of ours." Gwen's life choices bore out the many and conflicting ways she interpreted her mother's life story. In the absence of a strong culturally and socially based counterhegemonic ideal of mothering, Gwen's mother's experience served simultaneously as outlier, role model, and cautionary tale.

In analyzing the life trajectories of the mothers-employers I interviewed and how they interpreted their own mothers' relationships to work, I found that the *fact* of growing up with a working mother did not provide a sufficient positive role model in the face of intensive mothering ideologies. The mother-workers I interviewed also had more career opportunities and more demanding and fulfilling jobs than their mothers had had. This fact did not mitigate the effects of intensive mothering or how they used their mothers' life histories to think about their own mothering trajectories. How their mothers interpreted their experiences of combining work and family shaped how these daughters carried forward their mothers' relationship to work. And, for the mother-employers who entered into partnerships with their caregivers, having had working-mother role models was not sufficient to help them challenge aspects of intensive mothering; a successful challenge drew on counterhegemonic cultural beliefs, not individual biography.

Challenging Intensive Work: Part-Time Working Mothers and
the Threshold of Connection

In the first wave of data collection for the study, the mother-employers I interviewed worked full-time. When I looked back over these interviews and compared
the full-time workers to the part-time and flextime workers I interviewed in the
second phase of data collection, I noted that mothers who worked full-time in
male-pattern careers often felt so out of touch with what went on at home that
they had little or no experience of the responsibilities they were delegating to their
caregivers. As discussed in chapter 5, lack of experience led puppeteer managers
to impose unrealistic schedules on their children and nannies. Furthermore, many
feared that their nannies or au pairs might be doing their jobs too well, and thus
encroaching on the mothers' emotional territory. Preverbal children, in particular,
communicate a tremendous amount of information simply through subtle changes
in their responses to daily routines. As previous chapters have shown, mother-
employers who feel disconnected from these everyday routines often seek to gain
a sense of control by imposing policies that may not be reasonable for the child
or the caregiver. They also may seek to compensate by attempting to appear in
control and knowledgeable, and thus may seem to the caregiver to be crowding
her out and denying her knowledge. These concerns point to an important and
unexplored question: how much connection do mothers need in order to feel
secure in their relationships with their children?

All the mother-employers in the study stated that their ideal work schedule
would involve some kind of part-time arrangement. Those who had jobs that
demanded especially long hours and/or those with brief maternity leaves were
particularly frustrated with the imbalance between work and motherhood in their
lives. More important, many of these working mothers, especially those with very
young children, expressed a deep sense of insecurity about their mothering skills
and about the security of the bond between them and their children. They felt
inadequate when their children preferred their nannies or fathers to them. They
were disconcerted and sometimes dispirited when parents they did not know
said hello to their children in the supermarket or at the park. These encounters
underscored the painful reality that their children lived substantial periods of their
lives in communities that were foreign to them. As Suzanne remarked, they often
did not know what developmental stage their children were entering until it "was
about to hit me in the face." These mother-employers felt that they never reached
their own "threshold of connection," and their resulting insecurities played out in
interactions with their nannies.

Jessica was the most adamant of those who felt that their threshold of connection had not been met. When I asked her if she felt that social pressures to be a
stay-at-home mother had played a role in her decision to quit work, she replied,

"After I've been home for a while, maybe I would start [to feel that pressure], or if I was secure in my relationship with my child. My need for my relationship with my child is dominant now. And this is just my own personal thing. I mean, maybe if I felt good about being at work, I would feel like, 'Gosh, there's so many people who feel you should be home to raise a child properly.'" Here Jessica raises an important distinction between a *personal* need for adequate connection and *socially prescribed* expectations concerning good mothering. The distinction she draws between the two raises the question of whether simply changing cultural scripts would address the deep ambivalence she experienced. In her case, it was her personal sense of a loss of connection with her child that led her to decide to leave her lucrative career. Once she had been home with her son long enough to heal that wound, she felt she would be better able to assess how she wanted to use her time, whether it was entirely as a mother, some combination of part-time work and parenting, or returning to a full-time job.

Suzanne echoed Jessica's sentiments, stating that she would prefer a "part-time situation . . . where you can still get some satisfaction out of your work, but still have enough time to focus on cultivating a nice family environment." She referred to a friend who had what Suzanne considered the "ideal situation," in which "she has time to arrange for her kids to play, she knows all her kids' friends, and organizes activities." The culture of play dates and organized activities are clearly class-specific and stem from professional-class mothers' interpretations of intensive mothering. The desire for sufficient time to know one's children's friends and to be a part of their daily activities, however, are nearly universal parental desires. Suzanne's wishes do not seem excessive, but the demands of her job put even these simple actions in the category of out-of-reach luxuries.

Most of the research on dual-income families posits access to better childcare or more participation by fathers in childrearing as solutions to the "role strain" experienced by working mothers. Yet even the financial resources to purchase high-quality childcare and the presence of relatively participatory fathers were not sufficient to allow many of the mother-employers I interviewed to feel secure in their work-family arrangements. Paradoxically, for some, their husbands' participation and their caregivers' devotion to their children enhanced their feelings of inadequacy and insecurity.[16]

That fathers also feel this sense of loss seems less likely. Most of the husbands of the working women I interviewed were significantly more present in their children's lives than their own fathers had been in theirs. The mothers I interviewed, whether or not they wanted to replicate their own upbringing, were aware of the ways that their mothering diverged from, and might fall short of, their mothers' care. More important, however, there was a threshold beyond which mothers felt unacceptably absent from their children's lives. The locations of this threshold varied but, as mentioned earlier, all of the mothers stated that their ideal job would entail some form of part-time work or a graduated return to full-time work.

In the second round of interviews, I sought women who worked part-time or flextime schedules. Based on my experience with Elaine and Christine, I wanted to explore the idea that if a mother's threshold of connection had been met—and I assumed that meeting this threshold would vary from one respondent to another—she would feel secure enough in her connection with her children to delegate parts of that relationship to someone else. The part-time and flextime working mothers confirmed this notion. Because they had fulfilled their own need for what Suzanne called "at-homeness," they were less threatened by their nannies and more reasonable in their expectations of themselves and their children.

Libby was a perfect example of a flextime working mother. Her job was full-time but she could leave early or go in late whenever she needed to. During the summers when her husband, a teacher, was at home, she worked four long days so she could have three-day weekends with her family. This arrangement helped her to feel comfortable enough in her sense of herself as a mother to acknowledge that she would never want to stay home full-time. When I asked if it was something she ever considered, she laughed and responded, "Never. I would be just—Rob and I laughed about it this weekend. I would be miserable, he would be miserable, the children would be miserable. 'Know thy weaknesses.' That's my weakness. I can't stay home. Fortunately, we live in a day and age that I don't have to feel ashamed about that." Libby's sense of guiltlessness, however, was not widely shared. Most of the mothers from the first wave of interviews felt ashamed of their lack of desire to stay home with their children full-time. They felt they should at least *want* to be at home, or at least that their children should want them to want to. As a result, they unintentionally created a situation in which they believed that they and their children should feel deprived.[17]

By contrast, Libby did not feel threatened when her children chose Grace over her: "I assume the kids are going to run to Grace. They should, when she's here. And if it's between her and me, I don't know. I guess it's also how you perceive your role as a mother. And my role as a mother is not—[*pause*] I'm not going to be the sole loving female adult in their life." This is a radical statement in comparison to the views expressed by the other mother-employers I interviewed. I suggest that the flexibility in her work schedule allowed her to develop such a level of confidence in her status as mother that she could easily accept another significant maternal figure in her children's lives.

Andrea and her nanny, Bridget, provide another example of the kind of satisfactory relationship that employers and nannies can create if the threshold of connection is met. Andrea, at age thirty-six, worked part-time as a medical educator and was the mother of five children ranging in age from one to eight, with two-year-old twins and a six-year-old in the middle. Bridget brought her two-year-old son, Owen, to work with her, so when she was at Andrea's house, she cared for six children.

Andrea described how her expectations of Bridget's interactions with the children differed from those of her friends who worked full-time: "Someone could say, 'For an hour I want you to color with them.' Well, I know from being home with them, they're not going to last an hour. I can see if you weren't home you would have this grand scheme, you know, in your head . . . but it doesn't work that way . . . like this one's going to be out of control, that one's going to be crying about nothing, and things just happen that you don't think are going to happen." One of the benefits of part-time work is that mother-employers have a clear picture of exactly what duties and responsibilities they delegate. This knowledge, in turn, makes them more likely to have realistic expectations.

Mothers in partnerships were also less likely to need to believe that their children behaved perfectly all the time. Andrea added, "We'll kind of learn stuff from each other, about how they've been with her, or how they've been with me. . . . One of them seems to be having a bad week and she'll be very honest about, 'Oh yeah, she's been like this,' or, 'This week, she's been absolutely fine with me.'" This kind of mutual learning emerges on a daily basis when neither party sees the other's knowledge as a threat.

Bridget described working with Andrea and her children as "the perfect job." She got to be with Owen full-time and to be paid to do what she did best. In addition, "Owen has the best of both worlds. He's got me all day long and he's got other kids that he actually loves and adores." She also appreciated Andrea's efforts to ensure that she had full-time work. During the school year, Andrea hired Bridget to come to the house on the days she was away at work, and arranged for a relative to hire Bridget and Owen to provide childcare at their home on Andrea's days off. During the summertime, when Andrea did not work outside the home, she found a neighbor who needed three-day-a-week childcare and who was receptive to having Bridget bring Owen to work. Andrea's explanation—that her goal was to make it possible for Bridget "to stay as long as she wants to"—is revealing. She, like other mother-employers in partnerships with their caregivers, viewed the nanny as a whole person who was essential to her employer's family's well-being and whose needs had to be met in order to keep her with the family for the long haul. This perspective contrasts sharply with the view of puppeteer and paranormal employers, who typically considered the nanny a minor cog in their childrearing apparatus.

Andrea and Bridget took different approaches with the children. Bridget was more structured, Andrea a bit more "go-with-the-flow." Yet this difference was not a cause of conflict. Each appreciated what the other brought to the relationship. Andrea laughingly offered this example of their contrasting approaches: "Sometimes if I run home at lunchtime, they're all sitting around the table eating their lunch perfectly. And I feel like [when I do lunch], I have one here and the other over there, and I'm yelling, 'Sit down!' They don't look like my kids sitting down at the table eating their sandwich." At the same time, she admitted to being relieved to find that Bridget's son, Owen, who was approaching two, now "says, 'No! No!' and he's hitting her, and won't do what she's trying to get him to do . . . and I'm saying, 'Gee, Bridget, I thought you'd have the perfect child!' But we just write it off to the 'mother effect.'" Here, a misbehaving child was seen not as a failure on the part of the mother or the nanny but rather as a normal part of the challenges of parenting.

Ronda and Mary had a similar relationship, although they shared the care of only one child, Molly, who was still an infant. Mary was a first-time mother, and she had some of the same anxieties expressed by other new moms I interviewed. She did not feel jealous of Ronda's time with Molly, but she acknowledged that if she were working full- rather than part-time, she would "envy" her nanny: "I feel like I'm not missing that whole [infancy] experience. Like, if I were going to work all the time, there would be a real envy. In fact, we have this regular routine, and I feel like now Ronda is here 2.5 days a week, and I'm still part of the regular routine." Ronda appreciated the trust Mary and her husband placed in her. She compared them favorably to a previous employer who had stayed home full-time and was always "breathing over everybody's shoulder": "That makes people uncomfortable. She had a hard time finding a good nanny to stay with her because she's so busy looking over their shoulder, making sure. Maybe she feels that way because of Louise Woodward . . . but you still have to give somebody a little bit more room."[18] Ronda said her current situation was ideal. Mary worked part-time as a physician and worked with Ronda to keep the baby's routine consistent. Ronda also checked in with Molly's dad before she and the baby left the house and phoned Mary at work throughout the day. Unlike Ronda's unsatisfactory stay-at-home employer, however, neither Mary nor her husband engaged in the kind of "hovering" Ronda found so uncomfortable, and despite her regular check-ins with both parents, she felt she had a high degree of autonomy, which she interpreted as parental respect for her childcare skill.

Ida, one of Ronda's nanny friends from the playground, shared Ronda's sentiments regarding a part-time employed mother as a (potentially) ideal employer. Ida argued that her own employer's exposure to sustained periods of time at home with her young daughter helped the mother recognize that the child was "a handful." Elaborating, she said that when her employer stayed home, "She had to do stuff with her so she wouldn't get bored, put her down for her nap [which could be a struggle]." This experience, Ida felt, was "one reason she is more understanding."

These examples suggest that if their threshold of connection is met, employers feel more comfortable modifying their commitment to intensive mothering. Mothers were aware of social pressures to stay home full-time. If, however, they felt comfortable in their level of connection with their children, they also felt that they could choose to ignore that aspect of the intensive-mothering norm. Not surprisingly, the mother-employers in the second round of interviews who worked part-time or flextime were the most satisfied with their work and family arrangements. They were also more adept at working with their caregivers, especially when their children were younger than three. They had enough experience being with their children to understand the work they were delegating, and they were secure enough in their own connection with their children to welcome the help of another caring adult.

BENEFITS OF PARTNERSHIPS

Overcoming the Demands of Shadow Motherhood

The collaborative childrearing that was the hallmark of partnerships emulated the third-parent ideal sought by most nannies (see chapter 7), rather than the shadow-mother arrangement most of the mother-employers I interviewed felt they needed. As a result, nannies in partnerships were more satisfied in their work. At the same time, their employers felt more comfortable in their roles as mothers and as childcare employers.

For example, partnership mothers reinvented their view of what it meant to *them* to be a mother. Joyce shook her head with disdain when describing parents who engineered nanny turnover so that they could be sure that the nanny never usurped the mother's place: "I think that it's more important that he have a stable relationship with someone than, you know, people coming and going. Like, some people will say, 'How will he know [the difference between Mom and nanny]?' So if you keep getting rid of people and they come and go, then you will be the most constant person in his life and then it will be fine. And I think that's ridiculous. [*laughter*]" The hot-button topics that created tensions in shadow-mother arrangements did not seem to worry the women in partnerships. They did not require "mother-only tasks," nor were they overly concerned about whom their child addressed as "Mommy." Libby, for instance, dismissed her children's use of the word *mommy* as "no big deal." She recognized that her three-year-old son, in particular, sometimes referred to her as "Grace" and to Grace as "Mummy" in a deliberate effort to "get a rise out of either of us. He's definitely conscious of the game, and conscious of the distinction."

Similarly, these mothers, because they viewed themselves as one of several loving adults whose care and attention shaped their children's lives, did not make fetishes of their children's "firsts."[19] Joyce explained how she and her husband enlisted Stacy's help in recording Ellis's developmental milestones: "So we've said to Stacy, 'You know, if you see him doing something that's really great, put it on video so then we can see it. But, you know, I realize that I'm not gonna be able to see everything that he does." This openness to sharing "firsts" allowed parents and caregivers to collaborate in planning certain first-time events. In separate interviews, Grace and Libby described their collective effort to potty train Jaden. Grace said, "With Jaden, I just felt he was ready for potty training. And we call Mom and Dad and tell them, 'Jaden went pee-pee in the potty,' or 'Jaden went poo-poo in the potty,' or whatever it is. It's a big deal. We make a big deal of big steps." Libby's description of this process was a mirror image, with the addition of some office humor: "She [Grace] has the kids leave messages on my machine, about 'Mummy, I went poopy in the potty', which I save and replay, to everybody's great amusement."

Partnerships benefited both parties even when they had different styles. Mary's description of things she learned by being at home supports Ida's opinion that mother-employers who work part-time can gain a deep understanding and appreciation of what nannies do and can offer. Mary and Ronda had somewhat different styles—Ronda liked to dress Molly in frilly clothes; Mary preferred less "girly playclothes." Ronda was a "take charge" nanny who rearranged Molly's drawers and closets and kept a "baby log," even though Mary had not requested that she do so. Over time, Mary came to frame these sorts of differences as advantageous. At first, she said, she felt, " 'Oh, how can I let anybody else take care of my child?' And then I see that Ronda brings something totally different to Molly than I do. She's much more outgoing and gregarious and chatty than we are. . . . So there is a good side, too. It's not just making sure nothing terrible happens to your child. There's also this good side, which is that they get something from being with [another caregiver] that they might not get [otherwise]."

The mother-employers who had created successful partnerships with their nannies also felt comfortable sharing parenting with their husbands. Although several of the mothers I interviewed had husbands who worked from home at least some of the time, only those in partnerships encouraged their husbands to become part of the childcare team. Leah explained how her nanny, Ellie, and her husband, James, did many activities together: "James feels totally comfortable arranging things. . . . Now that he's home more, he's basically taken over [interacting with] the nanny." Leah felt that her husband's increased comfort level was the result of his being present and available to interact frequently with Ellie and the baby. She also saw that if she wanted to encourage this kind of teamwork, which she considered healthy, she had to get out of the way.

> I do think a lot of women act as gatekeepers. And I don't. . . . Once early on, when Alyssa was an infant, James always got up with her in the night. I'd had a terrible pregnancy and I was sick afterwards. . . . And he took care of things. And I remember once saying, "You're not doing the diaper right." And he said, "What do you mean, *right*? Are you, like, a baby nurse? Since when do you know how to diaper?" And

I thought, "You know, he's absolutely right. He's not going to do anything if I don't stop this."

Other mother-employers in partnership arrangements were similarly encouraging of paternal involvement. Rather than insisting on "mother-only" tasks, Andrea, for example, said that she and her husband tried to "split up" the five children between them. Each parent would take charge of their subgroup and do age-appropriate activities, or one adult might play with the younger children while the other helped the older children with their homework. This same flexibility in who does what with whom applied to the nanny as well.

Did mothers who shared parenting with fathers welcome nannies more comfortably into their lives? Or did a partnership with the childcare provider open the door to a broader definition of mothering and, thus, of parenting? Given the small size of the partnership sample, I cannot draw any causal conclusions, other than the clear indication from the mothers' descriptions that the two forms of sharing were clearly linked in their minds (as were all forms of maternal "gatekeeping"). I did not meet mothers who let fathers in but kept nannies out or vice versa, nor did I meet any mothers who had partnership relationships with their nannies who did not extend this to other family members. Clearly, these questions require further research.

Partnerships and Fair Pay

Finally, although most of the nannies I interviewed said they were willing to trade fair pay for recognition, nannies in partnership arrangements were well paid. As discussed in chapter 3, employers caught in the intensive-mothering/intensive-working knot tended to view the nanny's pay as a portion of their own salaries. They felt they needed to justify their "right" to work, and therefore calculated the nanny's salary as one of their own work-related expenses. As discussed in chapter 3, mothers who viewed their nannies as shadow mothers tended to calculate working hours and wages so that the nanny's hours fit *outside* the mother's workday, while her wages fit *inside* the mother's salary.

In partnership arrangements, however, the nanny's salary was calculated as a crucial component of the family budget. Employers who favored partnerships tended to describe nanny pay in the same "how much is my child worth to me" language that most nannies used. These employers spoke of their childcare expenses as second only to mortgage and health insurance in importance, and they were very critical of parents who tried to get childcare "on the cheap." Mary explained, "It's amazing what people will spend money on, and [childcare is] the first thing they think is too expensive. It's only ten dollars an hour, but they're driving around in God knows what for a car. . . . I'm not talking about the people who have to work full-time really to make ends meet, but people who have plenty of money but are trying to scrimp, you know, on childcare." In partnership households, the nanny's wage sometimes topped that of the lower earner in the family, which occasionally caused tensions when the lower earner was the husband. Leah said, "We used to joke, Cameron, that James was turning over all of his after-tax income to Ellie." James and Leah viewed Ellie's work as an essential aspect of family functioning, however, and paid her what they felt her work was worth.

Libby described a similar scenario in her family's negotiations over Grace's wages. Libby's salary as an executive was quite high; her husband, Rob, who was a schoolteacher, earned significantly less. This was a potential source of friction, so Libby "started out by what the going rate was . . . but about three months into it, I gave Grace a raise that I didn't tell my husband about for a couple of weeks because I knew it was going to upset him. But my feeling was, I couldn't pay this woman enough." When she approached Rob about the raise, he said, "Fine. As long as she's not getting paid more than I am." It was not long, however, before Grace was earning more than Rob. As Libby explained, laughingly, "He's a little frosted about that. It's turned into his favorite story to tell."

Elizabeth compared Lonehl's salary to that of her more important company employees, noting, "I pay her over half what we pay the employees who work here. And in fact I am a firm believer that someone who cares for children should be paid a living wage and that it is valuable work and we need to value it. . . . In my view, being linked into unemployment and social security and other things is very important. And for someone to spend multiple years doing [childcare] and having no credit in the larger system is very problematic." Not all the mothers I interviewed had the means to support their beliefs in fair pay for nanny work, but it is notable that nannies in partnerships tended to earn more, not because the mothers they worked for necessarily earned more, but because the nanny's wage was viewed as a necessary and important family expense, not a guilty replacement for the mother's time at home.

CONCLUSION

Joyce's comments about her relationship with Stacy provide a concise summary of the key attributes of partnership from an employer's perspective: "I think just the openness and being responsive to things that she has to say, and her opinion, that it counts, what she thinks. . . . But the other thing that I think is important, and I think that at least some people don't realize, is that it is a job; it's not a servant. And you have to think about yourself as an employer and what will be a good relationship and how to make that person want to stay doing what they're doing. Because [childcare] is something important." Similarly, nannies who reflected on their ideal relationship also emphasized the importance of communication and mutual respect.

My interviews with caregivers and mother-employers in partnerships offer a fruitful avenue of exploration. Since childcare workers are here to stay as crucial members of families' childrearing strategies, it is essential to determine best practices that facilitate successful communication and mutual recognition in parent-caregiver relationships. Although my sample is limited to one form of childcare, workers in other childcare settings complain of the same problems: lack of recognition and respect, poor communication, and poor pay.[20] The principles of partnerships can be applied to all childcare relationships, as discussed in the next chapter.

Untangling the Mother-Nanny Knot

Rather than confirming the home as a haven from the heartless world, this study has revealed the heartlessness of the system in which both mothers and nannies are caught. The preceding chapters detailed the ways in which these women's efforts to meet unrealistic ideals of mothering pit them against each other; too often, self-destructive conflicts fill the space that might otherwise be used to form mutually supportive partnerships that would enhance children's care. But such partnerships *are* possible. The study participants' experiences pointed to two important enabling factors: personal experience with and access to counterhegemonic mothering ideologies, and flextime or part-time schedules that allowed working mothers to reach their individual threshold of connection with their children, thus helping them feel more secure and more willing to share mothering work with others.[1] These changes on the employer side of the mother-nanny dyad also empowered caregivers to exercise greater control over their time and in their relationships with employers. The data are not exhaustive, but these findings suggest that when both mother-employers and nannies have frequent opportunities for real control over their own work, their relationship is likely to produce strongly positive results for everyone, including the children.[2]

By taking a sociological perspective, the preceding chapters turned the focus away from the personality traits and personal quirks of individuals in mother-nanny dyads and drew attention, instead, to the constraints of each party's social location and to the separate and combined pressures of ideology and the market. Mother-employers' demanding and inflexible work schedules undermined their sense of control over, or even familiarity with, the home front. This in turn made them likely to impose unreasonable rules and regulations on nannies. And the ever more competitive, high-stakes educational lottery their children were likely to face made these professional-class working mothers feel less confident about being able to achieve their mothering goals. Thus, they hired in-home caregivers and tried to control their every move, hoping that by doing so they would ensure that their children received optimal time and attention. Elements of the logic of professional-class intensive mothering—the importance of mother-only attachment, the birth-to-three fetish, and the necessity of developing children's skills and attributes sufficiently to ensure them a competitive edge—became more anxiety-producing to working mothers as their distance from the daily work of childrearing increased. Otherwise reasonable and well-intentioned mother-employers, even women who identified as feminists, became the puppeteer and paranormal managers of chapter 5, who then made the shadow-mothering demands of chapter 6. As workers who had very little power over their own work schedules and thus very little control over the time they were able to spend with their children, they became employers who withheld this kind of power and control from their nannies.

Not surprisingly, their nannies were acutely aware of and unhappy with their lack of autonomy, and they resented their employers' failure to recognize them as responsible adults and skilled workers, leading to the "third-parent" ideal and resistance strategies discussed in chapters 7 and 8. They also approached their work with a set of class-based mothering values very different from those of their employers. The caregivers I interviewed came from a wide range of backgrounds. Their levels of motivation as nannies were equally diverse, ranging from reluctance and resentment to passionate commitment. Nevertheless, they all embraced a working-class approach to intensive mothering as their work ethic. This work ethic stood in direct opposition to the belief in intensive mothering by proxy that the majority of their employers brought to the relationship. Nannies' poor pay and lack of benefits, and the long hours they spent working within the context of family norms, also meant that these caregivers typically sought interpersonal recognition for the value of their relationships with the children in their care as a substitute for the other forms of compensation they so clearly lacked. And, as I discuss later, even with fair pay and reasonable working conditions, work of this kind engages such deep aspects of the self that most caregivers still seek recognition for their personal value to individual children, as well as for the value of their mothering ethic.

The phenomenon of shadow mothering examined in this book seems more likely to spread than to recede over time. Its underlying causes have in no way diminished: the goal of child perfectibility continues to drive middle-class parents' childrearing strategies; the logic of competitive mothering that results still combines with male-pattern careers to make achieving intensive mothering ideals unattainable for professional-class mothers; cultural pressures and these women's internalized desires and expectations are no less likely to lead them to try to accomplish the unattainable via their working-class nannies; and their use of nannies as a tool in this highly competitive production system remains a key reason why working mothers tend to treat caregivers as disposable, interchangeable cogs rather than as important individuals in their children's lives.

Is there a way to break this cycle? This study's findings suggest the answer is maybe. My analysis shows how the combination of the logics of all-consuming careers, intensive mothering, and high-stakes childrearing goals drive professional- and managerial-class mothers to self-defeating strategies. But those findings also suggest that crafting enduring solutions to work/family conflict will require broad social, cultural, and economic change. Here, too, however, the study is helpful. The findings raise important questions about the nature of work and the role of class and culture in defining our values and shaping our assumptions. What does nanny work tell us about other forms of childcare? Is childcare in general destined to be undervalued and underpaid? Must the labor done for love always conflict with working for money? If not, what needs to change? What about mothers employed outside the home? Must the "rational self-interest" of the workplace inevitably collide with the "altruistic" values of intensive mothering?[3] My findings also point to steps that might be taken to begin reclaiming alternative values of care and personhood.

VALUING CHILDCARE IN TWO LANGUAGES: VOCABULARIES OF SKILL AND VOCABULARIES OF VIRTUE

Childcare workers' concerns regarding low pay and the lack of recognition they receive from the families they serve and from society at large are widely shared. Studies of daycare center workers, family daycare providers, and those who provide care to a wide range of client populations document similar concerns.[4] Although some scholars suggest that nanny work is inherently more demeaning than other forms of childcare,[5] both the researchers who have studied childcare in other settings and the nannies in this study with experience working in these other arrangements would disagree.

In advocating for themselves, childcare workers, and indeed all care-workers, face a fundamental tension between the competing languages of the market and morality. Elsewhere I have termed these the "vocabulary of skill" and the "vocabulary of virtue."[6] The former makes claims for fair pay for skilled labor by framing childcare as "like teaching" rather than "like mothering." This approach gains economic ground but devalues care and undermines childcare workers' core values. The vocabulary of virtue, in contrast, prioritizes altruism and self-sacrifice, but in doing so risks the economic devaluation of care-work.

A strict "love or money" bifurcation fails to recognize care-workers' need to be recognized and compensated for *both*.

Successful campaigns to value care-work must advocate simultaneously in both languages. Care-workers deeply invest themselves in their work; they are unwilling to sacrifice fair pay for altruism or to sacrifice the personal rewards of altruistic relations of care for fair pay. When these dual needs are not met through their communities or their clients, caregivers seek to value their own work using their own cultural logics. Sometimes, these logics are self-defeating. The "race to the bottom" described in chapter 8 is one example. Another is provided by the family daycare providers Margaret Nelson studied. These women found meaning in their work, despite its low pay and devaluation by the client families, because they themselves gave inherent value to at-home mothering. Ultimately, however, this strategy ran afoul of the realities of their situation. Because of the presence of clients' children, they did not have the freedom to mother their own children as they would have liked, and they felt conflicted about "providing a service in which they don't really believe" to the other families.[7]

The African American family daycare providers Mary Tuominen studied also were underpaid and felt denied the respect due them. They drew on religious values to dignify their own work as reflecting their "call to serve their communities," and as providing racial safety and cultural pride to the children in their care.[8] Still, like the nannies I interviewed, these women found that the meaning they assigned their work often prevented them from seeking higher pay or improved working conditions from the families they served. Center-based care-workers face similar tensions between claiming skill and asserting virtue. Several studies have shown that even when daycare workers achieve greater status and pay for their work by framing it in a vocabulary of skill and claiming a status "like teachers," they still find that parents refuse to recognize their role in the children's lives.[9]

As important as fair pay is, it does not fully address the problems this study found in the nanny job. This research joins studies of other childcare settings in pointing to the need for greater respect for the interpersonal relationships that undergird real care. One advocate for childcare center workers, in explaining why their organization chose not to adopt "early childhood education" terminology, said, "We're trying to reclaim the word 'care' and proclaim its value for what it is. . . . [W]hen we start dropping off the word 'care,' we're just saying that's a whole part of it that isn't really valuable."[10] Tensions between skill and caring, labor for love and labor for money, are enduring but false dichotomies that can tempt care-workers of all types to "break their own contracts" in the name of upholding the value of care.[11] Real change in the working conditions of nannies and other care providers will require a broad recalibration of the importance and value of this kind of work. In fact, when we look back at chapter 9's partnerships using this lens, it is not surprising that those nannies whose contributions to family life were economically valued were interpersonally valued as well. Likewise, all successful campaigns to raise wages for childcare workers have begun by enlisting parents to recognize the emotional and moral value of paid childcare to their own children and families.

To be truly successful, however, movements for fair pay and decent working conditions for childcare workers in all settings must reach beyond parents, mobilizing on the basis of the long-term *public* benefits of high-quality childcare, including advantages that accrue to "free riders" who gain from well-adjusted children who are not their own.[12] In fact, many prominent scholars have advocated for such a "care movement" to increase the perceived value of paid and unpaid childcare, eldercare, and care for the ill and disabled.[13] For this kind of a campaign to be successful in the realm of childcare, however, the grip of the ideology of intensive mothering must be loosened.

BREAKING THE INTENSIVE MOTHERING MOLD

Paradoxically, the same beliefs that fueled the sense of threat among the working mothers I interviewed, and led them to devalue the work of their caregivers, were also a source of misery to them. The women who had the most difficulty combining work and mothering into an effective mother-employer role were those who were most committed to both intensive mothering and intensive working. Numerous scholars have suggested that the solution to this problem can be found in a more flexible workplace with more "family-friendly" policies, such as care leave and part-time and flextime options. My findings suggest that a shift of this kind could encourage formation of partnerships by increasing the actual and perceived control that employed mothers have on the job.

The mothers I interviewed, however, were careful to distinguish between flextime that allowed them to remain involved at work and family-friendly policies that marginalized and mommy-tracked them despite their continued productivity and commitment. These women were high achievers who valued being held accountable at work, and they speak for many who consider it very woman-unfriendly to "solve" the work-family dilemma by channeling mothers away from the most stimulating jobs in the name of being more family friendly. Workplace policies certainly need to change. In particular, employers need to offer a broader range of choices, including flextime and flexi-place, more flexible leave time, and job-sharing opportunities. Nonetheless, there will always be a subset of jobs that require travel, long hours, and a high level of commitment. And there will always be some women who will want to take those jobs and still be able to have families. Why should they not have this option?

The easy answer is because fathers have not changed as much as mothers have. For at least the previous three decades, a now voluminous literature has been calling for greater involvement by fathers as a solution to women's work-family dilemmas. Male participation in second-shift work does appear to be slowly growing, and will certainly help mothers with the time pressures of trying "to do it all."[14] But my research suggests that even greatly increased male participation in parenting is not likely to be a solution unless working mothers are able to come to terms with the cultural logic of intensive mothering and the anxiety it produces. After all, when nannies relieved their employers of many hours of work and became emotionally close to the children, mothers often felt more threatened and unhappy. They grew overcontrolling and unreasonable rather than relieved and relaxed. Fathers, too, may find that getting more involved in childcare does not bring the immediate rewards they anticipated in their relationships with their spouses. Like many nannies, these men may either withdraw or fight for control. My study does not address this question, but it does suggest how valuable such research would be. With regard to the question of gender equality in families, my findings are more than suggestive; they leave little doubt that making serious progress in this area will require broad cultural change rather than just individual negotiations.

Working mothers in demanding careers must make peace with the fact that, even though they are unquestionably their children's mothers, other loving adults—including spouses, other relatives, and/or paid caregivers—must be and are actively involved in raising their children. The logic of intensive mothering, particularly as it applies to middle- and upper-middle-class mothers, therefore seems to be the greatest barrier to solving the problems detailed in this book. That insight leads directly to another: intensive mothering is inherently class based. This point is not emphasized nearly enough in the mothering literature.[15] Certainly, some aspects of contemporary intensive mothering affect working mothers across classes. Nearly all mothers, for instance, feel they ought to be at home with their children, ought to want to be at home with their children, and ought to be their children's primary parent.[16] Likewise, across classes, working mothers in the United States place a high priority on finding childcare that provides a clean, loving, and safe environment where their children will learn to play well with others. But these very broad commonalities contain differences.

For example, as I noted in chapter 1, mothers whose incomes are necessary for putting food on the family table have a socially acceptable excuse for their absence from the home. There is no such cultural pass for "Volvo-class" working mothers. And although the vast majority of employed mothers voice similar concerns about finding care that ensures their children's safety, sufficient nurturance, and an acceptable ratio of childcare workers to children in their care,[17] they may not be as committed to the transmission of class-specific cultural capital as the mothers I interviewed. *How* intensive mothering is expressed is cued by class. The kinds of guilt women feel when away from their children, what outcomes they worry their absence might cause, what aspects of their mothering responsibilities they prioritize—all vary by class. Similarly, the kinds of mothering practices that women value are class specific.

Like their counterparts in other classes, mothers in the professional and upper-middle classes perceive their duty as mothers as forming a solid attachment with their children. But in addition to this, these mothers hold themselves responsible for successfully transmitting status to their children. They must pass on their education and skills in the form of human capital; they must pass on their class-based habitus in the form of cultural capital; and they must give their children the right connections through social capital. Most studies of motherhood underestimate the pressure that middle- and upper-middle-class women feel to ensure their children's upward mobility—or at least status stability—particularly in a time of great risk and volatility. Existing research often seems to assume that status attainment is a "natural process" that takes no particular effort, provided that parents have the proper educational background themselves, or that the family has adequate financial resources to provide for college.

As the preceding shows, however, status attainment is hard work, and it is primarily women's work. Professional and upper-middle-class mothers start as early as possible, investing their time, money, and concern in the struggle to give their children "every advantage." They begin preparing their young for admittance to the right college by assuring that, from toddlerhood, their children have the right kinds of cognitive stimulation, the right kinds of activities, and the right kinds of friends. Such careful preparation helps position children for acceptance into the right preschool, the right elementary school,[18] and so forth. But all this effort does not allay professional and upper-middle-class mothers' anxieties; constant worry remains a feature of their mothering experience.

It is easy to dismiss this kind of pressure as something that employed mothers can slough off, but based on my interviews and on conversations with friends over many years, it is clear that the pressure to give one's child every possible opportunity to succeed is intense. Even women who vocally dismiss the culture of competitive mothering still express worries about whether or not something they have done or have failed to do will exact a toll in the future. They are haunted by the possibility that, in some unknown way, they may have deprived their child of something essential and that the implications of this deprivation will not become evident until the child reaches adulthood. This sense of blanket accountability, the never-ending responsibility for how their children turn out, haunts mothers as a panoptic gaze.[19]

Sharon Hays has influentially argued that it is simply irrational for women to simultaneously embrace the logic of rational self-interest inherent in the market *and* the logic of self-sacrifice demanded by intensive mothering because these logics are fundamentally contradictory. The underlying values of the market and the care relationship are indeed in tension. But, as the twin vocabularies of skill and virtue demonstrate, "the cultural contradictions of mothering" are not always so contradictory. Mothers are not always, as Hays argues, investing their energies in intensive mothering as an expression of "an explicit and systematic rejection of individualistic, competitive, and impersonal relations."[20] They are also using intensive mothering as a means of mastering the demands of the market itself. In other words, by embracing intensive mothering, professional-class women do not, as Hays suggests, hold the line against the encroachment of capitalist values at the expense of their own economic self-interest. Instead, the cultural logic governing the interaction of intensive mothering and market logics varies by social class.

Working-class women, for example, may find meaning in a monotonous job by embracing motherhood as their "real" identity and by pointing out that their time away from their children is necessary in order to provide for these children's basic needs. Here, they reverse the image of self-sacrifice offered by at-home mothers and their defenders, who see such "traditional" mothering as the last bulwark against the encroaching values of the market, just as Hays suggests. The language of sacrifice is readily available for mothers whether they are at home full-time or not, and the anxieties in these self-justifications fuel much of the heat in the "mommy wars." But the upper-middle-class and professional-class women I interviewed framed intensive mothering around *both* market and mothering logics. They did not value intensive mothering as a means of resisting the values the market embraces. Rather, they sacrificed sleep, time alone, and time with their partners, spending the vast majority of their nonworking hours with their children, in order to ensure that the children would have all the right tools for achievement. The market does not differentially value these children's SAT scores and their mothers' paychecks. Professional-class mothers base their efforts to succeed in both arenas on a market-centered calculus.

MOTHERING, SOCIAL CLASS, AND GENDER

If church attendance is the most racially segregated activity in the United States, parenting is one of our most class-segregated practices. Thus, the cross-class child-rearing relationships that are the focus of this book provide a rare opportunity to see class-based mothering values come into contact and conflict. Tensions between nannies and their employers are not, for the most part, an expression of resentment that one party earned more than the other or that one has authority over the other. These conditions are taken for granted. How the highly gendered work of mothering is enacted in class-based ways generates most of the conflict in these relationships. The performance of class *via gender and through mothering* locks both sets of women into value-laden conflicts that are difficult to overcome.

Letting go of the shadow-mother imperative not only means giving up the idea that the mother will be the primary adult in her child's life and challenging the competitive ideal of childrearing for the marketplace, but it also means abandoning the idea that the family's class-based assumptions will be the only values to which a child will be exposed. The mother-nanny relationship is one of the few places where different versions of motherhood come into intimate and repeated contact. Here, unlike in other venues of daily life, the link between values and class position is unavoidably evident. Neither employers nor nannies can simply take for granted the rightness of their childrearing practices, as parents normally do when surrounded by others who share their class-based assumptions. They have to articulate, rationalize, and justify these values to themselves and to the other party. My research thus points to how invisible class is as a cultural phenomenon—one in which values, and not simply economic status, define our understanding of our own and others' class location.

Class does not exist in and of itself; it has to be enacted. Motherhood is classed, but social class is also actively transmitted through mothering practices. This reality was particularly problematic for the mother-employers I interviewed. For them, status transmission was an important aspect of successful motherhood, but in order to fulfill this key responsibility, they had to rely on the work of a caregiver who was not "naturally" endowed with the class-based mores these mother-employers needed to pass on. The work of class transmission is evident, for example, in mother-employers' efforts to reproduce (even when doing so seems so obviously counterproductive) their own mothers' practices. And of course, those practices themselves were efforts to transmit class, status, and power to the next generation. Nannies do likewise, but also quite consciously try to temper their own "instincts" because reproducing *their* class is likely to get them fired.

When study participants clashed, it was most frequently over class-based mothering values. Both sets of women were strongly committed to reproducing those class-based values for their *own* children. What so often made their conflicts heated and difficult to resolve was not that commitment, however, but the question of whose practices and mores would ultimately be valued and recognized in the rearing of the employers' children. In most cases, nannies ceded to the mother-employers' norms. In mother-nanny relationships in general, however, as well as those analyzed in this book, mother-employers often reach a point where they no longer value their nanny because, as children grow beyond toddlerhood, the caregiver cannot transmit the required class-based cultural, social, and human capital to them. Not uncommonly, the nanny begins to fight back against such "impractical book parents." This painful and familiar scenario is not normally recognized for what it is—a class conflict via mothering values. Other analysts of these relationships have mistakenly diagnosed the problem as merely a class conflict and have argued that the solution is to distance the parties by placing children in daycare centers where the differences in class-based mothering norms would be mediated by curriculum.

I argue that these problems would not go away; they would simply go underground. This is because social class does not stand alone but must be performed in a social context and through social roles. At a daycare center, class might be performed through arguments over the menu, or in the parents' priorities for getting in that extra hour at work vs. arriving on time to pick up their children. In the more intimate, one-on-one shared-mothering relationship I examined, class differences come out into the open, but in complicated and nuanced ways. This study has illuminated how much of the mothering function is about class transmission, and how much active performance social class requires—in this case, through gender, in interaction with children, and within a mothering role.

CHILDCARE—HERE TO STAY

If I have succeeded, I have convinced the reader that childcare workers already play a fundamental, if unrecognized, role in the lives of contemporary families. This fact is not problematic in itself, though millions have been spent in attempts to determine whether or not childcare in and of itself is damaging and, if so, what kinds of childcare are best or worst for children. Instead of adding to the volumes already devoted to this debate, I have examined the costs—to childcare workers, to employers, and, by association, to children—of the *invisibility* of childcare workers in children's lives. For too long, childcare workers have been the dirty secret at the foundation of working family life.

And yet, in chapter 9, we see mothers, fathers, and paid caregivers openly sharing the work of care—across boundaries of gender, class, and family status. In these cases, childcare is valued as a family expense, not as a deduction from the wife's salary, and a child's attachment to the paid caregiver is cause for celebration, not family shame. Counterhegemonic mothering ideals and the flexibility at work that allows mothers to meet the threshold of connection at home both contribute to, but are not sufficient to create, these kinds of arrangements.

In the preceding pages we have seen how the work of status reproduction is central to women's views of mothering. By embracing this particular brand of intensive mothering, mothers model for their children a set of unhealthy class anxieties and their attendant dysfunctional childcare management strategies. Their children can learn only that paid caregivers are replaceable automata with predefined expiration dates. In contrast, those employers not as anxious about the direct reproduction of social class can create a home and work environment that respects the contributions of everyone involved. They can also value the caregivers' relationships with children over the long haul, and teach their children to value relationships with a variety of loving adults.

Research Methods

THE RESPONDENTS

This study draws on in-depth interviews with eighty women. Although the sample was primarily a sample of convenience, I used a theoretical sampling strategy to ensure that respondents represented the broadest possible range within the realm of commodified in-home care.[1] For example, I sought nannies and au pairs from various backgrounds and with differing levels of experience. I also interviewed mother-employers with one to five children and with differing on-the-job pressures and demands. The following is a breakdown of the group of respondents I interviewed for the study:

15 American-born nannies[2]	9 mothers who employ them
10 European au pairs	9 mothers who employ them
25 immigrant nannies	12 mothers who employ them

Of the American-born nannies, seven were from Boston, and the other eight were from the Midwest. Of the au pairs, five were from Scandinavia, four were from Great Britain, and one was from Spain. Two of the immigrant nannies were from China, one was from Africa, four migrated from Great Britain (primarily Ireland), nine were from Caribbean islands, and nine were from South and Central America. Approximately one-half of the caregivers worked on a live-in basis (primarily au pairs and American-born nannies), while the others worked full-time in their employers' homes but maintained their own residences off-site.

The mother-employers I interviewed were predominantly white professional workers. Although one family was going through a divorce at the time of the study and one employer was a single mother by choice, the vast majority of mother-employers were in dual-career marriages. In addition, although I sought ethnic variation, the majority of mother-employers were white (the study includes interviews with one Chinese American mother-employer, four Latina mother-employers, and three African American mother-employers).

In general, I found that most of the women of color I encountered who used in-home care employed relatives or neighbors as caregivers, thus making them ineligible for this study.[3]

I chose not to interview fathers or children in the families I studied for several reasons. First, the children were generally too young to be interviewed, for both practical and ethical reasons. Second, although I did initially consider interviewing fathers, my initial interviews with mother-employers and nannies in the pilot study convinced me that they viewed fathers as peripheral to their relationships. Most of the women described themselves as sharing the same "role" or "domain," and viewed the men in the family as external to their relationship. Finally, my research question emphasized how delegated care shapes the way mother-employers and caregivers think about motherhood, and how beliefs concerning motherhood affect the division of labor between them. Therefore, despite the fact that others (fathers, extended kin, children, etc.) were part of the overall childcare scenario, it made sense to limit my study to interviews with mother-employers and paid caregivers.

Because the study focuses on the effects of the intensive mothering ideology, I limited my recruitment to families with at least one child younger than age three during the period in which they used in-home care. And, since my interest is in how working mothers delegate childrearing, the first round of interviews was limited to families in which the mother worked at least thirty-five hours per week outside of the home, and therefore had to rely on a childcare provider for at least thirty-five hours per week. Finally, I limited the study to commodified care arrangements—that is, childcare relationships that began as employer-employee relationships rather than childcare arrangements with friends, neighbors, or kin.

During the second round of interviews, I maintained my focus on commodified childcare but sought to test hypotheses generated from the first round by interviewing a small sample of mother-employers who worked part-time.

Recruiting Respondents

I located respondents using a variety of means: using personal contacts, advertising in local newspapers, visiting playgrounds, contacting nanny agencies, and posting flyers. Most respondents, however, were contacted through a modified snowball method. In order to avoid too much overlap among respondents, I interviewed no more than two women from the same referral source. Others were approached at playgrounds or responded to advertisements in newspapers such as the *Boston Parents' Paper* and the *Tab*. Certain populations were targeted through advertising and cold-calling. To find Latina caregivers, for example, I placed ads in *El Mundo* and hired Spanish-speaking research assistants to contact community groups serving local Hispanic communities. Table 2 provides a breakdown of the referral sources used to recruit the fifty caregivers interviewed for this study. Two research assistants fluent in Spanish recruited and interviewed Latin American immigrant nannies.[4]

In general, I found mother-employers more difficult to locate than nannies, and when I did locate them, I found that they were more likely to decline to participate in the study.[5] Of the contacted mother-employers, nine refused to be interviewed, three others scheduled interviews and subsequently changed their minds and canceled, and one withdrew from the study after being interviewed. Those who chose not to participate cited time constraints and the personal nature of their childcare arrangements as reasons to decline.

TABLE 2   Referral Sources Used to Recruit Caregivers for This Study

Referral Source	Type of Caregiver Recruited		
	U.S.-born	Au Pair	Immigrant
Employer	3	3	6
Other Nanny	4	4	5
Agency or church		2	1
Responded to ad	6		5
Approached at park	1		8
Other personal contact	1	1	

I believe caregivers were more interested in being interviewed because they rarely had the opportunity to talk about their work. Undocumented immigrants were the only care-givers who were difficult to recruit, for understandable reasons. I did interview a few who had been referred to me by their employers, but they were less willing to speak openly than their au pair and American-born peers. I ultimately solved this problem by a two-stage recruitment process aimed at bringing immigrant nannies into the study. First, my Spanish-speaking research assistant and I conducted informal surveys at parks and playgrounds in Boston, Cambridge, and surrounding suburbs during the critical pre- and post-nap hours of 9–11 a.m. and 1–3 p.m.[6] We asked all adults in these parks if they were parents or childcare workers and, if the latter, what kind of childcare work they did. This survey in itself gave us valuable insight into the dispersion of different types of childcare providers throughout the region. In addition to the differences noted in chapter 3, we found that at-home mothers predominated in the wealthier suburbs, whereas nannies, daycare center workers, and family daycare providers were more frequently found in the less-affluent suburbs and in the cities.

During the survey, if a respondent identified herself as a nanny we asked further ques-tions, including how long she had been working, basic wage information, and where she was from. If she was an immigrant, we asked if she would be willing to be interviewed. Usually these women said no. We now knew the parks where they and their friends could be found, however, and proceeded to "hang out" there. It took us weeks, sometimes months, to gain the trust of these nannies and their friends. Sometimes we began with informal focus groups. Other times we had to prove ourselves by being willing to go on snack runs or help watch the children before individual nannies would agree to be interviewed. They were paid the standard rate (see below), and by the time of the individual interviews we had established a secure rapport. Ironically, one of the nannies who was most reluctant to speak to me became the biggest advocate for this book. Every time I passed the park where she and her friends worked, she would shout, "Hey! Where's that nanny book?" I hope that this publication brings a smile to her face.

Analysis of Recruitment Patterns

We can learn quite a bit simply by studying variations in recruitment patterns. Table 3 gives a breakdown of the referral sources used to recruit mother-employers for this study (broken down by type of caregiver employed). Several notable features emerge from the

TABLE 3 Referral Sources Used to Recruit Mother-Employers for This Study

	Type of Caregiver		
Referral Source	U.S.-born	Au Pair	Immigrant
Nanny	3	2	1
Another mother	4	2	5
Agency	0	2	0
Responded to ad	3	1	0
Other personal contact	5	3	6

contrast between our access to nannies and our access to mother-employers in this study. For example, more caregivers than mother-employers responded to advertising—more than half of the caregivers responded to an advertisement in the *Boston Parents' Paper* I had placed in hopes of recruiting working mothers who employed in-home childcare providers.[7] This speaks to the fact that more nannies than mother-employers in my study read the *Parents' Paper,* looking for child-friendly activities, and had the *time* to read newspapers and respond to ads.

Worth noting, too, is the fact that although twelve caregivers were referred to the study by their employers, only six mother-employers were referred by their caregivers. This difference may not seem significant, but when we look at the types of employer-employee arrangement in this category, it is striking that most of the caregivers referred by employers were immigrants, and most of the mother-employers who were referred by nannies were referred by Caucasian American employees. I believe this distinction reflects the greater asymmetry in employer-employee relations between immigrant nannies (both documented and undocumented) and their employers. All but one of the immigrant nannies accessed through other sources (ads, the park) were unwilling or afraid to refer me to their employers.

Sixteen of the caregivers I interviewed worked for fourteen of the mother-employers I interviewed.[8] Therefore, approximately one-half of the interviews represent data from mother-nanny dyads. The dyads represent the spectrum of in-home childcare arrangements: six mother-employers with Caucasian American nannies, four mother-employers with au pairs, and four mother-employers with immigrant nannies.

Interviewing

The majority of the interviews took place at the respondent's home or workplace. I interviewed some respondents two or three times over a period of years, but most were interviewed only once. Interviews ranged from ninety minutes to four hours in length. In some cases, especially with the mother-employers, a single interview took two or more visits. For example, in interviewing a busy psychologist, I visited her office during cancellations, using three forty-minute sessions to complete the interview. Nannies and au pairs were paid fifteen dollars per hour for their time. Since the mothers had substantially greater economic resources than I did, I found it more practical to pay them in information. So, for example, when a new article from the NICHD was released, especially if it offered reassurance to working mothers, I would offer it as a parting gift to the mother-employer.

The interviews covered a number of topics, ranging from the choices that led them to their current situation, to the events of a typical day, to their feelings and beliefs about their child-rearing relationships. Although I followed the same topic guide for all of the interviews, they were loosely structured, allowing room for respondents to raise questions and issues that they deemed salient. This format encouraged respondents to construct their own stories concerning their experiences, yet also allowed me to probe, where necessary, and to raise topics that might not arise otherwise. After receiving each respondent's informed consent, I tape recorded and transcribed each interview. In addition, I asked each respondent to complete a data sheet that established baseline demographic information (see tables 4 and 5).

In conducting the interviews, I followed a logic I call "climbing the ladder of abstraction." Initially, I asked questions seeking to elicit *narratives* about the women's experiences with motherhood and childcare work. During this phase of the interview, I listened carefully for allusions to topics I might want to probe later, but I refrained from interrupting. The goal at this stage was to allow the women to frame their experience in their own words and to create a common narrative on which we could both draw in discussing their experience. I then posed questions intended to probe those areas that seemed important to the respondent and asked focused questions aimed at eliciting *feelings* and *opinions* concerning the narrative. Finally, during the third stage of interviewing, I asked respondents to reflect on the experiences they had just related to me, and to *theorize* about what they meant.

Sometimes a respondent would begin by responding with the highest level of abstraction, *theorizing*, as in "Well, you know, if you don't have a green card you're just screwed." I would then take the respondent down to the most concrete level and ask if she or anyone she knew had experiences that could illustrate her argument. I would then move to midlevel questions, such as "how did that make you feel?" or "what do you think should be done about that?" The key in this form of interviewing is to be sure to hit on each of the three levels of abstraction for every topic area. This approach not only creates richly textured data ("thick description") for analysis but also allows the interviewer later to triangulate between three different levels of interpretation of the same topic within one interview. It was not uncommon, for example, for respondents to offer a story that contradicted their stated opinion, or to theorize causal relations that went far beyond what their narrative could illustrate. All of these utterances, as well as the relations between them, made for useful data.

Limitations of the Sample

As an in-depth qualitative study based on a purposive sample, this study does not claim to be generalizable. In fact, by selecting a form of childcare that, by its very nature, *increases* the need for interpersonal communication, I chose an "ideal type" that would emphasize some of the relational factors that I sought to study. My aim was to generate what ethnographers refer to as "concepts that travel," patterns of interaction related to social and cultural systems that are reproduced in multiple caregiving contexts.

Because I was able to interview most of the respondents only once, I also limited my data collection to snapshots of ongoing relationships at one point in time. This was primarily a function of the relatively short duration of these relationships. I cannot draw conclusions, therefore, about how these relationships might have evolved over time, as more children arrived in a given family or as the children aged. I did study enough of the relationships over time to be able to assert that most did not alter significantly. Given that my primary focus was on commodified care during the birth-to-three period, however, it made sense not to follow these families into their elementary school years.

Analyzing the Data

My analysis of the data was ongoing, but can be broken down into three main stages. The first stage involved recording in-depth field notes immediately after each interview. Usually, in addition to the notes I took during the interview itself, I would dictate all of my impressions at the end of the interview while driving home, and would transcribe those notes along with the interview data. These field notes were extremely useful in constructing my analysis as I proceeded with the research and served as a good record of the development of certain lines of inquiry.

Second, in transcribing the interviews, I did what Garey has termed "listening twice."[9] This means not only getting the words on paper but also using the transcription process as a means of listening for "how responses are structured, hearing where explanation is difficult, feeling the form in which content is presented."[10] I also based this listening process on DeVault's argument that many of women's experiences do not find a mode of articulation in standard (male) language. I therefore listened for moments when women stumbled, searching for a means to articulate their experience, moments when they asked for understanding in phrases such as "you know," and moments when they contradicted themselves. As Anderson and Jack have noted, "to hear women's perspectives accurately, we have to learn to listen in stereo, receiving both the dominant and muted channels clearly."[11] This meant listening for the dominant discourses of attachment and child development in addition to the more muted discourses regarding struggles over the timing of naps, appropriate playdate partners, and class-based approaches to discipline.

As I moved to coding the printed transcripts, several approaches were useful to me. I used the grounded theory method of "open" and "focused" coding, moving from a line-by-line analysis of everything that was said to coding that homed in on the themes that had emerged as most salient. I also looked for "in vivo" codes—themes that emerged from the respondents' own phrasing—and for those places where language seemed inadequate to express what the women were feeling and experiencing.[12] Finally, I coded the transcripts comparatively, first comparing the caregivers and mothers in general, and then focusing on the employer-nanny dyads, conducting a comparative analysis of their divergent accounts of childrearing work in the same family setting.

One of the challenges presented by this research topic involved interpretation of accounts, from two different sources, of life in the same household—accounts that sometimes diverged so radically as to make an observer question whether the two parties indeed worked together. I take seriously the notion that each party in these negotiations is situated in a cultural and institutional location that forms her particular standpoint. I argue, therefore, that the important task in interpreting the often conflicting accounts of the two sets of women quoted in this book is not to determine who is correct, but rather to uncover the underlying nature of their conflicts. Doing so reveals the institutional and cultural constraints that situate each party and form her perspective in competing definitions of family life and mother-work.

This understanding and use of the concept of standpoint brings me back to micropolitics. In choosing to study the small wars waged every day, I am not asserting that these are the only power struggles that still exist in a hypermodern age; quite the contrary. I examine the micropolitics of motherhood in order to trace its social origins. Through the study of symbolic battles over developmental firsts or the micromanagement of childcare, this book traces the path from the personal back to the political, from individual skirmishes at home to the broader cultural and institutional contexts that alternately empower and constrain both mother-employers and mother-workers.

PROFILES OF THE STUDY PARTICIPANTS

TABLE 4 Mother-Employers Interviewed for This Study

Mother-Employer's Pseudonym	Age	Occupation	Work Hours	Part Time?	Number of Children	Children's Ages	Management Style	Caregiver's Pseudonym	Caregiver's Origin
Alicia	29	writer	45	n	2	7 months, 2	paranormal	Leticia	Venezuela (immigrant)
Amy	34	manager	50	n	1	16 months	puppeteer	Sonja	Iceland (au pair)
Andrea	36	medical educator	20	y	5	1, 2, 2, 6, 8	partner	Bridget	Ireland (immigrant)
Bonnie	36	engineer	40	n	3	4 months, 2, 4	puppeteer	Astrid	Sweden (au pair)
Carol	43	college instructor	35	n	3	3, 5, 8	puppeteer	Karin and Berenice	Karin: Norway; Berenice: Spain (au pairs)
Caroline	35	professor	30	flex	3	4, 9, 11	paranormal	Aida	United States (black)
Debbie	34	attorney	50	n	2	6 months, 2	puppeteer	Annika and Ulle	Norway (au pairs)
Elaine	34	executive	35	Yes	2	6 months, 2	partner	Christine	United States (white)
Elizabeth	47	executive	55	n	1	3	partner	Lonehl	United States (black)
Gloria	45	teacher	30	n	2	6, 8	puppeteer	Sally	United States (black)
Gwen	34	professor	35	flex	2	2, 5	partner	Sylvia	Guatemala (immigrant)
Jane	34	executive	60	n	2	2, 8	puppeteer	Sarah	United States (white)
Janet	36	attorney	50	n	2	4, 7	paranormal	Colleen and Katya	Colleen: United States (white); Katya: Poland (immigrant)

Jeanette	39	P.R. executive	36	n	1	13 weeks	puppeteer	Peggy	United States (white)
Jessica	38	engineer	50	n	1	11 months	puppeteer	Anabel	England (au pair)
Joan	38	executive	55	n	1	11 months	paranormal	Melanie	United States (white)
Joyce	37	physician	60	n	1	11 months	partner	Stacy	United States (white)
Leah	44	Attorney	45	n	1	5	partner	Ellie	United States (white)
Leigh	38	physician	50	n	2	3, 5	paranormal	Hillary	England (au pair)
Libby	42	executive	35	flex	2	4, 6	partner	Grace	Scotland (immigrant)
Linda	39	attorney	30	y	3	2, 5, 7	paranormal	Josephine	United States (black)
Mary	37	physician	30	y	1	6 months	partner	Ronda	United States (white)
Mary Anne	34	scientist	45	n	1	2	puppeteer	Esther	China (immigrant)
Min	37	scientist	40	n	2	9 months, 3	partner	Li Chan	China (immigrant)
Naomi	36	physician	40	n	2	14 months, 3	paranormal	Yvonne and Carla	Yvonne: Jamaica; Carla: Trinidad (immigrants)
Pat	42	military officer	65	n	2	7, 9	puppeteer	Dagmar	Sweden (immigrant)
Paula	39	psychologist	40	n	3	3, 7, 9	paranormal	Paloma	Spain (au pair)
Suzanne	30	executive	50	n	1	16 months	puppeteer	Violet	St. Lucia (immigrant)
Teresa	33	math professor	45	flex	2	1, 2	paranormal	Angelina	Honduras (immigrant)
Vivian	43	executive	45	n	2	3, 5	partner	Luz	Chile (immigrant)

TABLE 5 Caregivers Interviewed for This Study

Caregiver's Pseudonym	Age	Origin	Monthly Wage (dollars)	Live-in?	Weekly Hours	Health Insurance	Sick Pay	Vacation	FICA	Taxes
Anabel	18	Scotland (au pair)	400	y	50	y	n	n	n	n
Anne	34	Jamaica (immigrant)	2,400	n	50	n	n	y	n	n
April	24	United States (white)	1,280	n	45	n	n	n	y	y
Astrid	19	Sweden (au pair)	400	y	45	y	n	n	n	n
Berenice	25	Spain (au pair)	400	y	45	y	n	n	n	n
Bridget	32	Ireland (immigrant)	1,081	n	30	n	n	y	n	n
Carmela	27	Puerto Rico (immigrant)	240	n	30	n	n	n	n	n
Cassie	27	United States (white)	750	n	20	y	y	y	y	y
Celine	42	Trinidad (immigrant)	800	n	25	n	y	y	n	n
Chantal	42	St. Lucia (immigrant)	1,500	n	50	n	n	n	n	n
Charmaine	50	St. Lucia (immigrant)	1,200	n	40	n	n	n	n	n
Christine	21	United States (white)	450	n	52	n	n	n	y	n
Colleen	25	United States (white)	1,625	y	44	half	y	y	y	y
Corinne	28	Kenya (immigrant)	1,800	n	45	n	n	y	n	n
Ellie	30	United States (white)	1,500	n	50	n	n	y	y	y
Elsa	20	Sweden (au pair)	400	y	50	y	n	n	n	n
Esther	64	China (immigrant)	280	n	40	n	n	n	n	n
Fiona	30	Ireland (immigrant)	1,500	n	50	n	n	y	y	y
Grace	30	Scotland (immigrant)	2,000	n	50	n	y	y	n	n
Helene	29	United States (white)	1,600	n	40	y	y	y	y	n
Hillary	26	Britain (au pair)	400	y	50	y	n	n	n	n
Ida	38	Trinidad (immigrant)	1,680	n	42	n	y	y	y	y
Julie	20	United States (white)	800	y	60	n	n	n	y	y
Karin	20	Norway (au pair)	400	y	45	y	n	n	n	n

Kristina	21	Sweden (au pair)	400	y	45	y	y	n	n	n
Li Chan	56	China (immigrant)	800	n	45	n	y	y	n	n
Liv	21	Sweden (au pair)	400	y	45	y	y	n	n	n
Lonehl	35	United States (black)/ Barbados (dual citizen)	2,000	n	60	y	y	y	y	y
Lucy	34	Barbados (immigrant)	1,200	n	45	n	n	n	n	n
Lupe	29	Mexico (immigrant)	800	n	30	n	n	n	n	n
Lura	31	United States (white)	1,500	y	37	y	y	y	y	y
Luz	26	Chile (immigrant)	1,600	n	48	y	y	y	n	n
Margaret	24	Britain (au pair)	600	y	50	n	n	n	n	n
Margarita	49	Ecuador (immigrant)	400	n	45	n	n	n	n	n
Marisol	37	Nicaragua (immigrant)	1,536	n	50	n	n	n	n	n
Marjorie	25	Britain (au pair)	600	y	50	n	y	y	n	n
Melanie	24	United States (white)	1,600	n	50	y	y	y	n	n
Miriam	22	United States (white)	1,920	n	45	n	n	n	n	n
Nilda	26	Montserrat (immigrant)	1,800	n	45	n	n	n	n	n
Penelope	24	England (immigrant)	1,800	n	45	n	n	n	n	n
Pia	30	Ecuador (immigrant)	1,000	n	50	n	n	n	n	n
Pilar	21	El Salvador (immigrant)	480	n	55	n	n	n	n	n
Ronda	34	United States (black)	1,280	n	32	n	n	n	n	n
Rosa	32	Honduras (immigrant)	600	y	50	n	n	n	n	n
Sarah	24	United States (white)	900	y	60	y	n	n	n	n
Stacy	21	United States (white)	1,050	y	53	n	y	y	y	y
Sylvia	34	Guatemala (immigrant)	1,200	y	20	y	y	y	y	y
Valerie	22	United States (white)	960	n	45	y	y	y	n	n
Violet	41	St. Lucia (immigrant)	1,000	y	50	n	n	n	n	n
Ynez	46	Honduras (immigrant)	320	n	50	n	n	n	n	n

CHAPTER 1

1. U.S. Department of Labor, Bureau of Labor Statistics, *Labor Force Statistics from the Current Population Survey, 2003* (Washington, DC: U.S. Department of Labor, 2003), table 5, "Employment status of the population by sex, marital status, and presence and age of own children under 18, 2002–03 annual averages."

2. Matthew died on February 9, 1997, five days after being admitted to the hospital with a subdural hematoma and falling into a coma. At issue in the trial was the timing of the injury. He also had a fractured wrist and retinal hemorrhages typical of shaken baby syndrome. Shaken baby syndrome can take days or even weeks to become evident, however, and Louise passed polygraph tests and continued to assert her innocence into 1998. She was found guilty of second-degree murder, but on appeal her conviction was reduced to involuntary manslaughter and her sentence reduced to time served. For a more detailed description of the trial, see Susan Chira, *A Mother's Place: Choosing Work and Family without Guilt or Blame* (New York: HarperCollins, 1998), chapter 1.

3. Peter S. Canellos, "Societal, Legal Change Is Legacy of a Public Trial: The Au Pair Case / Zobel Ruling Affirmed," *Boston Globe*, 1 June 1998; Chira, *A Mother's Place*.

4. This was neither the first nor the last of the public debates over nannies that would strike at the heart of the so-called mommy wars. Renee Chou, "Child Abuse Charges Filed in 'Nanny Cam' Case," WRAL, 3 July 2008, www.wral.com/news/local/story/2561722/; Richard Lake, "Child Care: Abuse by Nannies Unusual. Still, Experts Say Parents Need to Take Standard Precautions," *Las Vegas Review Journal*, 9 January 2005, www.reviewjournal.com/lvrj_home/2005/Jan-09-Sun-2005/news/25623713.html; NBC6 News Team, "Police Release New 'Nanny Cam' Video in Abuse Probe: Parents 'Horrified' by Alleged Abuse Caught on Tape," NBC6, 3 July 2008.

5. Doreen Vigue, "For Grieving Mother, a Daily Ordeal: Deborah Eappen Struggles to Find Answers," *Boston Globe*, 7 November 1997.

6. It also takes the form of "reporting" on Web sites such as isawyournanny.blogspot. com. For an excellent discussion of this blog, see Margaret K. Nelson, "'I Saw Your Nanny': Gossip and Shame in the Surveillance of Child Care," in *Who's Watching? Daily Practices of Surveillance among Contemporary Famlies*, ed. Margaret K. Nelson and Anita Ilta Garey (Nashville: Vanderbilt University Press, 2009), 107–33.

7. Pew Research Center for People and the Press, "The 2004 Political Landscape: Evenly Divided and Increasingly Polarized," 5 November 2003, http://people-press.org/reports/ pdf/196.pdf; ABC News/Washington Post, "Poll: Moms Make It Work," ABC News, 24 April 2005.

8. A survey of parents showed that 73 percent agreed that it was more important for mothers receiving public assistance to work than to stay home with their children, even if that meant the children would be in child care: Public Agenda, *Red Flag: Neither Liberal nor Conservative Approaches to Welfare* (Washington, DC: Public Agenda, 2008).

9. Among all women with infants, the percentage who work outside the home is slightly lower: 59 percent in 2005 (U.S. Department of Commerce, Census Bureau, "Mother's Day: May 8, 2005," press release, 2 May 2005). Today that number has declined slightly to 55 percent. It is not clear if this slight decline is a "blip" or part of a larger trend. For an excellent discussion of the so-called opt-out revolution, see Pamela Stone, *Opting Out? Why Women Really Quit Careers and Head Home* (Berkeley: University of California Press, 2007).

10. Of course, single mothers work even longer hours outside the home than mothers in dual-earner households do. Lawrence Mishel, Jared Bernstein, and John Schmitt, *The State of Working America* (Washington, DC: Economic Policy Institute, 1999); Lawrence Mishel, Jared Bernstein, and Sylvia Allegretto, *The State of Working America, 2006/2007*, 10th ed. (Ithaca, NY: ILR Press, 2007).

11. On "raising the bar," see Pierrette Hondagneu-Sotelo, *Domestica: Immigrant Workers Cleaning and Caring in the Shadows of Affluence* (Berkeley: University of California Press, 2001), 24.

12. Molly Ladd-Taylor, *Mother-Work: Women, Child Welfare, and the State, 1890–1930* (Urbana: University of Illinois Press, 1994). My research focuses on Ladd-Taylor's first component of mother-work.

13. I refer to the employers in this study interchangeably as "working mothers" and as "mother-employers" because they are simultaneously working mothers and the employers of women who themselves frequently are working mothers. I also use the term "mother-workers" to refer to childcare providers, since they are doing *paid* mother-work, as opposed to the equally valuable unpaid mother-work they provide in their own homes and that their employers provide their own children when the workday ends.

14. The concept of micropolitics has been used in discourse analysis and in postmodern theory. Some postmodern theorists argue that micropolitics have taken the place of politics writ large, such that "in a postmodern world, power is used and structured into social relations so that it does not appear to be 'used' at all." J. Blase and G. Anderson, *The Micropolitics of Educational Leadership: From Control to Empowerment* (New York: Teachers College Press, 1995), quoted in Louise Morley, *Organising Feminisms: The Micropolitics of the Academy* (New York: St. Martin's Press, 1999), 5. I do not use the concept this way;

rather I use it to trace the small battles that take place in private spaces back to the cultural and institutional structures that give these battles power and meaning.

15. Caitlin Flanagan, "Dispatches from the Nanny Wars: How Serfdom Saved the Women's Movement," *The Atlantic*, March 2004, 127.

16. Arlie Russell Hochschild, *The Managed Heart: Commercialization of Human Feeling* (Berkeley: University of California Press, 1983). Hochschild defines emotional labor as "the management of feeling to create a publicly observable facial and bodily display" (7n).

17. Arlie Russell Hochschild with Anne Machung, *The Second Shift: Working Parents and the Revolution at Home* (New York: Viking, 1989).

18. See, for example, Suzanne M. Bianchi et al., "Is Anyone Doing the Housework? Trends in the Gender Division of Labor," *Social Forces* 79, no. 1 (2000): 191–228; Myra Marx Ferree, "The Gender Division of Labor in Two-Earner Marriages: Dimensions of Variability and Change," *Journal of Family Issues* 12, no. 2 (1991): 158–80; Julie Brines, "Economic Dependency, Gender, and the Division of Labor at Home," *American Journal of Sociology* 100, no. 3 (1994): 652–88; Beth Anne Shelton, "The Division of Household Labor," *Annual Review of Sociology* 22 (1996): 299–322; Michael Bittman et al., "When Does Gender Trump Money? Bargaining and Time in Household Work," *American Journal of Sociology* 109, no. 1 (2003): 186–214; Liana C. Sayer, "Gender, Time, and Inequality: Trends in Women's and Men's Paid Work, Unpaid Work, and Free Time," *Social Forces* 84, no. 1 (2005): 285–303; Scott Coltrane, "Research on Household Labor: Modeling and Measuring the Social Embeddednes of Routine Family Work," *Journal of Marriage and the Family* 62, no. 4 (2000): 1208–33; and Marybeth J. Mattingly and Suzanne M. Bianchi, "Gender Differences in the Quantity and Quality of Free Time: The U.S. Experience," *Social Forces* 81, no. 3 (2003): 999–1030.

19. Mary Dorinda Allard et al., "Comparing Childcare Measures in the ATUS and Earlier Time-Diary Studies," *Monthly Labor Review* 130, no. 5 (2007): 27–36; Suzanne Bianchi, John P. Robinson, and Melissa A. Milkie, *Changing Rhythms of American Family Life* (New York: Russell Sage Foundation, 2006), 72.

20. See Harriet B. Presser, *Working in a 24/7 Economy: Challenges for American Families* (New York: Russell Sage Foundation, 2003); Rosanna Hertz, "Making Family under a Shiftwork Schedule: Air Force Security Guards and Their Wives," *Social Problems* 36, no. 5 (1989): 491–507; and Anita Ilta Garey, "Constructing Motherhood on the Night Shift: 'Working Mothers' as 'Stay-at Home Moms,'" *Qualitative Sociology* 18, no. 4 (1995): 415–37. Not all jobs are open to shiftwork schedules, however, and the mothers studied here did not have a shiftwork option.

21. Carole E. Joffe, *Friendly Intruders: Child Care Professionals and Family Life* (Berkeley: University of California Press, 1977). Joffe's study was one of the first to explore the role of childcare workers in family life.

22. Evelyn Nakano Glenn, "Social Constructions of Mothering: A Thematic Overview," in *Mothering: Ideology, Experience, and Agency,* ed. Evelyn Nakano Glenn, Grace Chang, and Linda Renney Forcey (New York: Routledge, 1994), 1–32; Sharon Hays, *The Cultural Contradictions of Motherhood* (New Haven, CT: Yale University Press, 1996); Maxine L. Margolis, *Mothers and Such: Views of American Women and Why They Changed* (Berkeley:

University of California Press, 1984); Shari L. Thurer, *The Myths of Motherhood: How Culture Reinvents the Good Mother* (New York: Penguin, 1994).

23. Chira, *A Mother's Place;* Glenn, "Social Constructions of Mothering."

24. For a counterexample, see Lynet Uttal, *Making Care Work: Employed Mothers in the New Childcare Market* (New Brunswick, NJ: Rutgers University Press, 2002). Uttal's study of forty-eight working mothers' paid and unpaid childcare arrangements shows that many women do find ways to renegotiate mothering so that it includes paid caregivers as trusted partners. She warns, however, that "we still lack clearly articulated models for this relationship and clear definitions of the role of childcare providers" (169). To this valuable suggestion for future research I would add the stipulation that this work include the voices of childcare providers and not rely solely on the perspectives of mothers.

25. Prior to this period, children were looked after primarily by servants and elder siblings.

26. S. Weir Mitchell, "When the College Is Hurtful to the Girl," *Ladies' Home Journal,* June 1900.

27. Carl N. Degler, *At Odds: Women and the Family in America from the Revolution to the Present* (New York: Oxford University Press, 1980), 413.

28. Bianchi, Robinson, and Milkie, *Changing Rhythms of American Family Life.*

29. Thurer, *The Myths of Motherhood,* 291.

30. Ann Swidler, "Culture in Action: Symbols and Strategies," *American Sociological Review* 51 (April 1986): 279.

31. Hondagneu-Sotelo, *Domestica;* Rhacel Salazar Parreñas, *Servants of Globalization: Women, Migration, and Domestic Work* (Stanford, CA: Stanford University Press, 2001); Mary Romero, *Maid in the U.S.A.* (New York: Routledge, 1992); Judith Rollins, *Between Women: Domestics and Their Employers,* Labor and Social Change, eds. Paula Rayman and Carmen Sirianni (Philadelphia: Temple University Press, 1985); Shellee Colen, " 'With Respect and Feelings': Voices of West Indian Child Care and Domestic Workers in New York City," in *All American Women,* ed. Johnnetta B. Cole (New York: Free Press, 1986), 46–70; Barbara Ehrenreich and Arlie Russell Hochschild, eds., *Global Woman: Nannies, Maids, and Sex Workers in the New Economy* (New York: Metropolitan Books, 2003); Grace Chang, *Disposable Domestics: Immigrant Women Workers in the Global Economy* (Cambridge, MA: South End Press, 2000); Evelyn Nakano Glenn, *Issei, Nisei, War Bride: Three Generations of Japanese American Women in Domestic Service* (Philadelphia: Temple University Press, 1986); Julia Wrigley, *Other People's Children: An Intimate Account of the Dilemmas Facing Middle-Class Parents and the Women They Hire to Raise Their Children* (New York: Basic Books, 1995); Mary C. Tuominen, *We Are Not Babysitters: Family Child Care Providers Redefine Work and Care* (New Brunswick, NJ: Rutgers University Press, 2003); Margaret K. Nelson, *Negotiated Care: The Experience of Family Day Care Providers* (Philadelphia: Temple University Press, 1990).

32. Saskia Sassen, "Global Cities and Survival Circuits," in *Global Woman: Nannies, Maids, and Sex Workers in the New Economy,* ed. Barbara Ehrenreich and Arlie Russell Hochschild (New York: Metropolitan Books, 2003), 254–74; Ruth Milkman, Ellen Reese, and Benita Roth, "The Macrosociology of Paid Domestic Labor," *Work and Occupations* 25, no. 4 (1998): 483–510. The latter article demonstrates that the size of the gap between

rich and poor in these global cities predicts where the market for domestic workers will be the largest.

33. Arlie Russell Hochschild, "The Nanny Chain," *American Prospect,* 3 January 2000, 32–36; Hondagneu-Sotelo, *Domestica;* Rollins, *Between Women;* Romero, *Maid in the U.S.A.;* Parreñas, *Servants of Globalization;* Glenn, *Issei, Nisei, War Bride;* Chang, *Disposable Domestics;* Shellee Colen, "'Housekeeping' for the Green Card: West Indian Household Workers, the State, and Stratified Reproduction in New York," in *At Work in Homes: Household Workers in World Perspective,* ed. Roger Sanjek and Shellee Colen (Washington, DC: American Anthropological Association, 1990), 89–118; Evelyn Nakano Glenn, "From Servitude to Service Work: Historical Continuities in the Racial Division of Paid Reproductive Labor," in *Working in the Service Society,* ed. Cameron Lynne Macdonald and Carmen Sirianni (Philadelphia: Temple University Press, 1996), 115–56; Pei-Chia Lan, *Global Cinderellas: Migrant Domestics and Newly Rich Employers in Taiwan* (Durham, NC: Duke University Press, 2006).

34. Earlier works have explored the servant-mistress dynamic in great detail. They have not considered how class-based childrearing beliefs and practices may shape and further complicate this relationship, however. (See note 31.)

35. Flanagan, "Dispatches from the Nanny Wars," 126.

36. Janelle S. Taylor, Linda L. Layne, and Danielle F. Wozniak, eds., *Consuming Motherhood* (New Brunswick, NJ: Rutgers University Press, 2004), 4.

37. Jean Bethke Elshtain, *Who Are We? Critical Reflections and Hopeful Possibilities* (New York: William B. Erdmans, 2000), 47.

38. Julie A. Nelson, "Of Markets and Martyrs: Is It OK to Pay Well for Care?" *Feminist Economics* 5, no. 3 (1999): 43–59.

39. Barbara Katz Rothman, *Recreating Motherhood: Ideology and Technology in a Patriarchal Society* (New York: W. W. Norton, 1989), 200.

40. Viviana Zelizer, *The Purchase of Intimacy* (Princeton, NJ: Princeton University Press, 2005), 34–35.

41. For a full discussion of the research methods, see the appendix. For studies that examine these other mothering-related questions, see Linda M. Blum, *At the Breast: Ideologies of Breastfeeding and Motherhood in the Contemporary United States* (Boston: Beacon Press, 1999); Diane E. Eyer, *Mother-Infant Bonding: A Scientific Fiction* (New Haven, CT: Yale University Press, 1992); Ruth McElroy, "Whose Body, Whose Nation? Surrogate Motherhood and Its Representation," *European Journal of Cultural Studies* 5, no. 3 (2002): 325–42; and Susan Markens, *Surrogate Motherhood and the Politics of Reproduction* (Berkeley: University of California Press, 2007).

42. Because of the sample design, almost all of the children the nannies in the study cared for were younger than age three.

43. See table 4 in the appendix for employer characteristics.

44. Au pairs are young women, usually between the ages of eighteen and twenty-two, who are participants in a one-year cultural exchange program administered through the State Department's Bureau of Educational and Cultural Affairs. In exchange for forty-five hours per week of childcare, they receive a stipend of $125–$150 per week plus room and board.

45. See table 5 in the appendix for a breakdown of the race/ethnicity and national origin of all of the childcare workers.

46. Nannies represent 15 percent of paid childcare providers for children younger than age six; center-based care serves 39 percent of the families using hired childcare, and family daycare homes serve another 34 percent. See Tuominen's breakdown of paid childcare for children younger than age six. Mary C. Tuominen, "The Conflicts of Caring," in *Care Work: Gender, Labor, and the Welfare State*, ed. Madonna Harrington Meyer (London: Routledge, 2000), 114, table 8.1.

47. Terry Arendell, "A Social Constructionist Approach to Parenting," in *Contemporary Parenting: Challenges and Issues*, ed Terry Arendell (Thousand Oaks, CA: Sage, 1997), 28; Cynthia T. Garcia Coll, E.C. Meyer, and L. Brillon, "Ethnic and Minority Parents," in *Handbook of Parenting*, ed. M.H. Bornstein (Mahwah, NJ: Lawrence Erlbaum Associates, 1995), 2:189–209; T.J. Hamner and P.H. Turner, *Parenting in Contemporary Society*, 3rd ed. (Needham Heights, MN: Allyn & Bacon, 1996).

48. Annette Lareau, *Unequal Childhoods: Class, Race, and Family Life* (Berkeley: University of California Press, 2003).

49. See the critique in Anita Ilta Garey, *Weaving Work and Motherhood* (Philadelphia: Temple University Press, 1999).

50. Barbara J. Risman and Danette Johnson-Sumerford, "Doing It Fairly: A Study of Postgender Marriages," *Journal of Marriage and the Family* 60 (February 1998): 23–40.

51. For a fascinating account of the Baird case, see Diane Sampson, "Rejecting Zoe Baird: Class Resentment and the Working Mother," in *"Bad" Mothers: The Politics of Blame in Twentieth-Century America*, ed. Molly Ladd-Taylor and Lauri Umansky (New York: New York University Press, 1998), 310–18.

52. For television sources, see the series *Supernanny* and *Nanny 911*. In advice books, see Justine Walsh, Kim Nicholson, and Richard Gere, *Nanny Wisdom: Our Secrets for Raising Healthy, Happy Children—from Newborns to Preschoolers* (New York: STC Paperbacks, 2005); and Jo Frost, *Jo Frost's Confident Baby Care: What You Need to Know for the First Year from the UK's Most Trusted Nanny* (London: Orion, 2007). In film, see *The Hand That Rocks the Cradle*, dir. Curtis Hanson (Hollywood Films, 1992). In popular fiction, see Emma McLaughlin and Nicola Krause, *The Nanny Diaries* (New York: St. Martin's Press, 2002); and Fay Weldon, *She May Not Leave* (New York: Grove Press, 2007). And in nonfiction, see Lucy Kaylin, *The Perfect Stranger: The Truth about Mothers and Nannies* (New York: Bloomsbury Press USA, 2007); Jessika Auerbach, *And Nanny Makes Three: Mothers and Nannies Tell the Truth about Work, Love, Money, and Each Other* (New York: St. Martin's Press, 2007); Susan Davis and Gina Hyams, eds., *Searching for Mary Poppins: Women Write about the Relationship between Mothers and Nannies* (New York: Plume, 2007); and Susan Carlton and Susan Myers, *The Nanny Book: The Smart Parent's Guide to Hiring, Firing, and Every Sticky Situation in Between* (New York, NY: St. Martin's Griffin, 1999).

53. Garey, *Weaving Work and Motherhood*, 4–5, points out that both scholarly and popular-culture accounts of working mothers overrepresent professional and managerial women. The "normal" working mother is more likely to be a waitress, a sales clerk, a secretary, or a nurse.

54. Matthew B. Miles and A. Michael Huberman, *Qualitative Data Analysis: An Expanded Sourcebook*, 2nd ed. (Thousand Oaks, CA: Sage, 1994).

55. All respondents were assigned pseudonyms, and in many cases, identifying informa- tion, such as occupation or home town, was changed to protect anonymity.

56. For discussions of similar challenges facing professional-class working mothers, see Mary Blair-Loy, *Competing Devotions: Career and Family among Women Executives* (Cambridge, MA: Harvard University Press, 2003); and Stone, *Opting Out?*

57. Garey, *Weaving Work and Motherhood*, 32.

58. The breakdown of these added participants is as follows: eight mother-employers, their eight nannies, and six additional nannies.

CHAPTER 2

1. For a discussion of the work pressures faced by men who are involved fathers, however, see Nicholas W. Townsend, *The Package Deal: Marriage, Work, and Fatherhood in Men's Lives* (Philadelphia: Temple University Press, 2002).

2. Some academic fields (for example, nursing and English) are female dominated. The mother-employers who worked in these fields had an easier time maintaining professional standing and justifying flextime or flexi-place. See chapter 9 for further discussion of these women and their childcare arrangements.

3. The participants' average age at the birth of their first child was nearly a decade older than the average for women in the United States in 2002 (25.1 years), and nearly fifteen years older than the average in 1970 (21.4). See http://www.kaisernetwork.org/daily_reports/ rep_index.cfm?DR_ID = 21410.

4. Joan Williams, *Unbending Gender: Why Family and Work Conflict and What to Do about It* (New York: Oxford University Press, 2000).

5. Sharon Hays, *The Cultural Contradictions of Motherhood* (New Haven, CT: Yale University Press, 1996).

6. See, for example, Pierre Bourdieu, *Distinction: A Social Critique of the Judgement of Taste,* trans. Richard Nice (Cambridge, MA: Harvard University Press, 1984); and Jay Macleod, *Ain't No Makin' It: Aspirations and Attainment in a Low-Income Neighborhood,* 3rd ed. (Boulder, CO: Westview Press, 2008).

7. Pierrette Hondagneu-Sotelo, *Domestica: Immigrant Workers Cleaning and Caring in the Shadows of Affluence* (Berkeley: University of California Press, 2001), 26. Although she refers to the "rhetoric of competitive mothering," Hondagneu-Sotelo does not elaborate on the concept or address its consequences for childcare workers.

8. Maternal gatekeeping is described as the "emotional hoarding" of children by mothers. Arlie Russell Hochschild with Anne Machung, *The Second Shift*, 2nd ed. (New York: Penguin, 2003), 227.

9. Hays, *The Cultural Contradictions of Motherhood*, 69.

10. See Mary D. Salter Ainsworth et al., *Patterns of Attachment: A Psychological Study of the Strange Situation* (Hillsdale, NJ: Lawrence Erlbaum Associates, 1978). This measure- ment method has come under increased scrutiny now that more children are in childcare and thus more likely to be accustomed to interacting with multiple adults.

11. NICHD Early Child Care Research Network, "Familial Factors Associated with the Characteristics of Nonmaternal Child Care," *Journal of Marriage and the Family* 59 (1997): 389–408; NICHD Early Child Care Research Network, "Early Child Care and Self-Control,

Compliance and Problem Behavior at Twenty-Four and Thirty-Six Months," *Child Development* 69 (1998): 1145–1170; NICHD Early Child Care Research Network, "Characteristics and Quality of Child Care for Toddlers and Preschoolers," *Applied Developmental Science* 4 (2000): 116–35.

12. Margaret Talbot, "Attachment Theory: The Ultimate Experiment," *New York Times*, 24 May 1998, Sunday magazine.

13. "Bringing Up Baby," interview with Jay Belskey, Kathleen McCartney, and Anne Goldstein by Juan Williams, dir. K. J. Lopez, *Talk of the Nation*, National Public Radio, 24 April 2001.

14. John T. Bruer, *The Myth of the First Three Years: A New Understanding of Early Brain Development and Lifelong Learning* (New York: Free Press, 1999). The 1997 Starting Points conference strongly endorsed the view that "how individuals function from the preschool years all the way through adolescence and even adulthood hinges, to significant extent, on the experiences children have in their first three years." Carnegie Corporation of New York, *Starting Points: Meeting the Needs of Our Youngest Children* (New York: Carnegie Corporation of New York, 1994); Rima Shore, *Rethinking the Brain: New Insights into Early Development* (New York: Families and Work Institute, 1997). The birth-to-three fetish began in 1975 with the publication of Burton L. White, *The First Three Years of Life* (New York: Avon, 1975). It became a fixation in the American public imagination during the late 1990s.

15. Quoted in Bruer, *The Myth of the First Three Years*, 23.

16. Ibid., 52.

17. Ann Hulbert, *Raising America: Experts, Parents, and a Century of Advice about Children* (New York: Alfred A. Knopf, 2003), 312.

18. Quoted in Debra Rosenberg and Larry Reibstein, "Pots, Blocks, and Socks," *Newsweek*, spring/summer 1997, 34–35.

19. Quoted in Mary Leonard, "Mother's Day: A Guilt-Edged Occasion," *Boston Globe*, 11 May 1997, E3.

20. Hays notes that in 1981, 97 percent of American mothers read at least one childrearing manual, and nearly 75 percent read two or more. Hays, *The Cultural Contradictions of Motherhood*, 51. It is likely that these numbers have increased, as five times as many childrearing advice books were published in 1997, when my interviews took place, as in 1975. Hulbert, *Raising America*.

21. The more highly educated a mother is, the more advice literature she is likely to read and the less satisfied she is likely to be with her own childrearing. The 1997 Pew Study on Women, Family, and Work found that although most women considered themselves inadequate as mothers, the least satisfied mothers were college-educated; 72 percent of the at-home mothers in this group were "less satisfied" with their mothering skills, and 68 percent of the working mothers were unsatisfied. For the Pew Study, see Leonard, "Mother's Day"; for a discussion of social class and advice books, see Terry Arendell, "A Social Constructionist Approach to Parenting," in *Contemporary Parenting: Challenges and Issues*, ed. Terry Arendell (Thousand Oaks, CA: Sage, 1997), 1–44; and Annette Lareau, *Unequal Childhoods: Class, Race, and Family Life* (Berkeley: University of California Press, 2003), 5.

22. Middle- and professional-class mothers are the most susceptible to the tenets of contemporary childrearing, but other groups of mothers feel the strain as well. Most hold

themselves accountable to the intensive mothering ideal whether or not this cultural standard is realistically attainable, and regardless of their marital status and social class. See, especially, Margaret K. Nelson, *The Social Economy of Single Motherhood: Raising Children in Rural America* (New York: Routledge, 2005); and Anita Ilta Garey, *Weaving Work and Motherhood* (Philadelphia: Temple University Press, 1999).

23. Hondagneu-Sotelo, *Domestica*.

24. Lareau, *Unequal Childhoods*.

25. The meaning of Bourdieu's concept has been variously interpreted and vigorously debated. At its most basic level, *habitus* is meant to capture "dispositions," the second-nature habits, styles, preferences, views, and so on that we use to "perceive, judge, and act in the world," and which we acquire by virtue of growing up in a particular family, located in a specific social class and historical time. See Loic Wacquant, "Pierre Bourdieu," in *Key Contemporary Thinkers*, ed. Rob Stones, 2nd ed. (New York: Macmillan, 2008), 267.

26. In her study of executive women, Mary Blair-Loy found that those who "opted out" of their careers were "busily engaged in transmitting an upper-class capital to their children." Mary Blair-Loy, *Competing Devotions: Career and Family among Women Executives* (Cambridge, MA: Harvard University Press, 2003), 54.

27. Lareau, *Unequal Childhoods*, 276.

28. Suzanne Bianchi's research shows that contemporary mothers actually spend slightly more time with their children than their own mothers did: 5.8 waking hours with their children per day in 1998, compared to 5.6 hours per day in 1965, even though 72 percent of mothers were in the workforce in 1998, compared to 30 percent in 1965. Liana C. Sayer, Suzanne M. Bianchi, and John P. Robinson, "Are Parents Investing Less in Children? Trends in Mothers' and Fathers' Time with Children," *American Journal of Sociology* 110, no. 1 (2004): 1–43; Sharon Cohany and Emily Sok, "Trends in the Labor Force Participation of Married Mothers of Infants," *Monthly Labor Review*, February 2007, 9–16.

29. Nine of the thirty mother-employers had mothers who had worked outside the home at some time during their childhood. The few mothers I found who had been raised in communities in which working mothers were the *norm* tended to be more willing and able to reinterpret intensive mothering and create their own mothering beliefs. See chapter 9.

30. There are many examples. During the period of my field research in the Boston area, the following accounts were very much on the minds of the women I interviewed: the 1999 *New York Times* coverage of Lois Beard, who had been slated to become the first woman U.S. Army general but instead opted to stay home with her sixteen-year-old daughter; the *Boston Globe's* photo spread the following summer spotlighting Liz Walker, the only African American to hold the prestigious night anchor position in Boston news, and her decision to give up her job to stay home with her son; and, in August 2001, *Newsweek's* touting of Generation X women who were choosing to stay home "and not rely on babysitters as their mothers did." For additional analysis of media treatment of working mothers, see Janna Malamud Smith, *A Potent Spell: Mother Love and the Power of Fear* (Boston: Houghton Mifflin, 2003).

31. The maximum thirty-five-hour workweek in France and the move by the European Union to ensure high-quality part-time work are examples of structural support for good jobs with reasonable hours. Leave policies for mothers, and in Scandinavia for fathers,

allow parents to take up to fifteen months of paid parental leave over an eight-year period. In Sweden and Norway, parents have the option of taking these leaves simultaneously, sequentially, or in combination with part-time work. The availability of publicly provided childcare also supports working families in many EU countries. See Janet C. Gornick and Marcia K. Meyers, *Families That Work: Policies for Reconciling Parenthood and Employment* (New York: Russell Sage Foundation, 2003).

32. Julia Wrigley, "Hiring a Nanny: The Limits of Private Solutions to Public Problems," *Annals of the American Academy of Political and Social Science* 563 (1999): 162–74; Myra Marx Ferree, "The Gender Division of Labor in Two-Earner Marriages: Dimensions of Variability and Change," *Journal of Family Issues* 12, no. 2 (1991):158–80; Julie Brines, "Economic Dependency, Gender, and the Division of Labor at Home," *American Journal of Sociology* 100, no. 3 (1994): 652–88.

33. Nelson, *The Social Economy of Single Motherhood.*

34. Arlie Russell Hochschild, "Inside the Clockwork of Male Careers," in *Women and the Power to Change,* ed. Florence Howe (Berkeley: Carnegie Foundation for the Advancement of Teaching, 1975); Felice N. Schwartz, "Management Women and the New Facts of Life," *Harvard Business Review,* January–February 1989, 65–76; Rosanna Hertz, "Dual-Career Couples and the American Dream: Self-Sufficiency and Achievement," *Journal of Comparative Family Studies* 23, no. 2 (1991): 247–63; Rosanna Hertz, *More Equal Than Others: Women and Men in Dual-Career Marriages* (Berkeley: University of California Press, 1986); Blair-Loy, *Competing Devotions;* Williams, *Unbending Gender.*

35. On the concept of the "two-person career," in which the wife's backstage labor is necessary to her husband's success, see Hanna Papanek, "Men, Women, and Work: Reflections on the Two-Person Career," *American Journal of Sociology* 78 (1975): 852–72. On the gendered inequalities in backstage support, see also Arlie Russell Hochschild with Anne Machung, *The Second Shift: Working Parents and the Revolution at Home* (New York: Viking, 1989), 253.

36. Jerry A. Jacobs and Kathleen Gerson, *The Time Divide: Work, Family, and Gender Inequality* (Cambridge, MA: Harvard University Press, 2005).

37. Blair-Loy, *Competing Devotions,* 32. There is some debate concerning the *inherent* nature of work/family conflict in the U.S. context. Anita Garey, for instance, argues that the dominant cultural portrayals of "work orientation" and "home orientation" unnecessarily place these two spheres in opposition. Garey's research, however, focuses on women in female-dominated careers such as nursing, where, arguably, there is greater flexibility and in which being a worker and a caregiver are *not* conflicting roles. Garey, *Weaving Work and Motherhood.*

38. Six of the mother-employers reported no discriminatory attitudes in the workplace in response to their pregnancies and little pressure to work longer than their normal work-week, whether it was a part-time thirty-hour week or a full-time fifty-hour week. These respondents were also the only ones who worked in predominantly female environments where combining a career with childbearing was the norm.

39. Other studies have reported similar phenomena. Lindy Fursman describes what she calls "social pregnancy," whereby a pregnant worker's workplace peers and managers "redefin[e] the woman as forgetful and scatter-brained, and then structur[e] her responsi-

bilities accordingly." Lindy Fursman, "Conscious Decisions, Unconscious Paths: Pregnancy and the Importance of Work for Women in Management" (working paper no. 23, Center for Working Families, University of California, Berkeley, April 2001), 25. Helen Pattison found that the master role of mother overshadowed women's roles as managers or professionals and diminished the degree to which their coworkers and supervisors perceived them as competent. Helen M. Pattison, Helen Gross, and Charlotte Cast, "Pregnancy and Employment: The Perceptions and Beliefs of Fellow Workers," *Journal of Reproductive and Infant Psychology* 15, nos. 3–4 (1997): 303–13. See also Martha McMahon, *Engendering Motherhood: Identity and Self-Transformation in Women's Lives* (New York: Guilford Press, 1995).

40. Hertz, *More Equal Than Others;* Hertz, "Dual-Career Couples and the American Dream," 254.

41. Schwartz, "Management Women and the New Facts of Life."

42. Ann Crittenden, *The Price of Motherhood: Why the Most Important Job in the World Is Still the Least Valued* (New York: Metropolitan Books, 2001), 29.

43. This finding is similar to Mindy Fried's findings about male workers in companies that offered paternity leave. Although the policy offered them leave time, they tended not to take it because the corporate culture and the demands of their jobs dictated that they continue to work. Mindy Fried, *Taking Time: Parental Leave Policy and Corporate Culture* (Philadelphia: Temple University Press, 1998). See also Townsend, *The Package Deal.* It is important to note, however, that even when they exercised only part of their parental leave options, most of the mother-employers I interviewed had significantly more benefits than mothers who work hourly jobs.

44. Sylvia Ann Hewlett, *Off-Ramps and On-Ramps* (Cambridge, MA: Harvard Business School Press, 2007), 46.

45. Although the case-by-case nature of "situationally defined" maternity leave makes it seem like an individual problem for specific women in particular jobs, studies of women in high-level positions indicate that the career costs of taking maternity leave are more systemic. See Blair-Loy, *Competing Devotions,* 147–48. Also see Crittenden, *The Price of Motherhood;* Jennifer Glass, "Blessing or Curse? Work-Family Policies and Women's Wage Growth over Time," *Work and Occupations* 31, no. 3 (2004): 367–94; M. J. Budig and P. England, "The Wage Penalty for Motherhood," *American Sociological Review* 66, no. 2 (2001): 204–25; and Fried, *Taking Time.*

46. Hewlett found that 35 percent of businesswomen experienced stigma for going part-time, and 26 percent felt stigmatized for choosing flextime work. Hewlett, *Off-Ramps and On-Ramps,* 33. Among part-time attorneys, Epstein found not only stigma but also blocked mobility in the form of poor-quality assignments, lateral promotions, and a lack of mentoring. Cynthia Epstein et al., *The Part-Time Paradox: Time Norms, Professional Life, Family and Gender* (New York: Routledge, 1999), 64–67.

47. Joan C. Williams, "The Interaction of Courts and Legislatures in Creating Family-Responsive Workplaces," in *Working Time for Working Families: Europe and the United States, Contributions to a Program of the Washington Office of the Friedrich Ebert Foundation in Cooperation with the WorkLife Law Program at American University Washington College of Law and the Hans Böckler Foundation, Held in Washington, DC on June 7–8, 2004,* ed.

Ariane Hegewisch et al. (Washington, DC: Friedrich-Ebert-Stiftung, 2005), 22–34. www
.uchastings.edu/site_files/WLL/FESWorkingTimePublication.pdf.

48. Current Population Survey data indicate that nationwide, in 2000, 30 percent of
women in professional/managerial careers worked more than forty hours per week, and
18 percent of these women worked an average of forty-nine or more hours. It is not clear,
however, how many of these women are classified as "part-time." Fursman, "Conscious
Decisions, Unconscious Paths," 8.

49. Comparative studies of working-class and professional-class working mothers
found that professional women in part-time positions worked 27–30 hours per week
without taking breaks, whereas working-class part-timers worked 16–24 hours per week,
including lunch breaks. Of course, the differences in earnings were no doubt equally significant. Karen Walker, "Class, Work, and Family in Women's Lives," *Qualitative Sociology*
13, no. 4 (1990): 297–320.

50. The part-time work arrangement most frequently described as ideal was a three-
day workweek with long days, but some interviewees said their preference would be five
six-hour days.

51. Some mothers asserted that the need to be constantly vigilant and up-to-date was
not real but rather was manufactured by their superiors and used as another form of gender
discrimination.

52. Income ranges and number of mother-employers within those ranges are as follows:
$15,000–$35,000 (4); $36,000–$50,000 (3); $51,000–$100,000 (13); $101,000–$150,000 (4);
$151,000–$200,000 (4); and more than $200,000 (2). Seventeen of the thirty mother-
employers earned at least 50 percent of their household's income.

53. Baby boomers are the first generation to find that a "middle-class lifestyle mandate[s]
a two-income household." Katherine S. Newman, *Declining Fortunes: The Withering of the
American Dream* (New York: Basic Books, 1993), 21.

54. Ibid. This trade-off is not always the only option, however. See Rosanna Hertz and
Faith I. T. Ferguson, "Childcare Choice and Constraints in the United States: Social Class,
Race and the Influence of Family Views," *Journal of Comparative Family Studies* 27, no. 2
(1996): 249–80. Hertz and Ferguson argue that African American professional women often
bore children at a relatively young age and then completed their professional training using
family support for childcare. This trend may be abating, however. See Karin L. Brewster
and Irene Padavic, "No More Kin Care? Change in Black Mothers' Reliance on Relatives
for Child Care, 1977–1994," *Gender and Society* 16, no. 4 (2002): 546–63.

55. Susan Chira, "Working Mom in D.C. Loses Custody Fight to Ex-Husband," *Houston
Chronicle*, 20 September 1994, sec. A; Elizabeth Wasserman, "Career vs. Time with Kids:
Simpson Prosecutor's Custody Dispute Fuels Battle-of-Sexes Debate," *San Jose Mercury
News*, 4 March 1995, morning final edition, front section; "A Working Mom's Battle; Job vs.
Custody in NBC Special," *Chicago Sun-Times*, 21 November 1994, late sports final edition,
features section.

56. See Hochschild with Machung, *The Second Shift*, 1st ed. Also see Ferree, "The Gender
Division of Labor in Two-Earner Marriages"; and Harriet Presser, "Employment Schedules
among Dual-Earner Spouses and the Division of Household Labor by Gender," *American
Sociological Review* 59, no. 3 (1994): 348–65.

57. For more on the concept of "maternal gatekeeping," see Sarah J. Schoppe-Sullivan et al., "Maternal Gatekeeping, Coparenting Quality, and Fathering Behavior in Families with Infants," *Journal of Family Psychology* 22 (2008): 389–98; Sarah M. Allen and Alan J. Hawkins, "Maternal Gatekeeping: Mothers' Beliefs and Behaviors That Inhibit Greater Father Involvement in Family Work," *Journal of Marriage and the Family* 61, no. 1 (1999): 199–212; Ruth Gaunt, "Maternal Gatekeeping: Antecedents and Consequences," *Journal of Family Issues* 29 (2008): 373–95; and J. Fagan and M. Barnett, "The Relationship between Maternal Gatekeeping, Paternal Competence, Mothers' Attitudes about the Father Role, and Father Involvement," *Journal of Family Issues* 24 (2003): 1020–43.

58. Real sharing occurs most frequently among working-class couples who do shift work, with the mother and father taking complementary shifts and trading off childcare responsibilities. Anita Ilta Garey, "Constructing Motherhood on the Night Shift: 'Working Mothers' as 'Stay-at Home Moms,'" *Qualitative Sociology* 18, no. 4 (1995): 415–37; Rosanna Hertz, "Making Family under a Shiftwork Schedule: Air Force Security Guards and Their Wives," *Social Problems* 36, no. 5 (1989): 491–507. The most recent time-diary statistics, however, show that in 2005, employed mothers of children younger than six performed on average 3.56 hours of combined housework, food preparation/cleanup, and childcare work, whereas employed men performed these same tasks an average of 2.67 hours per day. U.S. Department of Labor, Bureau of Labor Statistics, *Highlights of Women's Earnings in 2005* (Washington, DC: U.S. Department of Labor, 2006). Suzanne Bianchi, John P. Robinson, and Melissa A. Milkie, *Changing Rhythms of American Family Life* (New York: Russell Sage Foundation, 2006).

59. Since I did not interview any fathers, my discussion here refers only to how fathers' attitudes and actions were perceived by their wives and by their children's nannies, not to the men's own perceptions of family life.

60. Nannies and mothers who engaged in "partnerships" were the exception to this rule. See chapter 9 for a full discussion.

61. Julia Wrigley also found this to be the case. Julia Wrigley, *Other People's Children: An Intimate Account of the Dilemmas Facing Middle-Class Parents and the Women They Hire to Raise Their Children* (New York: Basic Books, 1995).

62. Judith Rollins, *Between Women: Domestics and Their Employers* (Philadelphia: Temple University Press, 1985).

63. The median weekly salary for all working mothers in 2005 was $574. See U.S. Department of Labor, Bureau of Labor Statistics, *Highlights of Women's Earnings in 2005*.

CHAPTER 3

1. This phrase in Spanish translates roughly into "poorly brought up" or "having poor manners."

2. During the study period, the average wage for daycare center workers in Massachusetts ranged from $8.49 per hour for assistants to $10.50 per hour for teachers, while the average wage for family daycare providers was $7.32 per hour before expenses. Center for the Childcare Workforce, "Current Data on the Salaries and Benefits of the U.S. Early Childhood Education Workforce" (Center for the Childcare Workforce / American Federation

of Teachers Educational Foundation, 2004). The average wage for a live-out nanny with working papers in this study was a surprisingly high $1,450.00 per month, making them among the highest-paid childcare workers; the au pairs earned as little as $100 per week for a live-in job; and the undocumented immigrants earned as little as $80 per week for live-out employment.

3. There are a few exceptions. In Nelson's study of family daycare providers, clients and caregivers were roughly of the same class background. Margaret K. Nelson, *Negotiated Care: The Experience of Family Day Care Providers* (Philadelphia: Temple University Press, 1990). This is probably the only category of childcare worker in which such similarity occurs. Some workers at "enrichment" daycare centers, such as Head Start, may be more educated and better paid than their clients, but the majority of childcare center workers are poorly paid and come from a lower class background than their clients.

4. For representative studies, see Shellee Colen, "'Housekeeping' for the Green Card: West Indian Household Workers, the State, and Stratified Reproduction in New York," in *At Work in Homes: Household Workers in World Perspective,* ed. Roger Sanjek and Shellee Colen (Washington, DC: American Anthropological Association, 1990), 89–118; Pierrette Hondagneu-Sotelo, *Domestica: Immigrant Workers Cleaning and Caring in the Shadows of Affluence* (Berkeley: University of California Press, 2001); Grace Chang, *Disposable Domestics: Immigrant Women Workers in the Global Economy* (Cambridge, MA: South End Press, 2000); and Julia Wrigley, *Other People's Children: An Intimate Account of the Dilemmas Facing Middle-Class Parents and the Women They Hire to Raise Their Children* (New York: Basic Books, 1995). The differences I find result in large part from the fact that I define the job as childcare-*only.* Other researchers study "nanny-housekeepers" and "cleaners." These job categories, as chapter 4 explains, carry very different "ethnic logics."

5. For the original discussion of stratified reproduction, see Shellee Colen, "'Like a Mother to Them': Stratified Reproduction and West Indian Childcare Workers and Employers in New York," in *Conceiving the New World Order: The Global Politics of Reproduction,* ed. Faye D. Ginsburg and Rayna Rapp (Berkeley: University of California Press, 1995), 78–102.

6. Colen, "'Like a Mother to Them,'" 78.

7. For more on the racial-ethnic distinctions between housework and caring labor, see Dorothy E. Roberts, "Spritual and Menial Housework," *Yale Journal of Law and Feminism* 9, no. 51 (1997): 51–80.

8. Two of the immigrant nannies were from China, one from Africa, four from Great Britain (mostly Ireland), nine from Caribbean islands, and nine from South and Central America. I conducted all interviews personally, except those with Latina women who spoke little or no English. I thank my Spanish-speaking research assistants Sandra Olarte and Sylvia Gutierrez for their help in recruiting and interviewing these women.

9. Some were legally in the United States but did not have working papers; others had green cards. Two were naturalized citizens. Understandably, most were reluctant to discuss their immigration status in much detail.

10. This is one of many differences between the Boston area and Los Angeles, where many studies of immigrant caregivers have been conducted. In Boston, immigrant communities are located within close proximity to public transportation, allowing these women to live with relatives or countrymen, and to work on a live-out basis and take home higher

wages. The majority of live-in nannies I encountered in my years of fieldwork were either young white migrants from the Midwest or European au pairs.

11. Similarly, Grace Chang, "Undocumented Latinas: The New 'Employable Mothers,'" in *Mothering: Ideology, Experience, and Agency,* ed. Evelyn Nakano Glenn and Grace Chang (New York: Routledge, 1994), 55, cites a survey of New York nanny agencies finding that "'illegal' workers earned as little as 175 dollars per week and 'legal' workers as much as six hundred dollars."

12. Pierrette Hondagneu-Sotelo and Ernestine Avila, "'I'm Here, but I'm There': The Meanings of Latina Transnational Motherhood," *Gender and Society* 11, no. 5 (1997): 548–71, found that 40 percent of the immigrant domestic workers they surveyed who had children had left at least one child in their home country. Leaving children behind often is necessary in order to mask the permanency of the immigrant's stay. Not bringing children implies that the immigrant has a "stake in returning home," which in turn protects the worker's "visitor" status. James Lardner, "Separate Lives," *DoubleTake,* no. 13 (1998): 56.

13. My thanks to Muzaffar Chishti, the director of the Migration Policy Institute at NYU School of Law, for his clear and concise explanation of these legal changes. Although the category "nanny" has recently been reclassified as low-level "skilled" labor, it is unlikely that this change will make a significant change in the time and hassle involved in employer sponsorship.

14. This may explain why, among the fifteen immigrant nannies interviewed for this study and the thirty-seven immigrants who contacted us but were ineligible for this study, only one had received a green card through employer sponsorship.

15. On the drawbacks of the earlier laws, see Abigail B. Bakan and Daiva Stasiulis, eds., *Not One of the Family: Foreign Domestic Workers in Canada* (Toronto: University of Toronto Press, 1997); on exploitation in the wake of the new laws, see Samar Collective, "One Big, Happy Community? Class Issues within South Asian American Homes: The Samar Collective," *Samar: South Asian Magazine for Action and Reflection* 4 (winter 1994): 10–15.

16. See also Pierrette Hondagneu-Sotelo, "Blowups and Other Unhappy Endings," in *Global Woman: Nannies, Maids, and Sex Workers in the New Economy,* ed. Barbara Ehrenreich and Arlie Russell Hochschild (New York: Henry Holt, 2002), 55–69. Although there were no cases of physical abuse or slavery among the women we interviewed (probably a result of the self-selection process), such stories circulated at the playgrounds where we met and interviewed immigrant nannies. The fact that immigration laws are increasingly punitive makes all immigrant workers more vulnerable and even less likely to leave or expose an employer as a perpetrator of abuse or exploitation.

17. It was Ynez's need for a new job that prompted her to respond to outreach efforts my Spanish-speaking graduate assistants had initiated with local agencies assisting Latin American immigrants. As the possibilities of employer sponsorship have dwindled, stories of abuse by relatives or countrymen have proliferated. See Guy Sterling, "A Complex West Orange Slave Case Languishes," *Star-Ledger* (New Jersey), 9 July 2007, final edition; U.S. Department of Justice, "Cameroonian Couple Sentenced on Human Trafficking Charges" (press release, 31 May 2007); Lisa Sink, "Verdict Awaited in Maid Case; Jury to Decide Whether Illegal Immigrant Was 'House Slave,'" *Milwaukee Journal Sentinel,* 26 May 2006, final edition, B6; Frankie Edozien and Adam Miller, "Immigrant 'Slave' Lived a Nightmare,"

New York Post, 16 July 1999; Frank Eltman, "NY Millionaires' Slavery Trial Opens: Trial Opens for Millionaire Couple Accused of Slavery on NY's Long Island," Associated Press, 29 October 2007, http://abcnews.go.com/thelaw/wirestory?id = 3790694; and Samar Collective, "One Big, Happy Community?" The expanding demand for inexpensive childcare also contributes to this problem. Bob Egelko, "Domestic Workers Vulnerable to Exploitation," *San Francisco Chronicle,* 14 October 2009, Bay Area section; Chang, "Undocumented Latinas."

18. Chang, "Undocumented Latinas"; Lardner, "Separate Lives."

19. Chang, "Undocumented Latinas," 261.

20. Robin F. DeMattia, "Help from Overseas in Raising Youngsters," *New York Times,* 28 July 1996, final edition, sec. 13CN, 8.

21. Approximately half of the interviews I conducted with au pairs took place before program reforms raised their weekly stipends from $100 to $125. The tuition payment was intended to help offset the cost of the mandatory six hours of academic credit au pairs are required to earn from an institution of higher education during their year stay in the United States.

22. Recent reforms allow families and au pairs to apply for a second year if the arrangement is working particularly well.

23. For information about the USIA's administration of cultural exchange programs, see Debbi Wilgoren and Michael D. Shear, "Regulation of Au Pairs Lags behind the Reality," *Washington Post,* 14 August 1994, B1, B6. A provision of the federal Foreign Affairs Reform and Restructuring Act (1998) dissolved the forty-six-year-old agency effective October 1, 1999. Information regarding the USIA's mission and history is available at the agency's archived web site at http://dosfan.lib.uic.edu/usia.

24. Riner was later found not guilty on all charges. The murder remained unsolved, but Riner's employer was a key suspect. Several cases since the Riner one, including the Louise Woodward "shaken baby" case in the Boston area, have kept au pair programs under critical scrutiny. Barbara Carton, "Minding the Au Pairs: Oversight Sought as Programs Grow," *Boston Globe,* 2 January 1992; Ric Kahn, "Murder Charge Lodged against Au Pair," *Boston Globe,* 12 February 1997, B1, B4; Jetta Bernier, "Au Pair Anxiety," *Boston Globe,* 16 February 1997, D1, D2.

25. One agency sent its clients a letter regarding the age-limit provision, stating that 60 percent of their client families had children younger than age two, while only 20 percent of their au pairs were older than twenty-one. Bernier, "Au Pair Anxiety."

26. Jennifer Peltz, "Au Pair Popularity May Expand Rules: Government Studies Allowing More Time," Associated Press, 29 June 2008, www.commercialappeal.com/news/2008/Jun/29/au-pair-popularity-may-expand-rules; Lorna Duckworth, "Fallout from Woodward Case Hits Au Pair Industry," *Independent,* 2 March 2002; Julia Meurling, "Bulletin Board; a Child Care Solution: Help from Overseas," *New York Times,* 1 September 2002; "Au Pair Supply Increases from Eastern Europe and South Africa," *Newswire, PR,* 13 May 1999, www.lexisnexis.com/us/lnacademic/results/docview/docview.do?docLinkInd=true&risb=21_T4462345904&format=GNBFI&sort=RELEVANCE&startDocNo=26&resultsUrlKey=29_T4462345911&cisb=22_T4462345910&treeMax=true&treeWidth=0&csi=8054&docNo=32; Lisa W. Foderaro, "New Breed of Au Pair Packs a Shaving Kit," *New York Times,* 14 June

1999, http://query.nytimes.com/gst/fullpage.html?res=9C04E4D91338F937A25755C0A96F958260&sec=&spon=&pagewanted=all.

27. See also chapters 7 and 8 for au pair and nannies' perspectives on their work lives.

28. The only caregivers interviewed for this study who wanted to work in center-based care were Scandinavian. Center-based care is the norm in Northern Europe and, more important, it is government subsidized and decently paid, making daycare center work a viable career choice. C. Philip Hwang and Anders G. Broberg, "The Historical and Social Context of Child Care in Sweden," in *Child Care in Context: Cross-Cultural Perspectives,* ed. Michael Lamb et al. (Hillsdale, NJ: Hove and London, 1992), 27–53.

29. Three of the interviewees were college graduates; the remainder either had no post-secondary education or had completed only one or two years of college.

30. Median weekly wages for childcare center workers in 2000 were $297 versus the $197 earned by family childcare providers. See Mary C. Tuominen, *We Are Not Babysitters: Family Child Care Providers Redefine Work and Care* (New Brunswick, NJ: Rutgers University Press, 2003), 9.

31. These views also present a twist on Wong's concept of "diverted motherhood." This concept refers to the practice of the woman of color who puts her own pregnancy, childbearing, and mothering on hold in order to nurture her white employer's family. Among the American-born nannies, it is not women of color but rather white women who intentionally use childcare work as a means of fulfilling their own intensive mothering ideal. Sau-ling C. Wong, "Diverted Mothering: Representations of Caregivers of Color in the Age of 'Multiculturalism,'" in *Mothering: Ideology Experience, and Agency,* ed. Evelyn Nakano Glenn and Grace Chang (New York: Routledge, 1994), 67–91.

32. Rhacel Parreñas also found this phenomenon among the immigrant nannies she studied. Rhacel Parreñas, *Children of Global Migration: Transnational Families and Gendered Woes* (Stanford, CA: Stanford University Press, 2005). Hondagneu-Sotelo and Avila, "'I'm Here, but I'm There'"; Arlie Russell Hochschild, "The Nanny Chain," *American Prospect,* 3 January 2000, 32–36; Mary Romero, "Unraveling Privilege: Workers' Children and the Hidden Costs of Paid Childcare," in *Global Dimensions of Gender and Carework,* ed. Mary K. Zimmerman, Jacquelyn S. Litt, and Christine E. Bose (Stanford, CA: Stanford University Press, 2006), 240–53.

33. The insights (and the terminology) regarding class-based childrearing strategies described here are drawn from Annette Lareau's work. See Annette Lareau, *Unequal Childhoods: Class, Race, and Family Life* (Berkeley: University of California Press, 2003). It is important to note that Lareau studied the childrearing practices of parents of elementary school children. Interestingly, as this section shows, her findings also apply to class-based childrearing beliefs and practices among parents of preschool children.

34. Ibid.

35. All au pairs have minimal health insurance based on au pair regulations; of the forty non–au pairs I interviewed, nine had employer-provided insurance.

36. Kirk Johnson, "Earning It: The Nanny Track, a Once-Simple World Grown Complicated," *New York Times,* 29 September 1996, sec. 3.

37. Katharine Silbaugh, "Turning Labor into Love: Housework and the Law," *Northwestern University Law Review* 91, no. 1 (1996): 72, emphasis in the original. See also Peggie

Smith, "Regulating Paid Household Work: Class, Gender, Race, and Agendas of Reform," *American University Law Review* 48, no. 4 (1999): 851–924.

38. The overtime provision does not apply to live-in nannies or other domestics.

39. The NLRA specifically excludes "any individual employed . . . in the domestic service of any family or person at his home" (quoted in Silbaugh, "Turning Labor into Love," 74). Note that this does not mean that domestics have not attempted to unionize, only that their right to do so is not protected by law. Donna Van Raaphorst, *Union Maids Not Wanted: Organizing Domestic Workers, 1870–1940* (New York: Praeger, 1988).

40. There is some hope for change. Since the time of my interviews, some relatively successful mobilization efforts have occurred. In New York, the state legislature is considering a minimum wage of $14 per hour for domestic workers. This "Domestic Worker's Bill of Rights" represents an attempt to bypass the NRLA by writing labor standards into law. Notably, however, even these changes will not help the most vulnerable workers in my study, the foreign au pairs and the undocumented immigrants. Steven Greenhouse, "Report Shows Americans Have More 'Labor Days,'" *New York Times,* 1 September 2001; Steven Greenhouse, "Legislation Pushed to Require Minimum Wage for Domestic Workers," *New York Times,* 27 June 2007, region section; Russ Buettner, "For Nannies, Hope for Workplace Protection," *New York Times,* 2 June 2010, region section.

41. For examples of these campaigns, see, e.g., Mary Tuominen, "Exploitation or Opportunity? The Contradictions of Child-Care Policy in the Contemporary United States," *Women and Politics* 18, no. 1 (1997): 53–80; Tuominen, *We Are Not Babysitters;* Dorothy Sue Cobble and Michael Merrill, "The Promise of Service Sector Unionism," in *Service Work: Critical Perspectives,* ed. Marek Korczynski and Cameron L. Macdonald (New York: Routledge, 2008), 153–74; Cameron L. Macdonald and David A. Merrill, "'It Shouldn't Have to Be a Trade': Recognition and Redistribution in Care Work Advocacy," *Hypatia: A Journal of Feminist Philosophy* 17, no. 2 (2002): 67–83; Peggie R. Smith, "Laboring for Childcare: A Consideration of New Approaches to Represent Low-Income Service Workers," *University of Pennsylvania Journal of Labor and Employment Law* 8, no. 3 (2006): 583–621; and Peggie R. Smith, "Welfare, Child Care, and the People Who Care: Union Representation of Family Child Care Providers," *University of Kansas Law Review* 55, no. 2 (2007): 321–64.

42. The only successful legal findings in favor of nannies in abusive work situations have been in cases brought by immigrants' rights groups, not by unions or domestic worker collectives. For examples of successful antislavery cases, see note 17 in this chapter. For an excellent discussion of labor mobilizing by immigrant groups, see Kathleen Coll, *Remaking Citizenship: Latina Immigrants and the New American Politics* (Stanford, CA: Stanford University Press, 2010).

43. In her study of family daycare providers, Margaret Nelson found that depending on their situation and their needs, parents and providers vacillated between applying the norms of a "*market* exchange with clearly specified obligations, stated rules, and social distance," and those of a "*social* exchange with diffuse obligations, negotiated decision-making based on trust, and intimacy." Nelson, *Negotiated Care,* 48, emphasis in the original.

44. On employers' strategies for bringing the logic of kin ties into the domestic labor arrangement, see, e.g., Shellee Colen, "'With Respect and Feelings': Voices of West Indian Child Care and Domestic Workers in New York City," in *All American Women,* ed. Johnnetta

B. Cole (New York: Free Press, 1986), 46–70; Bonnie Thornton Dill, "'Making Your Job Good Yourself': Domestic Service and the Construction of Personal Dignity," in *Women and the Politics of Empowerment,* ed. Anne Bookman and Sandra Morgen (Philadelphia: Temple University Press, 1988), 33–52; Rosanna Hertz, *More Equal Than Others: Women and Men in Dual-Career Marriages* (Berkeley: University of California Press, 1986); Judith Rollins, *Between Women: Domestics and Their Employers* (Philadelphia: Temple University Press, 1985); Mary Romero, *Maid in the U.S.A.* (New York: Routledge, 1992); and Wrigley, *Other People's Children.*

45. See chapter 8 for additional discussion of the role of self-sacrifice among childcare providers.

46. See chapter 7 for more on the nannies' perspective.

47. Although most of the live-in nannies I interviewed had separate quarters, usually in the basement or attic, lack of personal space or privacy is frequently mentioned in other accounts of nanny work, especially among live-in immigrant domestics. See Samar Collective, "One Big, Happy Community?"; Doreen Carvajal, "For Immigrant Maids, Not a Job but Servitude," *New York Times,* 25 February 1996, metro section; and Lardner, "Separate Lives."

48. See chapters 7 and 8 for further discussion of the caregivers' expectations and frustrations.

49. Rollins, *Between Women.*

50. Most of the mothers I interviewed spoke of paying the nanny out of their own salaries and of needing to earn enough to make it economically "worthwhile" for them to work outside the home. See chapter 9 for a discussion of the exceptions to this rule.

51. But see chapter 9 for exceptions. .

52. See chapters 7 and 8 for detailed discussion of caregivers' perspectives.

CHAPTER 4

1. Shellee Colen, "'With Respect and Feelings': Voices of West Indian Child Care and Domestic Workers in New York City," in *All American Women,* ed. Johnnetta B. Cole (New York: Free Press, 1986), 46–70; Shellee Colen, "'Housekeeping' for the Green Card: West Indian Household Workers, the State, and Stratified Reproduction in New York," in *At Work in Homes: Household Workers in World Perspective,* ed. Roger Sanjek and Shellee Colen (Washington, DC: American Anthropological Association, 1990), 89–118; Shellee Colen, "'Like a Mother to Them': Stratified Reproduction and West Indian Childcare Workers and Employers in New York," in *Conceiving the New World Order: The Global Politics of Reproduction,* ed. Faye D. Ginsburg and Rayna Rapp (Berkeley: University of California Press, 1995), 78–102; Pierrette Hondagneu-Sotelo, *Domestica: Immigrant Workers Cleaning and Caring in the Shadows of Affluence* (Berkeley: University of California Press, 2001); Julia Wrigley, *Other People's Children: An Intimate Account of the Dilemmas Facing Middle-Class Parents and the Women They Hire to Raise Their Children* (New York: Basic Books, 1995).

2. David Swartz, *Culture and Power: The Sociology of Pierre Bourdieu* (Chicago: University of Chicago Press, 1997); Pierre Bourdieu, "The Forms of Capital," in *Handbook of Theory and Research for the Sociology of Education,* ed. J.G. Richardson (New York: Greenwood Press, 1986), 241–58.

3. See Robin Leidner, *Fast Food, Fast Talk: Service Work and the Routinization of Everyday Life* (Berkeley: University of California Press, 1993).

4. For example, Hochschild notes that in most interactive service work, "the emotional style of offering the service is part of the service itself." Arlie Russell Hochschild, *The Managed Heart: Commercialization of Human Feeling* (Berkeley: University of California Press, 1983), 8. See also Cameron Macdonald and Carmen Sirianni. "The Service Society and the Changing Nature of Work," in *Understanding Society: An Introductory Reader,* ed. Margaret Anderson, Kim Logio, and Howard Taylor, 3rd ed. (New York: Wadsworth, 2009), 421–28.

5. Robin Leidner, "Rethinking Questions of Control: Lessons from McDonald's," in *Working in the Service Society,* ed. Cameron Lynne Macdonald and Carmen Sirianni (Philadelphia: Temple University Press, 1996), 29–49.

6. William T. Bielby, "Minimizing Workplace Gender and Racial Bias," *Contemporary Sociology* 29, no. 1 (2000): 120–29.

7. Barbara Reskin, "Getting It Right: Sex and Race Inequality in Work Organizations," *Annual Review of Sociology* 26 (2000): 707–9, citing Susan Fiske, "Stereotyping, Prejudice, and Discrimination," in *The Handbook of Social Psychology,* ed. S. T. Fiske, D. T. Gilbert, and G. Lindzey (Boston: McGraw-Hill, 1998), 357–411.

8. Ann Swidler, "Culture in Action: Symbols and Strategies," *American Sociological Review* 51 (April 1986): 273–86.

9. Ann Swidler, *Talk of Love: How Culture Matters* (Chicago: University of Chicago Press, 2001), 83.

10. Pierre Bourdieu, *Outline of a Theory of Practice,* trans. Richard Nice (Cambridge: Cambridge University Press, 1977), 86.

11. As Geertz has pointed out, "when one deals with meaningful forms, the temptation to see the relationship among them as immanent, is virtually overwhelming . . . but meaning is not intrinsic in the objects, acts, processes, and so on which bear it." Clifford Geertz, *The Interpretation of Cultures* (New York: Basic Books, 1973), 404.

12. Swartz, *Culture and Power,* 69.

13. Swidler, *Talk of Love,* 178.

14. It is important to note that hiring into networks to meet the needs of the customer, in this case the child, is a different process from hiring within an ethnic network to create employee solidarity. On how domestic workers use informal ethnic networks to find employment, see, for example, Pierrette Hondagneu-Sotelo, "Regulating the Unregulated? Domestic Workers' Social Networks," *Social Problems* 41, no. 1 (1994): 50–64; Thomas Bailey and Roger Waldinger, "Primary, Secondary, and Enclave Labor Markets: A Training Systems Approach," *American Sociological Review* 56, no. 4 (1991): 432–45; James R. Elliot, "Referral Hiring and Ethnically Homogenous Jobs: How Prevalent Is the Connection and for Whom?" *Social Sciences Research* 30, no. 3 (2001): 401–25; and Roberto M. Fernandez, Emilio J. Castilla, and Paul Moore, "Social Capital at Work: Networks and Employment at a Call Center," *American Journal of Sociology* 105, no. 5 (2000): 1288–1356.

15. Employers with large homes that could accommodate live-in help often ended up paying the least for childcare because the capacious living area that came with the nanny's position offset the low wages she was offered. Ironically, these employers were also among the wealthiest study participants.

16. It is worth noting that Hondagneu-Sotelo argues that hiring among domestics takes place primarily through employer networks. Hondagneu-Sotelo, *Domestica*. I found this process to be more complex. When employers did hire into networks, they were more likely to hire into existing *nanny networks* than from references from friends. In fact, most nannies felt strongly that they should hire their replacements as part of their duty to the children in their care.

17. Jay Belsky, "Parental and Nonparental Child Care and Children's Socioemotional Development: A Decade in Review," *Journal of Marriage and the Family* 52 (November 1990): 890. Wrigley, *Other People's Children,* found that parents became concerned about a new set of issues (e.g., language skills) as their children moved from infancy to toddler-hood and then into early childhood. She argues that class operates in these choices in terms of the relationship to the parent, not the child. Wrigley referred to the two groups of nannies as "class peers" and "class subordinates." In truth, they are ethnic equals and ethnic subordinates. It is doubtful that any nanny shares her employer's class standing, be it upbringing, education, or prospects; however, as Wrigley points out, in childcare work, ethnic differences serve as a marker for different skill levels.

18. Note that a similar ethnic logic currently favors a new group of nannies—those from Tibet. Katherine Zoepf, "Wanted: Tibetan Nannies," *New York Observer,* 27 September 2009.

19. Note, however, that parents almost never considered employing male nannies for preschool-age children. Stereotypes about the "kind" of male who would want to work with young children made it virtually impossible for male nannies to find employment.

20. The 1996 welfare reform legislation makes the same class-based assumption. Unlike middle-class mothers, poor mothers are viewed as eminently replaceable, and welfare reform laws implicitly argue that poor children would be better off spending time in formal childcare settings than with their own mothers.

21. Lynet Uttal, "'Trust Your Instincts': Cultural Similarity, Cultural Maintenance, and Racial Safety in Employed Mothers' Childcare Choices," *Qualitative Sociology* 20, no. 2 (1997): 266.

22. See, for example, Jodi Kantor, "Memo to Nanny: No Juice Boxes," *New York Times,* 8 September 2006, G1.

23. In 41 of the 60 arrangements, race or language was shared; in 22 of the 60, ethnic group or national origin were shared. I distinguish here among race, ethnicity, and national origin because one frequently served as a stand-in for the other. I refer to 60 *arrangements* because, although I interviewed 80 women, some were part of the same childcare arrangement. For example, I interviewed both Joyce and Stacy, two halves of one relationship.

24. U.S. Department of Commerce, Census Bureau, *2000 Census* (Washington, DC: U.S. Department of Commerce, 2000), table DP-1, "Profile of General Demographic Characteristics, Massachusetts."

25. Given the context, Rosa likely compares the "Mexican" Spanish—that is, those from Mexico and Central and South America—to Spanish-speakers from the Caribbean, particularly Puerto Rico and the Dominican Republic, whose accents bespoke lower-class origins.

26. E.S. Phelps, "The Statistical Theory of Racism and Sexism," *American Economic Review* 62 (1972): 659–61.

27. Anne S. Tsui, Terri D. Egan, and Charles A. O'Reilly III, "Being Different: Relational Demography and Organizational Attachment," *Administrative Science Quarterly* 37, no. 4 (1992): 549–79.

CHAPTER 5

1. Twenty-two of the thirty mothers interviewed used "intensive mothering by proxy" as a management strategy.

2. Lynet Uttal ("Custodial Care, Surrogate Care, and Coordinated Care: Employed Mothers and the Meaning of Child Care," *Gender and Society* 10, no. 3 [1996]: 291–311), for example, argues that the very nature of delegating childcare challenges traditional mothering ideologies. She studies *all* types of nonmaternal care, however, including care by relatives and by the father, so it is difficult to discern how her findings apply to paid care.

3. Partnerships were the only employer-employee relationships that explicitly challenged the ideology of intensive mothering by acknowledging the contributions of paid caregivers to childrearing. See chapter 9 for details.

4. Arlie Russell Hochschild with Anne Machung, *The Second Shift: Working Parents and the Revolution at Home* (New York: Viking, 1989), 258.

5. Thanks to Anita Garey for suggesting this term.

6. These figures refer to the management strategy in place when the initial interview took place. Management strategies are likely to change as the mother becomes more experienced in delegating care, as children age, or as caregivers are replaced.

7. Robin Leidner, *Fast Food, Fast Talk: Service Work and the Routinization of Everyday Life* (Berkeley: University of California Press, 1993).

8. These two approaches to managing nannies mirror the dominant methods of managing service workers in general. Some might argue that childcare differs too much from other forms of service work for this generalization to be relevant, but the same crucial puzzles exist: (1) the manager, in this case the mother, cannot directly supervise the interaction, which is, in effect, the product; and (2) the manager must therefore find another way to ensure that the customer (in this case, the child) gets the desired or needed interaction. Cameron Lynne Macdonald and Carmen Sirianni, eds., *Working in the Service Society* (Philadelphia: Temple University Press, 1996). Some managers take a "production line" approach, in which all interactions are strictly routinized and scripted. Others take an "empowerment" approach, in which employees are selected for particular personal qualities, which are then shaped and enhanced by management.

9. See chapters 7 and 8 for a full discussion of the nannies' perspectives.

10. Julia Wrigley and Joanna Dreby, "Fatalities and the Organization of Childcare in the United States, 1985–2003," *American Sociological Review* 70 (2005): 729–57.

11. Julia Wrigley, *Other People's Children: An Intimate Account of the Dilemmas Facing Middle-Class Parents and the Women They Hire to Raise Their Children* (New York: Basic Books, 1995), 137.

12. See, for example, Noel Cazaneve and Murray Straus, "Race, Class, Network Embeddedness, and Family Violence: A Search for Potent Support Systems," in *Physical Violence in American Families: Risk Factors and Adaptations to Violence in 8,145 Families*, ed. Murray

Straus and Richard Gelles (New Brunswick, NJ: Transaction Publishers, 1990), 321–39; Frank J. Moncher, "Social Isolation and Child Abuse Risk," *Families in Society* 76, no. 7 (1995): 421–33; and Diane DePanfilis, "Social Isolation of Neglectful Families: A Review of Social Support Assessment and Intervention Models," *Child Maltreatment* 1, no. 1 (1996): 37–52.

13. Rosanna Hertz, *More Equal Than Others: Women and Men in Dual-Career Marriages* (Berkeley: University of California Press, 1986), 187.

CHAPTER 6

1. Dorothy Smith refers to the fissures experienced by women in academe between their grounded understanding of the reproductive labor they perform every day to sustain family life and the rarified knowledge that "counts" in the academic setting as *lines of fault*. Dorothy E. Smith, *The Everyday World as Problematic* (Boston: Northeastern University Press, 1987). I use the term here to refer to the disjunctions in consciousness and experience of childrearing between the two sets of women.

2. Emotional labor is work that "requires one to induce or suppress feeling in order to sustain the outward countenance that produces the proper state of mind in others." Arlie Russell Hochschild, *The Managed Heart: Commercialization of Human Feeling* (Berkeley: University of California Press, 1983), 7.

3. With the advent of reproductive technologies, other forms of mothering (conception, gestation, various aspects of the biological tie) have also become divisible. This book focuses only on the division of mother-work, not on the division of other forms of mothering and their implications. Two historical changes also have contributed to anxiety about the fuzzy boundaries between mother and "not-mother." The legal definition of motherhood has blurred in the wake of more widespread use of reproductive technologies. Although for centuries common law has defined the mother as the person "having given birth" to the child, new definitions, such as the genetic mother or the contracting mother now appear in custody cases involving reproductive technologies. Tensions regarding what constitutes parenthood in practice appeared in custody and divorce cases long before the advent of surrogacy or egg donation, however. The invention of the concept of "psychological par-enthood," the notion that what counts in making custody decisions is the extent to which each of the parties has formed a secure attachment to the children by being present in their daily lives, by loving and caring for them on a consistent basis over time, has its roots in these legal contests. See, for example, Barbara Katz Rothman, *Recreating Motherhood: Ideology and Technology in a Patriarchal Society* (New York: W. W. Norton, 1989); and Susan Markens, *Surrogate Motherhood and the Politics of Reproduction* (Berkeley: University of California Press, 2007).

4. Chapter 7 focuses on caregivers' needs and desires.

5. Ivan Illich, *Shadow Work* (Boston: M. Boyars, 1981).

6. Arlene Kaplan Daniels, "Invisible Work," *Social Problems* 34, no. 5 (1987): 403–15.

7. Deborah Phillips, Carollee Howes, and Marcy Whitebook, "Child Care as an Adult Work Environment," *Journal of Social Issues* 47, no. 2 (1991): 49–70; Katharine Silbaugh, "Turning Labor into Love: Housework and the Law," *Northwestern University Law Review* 91, no. 1 (1996): 1–86.

8. Feminist scholars have long documented that reproductive labor is essential to human survival. See, for example, Marjorie L. DeVault, *Feeding the Family: The Social Organization of Caring and Gendered Work* (Chicago: University of Chicago Press, 1991); and Dorothy Smith, "From Women's Standpoint to a Sociology for People," in *Sociology for the Twenty-first Century*, ed. Janet Abu-Lughod (Chicago: University of Chicago Press, 1999), 65–82.

9. Daniels, "Invisible Work."

10. On the care penalty, see Paula England and Nancy Folbre, "The Cost of Caring," *Annals of the American Academy of Political and Social Science* 561, no. 1 (1999): 39–51. On unionization of care-workers, see Katharine Silbaugh, "Commodification and Women's Household Labor," *Yale Journal of Law and Feminism* 9, no. 1 (1997): 81–122; Cameron L. Macdonald and David A. Merrill, "'It Shouldn't Have to Be a Trade': Recognition and Redistribution in Care Work Advocacy," *Hypatia: A Journal of Feminist Philosophy* 17, no. 2 (2002): 67–83; and Dorothy Sue Cobble and Michael Merrill, "The Promise of Service Sector Unionism," in *Service Work: Critical Perspectives*, ed. Marek Korczynski and Cameron L. Macdonald (New York: Routledge, 2008), 153–74.

11. Dorothy E. Roberts, "Spritual and Menial Housework," *Yale Journal of Law and Feminism* 9, no. 51 (1997): 51–80.

12. Hochschild, *The Managed Heart*.

13. Christena Nippert-Eng, *Home and Work: Negotiating Boundaries through Everyday Life* (Chicago: University of Chicago Press, 1996).

14. Margaret K. Nelson, *Negotiated Care: The Experience of Family Day Care Providers* (Philadelphia: Temple University Press, 1990), 136.

15. Hochschild, *The Managed Heart*, 56.

16. Ibid., 90.

17. Lynet Uttal and Mary Tuominen, "Tenuous Relationships: Exploitation, Emotion, and Racial Ethnic Significance in Paid Child Care Work," *Gender and Society* 136 (December 1999): 763.

18. Chapter 8 explores this topic.

19. Most of the nannies I interviewed had one-year contracts that were up for annual renewal and renegotiation, and that could be extended indefinitely. Au pairs are limited to a one-year stay in the United States by the nature of their visas. Recently, the U.S. State Department has made it possible for au pairs and host families to apply for a one-time one-year extension to the au pair contract.

20. In describing the transition from an agrarian to an industrial economy, Tamara Hareven distinguishes between the experiences of "industrial time," with its fixed schedules and rigid time clock, and "family time," which was more flexible. Tamara K. Hareven, "Modernization and Family History: Perspectives on Social Change," *Signs* 2, no. 1 (1976): 190–206.

21. Arlie Russell Hochschild, *The Time Bind: When Work Becomes Home and Home Becomes Work* (New York: Metropolitan Books, 1997), 77.

22. Everett Hughes coined the distinction between "respectable" and "dirty" work. Everett C. Hughes, *Men and Their Work* (Glencoe, Il: Free Press, 1958).

23. Chapters 7 and 8 discuss nannies' perspectives on discipline.

24. Wrigley argues that parents keep "crucial aspects of care to perform themselves," but refers primarily to class-based tasks, such as reading to children or supervising their

homework, tasks that middle-class parents often do not trust "class subordinate" caregivers to perform adequately. Julia Wrigley, *Other People's Children: An Intimate Account of the Dilemmas Facing Middle-Class Parents and the Women They Hire to Raise Their Children* (New York: Basic Books, 1995), 121.

25. Although Meltz is referring here to daycare center workers, the same advice clearly applies to in-home childcare providers. Barbara Meltz, "When Jealousy Strikes the Working Parent," *Boston Globe*, 15 March 1991, 69.

CHAPTER 7

1. See the appendix for a discussion of interpreting conflicting accounts.

2. Jennifer Steinhauer, "City Nannies Say They, Too, Can Be Mother Lions," *New York Times*, 16 July 2005, A1.

3. Ibid.

4. Two-thirds of my interviews were conducted before the Louise Woodward trial made front-page news. In the remaining one-third, interviewees referred to the case, but because I did not discuss it with all of the respondents, I do not address any interpretations of the case here.

5. Other childcare workers across various settings face similar challenges. Rutman's study of Canadian daycare workers and family daycare providers showed that caregivers were most frustrated by the lack of respect for their expertise, in terms of "knowledge about caring for children in general or about the needs of individual children in their care." Deborah Rutman, "Child Care as Women's Work: Workers' Experiences of Powerfulness and Powerlessness," *Gender and Society* 10, no. 5 (1996): 635. The foremost nationwide study of U.S. daycare center workers found that feeling that their work was devalued by parents and by the public was one of the most common indicators of job dissatisfaction, second only to salary and benefit concerns. Deborah Phillips, Carollee Howes, and Marcy Whitebook, "Child Care as an Adult Work Environment," *Journal of Social Issues* 47, no. 2 (1991): 49–70. See also Elaine Enarson, "Experts and Caregivers: Perspectives on Underground Day Care," in *Circles of Care: Work and Identity in Women's Lives*, ed. Emily K. Abel and Margaret K. Nelson (Albany: SUNY Press, 1990), 233–45; and Margaret K. Nelson, *Negotiated Care: The Experience of Family Day Care Providers* (Philadelphia: Temple University Press, 1990).

6. This was particularly true of April and Melanie, who were the most educated of the American-born nannies.

7. Other childcare workers also seek to "professionalize" their work by using these two models. Many daycare center workers take on an early childhood education teacher role; most family daycare providers take on a mothering role. See Heather M. Fitz Gibbon, "Child Care across Sectors: A Comparison of the Work of Childcare in Three Settings," in *Child Care and Inequality: Rethinking Carework for Children and Youth*, ed. Francesca M. Cancian et al. (New York: Routledge, 2002), 145–58; and Nelson, *Negotiated Care*. Family daycare providers of color often draw on a long tradition of "Community Othermothers," viewing their work as providing a necessary service to their neighborhood community as well as to their racial/ethnic group. Mary C. Tuominen, *We Are Not Babysitters: Family Child Care Providers Redefine Work and Care* (New Brunswick, NJ: Rutgers University Press, 2003); Patricia Hill-Collins, "Black Women and Motherhood," in *Rethinking the*

244 NOTES TO CHAPTER 7

Family: Some Feminist Questions, ed. Barry Thorne and Marilyn Yalom, 2nd ed. (Boston: Northeastern University Press, 1992), 215–81. Both the mother and the teacher models have potential drawbacks. Enarson, "Experts and Caregivers," found that family daycare providers resist the teacher model imposed on them by state regulatory agencies because it denies the expertise involved in mothering and ignores its value as a form of care for the very young. See also Cameron L. Macdonald and David A. Merrill, "'It Shouldn't Have to Be a Trade': Recognition and Redistribution in Care Work Advocacy," *Hypatia: A Journal of Feminist Philosophy* 17, no. 2 (2002): 67–83. Susan Murray points out that alignment with the motherhood model "genders" the occupation and thus trivializes the work. Susan B. Murray, "Child Care Work: The Lived Experience" (Ph.D. Dissertation, University of California, Santa Cruz, 1995).

8. See also Pierrette Hondagneu-Sotelo, *Domestica: Immigrant Workers Cleaning and Caring in the Shadows of Affluence* (Berkeley: University of California Press, 2001).

9. Julia Wrigley also found this to be the case: "Denied adult freedoms, caregivers in restrictive households occupy an intermediate status, not children but not full adults either. They have a lot of responsibility, but in their daily lives they can be denied normal symbols of respect and trust." Julia Wrigley, *Other People's Children: An Intimate Account of the Dilemmas Facing Middle-Class Parents and the Women They Hire to Raise Their Children* (New York: Basic Books, 1995), 138.

10. Mothers in "partnerships" with their caregivers were the exception to this pattern. See chapter 9.

11. This distinction between head/conception (management) and hands/execution (worker) was initially outlined in Harry Braverman, *Labor and Monopoly Capital: The Degradation of Work in the Twentieth Century* (New York: Monthly Review Press, 1974), 113.

12. Others who have studied childcare workers in various settings have noted the "everydayness" of these workers' knowledge. See Susan B. Murray, "Child Care Work: Intimacy in the Shadows of Family Life," *Qualitative Sociology* 21, no. 2 (1998): 149–68; and Rutman, "Child Care as Women's Work."

13. Another five had never babysat as children but had mothering experience from having older children of their own. This is another way in which mothering is inherently classed. It is highly unlikely that a poor or working-class woman would reach adulthood without having done some childcare, whether for family or neighbors.

14. Kari Waerness, "The Rationality of Caring," *Economic and Industrial Democracy* 5 (1984), 198.

15. In describing what motherwit encompasses, Wendy Luttrell comments, "Motherwise knowledge is difficult to universalize because it is emotional, relational, individual, and particularized." Wendy Luttrell, *Schoolsmart and Motherwise: Working-Class Women's Identity and Schooling* (New York: Routledge, 1997), 31. The mother-employers did possess motherwit, but they usually favored book knowledge.

16. Evelyn Nakano Glenn, "Social Constructions of Mothering: A Thematic Overview," in *Mothering: Ideology, Experience, and Agency,* ed. Evelyn Nakano Glenn, Grace Chang, and Linda Renney Forcey (New York: Routledge, 1994), 13.

17. Elsewhere, I explain the bind created by caregivers' use of what I term the "vocabulary of virtue" (i.e., defining themselves as "like mothers") and the "vocabulary of skill"

(i.e., defining themselves as "like teachers"). See Macdonald and Merrill, "'It Shouldn't Have to Be a Trade.'"

CHAPTER 8

1. If a nanny was satisfied with her job and confident with her employer, she would refer me to the mother for an interview. In less stable relationships, I heard only one side.

2. Axel Honneth, *The Struggle for Recognition: The Moral Grammar of Social Conflicts* (Cambridge, MA: MIT Press, 1996).

3. Pierrette Hondagneu-Sotelo, "Blowups and Other Unhappy Endings," in *Global Woman: Nannies, Maids, and Sex Workers in the New Economy,* ed. Barbara Ehrenreich and Arlie Russell Hochschild (New York: Henry Holt, 2002), 55–69. She describes the "blowups" and abrupt departures she observed among the Latina maids and nannies she interviewed. This kind of departure was a rarity among the women I interviewed, perhaps because their jobs were defined as "childcare only" and because of the strong attachments they developed.

4. The Louise Woodward case, which occurred after I had conducted most of my interviews, stirred up fears about hiring an au pair who, like Woodward, had left her original host family. The case has tainted all au pairs who want to leave their posts, making exit difficult even when the grievances are significant.

5. Hondagneu-Sotelo also found this to be the case among the Latina domestics she interviewed. Pierrette Hondagneu-Sotelo, *Domestica: Immigrant Workers Cleaning and Caring in the Shadows of Affluence* (Berkeley: University of California Press, 2001), 147.

6. Research on maids, housekeepers, and other domestic workers has shown that they resort to similar strategies, reinterpreting their unequal status with respect to their employers through strategies of denigration and ridicule. See Bonnie Thornton Dill, "'Making Your Job Good Yourself': Domestic Service and the Construction of Personal Dignity," in *Women and the Politics of Empowerment,* ed. Anne Bookman and Sandra Morgen (Philadelphia: Temple University Press, 1988), 33–52; Judith Rollins, *Between Women: Domestics and Their Employers* (Philadelphia: Temple University Press, 1985); Mary Romero, *Maid in the U.S.A.* (New York: Routledge, 1992).

7. For example, Cohen says of the Canadian domestic workers she studied, "One way to assert humanity and dignity is to perform little tricks, privately or with other maids, and celebrate small triumphs while still retaining the employer's favor." Rina Cohen, "Women of Color in White Households: Coping Strategies of Live-in Domestic Workers," *Qualitative Sociology* 14, no. 2 (1991): 211. For a complete treatment of microresistance stratagems, see James C. Scott, *Weapons of the Weak: Everyday Forms of Peasant Resistance* (New Haven, CT: Yale University Press, 1985).

8. Rollins makes this argument. She notes that "domestics' highly developed observational skills may grow out of the need for maneuvering and for indirect manipulation in this occupation, but the resulting knowledge and understanding is critically beneficial to the maintenance of their sense of self-worth vis-à-vis their employers." Rollins, *Between Women,* 213.

9. This is an interesting contrast with the "nanny-housekeepers" interviewed by Hondagneu-Sotelo (in *Domestica*) who stated that the children behaved better for their parents.

Perhaps this is because some of the employers in her study did not work outside of the home, or because the children had become old enough to learn the significance of the differences of class and race between themselves and their caregivers. No nannies I interviewed ever stated that the children behaved better for their parents than they did for them.

10. Galinsky sees competency contests as an enactment of the "Child Savior Attitude," which essentially says, "Since this mother has gone off to work and abandoned her child, I will take better care of her than she could." Providers who take this attitude, she writes, are "parentist: no less destructive than someone who is ageist or racist." Quoted in Barbara Meltz, "When Jealousy Strikes the Working Parent," *Boston Globe*, 15 March 1991, 69.

11. This dilemma comes up frequently in studies of family daycare as well. Margaret K. Nelson, *Negotiated Care: The Experience of Family Day Care Providers* (Philadelphia: Temple University Press, 1990); Mary C. Tuominen, "The Conflicts of Caring," in *Care Work: Gender, Labor, and the Welfare State,* ed. Madonna Harrington Meyer (London: Routledge, 2000), 112–35. When disputes arise over pay or pickup or drop-off times, parents will use the childcare provider's attachment to the children as leverage, threatening to move them to another childcare provider.

12. This figure does not include the ten au pairs, who were limited by contract to one year. Including the au pairs, the average length of service with each family was 2.1 years.

13. Other scholars of childcare and caregiving work have noted that caregivers frequently make trade-offs between the inherent fulfillment of caregiving and fair pay. The theme of self-sacrifice and setting fees to meet a family's needs is not uncommon among childcare workers across settings. Lynet Uttal and Mary Tuominen argue that childcare workers in multiple settings frequently "break their own contracts" for the good of the children. Lynet Uttal and Mary Tuominen, "Tenuous Relationships: Exploitation, Emotion, and Racial Ethnic Significance in Paid Child Care Work," *Gender and Society* 136 (December 1999): 765. See also Nelson, *Negotiated Care;* Mary C. Tuominen, *We Are Not Babysitters: Family Child Care Providers Redefine Work and Care* (New Brunswick, NJ: Rutgers University Press, 2003); Deborah Rutman, "Child Care as Women's Work: Workers' Experiences of Powerfulness and Powerlessness," *Gender and Society* 10, no. 5 (1996): 629–49; and Cameron L. Macdonald and David A. Merrill, "'It Shouldn't Have to Be a Trade': Recognition and Redistribution in Care Work Advocacy," *Hypatia: A Journal of Feminist Philosophy* 17, no. 2 (2002): 67–83.

CHAPTER 9

1. Cameron L. Macdonald, "Working Mothers Manage Childcare: Puppeteers, Paranormals,.and Partnerships" (Center for Working Families, University of California, Berkeley, 2001); Cameron L. Macdonald, "Managing Childcare: Puppeteers, Paranormals and Partnerships" (paper presented at the Annual Meeting of the American Sociological Association, Special Panel on Carework, Anaheim, CA, 2001); Lynet Uttal, *Making Care Work: Employed Mothers in the New Childcare Market* (New Brunswick, NJ: Rutgers University Press, 2002). Uttal mentions a slightly different definition of mother-caregiver partnership, but she explores it only from the mother's perspective.

2. Unlike Elaine and Christine's relationship, which grew into a partnership over time, the relationship between the employers and nannies in these two cases included character-

istic elements of partnerships from the start. It was not feasible for me to revisit other dyads from the initial phase of data collection (conducted between 1995 and 1997). Au pairs' terms were short-lived by definition; and among the initial sample, the nannies I interviewed spent an average of only 1.5 years with any given employer. Although it is possible that other relationships also evolved into partnerships, this is not likely. None of the other long-term relationships described by first-round interviewees included signs of both parties engaging in the four relational characteristics associated with successful partnerships.

3. This form of hypothesis generation and testing based on observed social patterns is consistent with grounded theory analysis, as is the practice of "theoretical sampling" based on only one observation. With the latter, a unique pattern, such as that which emerged with Elaine and Christine, is not viewed as an outlier, but rather as a negative case that requires explanation. Kathy Charmaz, *Constructing Grounded Theory: A Practical Guide through Qualitative Analysis* (London: Sage, 2006), 101–13

4. This second phase of data collection took place in 1998 and 2000. Eight of the thirteen mother-employers were white; five were nonwhite. Note that the sample for this second round of interviews is not representative. Rather, it is purposive—I used data from the first round of interviews to generate hypotheses, which I then tested in the second round.

5. To qualify as a partnership, *both* the mother-employer and her care provider had to independently describe their relationship in the same terms. Although as a precondition for inclusion in the phase two sample, an employer either had to have been raised by a working mother or be working part-time or flextime, not all employers in either category were in partnership arrangements with their nannies. Of the five nonwhite employers raised by working mothers, three were in partnerships; among the white employers, of the six who had been raised by working mothers, two were in partnerships.

6. The initial round of interviews included twenty-two mother-employers and thirty-six caregivers. See the appendix for details regarding both stages of data collection. Elaine is counted as both a puppeteer and a partnership manager because of the dramatic shift in her management style in the course of her relationship with Christine.

7. Emphasis added.

8. Clearly, my findings speak only to *mother's* needs, but I prefer not to assume that only mothers have this need. Fathers may also have a "threshold of connection," an issue that needs to be explored.

9. Mary C. Tuominen, *We Are Not Babysitters: Family Child Care Providers Redefine Work and Care* (New Brunswick, NJ: Rutgers University Press, 2003); Denise A. Segura, "Working at Motherhood: Chicana and Mexican Immigrant Mothers and Employment," in *Mothering: Ideology, Experience, and Agency,* ed. Evelyn Nakano Glenn, Grace Chang, and Linda Ronnie Farrey (New York: Routledge, 1994), 211–31; Patricia Hill-Collins, "Black Women and Motherhood," in *Rethinking the Family: Some Feminist Questions,* ed. Barrie Thorne and Marilyn Yalom, 2nd ed. (Boston: Northeastern University Press, 1992), 215–45; Julia McQuillan et al., "The Importance of Motherhood among Women in the Contemporary United States," *Gender and Society* 22, no. 4 (2008): 477–96.

10. C. Wright Mills, "Situated Actions and Vocabularies of Motive," *American Sociological Review* 5, no. 6 (1940): 904–13.

11. It is important to note that although the characteristics I sought in potential partnership employers were a necessary precondition for partnerships with their nannies, not

all part-time working mothers or women of color in this study were in partnerships. For example, Gloria attempted paranormal management with African American nannies, only to find that they did not share her values. Her husband "flip-flopped" his working hours to a night shift because they ultimately felt that they could not find a satisfactory nanny within their relatively modest means.

12. *Concerted cultivation,* which is Annette Lareau's term, is discussed in chapter 2. Annette Lareau, *Unequal Childhoods: Class, Race, and Family Life* (Berkeley: University of California Press, 2003).

13. The question of whether ethnicity or class is the stronger cultural resource on which to draw in forming counterhegemonic mothering ideologies deserves more exploration. Because my sample is small and is a purposive sample drawn for convenience, I can offer only impressionistic findings—that culture of origin matters, and that women of color seemed to have more counterhegemonic childrearing cultural tools on which to draw than did white women.

14. Rosanna Hertz, *Single by Chance, Mothers by Choice: How Women Are Choosing Parenthood without Marriage and Creating the New American Family* (New York: Oxford University Press, 2006), 191.

15. Viviana Zelizer defines relational work as the ongoing negotiations required in all forms of intimacy and care, especially those involving compensation in other media in exchange for care. Viviana Zelizer, *The Purchase of Intimacy* (Princeton, NJ: Princeton University Press, 2005).

16. This is not to imply that some mothers in this study would not have preferred more active participation from their spouses, or that all were satisfied with the quality of their paid childcare providers. Once these needs are satisfied, however, another underlying need for a level of connection with their children that they considered "good enough" emerged.

17. Arlie Russell Hochschild, "Eavesdropping Children, Adult Deals, and Cultures of Care," in *The Commercialization of Intimate Life* (Berkeley: University of California Press, 2000), 172–81.

18. All the nannies I interviewed were adamant that they would never work for a full-time at-home mother and they cited this sort of oversupervision as the reason. Part-time working mothers were acceptable, provided that they allowed the nanny to be in charge during her "shift."

19. See chapter 6 for a discussion of the anxiety most mother-employers who were not in partnerships expressed about the possibility of missing their children's milestones.

20. For just a few examples, see Cameron L. Macdonald and David A. Merrill, "'It Shouldn't Have to Be a Trade': Recognition and Redistribution in Care Work Advocacy," *Hypatia: A Journal of Feminist Philosophy* 17, no. 2 (2002): 67–83; Lynet Uttal and Mary Tuominen, "Tenuous Relationships: Exploitation, Emotion, and Racial Ethnic Significance in Paid Child Care Work," *Gender and Society* 136 (December 1999): 758–80; Mary C. Tuominen, "The Conflicts of Caring," in *Care Work: Gender, Labor, and the Welfare State,* ed. Madonna Harrington Meyer (London: Routledge, 2000), 112–35; Elaine Enarson, "Experts and Caregivers: Perspectives on Underground Day Care," in *Circles of Care: Work and Identity in Women's Lives,* ed. Emily K. Abel and Margaret K. Nelson (Albany: SUNY Press, 1990), 233–45; Susan B. Murray, "Child Care Work: Intimacy in the Shadows of Family Life,"

Qualitative Sociology 21, no. 2 (1998): 149–68; and Heather M. Fitz Gibbon, "Child Care across Sectors: A Comparison of the Work of Childcare in Three Settings," in *Child Care and Inequality: Rethinking Carework for Children and Youth,* ed. Francesca M. Cancian et al. (New York: Routledge, 2002), 145–58.

CHAPTER 10

1. The fact that part-time and flextime working mothers made better employers does not suggest that at-home mothers made good ones. None of the nannies I interviewed would consider working for an at-home mother. For a popular-culture representation of this nightmarish childcare scenario, see Emma McLaughlin and Nicola Krause, *The Nanny Diaries* (New York: St. Martin's Press, 2002).

2. For an evocative and persuasive discussion of how adult framing of childcare arrangements affects children's perceptions of their care, see Arlie Russell Hochschild, "Eavesdropping Children, Adult Deals, and Cultures of Care," in *The Commercialization of Intimate Life* (Berkeley: University of California Press, 2000), 172–81.

3. This is Hays's conclusion. Although her argument doubtless makes sense for many who embrace the ideology of intensive mothering, I argue that the social class represented by the women I interviewed has a more complex relationship to this paradox. See Sharon Hays, *The Cultural Contradictions of Motherhood* (New Haven, CT: Yale University Press, 1996).

4. See, e.g., Margaret K. Nelson, *Negotiated Care: The Experience of Family Day Care Providers* (Philadelphia: Temple University Press, 1990); Cameron L. Macdonald and David A. Merrill, " 'It Shouldn't Have to Be a Trade': Recognition and Redistribution in Care Work Advocacy," *Hypatia: A Journal of Feminist Philosophy* 17, no. 2 (2002): 67–83; Mary C. Tuominen, "The Conflicts of Caring," in *Care Work: Gender, Labor, and the Welfare State,* ed. Madonna Harrington Meyer (London: Routledge, 2000), 112–35; Mary C. Tuominen, *We Are Not Babysitters: Family Child Care Providers Redefine Work and Care* (New Brunswick, NJ: Rutgers University Press, 2003); and Heather M. Fitz Gibbon, "Child Care across Sectors: A Comparison of the Work of Childcare in Three Settings," in *Child Care and Inequality: Rethinking Carework for Children and Youth,* ed. Francesca M. Cancian et al. (New York: Routledge, 2002), 145–58.

5. Julia Wrigley, *Other People's Children: An Intimate Account of the Dilemmas Facing Middle-Class Parents and the Women They Hire to Raise Their Children* (New York: Basic Books, 1995).

6. Macdonald and Merrill, " 'It Shouldn't Have to Be a Trade.' "

7. Nelson, *Negotiated Care,* 210.

8. Tuominen, *We Are Not Babysitters,* 187.

9. Fitz Gibbon, "Child Care across Sectors."

10. A childcare advocate quoted in Macdonald and Merrill, " 'It Shouldn't Have to Be a Trade.' "

11. Tuominen, "The Conflicts of Caring."

12. For the concept of economic "free riders" in care-work, see Paula England and Nancy Folbre, "The Cost of Caring," *Annals of the American Academy of Political and Social*

Science 561, no. 1 (1999): 39–51. For more on childcare mobilization strategies, see Marcy Whitebook and Abby Eichberg, "Finding the Better Way: Assessing Child Care Compensation Initiatives," *Young Children* 57, no. 3 (2002); Marcy Whitebook, Carollee Howes, and Deborah Phillips, *Worthy Work, Unlivable Wages: The National Staffing Study, 1988–1997* (Washington, DC: Center for the Child Care Workforce, 1998); Macdonald and Merrill, " 'It Shouldn't Have to Be a Trade' "; and Dorothy Sue Cobble and Michael Merrill, "The Promise of Service Sector Unionism," in *Service Work: Critical Perspectives,* ed. Marek Korczynski and Cameron L. Macdonald (New York: Routledge, 2008), 153–74.

13. Deborah Stone, "Why We Need a Care Movement," *Nation,* 13 March 2000, 84–94; Evelyn Nakano Glenn, "Creating a Caring Society," *Contemporary Sociology* 29, no. 1 (2000): 13–15.

14. Oriel Sullivan and Scott Coltrane, "Men's Changing Contribution to Housework and Child Care," Discussion Panel on Changing Family Roles, Council on Contemporary Families, 25–26 April 2008.

15. Except, for example, Annette Lareau, *Unequal Childhoods: Class, Race, and Family Life* (Berkeley: University of California Press, 2003).

16. For example, see Anita Ilta Garey, *Weaving Work and Motherhood* (Philadelphia: Temple University Press, 1999); Margaret K. Nelson, *The Social Economy of Single Motherhood: Raising Children in Rural America* (New York: Routledge, 2005); Evelyn Nakano Glenn, "Social Constructions of Mothering: A Thematic Overview," in *Mothering: Ideology, Experience, and Agency,* ed. Evelyn Nakano Glenn, Grace Chang, and Linda Renney Forcey (New York: Routledge, 1994), 1–32; Patricia Hill-Collins, "Black Women and Motherhood," in *Rethinking the Family: Some Feminist Questions,* ed. Barrie Thorne and Marilyn Yalom, 2nd ed. (Boston: Northeastern University Press, 1992), 215–45.

17. Elizabeth Puhn Pungello and Beth Kurtz-Costes, "Why and How Working Women Choose Child Care: A Review with a Focus on Infancy," *Developmental Review* 19 (1999): 31–96.

18. Although claims about the effectiveness of childhood "enhancement" tools are becoming less tenable. See Associated Press, "Disney Expands Refunds on 'Baby Einstein' DVDs," *New York Times,* 23 October 2009.

19. Michael Foucault famously used Bentham's "panopticon" to describe the sense of constant observation that is a hallmark of late modernity. In the panopticon, prisoners were held in cells always open to view by guards in a central tower; the prisoners could not discern when the guards were present or absent, leaving them with the sense of an ever-present observer, which ultimately resulted in their policing themselves.

20. Hays, *The Cultural Contradictions of Motherhood,* 157.

APPENDIX

1. Barney Glaser and Alselm Strauss, *The Discovery of Grounded Theory* (Chicago: Aldine, 1967), 45–47.

2. Two African American and nine Caucasian women. Note that in much of this discussion I use the term *nanny* to refer generically to any childcare provider who cares for children in the children's home.

3. Because this study focuses on commodified care, I did not study employer-employee relationships that began as family or neighbor relationships (with the exception of Ynez, whose story depicts the typical trajectory of nannies who work for family members).

4. I owe special thanks to Sandra Olarte and Sylvia Gutierrez for their diligent work on this aspect of the project. Their participation was valuable not only because of their excellent language skills but also because of their ability to generate trust among respondents who were undocumented immigrants and their ability to comprehend and translate cultural metaphors used by women from various Latin American countries. For more on the question of cross-cultural interviewing, see Catherine Kohler Riessman, "When Gender Is Not Enough: Women Interviewing Women," *Gender and Society* 1, no. 2 (1987): 172–207.

5. This was the case with all but immigrant nannies, who (as discussed in chapter 3) often did not fit the study or declined to participate because of immigration concerns.

6. We conducted surveys at ten parks in Boston, eleven in Brookline, twelve in Cambridge, twelve in Newton, six in Watertown, and ten in the suburbs of Weston, Wellesley, Wayland, and Concord. We selected the parks based on the likelihood of finding nannies there, and therefore avoided parks in poor neighborhoods. This is clearly not a representative sample, but it gives a broad overview of the patterns of nanny employment and was a successful recruitment strategy.

7. The other caregivers responded to newspaper ads in *El Mundo* and the *TAB*, both of which are primary publishers of employment listings for nannies. All of the immigrants who responded to advertisements responded to ads in these papers.

8. The slight imbalance stems from the fact that I interviewed two nannies who each worked for two of the mothers over a period of years.

9. Anita Ilta Garey, *Weaving Work and Motherhood* (Philadelphia: Temple University Press, 1999).

10. Marjorie L. DeVault, "Talking and Listening from Women's Standpoint: Feminist Strategies for Interviewing and Analysis," *Social Problems* 37, no. 1 (1990): 102–4.

11. Kathryn Anderson and Dana C. Jack, "Learning to Listen: Interview Techniques and Analyses," in *Women's Words,* ed. Sherna Berger Gluck and Daphne Patai (New York: Routledge, 1991), 11.

12. Kathy Charmaz, *Constructing Grounded Theory: A Practical Guide through Qualitative Analysis* (London: Sage, 2006), 55.

BIBLIOGRAPHY

ABC News / Washington Post. "Poll: Moms Make It Work." ABC News, 24 April 2005.

Ainsworth, Mary D. Salter, Mary C. Blehar, Everett Waters, and Sally Wall. *Patterns of Attachment: A Psychological Study of the Strange Situation.* Hillsdale, NJ: Lawrence Erlbaum Associates, 1978.

Allard, Mary Dorinda , Suzanne M. Bianchi, Jay Stewart, and Vanessa R. Wight. "Comparing Childcare Measures in the ATUS and Earlier Time-Diary Studies." *Monthly Labor Review* 130, no. 5 (2007): 27–36.

Allen, Sarah M., and Alan J. Hawkins. "Maternal Gatekeeping: Mothers' Beliefs and Behaviors That Inhibit Greater Father Involvement in Family Work." *Journal of Marriage and the Family* 61, no. 1 (1999): 199–212.

Anderson, Kathryn, and Dana C. Jack. "Learning to Listen: Interview Techniques and Analyses." In *Women's Words,* ed. Sherna Berger Gluck and Daphne Patai, 1–11. New York: Routledge, 1991.

Arendell, Terry. "A Social Constructionist Approach to Parenting." In *Contemporary Parenting: Challenges and Issues,* ed. Terry Arendell, 1–44. Thousand Oaks, CA: Sage, 1997.

Associated Press. "Disney Expands Refunds on 'Baby Einstein' DVDs." *New York Times,* 23 October 2009.

"Au Pair Supply Increases from Eastern Europe and South Africa." *Newswire, PR,* 13 May 1999, www.lexisnexis.com/us/lnacademic/results/docview/docview.do?docLinkInd= true&risb=21_T4462345904&format=GNBFI&sort=RELEVANCE&startDocNo=26&r esultsUrlKey=29_T4462345911&cisb=22_T4462345910&treeMax=true&treeWidth=0& csi=8054&docNo=32.

Auerbach, Jessika. *And Nanny Makes Three: Mothers and Nannies Tell the Truth about Work, Love, Money, and Each Other.* New York: St. Martin's Press, 2007.

Bailey, Thomas, and Roger Waldinger. "Primary, Secondary, and Enclave Labor Markets: A Training Systems Approach." *American Sociological Review* 56, no. 4 (1991): 432–45.

Bakan, Abigail B., and Daiva Stasiulis, eds. *Not One of the Family: Foreign Domestic Workers in Canada*. Toronto: University of Toronto Press, 1997.

Belsky, Jay. "Parental and Nonparental Child Care and Children's Socioemotional Development: A Decade in Review." *Journal of Marriage and the Family* 52 (November 1990): 885–903.

Bernier, Jetta. "Au Pair Anxiety." *Boston Globe*, 16 February 1997, D1, D2.

Bianchi, Suzanne M., Melissa A. Milkie, Liana C. Sayer, and John P. Robinson. "Is Anyone Doing the Housework? Trends in the Gender Division of Labor." *Social Forces* 79, no. 1 (2000): 191–228.

Bianchi, Suzanne, John P. Robinson, and Melissa A. Milkie. *Changing Rhythms of American Family Life*. New York: Russell Sage Foundation, 2006.

Bielby, William T. "Minimizing Workplace Gender and Racial Bias." *Contemporary Sociology* 29, no. 1 (2000): 120–29.

Bittman, Michael, Paula England, Liana Sayer, Nancy Folbre, and George Matheson. "When Does Gender Trump Money? Bargaining and Time in Household Work." *American Journal of Sociology* 109, no. 1 (2003): 186–214.

Blair-Loy, Mary. *Competing Devotions: Career and Family among Women Executives*. Cambridge, MA: Harvard University Press, 2003.

Blase, J., and G. Anderson. *The Micropolitics of Educational Leadership: From Control to Empowerment*. New York: Teachers College Press, 1995.

Blum, Linda M. *At the Breast: Ideologies of Breastfeeding and Motherhood in the Contemporary United States*. Boston: Beacon Press, 1999.

Bourdieu, Pierre. *Distinction: A Social Critique of the Judgement of Taste*. Trans. Richard Nice. Cambridge, MA: Harvard University Press, 1984.

———. "The Forms of Capital." In *Handbook of Theory and Research for the Sociology of Education*, ed. J. G. Richardson, 241–58. New York: Greenwood Press, 1986.

———. *Outline of a Theory of Practice*. Trans. Richard Nice. Cambridge: Cambridge University Press, 1977.

Braverman, Harry. *Labor and Monopoly Capital: The Degradation of Work in the Twentieth Century*. New York: Monthly Review Press, 1974.

Brewster, Karin L., and Irene Padavic. "No More Kin Care? Change in Black Mothers' Reliance on Relatives for Child Care, 1977–1994." *Gender and Society* 16, no. 4 (2002): 546–63.

Brines, Julie. "Economic Dependency, Gender, and the Division of Labor at Home." *American Journal of Sociology* 100, no. 3 (1994): 652–88.

"Bringing Up Baby." Interview with Jay Belsky, Kathleen McCartney, and Anne Goldstein by Juan Williams, dir. K. J. Lopez. *Talk of the Nation*, National Public Radio, 24 April 2001.

Bruer, John T. *The Myth of the First Three Years: A New Understanding of Early Brain Development and Lifelong Learning*. New York: Free Press, 1999.

Budig, M. J., and P. England. "The Wage Penalty for Motherhood." *American Sociological Review* 66, no. 2 (2001): 204–25.

Buettner, Russ. "For Nannies, Hope for Workplace Protection." *New York Times*, 2 June 2010, region section.

Canellos, Peter S. "Societal, Legal Change Is Legacy of a Public Trial; The Au Pair Case / Zobel Ruling Affirmed." *Boston Globe*, 1 June 1998, city edition, metro/region section, A1.

Carlton, Susan, and Susan Myers. *The Nanny Book: The Smart Parent's Guide to Hiring, Firing, and Every Sticky Situation in Between.* New York: St. Martin's Griffin, 1999.

Carnegie Corporation of New York. *Starting Points: Meeting the Needs of Our Youngest Children.* New York: Carnegie Corporation of New York, 1994.

Carton, Barbara. "Minding the Au Pairs: Oversight Sought as Programs Grow." *Boston Globe*, 2 January 1992.

Carvajal, Doreen. "For Immigrant Maids, Not a Job but Servitude." *New York Times*, 25 February 1996, metro section.

Cazaneve, Noel, and Murray Straus. "Race, Class, Network Embeddedness, and Family Violence: A Search for Potent Support Systems." In *Physical Violence in American Families: Risk Factors and Adaptations to Violence in 8,145 Families*, ed. Murray Straus and Richard Gelles, 321–39. New Brunswick, NJ: Transaction Publishers, 1990.

Center for the Childcare Workforce. "Current Data on the Salaries and Benefits of the U.S. Early Childhood Education Workforce." Center for the Childcare Workforce / American Federation of Teachers Educational Foundation, 2004.

Chang, Grace. *Disposable Domestics: Immigrant Women Workers in the Global Economy.* Cambridge, MA: South End Press, 2000.

———. "Undocumented Latinas: The New 'Employable Mothers.'" In *Mothering: Ideology, Experience, and Agency*, ed. Evelyn Nakano Glenn and Grace Chang, 259–86. New York: Routledge, 1994.

Charmaz, Kathy. *Constructing Grounded Theory: A Practical Guide through Qualitative Analysis.* London: Sage, 2006.

Chira, Susan. *A Mother's Place: Choosing Work and Family without Guilt or Blame.* New York: HarperCollins, 1998.

———. "Working Mom in D.C. Loses Custody Fight to Ex-Husband." *Houston Chronicle*, 20 September 1994, sec. A.

Chou, Renee. "Child Abuse Charges Filed in 'Nanny Cam' Case." WRAL, 3 July 2008. www.wral.com/news/local/story/2561722/.

Cobble, Dorothy Sue, and Michael Merrill. "The Promise of Service Sector Unionism." In *Service Work: Critical Perspectives*, ed. Marek Korczynski and Cameron L. Macdonald, 153–74. New York: Routledge, 2008.

Cohany, Sharon, and Emily Sok. "Trends in the Labor Force Participation of Married Mothers of Infants." *Monthly Labor Review*, February 2007, 9–16.

Cohen, Rina. "Women of Color in White Households: Coping Strategies of Live-in Domestic Workers." *Qualitative Sociology* 14, no. 2 (1991): 197–215.

Colen, Shellee. "'Housekeeping' for the Green Card: West Indian Household Workers, the State, and Stratified Reproduction in New York." In *At Work in Homes: Household Workers in World Perspective*, ed. Roger Sanjek and Shellee Colen, 89–118. Washington, DC: American Anthropological Association, 1990.

———. "'Like a Mother to Them': Stratified Reproduction and West Indian Childcare Workers and Employers in New York." In *Conceiving the New World Order: The Global*

Politics of Reproduction, ed. Faye D. Ginsburg and Rayna Rapp, 78–102. Berkeley: University of California Press, 1995.

———. "'With Respect and Feelings': Voices of West Indian Child Care and Domestic Workers in New York City." In *All American Women,* ed. Johnnetta B. Cole, 46–70. New York: Free Press, 1986.

Coll, Cynthia T. Garcia, E. C. Meyer, and L. Brillon. "Ethnic and Minority Parents." In *Handbook of Parenting,* ed. M. H. Bornstein, 2:189–209. Mahwah, NJ: Lawrence Erlbaum Associates, 1995.

Coll, Kathleen. *Remaking Citizenship: Latina Immigrants and the New American Politics.* Stanford, CA: Stanford University Press, 2010.

Coltrane, Scott. "Research on Household Labor: Modeling and Measuring the Social Embeddednes of Routine Family Work." *Journal of Marriage and the Family* 62, no. 4 (2000): 1208–33.

Crittenden, Ann. *The Price of Motherhood: Why the Most Important Job in the World Is Still the Least Valued.* New York: Metropolitan Books, 2001.

Daniels, Arlene Kaplan. "Invisible Work." *Social Problems* 34, no. 5 (1987): 403–15.

Davis, Susan, and Gina Hyams, eds. *Searching for Mary Poppins: Women Write about the Relationship between Mothers and Nannies.* New York: Plume, 2007.

Degler, Carl N. *At Odds: Women and the Family in America from the Revolution to the Present.* New York: Oxford University Press, 1980.

DeMattia, Robin F. "Help from Overseas in Raising Youngsters." *New York Times,* 28 July 1996, final edition, sec. 13CN, 8.

DePanfilis, Diane. "Social Isolation of Neglectful Families: A Review of Social Support Assessment and Intervention Models." *Child Maltreatment* 1, no. 1 (1996): 37–52.

DeVault, Marjorie L. *Feeding the Family: The Social Organization of Caring and Gendered Work.* Chicago: University of Chicago Press, 1991.

———. "Talking and Listening from Women's Standpoint: Feminist Strategies for Interviewing and Analysis." *Social Problems* 37, no. 1 (1990): 96–116.

Dill, Bonnie Thornton. "'Making Your Job Good Yourself': Domestic Service and the Construction of Personal Dignity." In *Women and the Politics of Empowerment,* ed. Anne Bookman and Sandra Morgen, 33–52. Philadelphia: Temple University Press, 1988.

Duckworth, Lorna. "Fallout from Woodward Case Hits Au Pair Industry." *Independent,* 2 March 2002.

Edozien, Frankie, and Adam Miller. "Immigrant 'Slave' Lived a Nightmare." *New York Post,* 16 July 1999.

Egelko, Bob. "Domestic Workers Vulnerable to Exploitation." *San Francisco Chronicle,* 14 October 2009, Bay Area Section.

Ehrenreich, Barbara, and Arlie Russell Hochschild, eds. *Global Woman: Nannies, Maids, and Sex Workers in the New Economy.* New York: Metropolitan Books, 2003.

Elliot, James R. "Referral Hiring and Ethnically Homogenous Jobs: How Prevalent Is the Connection and for Whom?" *Social Sciences Research* 30, no. 3 (2001): 401–25.

Elshtain, Jean Bethke. *Who Are We? Critical Reflections and Hopeful Possibilities.* New York: William B. Erdmans, 2000.

Eltman, Frank. "NY Millionaires' Slavery Trial Opens: Trial Opens for Millionaire Couple Accused of Slavery on NY's Long Island." Associated Press, 29 October 2007, http://abcnews.go.com/thelaw/wirestory?id=3790694.

Enarson, Elaine. "Experts and Caregivers: Perspectives on Underground Day Care." In *Circles of Care: Work and Identity in Women's Lives,* ed. Emily K. Abel and Margaret K. Nelson, 233–45. Albany: SUNY Press, 1990.

England, Paula, and Nancy Folbre. "The Cost of Caring." *Annals of the American Academy of Political and Social Science* 561, no. 1 (1999): 39–51.

Epstein, Cynthia, Carroll Seron, Bonnie Oglensky, and Robert Saute. *The Part-Time Paradox: Time Norms, Professional Life, Family and Gender.* New York: Routledge, 1999.

Eyer, Diane E. *Mother-Infant Bonding: A Scientific Fiction.* New Haven, CT: Yale University Press, 1992.

Fagan, J., and M. Barnett. "The Relationship between Maternal Gatekeeping, Paternal Competence, Mothers' Attitudes about the Father Role, and Father Involvement." *Journal of Family Issues* 24 (2003): 1020–43.

Fernandez, Roberto M., Emilio J. Castilla, and Paul Moore. "Social Capital at Work: Networks and Employment at a Call Center." *American Journal of Sociology* 105, no. 5 (2000): 1288–1356.

Ferree, Myra Marx. "The Gender Division of Labor in Two-Earner Marriages: Dimensions of Variability and Change." *Journal of Family Issues* 12, no. 2 (1991): 158–80.

Fiske, Susan. "Stereotyping, Prejudice, and Discrimination." In *The Handbook of Social Psychology,* ed. S. T. Fiske, D. T. Gilbert, and G. Lindzey, 357–411. Boston: McGraw-Hill, 1998.

Fitz Gibbon, Heather M. "Child Care across Sectors: A Comparison of the Work of Child Care in Three Settings." In *Child Care and Inequality: Rethinking Carework for Children and Youth,* ed. Francesca M. Cancian, Demie Kurz, Andrew S. London, Rebecca Reviere, and Mary C. Tourninen, 145–58. New York: Routledge, 2002.

Flanagan, Caitlin. "Dispatches from the Nanny Wars: How Serfdom Saved the Women's Movement." *Atlantic,* March 2004, 109–28.

Foderaro, Lisa W. "New Breed of Au Pair Packs a Shaving Kit." *New York Times,* 14 June 1999, http://query.nytimes.com/gst/fullpage.html?res=9C04E4D91338F937A25755C0A9 6F958260&sec=&spon=&pagewanted=all.

Foucault, Michel. *Discipline and Punish: The Birth of the Prison.* New York: Vintage, 1995.

Fried, Mindy. *Taking Time: Parental Leave Policy and Corporate Culture.* Philadelphia: Temple University Press, 1998.

Frost, Jo. *Jo Frost's Confident Baby Care: What You Need to Know for the First Year from the UK's Most Trusted Nanny.* London: Orion, 2007.

Fursman, Lindy. "Conscious Decisions, Unconscious Paths: Pregnancy and the Importance of Work for Women in Management." Working paper no. 23, Center for Working Families, University of California, Berkeley, April 2001.

Garey, Anita Ilta. "Constructing Motherhood on the Night Shift: 'Working Mothers' as 'Stay-at Home Moms.'" *Qualitative Sociology* 18, no. 4 (1995): 415–37.

———. *Weaving Work and Motherhood.* Philadelphia: Temple University Press, 1999.

Gaunt, Ruth. "Maternal Gatekeeping: Antecedents and Consequences." *Journal of Family Issues* 29 (2008): 373–95.

Geertz, Clifford. *The Interpretation of Cultures*. New York: Basic Books, 1973.

Glaser, Barney, and Alselm Strauss. *The Discovery of Grounded Theory*. Chicago: Aldine, 1967.

Glass, Jennifer. "Blessing or Curse? Work-Family Policies and Women's Wage Growth over Time." *Work and Occupations* 31, no. 3 (2004): 367–94.

Glenn, Evelyn Nakano. "Creating a Caring Society." *Contemporary Sociology* 29, no. 1 (2000): 13–15.

———. "From Servitude to Service Work: Historical Continuities in the Racial Division of Paid Reproductive Labor." In *Working in the Service Society*, ed. Cameron Lynne Macdonald and Carmen Sirianni, 115–56. Philadelphia: Temple University Press, 1996.

———. *Issei, Nisei, War Bride: Three Generations of Japanese American Women in Domestic Service*. Philadelphia: Temple University Press, 1986.

———. "Social Constructions of Mothering: A Thematic Overview." In *Mothering: Ideology, Experience, and Agency*, ed. Evelyn Nakano Glenn, Grace Chang, and Linda Renney Forcey, 1–32. New York: Routledge, 1994.

Gornick, Janet C., and Marcia K. Meyers. *Families That Work: Policies for Reconciling Parenthood and Employment*. New York: Russell Sage Foundation, 2003.

Greenhouse, Steven. "Legislation Pushed to Require Minimum Wage for Domestic Workers." *New York Times*, 27 June 2007, region section.

———. "Report Shows Americans Have More 'Labor Days.'" *New York Times*, 1 September 2001.

Hamner, T. J., and P. H. Turner. *Parenting in Contemporary Society*. 3rd ed. Needham Heights, MN: Allyn & Bacon, 1996.

The Hand That Rocks the Cradle. Dir. Curtis Hanson. Hollywood Pictures, 1992.

Hareven, Tamara K. "Modernization and Family History: Perspectives on Social Change." *Signs* 2, no. 1 (1976): 190–206.

Hays, Sharon. *The Cultural Contradictions of Motherhood*. New Haven, CT: Yale University Press, 1996.

Hertz, Rosanna. "Dual-Career Couples and the American Dream: Self-Sufficiency and Achievement." *Journal of Comparative Family Studies* 23, no. 2 (1991): 247–63.

———. "Making Family under a Shiftwork Schedule: Air Force Security Guards and Their Wives." *Social Problems* 36, no. 5 (1989): 491–507.

———. *More Equal Than Others: Women and Men in Dual-Career Marriages*. Berkeley: University of California Press, 1986.

———. *Single by Chance, Mothers by Choice: How Women Are Choosing Parenthood without Marriage and Creating the New American Family*. New York: Oxford University Press, 2006.

Hertz, Rosanna, and Faith I. T. Ferguson. "Childcare Choice and Constraints in the United States: Social Class, Race and the Influence of Family Views." *Journal of Comparative Family Studies* 27, no. 2 (1996): 249–80.

Hewlett, Sylvia Ann. *Off-Ramps and On-Ramps*. Cambridge, MA: Harvard Business School Press, 2007.

Hill-Collins, Patricia. "Black Women and Motherhood." In *Rethinking the Family: Some Feminist Questions*, ed. Barrie Thorne and Marilyn Yalom, 215–45. 2nd ed. Boston: Northeastern University Press, 1992.

Hochschild, Arlie Russell. "Eavesdropping Children, Adult Deals, and Cultures of Care." In *The Commercialization of Intimate Life*, 172–81. Berkeley: University of California Press, 2000.

———. "Inside the Clockwork of Male Careers." In *Women and the Power to Change*, ed. Florence Howe, 47–80. Berkeley: Carnegie Foundation for the Advancement of Teaching, 1975.

———. *The Managed Heart: Commercialization of Human Feeling*. Berkeley: University of California Press, 1983.

———. "The Nanny Chain." *American Prospect*, 3 January 2000, 32–36.

———. *The Time Bind: When Work Becomes Home and Home Becomes Work*. New York: Metropolitan Books, 1997.

Hochschild, Arlie Russell, with Anne Machung. *The Second Shift: Working Parents and the Revolution at Home*. New York: Viking, 1989.

———. *The Second Shift*. 2nd ed. New York: Penguin, 2003.

Hondagneu-Sotelo, Pierrette. "Blowups and Other Unhappy Endings." In *Global Woman: Nannies, Maids, and Sex Workers in the New Economy*, ed. Barbara Ehrenreich and Arlie Russell Hochschild, 55–69. New York: Henry Holt, 2002.

———. *Domestica: Immigrant Workers Cleaning and Caring in the Shadows of Affluence*. Berkeley: University of California Press, 2001.

———. "Regulating the Unregulated? Domestic Workers' Social Networks." *Social Problems* 41, no. 1 (1994): 50–64.

Hondagneu-Sotelo, Pierrette, and Ernestine Avila. "'I'm Here, but I'm There': The Meanings of Latina Transnational Motherhood." *Gender and Society* 11, no. 5 (1997): 548–71.

Honneth, Axel. *The Struggle for Recognition: The Moral Grammar of Social Conflicts*. Cambridge, MA: MIT Press, 1996.

Hughes, Everett C. *Men and Their Work*. Glencoe, IL: Free Press, 1958.

Hulbert, Ann. *Raising America: Experts, Parents, and a Century of Advice about Children*. New York: Alfred A. Knopf, 2003.

Hwang, C. Philip, and Anders G. Broberg. "The Historical and Social Context of Child Care in Sweden." In *Child Care in Context: Cross-Cultural Perspectives*, ed. Michael Lamb, Kathleen Sternberg, Carl Philip Hwang, and Anders Broberg, 27–53. Hillsdale, NJ: Hove and London, 1992.

Illich, Ivan. *Shadow Work*. Boston: M. Boyars, 1981.

Jacobs, Jerry A., and Kathleen Gerson. *The Time Divide: Work, Family, and Gender Inequality*. Cambridge, MA: Harvard University Press, 2005.

Joffe, Carole E. *Friendly Intruders: Child Care Professionals and Family Life*. Berkeley: University of California Press, 1977.

Johnson, Kirk. "Earning It: The Nanny Track, a Once-Simple World Grown Complicated." *New York Times*, 29 September 1996, sec. 3.

Kahn, Ric. "Murder Charge Lodged against Au Pair." *Boston Globe*, 12 February 1997, B1, B4.

Kantor, Jodi. "Memo to Nanny: No Juice Boxes." *New York Times*, 8 September 2006, G1.

Kaylin, Lucy. *The Perfect Stranger: The Truth about Mothers and Nannies*. New York: Bloomsbury Press USA, 2007.

Ladd-Taylor, Molly. *Mother-Work: Women, Child Welfare, and the State, 1890–1930*. Urbana: University of Illinois Press, 1994.

Lake, Richard. "Child Care: Abuse by Nannies Unusual. Still, Experts Say Parents Need to Take Standard Precautions." *Las Vegas Review Journal,* 9 January 2005. www .reviewjournal.com/lvrj_home/2005/Jan-09-Sun-2005/news/25623713.html.

Lan, Pei-Chia. *Global Cinderellas: Migrant Domestics and Newly Rich Employers in Taiwan.* Durham, NC: Duke University Press, 2006.

Lardner, James. "Separate Lives." *DoubleTake,* no. 13 (1998): 54–66.

Lareau, Annette. *Unequal Childhoods: Class, Race, and Family Life.* Berkeley: University of California Press, 2003.

Leidner, Robin. *Fast Food, Fast Talk: Service Work and the Routinization of Everyday Life.* Berkeley: University of California Press, 1993.

——. "Rethinking Questions of Control: Lessons from McDonald's." In *Working in the Service Society,* ed. Cameron Lynne Macdonald and Carmen Sirianni, 29–49. Philadelphia: Temple University Press, 1996.

Leonard, Mary. "Mother's Day: A Guilt-Edged Occasion." *Boston Globe,* 11 May 1997, E3.

Luttrell, Wendy. *Schoolsmart and Motherwise: Working-Class Women's Identity and Schooling.* New York: Routledge, 1997.

Macdonald, Cameron L. "Managing Childcare: Puppeteers, Paranormals and Partnerships." Paper presented at the Annual Meeting of the American Sociological Association, Special Panel on Carework, Anaheim, CA, 2001.

——. "Working Mothers Manage Childcare: Puppeteers, Paranormals and Partnerships." Center for Working Families, University of California, Berkeley, 2001.

Macdonald, Cameron L., and David A. Merrill. "'It Shouldn't Have to Be a Trade': Recognition and Redistribution in Care Work Advocacy." *Hypatia: A Journal of Feminist Philosophy* 17, no. 2 (2002): 67–83.

Macdonald, Cameron Lynne, and Carmen Sirianni. "The Service Society and the Changing Nature of Work." In *Understanding Society: An Introductory Reader,* ed. Margaret Anderson, Kim Logio, and Howard Taylor, 421–28. 3rd ed. New York: Wadsworth, 2009.

——, eds. *Working in the Service Society.* Philadelphia: Temple University Press, 1996.

Macleod, Jay. *Ain't No Makin' It: Aspirations and Attainment in a Low-Income Neighborhood.* 3rd ed. Boulder, CO: Westview Press, 2008.

Margolis, Maxine L. *Mothers and Such: Views of American Women and Why They Changed.* Berkeley: University of California Press, 1984.

Markens, Susan. *Surrogate Motherhood and the Politics of Reproduction.* Berkeley: University of California Press, 2007.

Mattingly, Marybeth J., and Suzanne M. Bianchi. "Gender Differences in the Quantity and Quality of Free Time: The U.S. Experience." *Social Forces* 81, no. 3 (2003): 999–1030.

McElroy, Ruth. "Whose Body, Whose Nation? Surrogate Motherhood and Its Representation." *European Journal of Cultural Studies* 5, no. 3 (2002): 325–42.

McLaughlin, Emma, and Nicola Krause. *The Nanny Diaries.* New York: St. Martin's Press, 2002.

McMahon, Martha. *Engendering Motherhood: Identity and Self-Transformation in Women's Lives.* New York: Guilford Press, 1995.

McQuillan, Julia, Arthur L. Greil, Karina M. Shreffler, and Veronica Tichenor. "The Importance of Motherhood among Women in the Contemporary United States." *Gender and Society* 22, no. 4 (2008): 477–96.

Meltz, Barbara. "When Jealousy Strikes the Working Parent." *Boston Globe*, 15 March 1991, city edition, At Home section, 69.

Meurling, Julia. "Bulletin Board: A Child Care Solution: Help from Overseas." *New York Times*, 1 September 2002.

Miles, Matthew B., and A. Michael Huberman. *Qualitative Data Analysis: An Expanded Sourcebook.* 2nd ed. Thousand Oaks, CA: Sage, 1994.

Milkman, Ruth, Ellen Reese, and Benita Roth. "The Macrosociology of Paid Domestic Labor." *Work and Occupations* 25, no. 4 (1998): 483–510.

Mills, C. Wright. "Situated Actions and Vocabularies of Motive." *American Sociological Review* 5, no. 6 (1940): 904–13.

Mishel, Lawrence, Jared Bernstein, and Sylvia Allegretto. *The State of Working America, 2006/2007.* 10th ed. Ithaca, NY: ILR Press, 2007.

Mishel, Lawrence, Jared Bernstein, and John Schmitt. *The State of Working America.* Washington, DC: Economic Policy Institute, 1999.

Mitchell, S. Weir. "When the College Is Hurtful to the Girl." *Ladies' Home Journal*, June 1900.

Moncher, Frank J. "Social Isolation and Child Abuse Risk." *Families in Society* 76, no. 7 (1995): 421–33.

Morley, Louise. *Organising Feminisms: The Micropolitics of the Academy.* New York: St. Martin's Press, 1999.

Murray, Susan B. "Child Care Work: Intimacy in the Shadows of Family Life." *Qualitative Sociology* 21, no. 2 (1998): 149–68.

———. "Child Care Work: The Lived Experience." Ph.D. dissertation. University of California, Santa Cruz, 1995.

NBC6 News Team. "Police Release New 'Nanny Cam' Video in Abuse Probe: Parents 'Horrified' by Alleged Abuse Caught on Tape." NBC6, 3 July 2008.

Nelson, Julie A. "Of Markets and Martyrs: Is It OK to Pay Well for Care?" *Feminist Economics* 5, no. 3 (1999): 43–59.

Nelson, Margaret K. "'I Saw Your Nanny': Gossip and Shame in the Surveillance of Child Care." In *Who's Watching? Daily Practices of Surveillance among Contemporary Families*, ed. Margaret K. Nelson and Anita Ilta Garey, 107–33. Nashville: Vanderbilt University Press, 2009.

———. *Negotiated Care: The Experience of Family Day Care Providers.* Philadelphia: Temple University Press, 1990.

———. *The Social Economy of Single Motherhood: Raising Children in Rural America.* New York: Routledge, 2005.

Newman, Katherine S. *Declining Fortunes: The Withering of the American Dream.* New York: Basic Books, 1993.

NICHD Early Child Care Research Network. "Characteristics and Quality of Child Care for Toddlers and Preschoolers." *Applied Developmental Science* 4 (2000): 116–35.

———. "Early Child Care and Self-Control, Compliance and Problem Behavior at Twenty-Four and Thirty-Six Months." *Child Development* 69 (1998): 1145–1170.

———. "Familial Factors Associated with the Characteristics of Nonmaternal Child Care." *Journal of Marriage and the Family* 59 (1997): 389–408.

Nippert-Eng, Christena. *Home and Work: Negotiating Boundaries through Everyday Life.* Chicago: University of Chicago Press, 1996.

Papanek, Hanna. "Men, Women, and Work: Reflections on the Two-Person Career." *American Journal of Sociology* 78 (1975): 852–72.

Parreñas, Rhacel Salazar. *Children of Global Migration: Transnational Families and Gendered Woes.* Stanford, CA: Stanford University Press, 2005.

———. *Servants of Globalization: Women, Migration, and Domestic Work.* Stanford, CA: Stanford University Press, 2001.

Pattison, Helen M., Helen Gross, and Charlotte Cast. "Pregnancy and Employment: The Perceptions and Beliefs of Fellow Workers." *Journal of Reproductive and Infant Psychology* 15, nos. 3–4 (1997): 303–13.

Peltz, Jennifer. "Au Pair Popularity May Expand Rules: Government Studies Allowing More Time." Associated Press, 29 June 2008, www.commercialappeal.com/news/2008/Jun/29/au-pair-popularity-may-expand-rules/.

Pew Research Center for People and the Press. "The 2004 Political Landscape: Evenly Divided and Increasingly Polarized." 5 November 2003. http://people-press.org/reports/pdf/196.pdf.

Phelps, E. S. "The Statistical Theory of Racism and Sexism." *American Economic Review* 62 (1972): 659–61.

Phillips, Deborah, Carollee Howes, and Marcy Whitebook. "Child Care as an Adult Work Environment." *Journal of Social Issues* 47, no. 2 (1991): 49–70.

Presser, Harriet. "Employment Schedules among Dual-Earner Spouses and the Division of Household Labor by Gender." *American Sociological Review* 59, no. 3 (1994): 348–65.

———. *Working in a 24/7 Economy: Challenges for American Families.* New York: Russell Sage Foundation, 2003.

Public Agenda. *Red Flag: Neither Liberal nor Conservative Approaches to Welfare.* Washington, DC: Public Agenda, 2008.

Pungello, Elizabeth Puhn, and Beth Kurtz-Costes. "Why and How Working Women Choose Child Care: A Review with a Focus on Infancy." *Developmental Review* 19 (1999): 31–96.

Reskin, Barbara. "Getting It Right: Sex and Race Inequality in Work Organizations." *Annual Review of Sociology* 26 (2000): 707–9.

Riessman, Catherine Kohler. "When Gender Is Not Enough: Women Interviewing Women." *Gender and Society* 1, no. 2 (1987): 172–207.

Risman, Barbara J., and Danette Johnson-Sumerford. "Doing It Fairly: A Study of Postgender Marriages." *Journal of Marriage and the Family* 60 (February 1998): 23–40.

Roberts, Dorothy E. "Spritual and Menial Housework." *Yale Journal of Law and Feminism* 9, no. 51 (1997): 51–80.

Rollins, Judith. *Between Women: Domestics and Their Employers.* Philadelphia: Temple University Press, 1985.

Romero, Mary. *Maid in the U.S.A.* New York: Routledge, 1992.

———. "Unraveling Privilege: Workers' Children and the Hidden Costs of Paid Childcare." In *Global Dimensions of Gender and Carework,* ed. Mary K. Zimmerman, Jacquelyn S. Litt, and Christine E. Bose, 240–53. Stanford, CA: Stanford University Press, 2006.

Rosenberg, Debra, and Larry Reibstein. "Pots, Blocks, and Socks." *Newsweek,* spring/ summer 1997, 34–35.

Rothman, Barbara Katz. *Recreating Motherhood: Ideology and Technology in a Patriarchal Society.* New York: W. W. Norton, 1989.

Rutman, Deborah. "Child Care as Women's Work: Workers' Experiences of Powerfulness and Powerlessness." *Gender and Society* 10, no. 5 (1996): 629–49.

Samar Collective. "One Big, Happy Community? Class Issues within South Asian American Homes: The Samar Collective." *Samar: South Asian Magazine for Action and Reflection* 4 (winter 1994): 10–15.

Sampson, Diane. "Rejecting Zoe Baird: Class Resentment and the Working Mother." In *"Bad" Mothers: The Politics of Blame in Twentieth-Century America,* ed. Molly Ladd-Taylor and Lauri Umansky, 310–18. New York: New York University Press, 1998.

Sassen, Saskia. "Global Cities and Survival Circuits." In *Global Woman: Nannies, Maids, and Sex Workers in the New Economy,* ed. Barbara Ehrenreich and Arlie Russell Hochschild, 254–74. New York: Metropolitan Books, 2003.

Sayer, Liana C. "Gender, Time, and Inequality: Trends in Women's and Men's Paid Work, Unpaid Work, and Free Time." *Social Forces* 84, no. 1 (2005): 285–303.

Sayer, Liana C., Suzanne M. Bianchi, and John P. Robinson. "Are Parents Investing Less in Children? Trends in Mothers' and Fathers' Time with Children." *American Journal of Sociology* 110, no. 1 (2004): 1–43.

Schoppe-Sullivan, Sarah J. G., G. L. Brown, E. A. Cannon, S. C. Mangelsdorf, and M. Szweczyk Sokolowski. "Maternal Gatekeeping, Coparenting Quality, and Fathering Behavior in Families with Infants." *Journal of Family Psychology* 22 (2008): 389–98.

Schwartz, Felice N. "Management Women and the New Facts of Life." *Harvard Business Review,* January–February 1989, 65–76.

Scott, James C. *Weapons of the Weak: Everyday Forms of Peasant Resistance.* New Haven, CT: Yale University Press, 1985.

Segura, Denise A. "Working at Motherhood: Chicana and Mexican Immigrant Mothers and Employment." In *Mothering: Ideology, Experience, and Agency,* ed. Evelyn Nakano Glenn, Grace Chang, and Linda Ronnie Farrey, 211–31. New York: Routledge, 1994.

Shelton, Beth Anne. "The Division of Household Labor." *Annual Review of Sociology* 22 (1996): 299–322.

Shore, Rima. *Rethinking the Brain: New Insights into Early Development.* New York: Families and Work Institute, 1997.

Silbaugh, Katharine. "Commodification and Women's Household Labor." *Yale Journal of Law and Feminism* 9, no. 1 (1997): 81–122.

———. "Turning Labor into Love: Housework and the Law." *Northwestern University Law Review* 91, no. 1 (1996): 1–86.

Sink, Lisa. "Verdict Awaited in Maid Case; Jury to Decide Whether Illegal Immigrant Was 'House Slave.'" *Milwaukee Journal Sentinel,* 26 May 2006, final edition, B6.

Smith, Dorothy E. *The Everyday World as Problematic.* Boston: Northeastern University Press, 1987.

———. "From Women's Standpoint to a Sociology for People." In *Sociology for the Twenty-first Century,* ed. Janet Abu-Lughod, 65–82. Chicago: University of Chicago Press, 1999.

Smith, Janna Malamud. *A Potent Spell: Mother Love and the Power of Fear.* Boston: Houghton Mifflin, 2003.

Smith, Peggie R. "Laboring for Childcare: A Consideration of New Approaches to Represent Low-Income Service Workers." *University of Pennsylvania Journal of Labor and Employment Law* 8, no. 3 (2006): 583–621.

———. "Regulating Paid Household Work: Class, Gender, Race, and Agendas of Reform." *American University Law Review* 48, no. 4 (1999): 851–924.

———. "Welfare, Child Care, and the People Who Care: Union Representation of Family Child Care Providers." *University of Kansas Law Review* 55, no. 2 (2007): 321–64.

Steinhauer, Jennifer. "City Nannies Say They, Too, Can Be Mother Lions." *New York Times,* 16 July 2005, A1.

Sterling, Guy. "A Complex W. Orange Slave Case Languishes." *Star-Ledger* (New Jersey), 9 July 2007, final edition.

Stone, Deborah. "Why We Need a Care Movement." *Nation,* 13 March 2000, 84–94.

Stone, Pamela. *Opting Out? Why Women Really Quit Careers and Head Home.* Berkeley: University of California Press, 2007.

Sullivan, Oriel, and Scott Coltrane. "Men's Changing Contribution to Housework and Child Care." Discussion Panel on Changing Family Roles, Council on Contemporary Families, 25–26 April 2008.

Swartz, David. *Culture and Power: The Sociology of Pierre Bourdieu.* Chicago: University of Chicago Press, 1997.

Swidler, Ann. "Culture in Action: Symbols and Strategies." *American Sociological Review* 51 (April 1986): 273–86.

———. *Talk of Love: How Culture Matters.* Chicago: University of Chicago Press, 2001.

Talbot, Margaret. "Attachment Theory: The Ultimate Experiment." *New York Times,* 24 May 1998, Sunday magazine.

Taylor, Janelle S., Linda L. Layne, and Danielle F. Wozniak, eds. *Consuming Motherhood.* New Brunswick, NJ: Rutgers University Press, 2004.

Thurer, Shari L. *The Myths of Motherhood: How Culture Reinvents the Good Mother.* New York: Penguin, 1994.

Townsend, Nicholas W. *The Package Deal: Marriage, Work, and Fatherhood in Men's Lives.* Philadelphia: Temple University Press, 2002.

Tsui, Anne S., Terri D. Egan, and Charles A. O'Reilly III. "Being Different: Relational Demography and Organizational Attachment." *Administrative Science Quarterly* 37, no. 4 (1992): 549–79.

Tuominen, Mary C. "The Conflicts of Caring." In *Care Work: Gender, Labor, and the Welfare State,* ed. Madonna Harrington Meyer, 112–35. London: Routledge, 2000.

———. "Exploitation or Opportunity? The Contradictions of Child-Care Policy in the Contemporary United States." *Women and Politics* 18, no. 1 (1997): 53–80.

———. *We Are Not Babysitters: Family Child Care Providers Redefine Work and Care.* New Brunswick, NJ: Rutgers University Press, 2003.

U.S. Department of Commerce, Census Bureau. *2000 Census.* Washington, DC: U.S. Department of Commerce, 2000.

———. "Facts for Features: Mother's Day: May 8, 2005." Press release, 2 May 2005. www
.census.gov/Press-Release/www/releases/archives/facts_for_features_special_editions
/004109.html.

U.S. Department of Justice. "Cameroonian Couple Sentenced on Human Trafficking
Charges." Press release, 31 May 2007.

U.S. Department of Labor, Bureau of Labor Statistics. *Highlights of Women's Earnings in
2005*. Washington, DC: U.S. Department of Labor, 2006.

———. *Labor Force Statistics from the Current Population Survey, 2003*. Washington, DC:
U.S. Department of Labor, 2003.

Uttal, Lynet. "Custodial Care, Surrogate Care, and Coordinated Care: Employed Mothers
and the Meaning of Child Care." *Gender and Society* 10, no. 3 (1996): 291–311.

———. *Making Care Work: Employed Mothers in the New Childcare Market*. New Brunswick,
NJ: Rutgers University Press, 2002.

———. "'Trust Your Instincts': Cultural Similarity, Cultural Maintenance, and Racial
Safety in Employed Mothers' Childcare Choices." *Qualitative Sociology* 20, no. 2 (1997):
253–74.

Uttal, Lynet, and Mary Tuominen. "Tenuous Relationships: Exploitation, Emotion, and
Racial Ethnic Significance in Paid Child Care Work." *Gender and Society* 136 (December
1999): 758–80.

Van Raaphorst, Donna. *Union Maids Not Wanted: Organizing Domestic Workers, 1870–1940*.
New York: Praeger, 1988.

Vigue, Doreen. "For Grieving Mother, a Daily Ordeal; Deborah Eappen Struggles to Find
Answers." *Boston Globe*, 7 November 1997, metro/region section, B1.

Wacquant, Loic. "Pierre Bourdieu." In *Key Contemporary Thinkers*, ed. Rob Stones, 261–77.
2nd ed. New York: Macmillan, 2008.

Waerness, Kari. "The Rationality of Caring." *Economic and Industrial Democracy* 5 (1984):
185–211.

Walker, Karen. "Class, Work, and Family in Women's Lives." *Qualitative Sociology* 13, no.
4 (1990): 297–320.

Walsh, Justine, Kim Nicholson, and Richard Gere. *Nanny Wisdom: Our Secrets for Raising
Healthy, Happy Children—from Newborns to Preschoolers*. New York: STC Paperbacks,
2005.

Wasserman, Elizabeth. "Career vs. Time with Kids: Simpson Prosecutor's Custody Dispute
Fuels Battle-of-Sexes Debate." *San Jose Mercury News*, 4 March 1995, morning final
edition, front section.

Weldon, Fay. *She May Not Leave*. New York: Grove Press, 2007.

White, Burton L. *The First Three Years of Life*. New York: Avon, 1975.

Whitebook, Marcy, and Abby Eichberg. "Finding the Better Way: Assessing Child Care
Compensation Initiatives." *Young Children* 57, no. 3 (2002): 1–24.

Whitebook, Marcy, Carollee Howes, and Deborah Phillips. *Worthy Work, Unlivable Wages:
The National Staffing Study, 1988–1997*. Washington, DC: Center for the Child Care
Workforce, 1998.

Wilgoren, Debbi, and Michael D. Shear. "Regulation of Au Pairs Lags behind the Reality."
Washington Post, 14 August 1994, B1, B6.

Williams, Joan C. "The Interaction of Courts and Legislatures in Creating Family-Responsive Workplaces." In *Working Time for Working Families: Europe and the United States, Contributions to a Program of the Washington Office of the Friedrich Ebert Foundation in Cooperation with the WorkLife Law Program at American University Washington College of Law and the Hans Böckler Foundation, Held in Washington, DC on June 7–8, 2004*, ed. Ariane Hegewisch et al., 22–34. Washington, DC: Friedrich-Ebert-Stiftung, 2005. www.uchastings.edu/site_files/WLL/FESWorkingTimePublication.pdf.

———. *Unbending Gender: Why Family and Work Conflict and What to Do about It*. New York: Oxford University Press, 2000.

Wong, Sau-ling C. "Diverted Mothering: Representations of Caregivers of Color in the Age of 'Multiculturalism.'" In *Mothering: Ideology, Experience, and Agency*, ed. Evelyn Nakano Glenn and Grace Chang, 67–91. New York: Routledge, 1994.

"A Working Mom's Battle: Job vs. Custody in NBC Special." *Chicago Sun-Times*, 21 November 1994, late sports final edition, features section.

Wrigley, Julia. "Hiring a Nanny: The Limits of Private Solutions to Public Problems." *Annals of the American Academy of Political and Social Science* 563 (1999): 162–74.

———. *Other People's Children: An Intimate Account of the Dilemmas Facing Middle-Class Parents and the Women They Hire to Raise Their Children*. New York: Basic Books, 1995.

Wrigley, Julia, and Joanna Dreby. "Fatalities and the Organization of Childcare in the United States, 1985–2003." *American Sociological Review* 70 (2005): 729–57.

Zelizer, Viviana. *The Purchase of Intimacy*. Princeton, NJ: Princeton University Press, 2005.

Zoepf, Katherine. "Wanted: Tibetan Nannies." *New York Observer*, 27 September 2009.

INDEX

Accomplishment of natural growth, 56
Advice literature, 74–76, 137–139, 226n21
African Americans: as childcare providers, 199; as parents, 80–81
Agencies, placement, 52–53, 63, 144
Ainsworth, Mary, 23
At-home mothers, 25–28, 54–55, 93, 141
Attachment, 123–124, 131; detached attachment, 114–118, 156; mother-child, 23, 89, 109, 178; and nanny's legacy, 156–158; recognition of, 145; and salary negotiation, 161–162; and third-parent ideal, 140–142
Au pairs, 49–52, 113, 117, 147, 223n44, 234n21
Autonomy, 132–134, 169–174

Baird, Zoe, 11
Birth-to-three fetish, 23–24
Bitch sessions, 143–146, 148
Blanket accountability, 13, 19, 39–41; and class transmission, 21; and counterideology, 25; and intensive mothering, 104
Body check, 98
Book parents, 138–140
Boundaries, mother-nanny, 112–113, 123–126
Bourdieu, Pierre, 26
Breastfeeding, 122
Bundling services, 74, 78

Car access, 93–94
Careers. See also Male-pattern careers: and childcare management, 89; and chil-

dren's' education, 35; and divorce, 35–36; and economic need, 34–35; and intensive mothering, 41, 168, 196–197; mommy-track, 30, 33, 200; and motherhood, 6, 18, 21–22; and part-time work, 32–33, 186–191, 196, 200, 229n46.230n48; and pregnancy, 29–32; and scaling back, 32–33; security, 33–36, 41; unencumbered worker, 22, 29–33; value of, 34
Caregivers, 45–47, 205–206. See also Nannies; devaluation of, 138, 140, 161, 198–200; and fair pay, 246n13; fathers as, 5, 36–37; and housekeeping, 133; and isolation, 101–102; management of, 89–90; and mothers, 3; prior qualifications of, 171; and racism, 2; and self-worth, 151; and shadow mothering, 110–112; and work negotiation, 3
Caribbean nannies, 75, 79
Chase, Richard, 24
Childcare. See Caregivers; Nannies
Childrearing. See also Partnerships: advice literature, 74–76; bundling services, 74; and class transmission, 25–26; and cognitive stimulation, 24; competency contests, 146, 151–155, 159; discipline, 57, 121, 149–151, 153–154; division of labor, 36–37, 111, 121, 135–136, 153; and ethnicity, 80; maternal gatekeeping, 36–40, 193; mother-infant bond, 23, 89, 109, 178; mother's control of, 36–40; and nanny turnover, 76–78; perfectible child hypothesis, 24–25; sharing, 182, 231n58; and social

Quality time, 37, 118–121

Race. *See also* Ethnicity: and caregiving, 2; and division of labor, 111; and hiring preferences, 46, 69–73, 75, 79–80; and working conditions, 47, 150
Race to the bottom, 160–162
Rationality of caring, 138
Recognition deficit, 145, 160–161, 197
Relational work, 248n15
Reproductive labor, 45–46, 61–62, 110–111, 241n1
Research methods, 207–213; analysis, 212–213; interviewing, 210–211; limitations, 211–212; profiles, 214–217; recruitment, 208–210; respondents, 207–208; terms of, 220n13
Resistance strategies, 145–163; breaking/remaking rules, 149–151; competency contests, 146, 151–155, 159; covert, 147–151; and intensive mothering, 160–162; quitting, 146–147; subterfuge, 148–149; wishful thinking, 155–160
Rethinking the Brain—New Insights into Early Development, 23
Riner, Olivia, 50
Roberts, Dorothy, 111–112
Rollins, Judith, 40, 62–63
Rothman, Barbara Katz, 8

Salaries. *See* Wages, childcare
Scripting, 71, 92
Second shift, 5
Selective sharing, 37–38
Separation, 117–118
Service-triangle employers, 70, 91, 240n8
Sexual harassment, 58
Shadow mothering, 11, 14, 19, 110–112; causes of, 197–198; enhancing mothers, 118–123; erasing nannies, 112–118; and intensive mothering, 126–127, 146, 158–159; mother-only tasks, 122–123, 132; and nannies' expertise, 137; and partnerships, 191–193; and social class, 201–205; and third-parent ideal, 142
Shadow work, 110–112
Silbaugh, Katherine, 58
Single mothers, 183–184, 220n10
Social class: and childrearing, 4, 55–57, 152, 201–205, 239n20; class transmission, 21, 25–26, 202–205; and daycare centers, 205; and gender, 204–205; and hiring practices, 80–81; and mothering ideals, 6, 15–16,

201–202, 203–205; and salary, 35, 232n3; and shadow mothering, 201–205
Socializing, nannies, 70, 92–93
Spanking, 150
Spiritual motherhood, 111–112, 118
Starting Points conference, 23, 226n14
Stereotyping, 71, 83
Stratified reproduction, 45–46, 61–62, 111
Structured play, 56–57, 155. *See also* Play dates
Study design, 9–12
Swidler, Anne, 7, 71–72

Theoretical sampling, 247n3
Third-parent ideal, 15, 131–142; and attachment, 140–142; autonomy, 132–134; and book parents, 138–140; division of labor, 135–136; and intensive mothering, 136–137, 141–142, 158; nannies' expertise, 135–140; and shadow mothering, 142
Threshold of connection, 177–178, 186–191
Thurer, Shari, 7
Time-outs, 57, 150
Tirado, Brunilda, 131
Trust, 169–172
Tuominen, Mary, 199

Undocumented immigrants, 147, 150
Unencumbered worker, 22, 29–33
Unexpected drop-in, 97
United States: au pairs in, 50–51; immigration law, 48–49; paid childcare in, 224n46; State Department, 50–51; working mothers in, 1, 9, 28, 220n9
United States Information Agency (USIA), 50
Unscheduled play, 56
Uttal, Lynet, 80

Vocabulary of skill, 198–200
Vocabulary of virtue, 198–200
Volunteer work, 180

Wages, childcare, 30–31, 231n2, 235n30; American-born nannies, 53; au pairs, 52; and class transmission, 35; domestic workers, 58; and housework, 133; immigrant nannies, 47–48; negotiating, 62–64, 161–162; and partnerships, 193–194; and recognition, 160–161, 197; and social class, 35, 232n3; and vocabularies of skill/virtue, 198–199
Weber, Max, 11
Williams, Joan, 29, 32

TEXT
10/12.5 Minion Pro

DISPLAY
Minion Pro

COMPOSITOR
Toppan Best-set Premedia Limited

INDEXER
Pierce Butler

PRINTER AND BINDER
Maple-Vail Book Manufacturing Group